WITNESS IN PALESTINE

A JEWISH AMERICAN WOMAN IN THE OCCUPIED TERRITORIES

"Even those who are familiar with the grim reality of the occupied territories will quickly be drawn into a world they had barely imagined by these vivid, searingly honest, intensely acute portrayals of unflagging courage, wanton cruelty, and enduring faith that through nonviolent resistance, fundamental decency will somehow prevail—an outcome that lies very much in our hands. I cannot find words to express my admiration for the solidarity workers and peacemakers, international and Israeli, and the people of Palestine whom they are supporting in their struggles to survive and to overcome."

–**Noam Chomsky**

"Baltzer's moving and vivid memoir tells the story of the daily struggle along the Wall in the West Bank, with stories and pictures that capture not just the hardships, but also the resilience of the Palestinian people. It also tells the story of courageous internationals like Baltzer, dedicating their time and energy to the struggle of the suffering, who give many of us hope that, with the people of the world working together, justice and peaceful coexistence in Israel/Palestine are possible."

–**Tanya Reinhart**,
author of *Israel/Palestine*

"By combining a lucid and captivating text with artistic photography, this book draws you into the life of an average Palestinian living under exceptional circumstances of occupation, oppression, and colonization. This vivid account is also a deeply personal story that will inspire you not only to have hope but to actively seek and work for peace and justice."

–**Mazin Qumsiyeh**, author of
Sharing the Land of Canaan

WITNESS IN PALESTINE

A JEWISH AMERICAN WOMAN IN THE OCCUPIED TERRITORIES

Anna Baltzer

Paradigm Publishers

Boulder • London

Published in the United States by
Paradigm Publishers
3360 Mitchell Lane Suite E
Boulder, CO 80301 • USA

Paradigm Publishers is the trade name of Birkenkamp & Company, LLC
Dean Birkenkamp, President and Publisher.

Library of Congress Cataloging-in-Publishing Data has been applied for.

ISBN: 978-1-59451-30-7

Printed and bound in Turkey on acid free paper that meets the standards of the American National Standard for Permanence of Paper for Printed Library Materials.

Printed, bound, and typeset by
Yorum Printing Publication Industry Ltd. Co.
İvedik Matbaacılar Sitesi, 35. Cadde No: 36-38
Yenimahalle • Ankara, Turkey
Phone: (90) 312 395 21 12 • Fax: (90) 312 394 11 09
www.yorummatbaa.com • info@yorummatbaa.com

Updated and revised edition
10 09 08 07 2 3 4 5

Table of Contents

PART I

2003

2004

2005

PART II

2007

List of Maps

MIDDLE EAST

Adapted from Central Intelligence Agency map 802983AI (R02107) 6-03 by Myriam Dousse

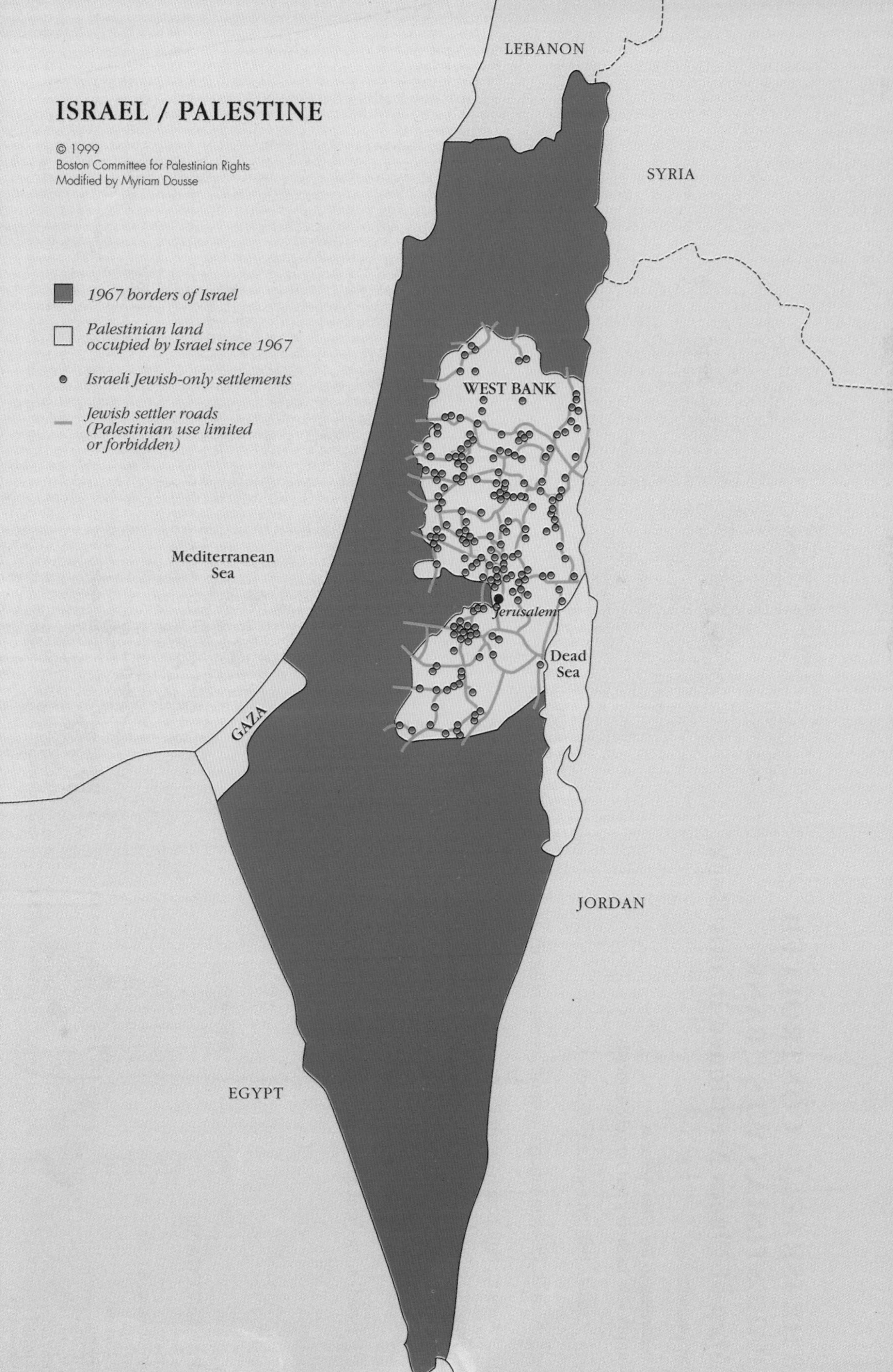

ISRAEL / PALESTINE
© 1999
Boston Committee for Palestinian Rights
Modified by Myriam Dousse
1967 borders of Israel
Palestinian land occupied by Israel since 1967
Israeli Jewish-only settlements
Jewish settler roads (Palestinian use limited or forbidden)
LEBANON
SYRIA
WEST BANK
Mediterranean Sea
Jerusalem
Dead Sea
GAZA
JORDAN
EGYPT

THE ISRAELI - CONTROLLED PALESTINIAN WEST BANK

Map of Places Mentioned in this Book

MAY 2002

According to the Oslo Accords (applicable in theory but largely ignored)

- Area A, Full Palestinian control
- Area B, Palestinian civil control, Israeli military control
- Area C, Full Israeli control
- The "Green Line," the internationally-recognized 1967 border between Israel and the West Bank
- Israeli settlement municipal and jurisdictional area

PALESTINIAN

A'ram	F9
Abu Dis	F10
Al Far'a Refugee Camp	G4
Al-Jiflik	H5
As-Sawiya	F6
Atara	F7
At-Tawani	E14
Aqraba	G6
Az-Zawiya	D6
Azzun	D5
Azzun Atma	D6
Balata Refugee Camp	F5

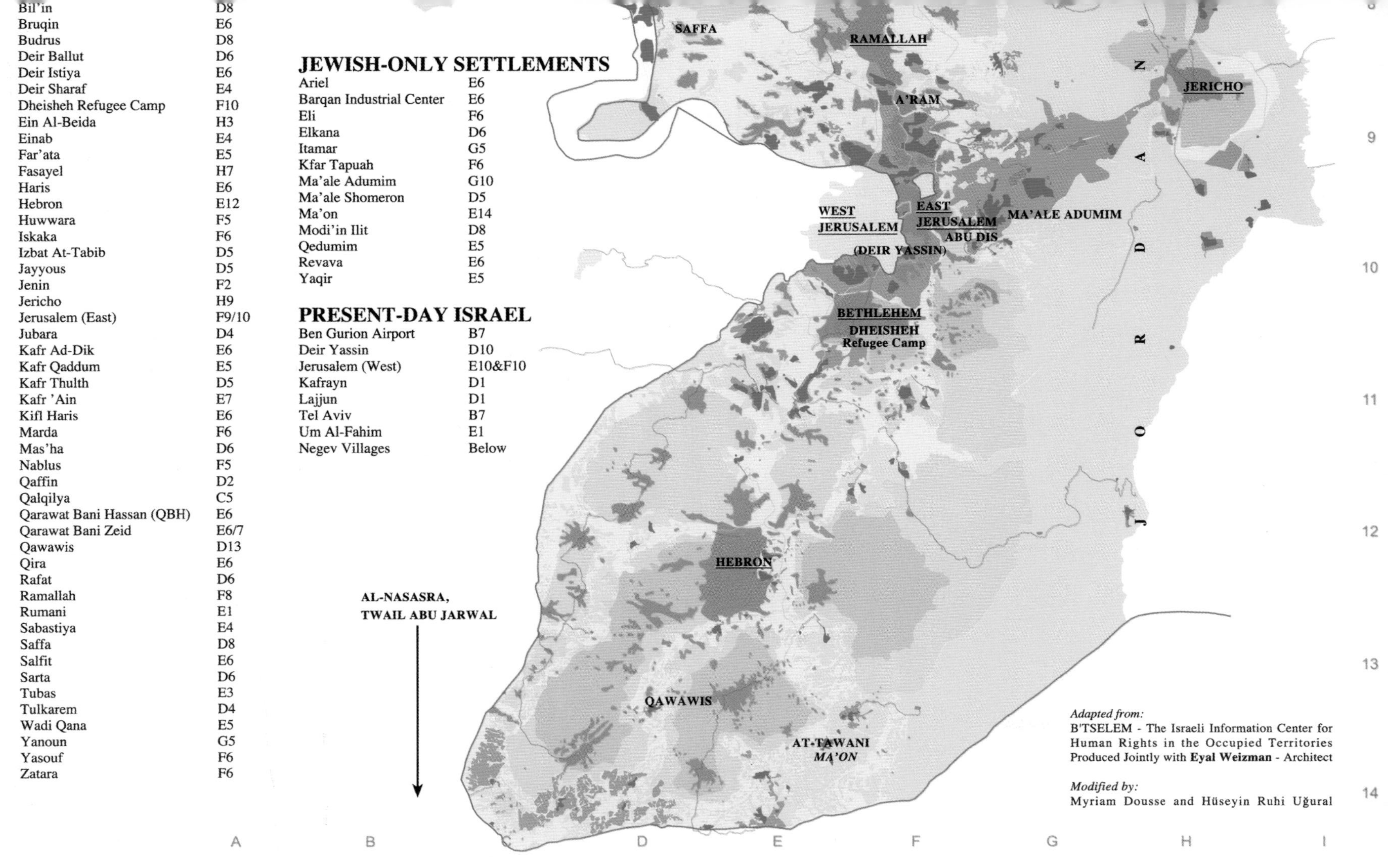

Bil'in D8
Bruqin E6
Budrus D8
Deir Ballut D6
Deir Istiya E6
Deir Sharaf E4
Dheisheh Refugee Camp F10
Ein Al-Beida H3
Einab E4
Far'ata E5
Fasayel H7
Haris E6
Hebron E12
Huwwara F5
Iskaka F6
Izbat At-Tabib D5
Jayyous D5
Jenin F2
Jericho H9
Jerusalem (East) F9/10
Jubara D4
Kafr Ad-Dik E6
Kafr Qaddum E5
Kafr Thulth D5
Kafr 'Ain E7
Kifl Haris E6
Marda F6
Mas'ha D6
Nablus F5
Qaffin D2
Qalqilya C5
Qarawat Bani Hassan (QBH) E6
Qarawat Bani Zeid E6/7
Qawawis D13
Qira E6
Rafat D6
Ramallah F8
Rumani E1
Sabastiya E4
Saffa D8
Salfit E6
Sarta D6
Tubas E3
Tulkarem D4
Wadi Qana E5
Yanoun G5
Yasouf F6
Zatara F6
JEWISH-ONLY SETTLEMENTS
Ariel E6
Barqan Industrial Center E6
Eli F6
Elkana D6
Itamar G5
Kfar Tapuah F6
Ma'ale Adumim G10
Ma'ale Shomeron D5
Ma'on E14
Modi'in Ilit D8
Qedumim E5
Revava E6
Yaqir E5
PRESENT-DAY ISRAEL
Ben Gurion Airport B7
Deir Yassin D10
Jerusalem (West) E10&F10
Kafrayn D1
Lajjun D1
Tel Aviv B7
Um Al-Fahim E1
Negev Villages Below
AL-NASASRA,
TWAIL ABU JARWAL
SAFFA
RAMALLAH
A'RAM
JERICHO
WEST
JERUSALEM
EAST
JERUSALEM
ABU DIS
MA'ALE ADUMIM
(DEIR YASSIN)
BETHLEHEM
DHEISHEH
Refugee Camp
HEBRON
QAWAWIS
AT-TAWANI
MA'ON
J O R D A N
Adapted from:
B'TSELEM - The Israeli Information Center for
Human Rights in the Occupied Territories
Produced Jointly with Eyal Weizman - Architect
Modified by:
Myriam Dousse and Hüseyin Ruhi Uğural
9
10
11
12
13
14
A B C D E F G H I

Introduction

Israel has always meant something to me. When I was young, my grandmother, who had fled Europe and lost most of her family in the Nazi Holocaust, used to talk about Israel as the one protection that our family and Jews everywhere had against persecution or murder in the future. When I first visited Israel myself, sponsored by a program called "Birthright Israel" that sends young non-Israeli Jews on a 10-day all-expenses-paid tour of the Holy Land, I saw nothing to make me think that Israel was anything other than a peace-seeking democracy. My image of Israel was of a tiny victimized country that simply wanted to live in peace but couldn't because of its aggressive, Jew-hating Arab neighbors.

I came to question my view of Israel during a trip through the Middle East. At the time, I was teaching English at a university in Ankara, Turkey on a Fulbright grant. During vacations, I traveled around Syria, Lebanon, and Iran. I was welcomed everywhere I went, particularly in southern Lebanon, where I was taken in by several families of Palestinian refugees. One family in particular not only showered me with hospitality and warmth, but accepted and respected me to an extent that I had rarely experienced even in my own communities back home. Through my friendship with the eldest son, Mahmoud, and his parents, siblings, and neighbors, I began to hear a different narrative about the state of Israel from the one I had heard growing up as a Jewish American.

My new friends told me stories of past and present military attacks, house demolitions, land confiscation, imprisonment without trial, torture, and government-sponsored assassination. It seemed that these aggressive actions were not carried out for the protection of the Jewish people, as I had previously been taught, but rather for the creation and expansion of a Jewish state at the expense of the rights, lives, and dignity of the non-Jewish people living in the region. It was hard for me to believe that Israel could act so unjustly. Questioning Israel in any way felt like a betrayal of my grandmother.

Nonetheless, it became important for me to arrive at my own understanding of the conflict through research and personal witnessing. I read books written from different perspectives and attended presentations by local activists reporting on their experiences in the Occupied Palestinian Territories, one place where my Birthright Israel tour bus had not stopped. To my disappointment, I began to see that Mahmoud and his family had been right: there was far more to Israel's past and present policies than I had been told. After extensive reading, the following aspects of the current situation in Israel and the Palestinian Territories became clear to me:

- Israel's ongoing 40-year Occupation of the West Bank, the Gaza Strip,[1] and East Jerusalem is illegal and violates the Fourth Geneva Conventions, as well as more

[1] When this book went to press, Israel had evacuated Gaza but continued to occupy it. For a post-disengagement update and discussion, see.p. 327.

than 60 United Nations resolutions.[2] Israel has violated more UN resolutions than any other country in the history of the organization.

- Palestinians in the Occupied Territories and in Israel are denied equal rights to Jews in the same areas purely on the basis of their religion and ethnicity.
- The Israeli military controls the movement of nearly four million Palestinians through a system of checkpoints, roadblocks, and segregated roads. By the same means, Israel also limits the supply of food, water, medical supplies, and other basic necessities to Palestinian civilians.[3]
- The Israeli army and government exercise virtually unchecked freedom to detain, threaten, arrest, imprison, torture, and assassinate Palestinians, often without charge or trial.
- The Israeli government sponsors the mass transfer of Jewish Israeli citizens from Israel to Jewish-only colonies, known as settlements, built illegally on internationally recognized Palestinian land in the Occupied Territories.
- Israeli settlers suffer practically no legal consequences for building new illegal (according to international and Israeli law) settlements, for expanding existing ones, or for threatening or physically attacking Palestinian civilians.
- Israel's human rights violations since September of 2000 have left more than four times more Palestinian civilians dead than the total number of Israelis (both civilians and soldiers) killed by Palestinians.[4]
- The Wall, or "Security Fence," that is currently under construction by Israel in the name of preventing terrorism in fact weaves *through*, not around, the West Bank, effectively separating hundreds of thousands of West Bank Palestinians from their land, jobs, hospitals, and schools, and from each other.
- Israel's policies of occupation and colonization have been consistent with a steady pattern of transferring the indigenous Palestinians out of Israel/Palestine, and confiscating their land, water, and resources for Jewish Israeli use. This process, similar to the ethnic cleansing carried out in North America, Australia, and the former Yugoslavia, began before Israel's creation in 1948, and continues today.

---

[2] Mazin Qumsiyeh, *Sharing the Land of Canaan* (London: Pluto Press, 2004).

[3] According to US, UN, European, and Palestinian research and relief agencies, Israel's restrictions on transportation are a major cause of widespread malnutrition, unemployment, and poverty (at 43% when this book went to press) among Palestinians in the Occupied Territories. Norman Finkelstein, *Image and Reality of the Israel-Palestine Conflict*, second edition (New York: Verso, 2003), p. xx; *Palestinian Academic Society for the Study of International Affairs: PASSIA* (2007 Diary).

[4] *Middle East Policy Council. www.mepc.org/resources/mrates.asp*
"Numbers *do not* include Palestinian suicide bombers (or other attackers) nor do they include Palestinians targeted for assassination, though bystanders killed during these assassinations are counted. However, [Israeli] soldiers killed during incursions into Palestinian lands *are counted.* Data collected from *B'tselem* (the Israeli Information Center for Human Rights in the Occupied Territories), the Palestinian Red Crescent Society, and the Israeli Ministry of Foreign Affairs"; The Red Cross estimates closer to 10 times more Palestinian civilians have been killed than Israelis. Qumsiyeh, p. 104.

- Every year, the US government funnels billions of American tax-dollars to Israel, which are used primarily to purchase American-made weapons to arm the occupying Israeli army and settlers.[5]

As an American taxpayer, I feel responsible for the role my money, government, and country play in the violations of international law and human rights. I feel doubly responsible as a Jewish American, since Israel's abuses are being carried out in the name of Jews everywhere. Although I have never been religious, Jewish culture and history have always been a part of my environment, and identifying as a Jew has never seemed so much a choice as a fact. According to prevailing Jewish law and explicit Israeli law, Judaism is based on heritage, not faith or religious practice. I am a member of the community that Israel claims to be protecting through its violations of international law and human rights.

In the fall of 2003, I decided to travel to the Occupied Palestinian Territories to see the situation for myself. I applied and was accepted to volunteer with the International Women's Peace Service (IWPS), a grassroots peace organization dedicated to documenting and nonviolently intervening in human rights abuses in the West Bank, and supporting the nonviolent movement to end the Occupation. This book is a narraration of the 8 months that I spent working with IWPS, spanning the past 5 years. It documents both the situation on the ground as I observed it and my personal emotional and intellectual journey piecing together my own understanding of the conflict.

I have tried to describe as accurately as possible what I saw in the West Bank. I do not claim that my presentation of the situation is unbiased—I cannot deny having strong opinions about the issue, which will inevitably be apparent in my narrative—but I have tried to keep my editorializing separate from my reporting. I also do not profess to offer a broad synthesis of the Arab-Israeli conflict or even of life in occupied Palestine. As a foreigner voluntarily working in a specific part of the region for a relatively short period of time, I cannot begin to understand what it means to be a Palestinian living under the Occupation. These accounts represent no "side" but my own. They are the observations and recordings of one woman's experience living and working in the West Bank.

A lot of details in this book are repeated: dozens of Palestinians detained at checkpoints, threatened by settlers, taunted, and harassed. I have not shied away from these details. It is my belief that to understand the effects of the Occupation one must look not just to the dramatic moments of violence that are represented (or misrepresented) in the news, but also to the small, everyday acts of violence and humiliation, and next to them the small, everyday acts of resistance and human dignity. If my accounts feature too many frustrating details of delays, searches, and abuse, I can only say that this is the nature of life under the Occupation.

This book was primarily intended for Americans and other Westerners who may be uninformed about the current situation in Palestine, but I believe it is suitable for readers everywhere, regardless of their political beliefs or previous knowledge of the subject. Important words and terms have been highlighted in the text and are defined in the Glossary. For those completely unfamiliar with the conflict, I have included a very brief outline of the region's history in Appendix III. Appendix IV addresses some of the major questions and myths that surround the issue, and Appendix V contains quotations from Israeli, Palestinian, and US leaders, as well as other significant voices articulating what I see as the key points of the conflict.

---

[5] For more details about US foreign aid to Israel, see the Conclusion.

I have divided this updated and revised edition into Parts I and II. Part I contains my writings from Palestine between 2003 and 2005, the bulk of this book's first edition. Wherever possible I have updated maps and statistics. Most new material can be found in Part II, which was written during my most recent stint with IWPS in 2007. Throughout the book, some names were changed for privacy or security, some quotations were reconstructed from detailed notes, and very minor chronological alterations were made for the sake of coherence. All reports are otherwise fully accurate to the best of my knowledge, and all errors are my own.

Readers may remark a change in my writing between Parts I and II. For example, in my earlier writings, I made an effort to avoid discussing pre-Occupation history, both because I am not an authority on the subject and because I saw it as a sore point and a distraction from addressing the urgency of the current situation in the Occupied Territories. I reasoned that many people who strongly disagreed about the past and future of Israel and Palestine could at least agree that Israel's policies of occupation and colonization were a step backwards from peace, from the point of view of justice for Palestinians and safety for Israelis. I still believe this to be true. With time, however, I have reoriented my research towards exploring the Zionist history and ideology underlying the current situation. I believe these things to be at the heart of the conflict, and thus unavoidable.

I do not expect—or even wish for—readers to blindly accept my assertions about Israel and the Occupation; I certainly did not believe such claims when I first encountered them. My hope is that readers will react individually to my stories and begin to develop their own understanding of the situation. Readers who do not wish to take my word for it certainly don't have to: there are dozens of Israeli, Palestinian, and international groups organizing tours in Israel/Palestine and documenting all aspects of the situation. Many of these organizations are highlighted in the text and listed in Appendices I and II: What You Can Do and the Resource Guide. These appendices also provide suggestions for further research on the subject, as well as various ways to get involved in the growing international nonviolent movement for peace and justice in Israel/Palestine.

Acknowledgements

I am deeply grateful to Josh Carney, Toni Mandry, Daniel Immerwahr, Kobi Snitz, Emma Hospelhorn, Robert West, Marc Wordsmith, Fatima Gabru, Beth Raymer, A. M. Poppy, Blake Lipsett, Andy Assad, and Knud Lambrecht for helping me transform a collection of my scattered emails into a coherent book. I am lucky to have such gifted and devoted friends. I want to thank Hannah, Luna, Renée, Amy, Omar, Gavriel, Hani, and Ayed for allowing me to quote their illuminating words and ideas, and everyone in the movement who permitted me to publish their photographs or faces in this book. Special thanks to my cousin Myriam for the cover and maps, and to Özhan, Engin, Chris, and the Yorum family for other graphics. Deep thanks to Jeff for his invaluable friendship, to Reem for being a mother and a sister to me in Palestine, to Josh for his openness and emotional wisdom, and to my parents for their unwavering love, support, and trust. Thank you most of all to the IWPS team and my Palestinian, Israeli, and international colleagues in the resistance, so many of whom have shown me through courageous actions not only how to work for peace, but that peace is possible.

Dedication

to Mahmoud and his family, for reminding me to seek the truth;
to Daniel, for reminding me to write;
and to Andrea, for reminding me to believe.

PART I

2003 - 2005

Tuesday, November 18, 2003

My first week in Palestine has been spent in the trees. Every morning I wake up at sunrise to walk with farmers to their olive groves, where we climb the ancient trees and fill our shirts with olives, taking occasional breaks to sip fresh sage tea and admire the scenery. It is fall, the time of the olive harvest, when hundreds of thousands of Palestinian olive trees burst with ripe purple olives to be plucked and marinated or pressed for fresh olive oil.

For many generations, local Palestinian farmers have depended on the fall harvest as a major source of income to support their families. However many farmers now say they are afraid to approach their trees alone. They have been traumatized by repeated harassment from soldiers and armed settlers from Israel, who for decades have been patrolling Palestinian land to ensure the protection and expansion of Jewish-only settlements.

Settlements are towns or communities built by Israel exclusively for Jews on internationally recognized Palestinian land. Israeli settlements are in violation of Article 49 of the Fourth Geneva Convention, which prohibits an occupying power from transferring citizens from its own population to the occupied territory, in this case the West Bank, the Gaza Strip,[1] and East Jerusalem. In many languages, like French, the general word for "settlement" is the same as the word for "colony." But in English and Hebrew, a more benign word is used: people living in Israeli settlements are referred to as "settlers," not "colonizers."

[1] When this book went to press, Israeli settlers had been evacuated from the Gaza Strip, although the territory remained under Israeli military siege. For a post-evacuation update and analysis, see p. 327

Har Homa settlement near Bethlehem

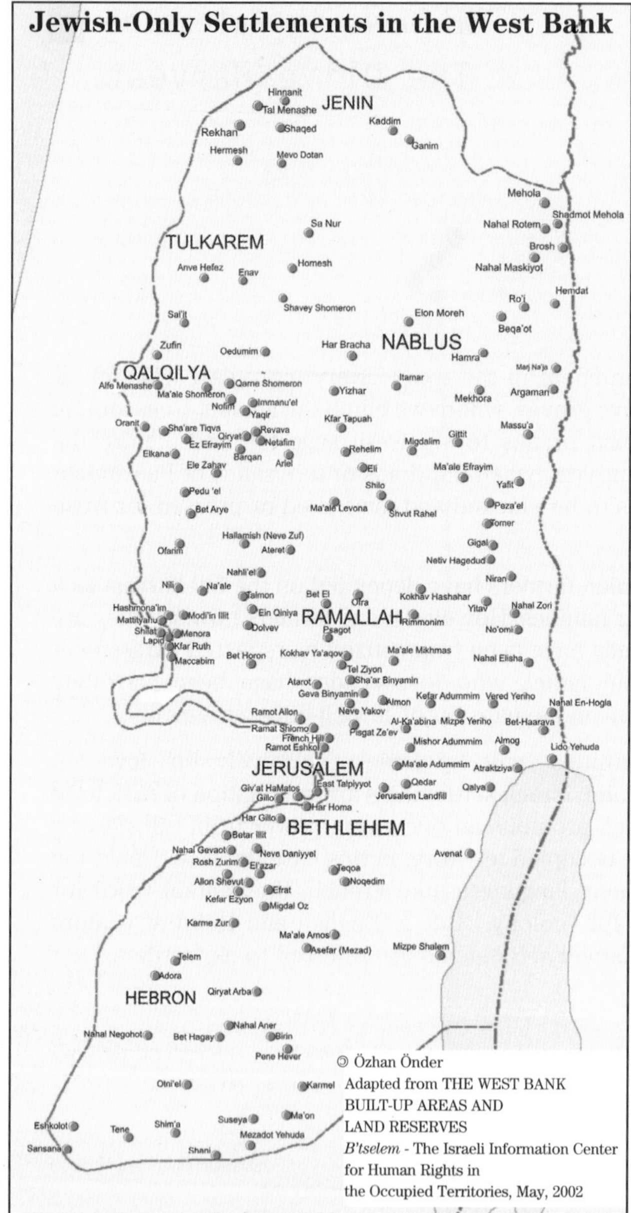

© Özhan Önder
Adapted from THE WEST BANK BUILT-UP AREAS AND LAND RESERVES
B'tselem - The Israeli Information Center for Human Rights in the Occupied Territories, May, 2002

In spite of international law, Israel not only condones the illegal settlements, but actively supports their establishment and growth. For example, the Israeli government subsidizes housing, water, electricity, transportation, and many other services for settlers. By declaring settlements "national priority areas," the illegal colonies are entitled to 65% more grants than local councils in Israel. The Israeli government provides individual setters with financial assistance by enabling them to lease land at rates well below the actual value.[2] Israel also offers tax breaks, business incentives, free schooling, and mortgage grants up to 95% in the settlements[3] to attract new Jewish citizens to become part of the occupying presence. The larger the Israeli population in the West Bank, Gaza, and Jerusalem, the stronger Israel's claim to that land becomes.

On an Israeli road outside of Ariel settlement near our house, a Hebrew billboard announces to passersby, "Now is the time to move to Ariel. Join our community, and you will receive 100,000 New Israeli Shekels." That's more than US$20,000. Advertisements like this appeal not to well-off Israelis, but rather to poorer Israelis, like young families, recent immigrants, or Israelis of color. These might be people who couldn't care less about the political or religious significance of the land itself. Maybe they are simply looking for a higher standard of living for themselves and their families.[4] In fact, most Israeli settlers move to the Palestinian Territories not because they think "This land is ours and nobody else's," but because, in one way or another, their government is paying them to do so (with American tax-dollars).

---

[2] "Occupation in Hebron," *Alternative Information Center: AIC* (2004), p. 29.

[3] *PASSIA* 2007, p. 313.

[4] The situation bears a striking resemblance to the US military, which fills its enlisted ranks with underprivileged young men, often black or Chicano, who fight not necessarily because they believe in the cause, but because they need the money and education that the army offers to them.

A minority of settlers choose to live in the Palestinian Territories primarily for political or religious reasons. Many of these "ideological"—as opposed to "economic"—settlers frequently threaten or attack Palestinian farmers and families because they believe the Palestinians are occupying land promised to the Jewish people by God. Due to the increasing danger of settler attacks, many farmers have started requesting accompaniment from Israeli peace groups and international organizations. The hope is that violent settlers or soldiers might exercise restraint in the presence of Israelis or internationals, either out of shame or because we might document the violence and transmit the news to Western media sources, where stories of Israeli settler or soldier violence often go untold.

A billboard outside of Ariel settlement offers Israelis 100,000 shekels (more than US$20,000) to move to the West Bank settlement.

One organization providing international accompaniment to Palestinian farmers is the International Women's Peace Service (IWPS), where I am volunteering for the next 2 months. IWPS is a grassroots peace organization dedicated to documenting and nonviolently intervening in human rights abuses in the West Bank, and to supporting Palestinian and Israeli nonviolent resistance to the Occupation. We are based in Haris, a small village in the West Bank's rural Salfit region. When farmers from the neighboring village of Deir Istiya contacted us recently to request accompaniment, three IWPS women (myself included) and five Israeli activists volunteered to go.

Although the Deir Istiya farmers' groves are not far from their homes, it was a long walk because Palestinians are not permitted to use the main road connecting their village with their land. That main road is a settler highway, built to connect nearby settlements with one another and with Israel proper. Most roads in the Occupied Territories are segregated, with older, sometimes dirt roads for Palestinians, and modern highways of up to four lanes for Israelis. The latter are built over demolished homes and olive groves of local Palestinian villages, but the road signs often give no indication of past or

Palestinian farmers from Haris village hurry across the settler highway that separates them from their olive groves. West Bank settler roads are built on Palestinian land, but West Bank Palestinians are forbidden from using them without a special permit.

Signs on a settler highway that was built on the land of Deir Istiya village (background) point the way to Israeli settlements and cities only. Some of the Arabic translations have been blacked out with spray paint.

present Palestinian communities. Signs point the way to Tel Aviv, Jerusalem, and nearby Israeli settlements. The ones we passed on the way to Deir Istiya's olive groves were printed in Hebrew, Arabic, and English, but the Arabic had been blacked out with spray-paint, we assumed by ideological settlers.

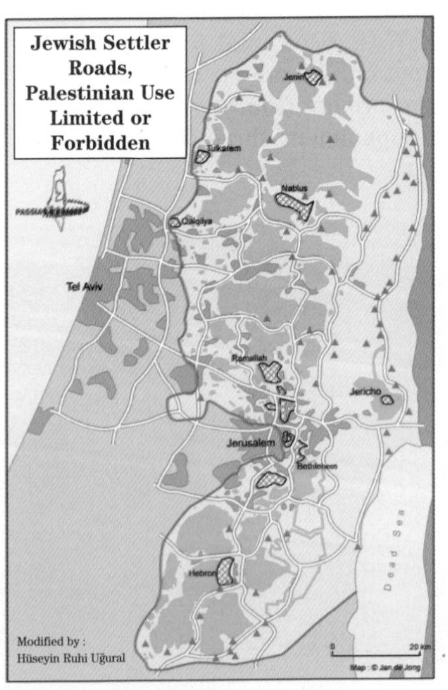

Our first days of harvesting with the farmers and Israeli activists were peaceful. I marveled at the technique of separating olives from leaves: everything is poured out of buckets from a high place, and the wind carries away the light leaves while the olives, heavy with oil, fall into a pile together. The atmosphere was pleasant, sorting olives, drinking tea, and chatting in the shade of the silvery trees. The Palestinians did their best in Hebrew and the Israelis and I tried to speak a little Arabic.

Today was less serene. As we moved west with the harvest, we came closer to the bulldozers plowing through Deir Istiya's groves. The bulldozers are leveling olive groves for the expansion of nearby Revava settlement. My friends from Deir Istiya fear their land will be next. While we were harvesting, a Revava settler with an M16 semiautomatic weapon approached us and asked the Palestinians for their identification papers. The farmers obliged. The other three IWPS women and I approached the settler to observe him, trying to be conspicuous but not threatening. We knew the settler had no right to ask the farmer for his ID—it is a Palestinian grove—but our policy is not to take the lead, rather to support Palestinians in their tactics as long as they are nonviolent. The farmer asked us to stay back, and we did. The farmer knew it was easier and safer to comply rather than refuse and risk facing violence from settlers or soldiers.

© IWPS 2003

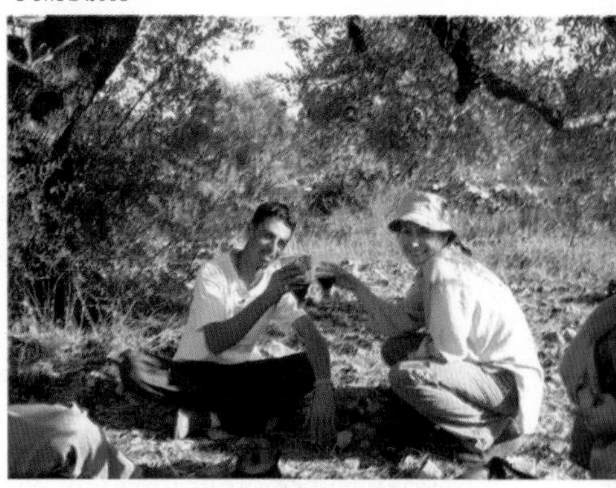

The author and a Palestinian friend take a break from picking olives to relax with a cup of tea.

After the settler left, I volunteered to keep an eye out for settlers or soldiers, and also to keep watch over the farmers' donkeys. (I had heard of recent cases of settlers stealing donkeys.) Half an hour later, three armed soldiers approached us and one asked if we had seen anyone around. We told him we'd seen a man with a gun. Alarmed, the soldier asked us to describe the man. We described the settler we had just seen and he relaxed visibly: "Just a Jew? Oh, his gun is necessary—he has to defend himself."

The soldiers asked how long we would be there and we said until sunset. When they were gone, we discussed the encounter and agreed that in the future we would translate questions into Arabic instead of answering them ourselves, even if the questions were simple. Our purpose is not to speak or fight for Palestinians, but to support their right both to be on their land and to resist the forces occupying it.

It was a long walk home after harvesting. In addition to taking a long detour around the settler road, we had to cart all of the olives from that day in one trip because there have apparently been recent incidents of settlers stealing olives in the area. When we arrived at our house in Haris, we learned that a farmer from a nearby village had been taken away by soldiers while he was picking olives with his family and three international volunteers who were accompanying them. Fortunately, several groups were notified and took action. Rabbis for Human Rights (RHR), an Israeli peace organization that fights human rights violations in Israel and the Occupied Territories in the Jewish tradition of *Tikkun olam*, or social action, is already working on getting the farmer released. CNN reporters who happened to be in the neighborhood at the time will probably have a story, too. We are optimistic because of the international media coverage and sympathetic Israeli presence, and some of us will go to the village tomorrow to help finish the harvest that was interrupted.

A farmer returns home with his olives after a day of harvesting.

Witness in Palestine
Farmer Kidnapped in Marda

Wednesday, November 19, 2003

Today was another long day. We began picking olives early and then received a call that a Palestinian farmer named Ismael was being denied access through Ariel settlement to his land. Ariel is home to about 20,000 settlers and is expanding. Many farmers like Ismael have been separated from their land by the settlement. Ismael has 500 trees full of olives that will go bad unless they are picked in the next few weeks. But he was told he must go the long way around—that is, hike 2 hours around the settlement and several hills to reach land that is only about 10 minutes away from his house—or not go at all. Ismael has an Israeli permit to go to his land in Ariel and has successfully traveled through the checkpoint in the past, but these days his permit isn't enough.

This morning, as Ismael struggled towards the settlement gate on his donkey-cart, some settlers in traffic taunted him, saying, "Do you take your donkey-cart to Jerusalem also?" The settlers know very well that Ismael, like most Palestinians living in the West Bank, cannot go to Jerusalem (whereas all Jews in the world can not only visit but even obtain immediate residency there if they wanted to). Rabbi Arik Ascherman from RHR came to help us lobby for Ismael's passage, but with no luck. Next week, Ismael will apply for another permit, the same as the first, to try again to reach his olive trees before it is too late.

After saying goodbye to Ismael, Rabbi Ascherman and I drove to Marda, where a farmer was taken away by soldiers yesterday afternoon. We were greeted by Chloe and Aldo, two international volunteers whom I recognized from a nonviolence training workshop we attended together in Bethlehem my first weekend. The workshop was conducted by the International Solidarity Movement (ISM), a Palestinian-led grassroots organization that enlists international volunteers to support nonviolent Palestinian resistance to the Occupation. At the training we practiced quick consensus-based decision-making in emergency situations as well as nonviolent direct action: physical action to restrain an oppressive force.

Israeli soldiers patrol the Palestinian West Bank with virtual impunity in the name of security.

Chloe and Aldo work with ISM, and yesterday they witnessed the abduction in Marda. They said three soldiers approached their group of olive-pickers and one soldier motioned to Amid, a farmer, to get into their jeep. Amid was very frightened and did as the soldier said. When Chloe and Aldo asked the soldier what he was doing, he replied sarcastically, "I am just a maniac." Chloe called the ISM office and took out her camera but the soldier threatened her so she put it away. The soldier drove away with Amid for 5 minutes and then returned with a bulldozer, saying he would come back that night to bulldoze all the family's trees. Tamir, the owner of the trees, was terrified. Chloe and Aldo agreed to stay with Amid's wife and children that night to show their support and to check on the trees from time to time.

Israeli volunteers from Rabbis for Human Rights help Palestinian farmers harvest olives on their threatened land.

An hour later, Rabbi Ascherman and about 50 RHR volunteers showed up to help finish picking the olives. Chloe said they carpeted the land and within half an hour the entire harvest was finished. Chloe's eyes lit up when she described the image of 50 Israeli activists coming to the aid of Amid's and Tamir's families. She also related something Tamir had said to the soldier who returned with the bulldozer: "Look at the way my children are looking at you. We are supposed to be negotiating peace, but imagine how you must appear in their eyes." She was heartened that the children's last impression of Israelis that day had been a positive one.

According to Chloe, 7 hours or so after being taken away, Amid returned home. His clothes were dirty, his hair matted, and he looked startled. He said the soldiers had forced him to lie down in the back of the jeep to avoid being seen as they drove. They took him to an abandoned building, blindfolded him, tied rags around his limbs to prevent bruising, and then beat him. Amid, who speaks fluent Hebrew from his years working in Israel, pleaded with the soldiers, asking what he had done wrong. The lead soldier replied, "I'm not doing this because you've done anything wrong. I'm doing this because you're Palestinian and I want you dead."

The lead soldier then took off Amid's blindfold and pointed a gun in his face, telling him to "prepare to die." At the last minute, another soldier reminded his colleague that one of the international volunteers had perhaps gotten a photograph of them. The lead soldier got scared and let Amid go.

When I met Amid he looked exhausted but was friendly and welcomed me into his home. Rabbi Ascherman began to talk to Amid about his rights to file a complaint about the abuse. Chloe had taken down the license plate number of the jeep when it first drove away, which will hopefully be enough to track the soldiers. It is not clear that the offending soldier will face charges for his crime, since the victim was Palestinian; generally, soldiers are only reprimanded for violence against Jews or internationals.

During my time with Rabbi Ascherman, we talked about Israeli culture and how it is changing. When I came to Israel last year anticipating the warm Jewish culture I had heard about, I was shocked and upset by the ubiquitous suspicion, soldiers, and guns that made me feel far more uneasy than secure. Rabbi Ascherman assured me that although in the last few years he has seen a deterioration of the values that first made him want to live in Israel (he is originally from the United States), he also believes there is a current movement of Jewish Israelis to "return to themselves," to return to the "strong passionate Jewish morality" that he sees as fundamental in the Jewish culture and religion.[5]

Israeli former soldiers who, like Rabbi Ascherman, "feel that service in the Occupied Territories and the incidents [Israeli soldiers have] faced have distorted and harmed the moral values on which [they] grew up" have formed a group called Breaking the Silence. Hundreds of regretful Israeli ex-soldiers have come forward to "tell [the truth] about everything that goes on [in the Occupied Territories] each and every day." According to former soldiers' investigations and testimonies, incidents of abuse and army brutality like the kidnapping in Marda are no longer the exception; they have become the norm.[6]

From what Amid could tell, the two other soldiers involved in the incident disapproved of the actions of their commanding officer, but were too intimidated to stop him. During my time here, I hope to encourage more soldiers to listen to their consciences instead of blindly following their superiors—I know that members of Breaking the Silence wish they had done so.[7] I am personally encouraged by the recent evidence that—as in Amid's case—an international presence can make a difference.

Israeli activist Yehoshua Rosen picks olives in solidarity with Abu Fouad, a farmer from Deir Istiya.

[5] Rabbi Ascherman talks about the need to create "an Israel that is not only physically strong but also morally strong" in a short film documenting Israelis and Palestinians rebuilding illegally demolished Palestinian homes in East Jerusalem: *www.icahd.org/eng/video.asp?menu=video&submenu=video*

[6] More information about Breaking the Silence can be found at *www.breakingthesilence.org.il*

[7] Here is one soldier's testimony of blindly following orders: *www.breakingthesilence.org.il/testimony_en.asp?full=334*

Checkpoint Watch in Deir Ballut & Jubara

Thursday, November 20, 2003

This morning I went on my first "Checkpoint Watch." Similar to border crossings between countries, checkpoints are barriers manned by soldiers or border police to restrict pedestrian and vehicular mobility. However, unlike border crossings, most checkpoints in the Occupied Palestinian Territories are installed *within* the West Bank and Gaza, not around them. The Israeli government claims checkpoints are necessary to prevent Palestinian attacks on Israelis, but checkpoints primarily restrict movement between Palestinian cities and villages, not between the Palestinian Territories and Israel.

Abuses by Israeli soldiers or police are so common at checkpoints that Israeli and international volunteers have developed Checkpoint Watch to witness those abuses and if possible, intervene to stop them. Today we observed the checkpoint that monitors movement into and out of Deir Ballut, a small village just east of the Green Line, the internationally recognized border between Israel and the West Bank. Last night the army unexpectedly closed the checkpoint into Deir Ballut and several villagers were stranded away from home. When we arrived in the early morning, the checkpoint was almost empty save for a few children on their way to school. In the old days, the students used to take a school bus, but the vehicle obstructions have rendered that option more hassle than it's worth. Instead, the children and teachers walk past snipers and electric fences on their way to class every morning, showing their IDs and opening up their book-bags to be searched. Since checkpoint wait-times are always unpredictable, so are their school hours.

Three female teachers came to the checkpoint after we arrived and the soldier motioned for them to come up one by one. The first woman approached the soldier, waited

Palestinians wait to show their IDs and be searched at a military checkpoint in the middle of the West Bank.

Two women from Deir Ballut cross the military checkpoint that blocks the village's main road. Pedu'el settlement occupies Deir Ballut land in the background.

while he searched her, and then continued when he nodded that she could pass. The next two women had brought their school identification but not their Israeli-issued identity papers. Apparently, school IDs had been enough in the past, but today's soldier said that wouldn't suffice. The women tried to explain to the soldier that if they went all the way back to the village to fetch their papers, they would be late for their classes. In the end, they went all the way back home and were late for their classes.

I asked the soldier if he was worried that the women were dangerous. He said it was against the rules to let them pass without papers. I took a step forward and asked him if he ever thought about the rules he was enforcing. He shouted at me to step back. I held my ground and said I just wanted to talk, but he barked at me to go back right away. I turned and walked back to the concrete blocks where my colleagues were observing. I felt terrible about the exchange. It seemed my questions had made him angrier, and I knew I would not

Palestinians wait in line at an Israeli military checkpoint inside the West Bank. Yellow-plated Israeli cars pass freely on their left.

be the one to suffer the consequences of my actions and his bad mood.

In everything internationals do, our first consideration must always be the effects our actions will have on the people around us, both long-term and short-term. I believe the questions I asked the soldier were good ones, but it may have been a mistake to ask them at that moment. I may be able to leave when things become heated, but most people here cannot.

At 9 a.m. we left Deir Ballut for the city of Tulkarem to visit two women who are setting up a cooperative for local seam-stresses. One woman asked me if I would help her sell locally-produced handicrafts abroad. I said I would inquire about possibilities, but I am not optimistic. Most Palestinian trade is restricted to countries maintaining good diplomatic relations with Israel, which excludes many neighboring

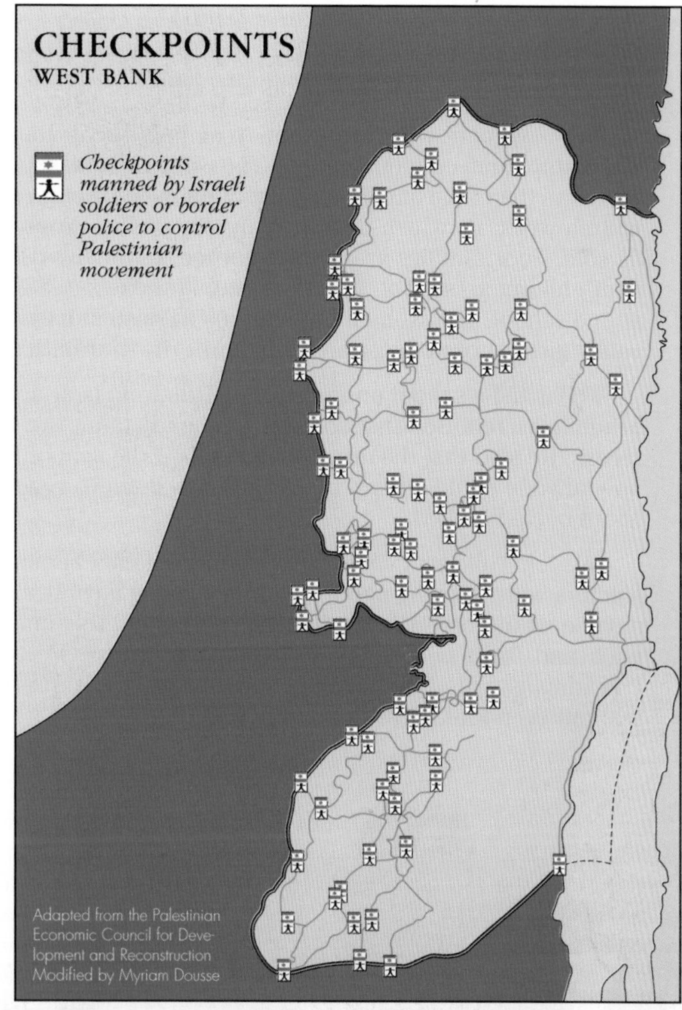

Soldiers monitor movement between Palestinian towns and villages.

Arab countries. Palestinian trade is also subject to Israeli taxes, which are sometimes higher than Palestinian merchants can afford to pay.

Both women work full-time teaching local female villagers about democracy, leadership, and communication. The women told us familiar stories of farmers denied access to their land at checkpoints, or allowed through but denied permission to return for up to a week, by which time their freshly picked crops had gone bad and could no longer be sold. Poor families are getting poorer, and many parents can no longer afford to send their children to school. It costs about 45 shekels (US$10) a year for a Palestinian child to attend school. The women implored us to raise money to help the children, many of them young girls whose education is not a priority in traditional families.[8]

We visited a school on the edge of Tulkarem near an Israeli military training camp. The headmaster reported that soldiers frequently taunt the children playing in the yard during recess. He said that the army once bombed the school from military planes. He wondered how anyone could expect the children to learn to read and write when they are worried about being bombed.

We left Tulkarem via the city's southern checkpoint, Jubara, which was in chaos. The soldiers were keeping people back by placing a rubber rod on the ground and threatening anyone who crossed it. We felt trapped behind this imaginary wall as the soldiers walked back and forth in front of us with large guns. Of course, the barrier applied only to Palestinians; when the soldiers saw our group of internationals, they waved us through without even looking at our passports.

A white-plated and green-plated (Palestinian) ambulance pulls over to allow yellow-plated (Israeli) vehicles to pass at Zatara checkpoint.

We were not the only privileged people there. Cars with yellow license plates drove straight through the checkpoint without stopping. Israelis and Palestinians have different colored license plates so that soldiers can easily identify whether a car is carrying Israelis or Palestinians. Israeli plates are yellow, while Palestinian plates are white and green. At Jubara checkpoint, as at others, yellow-plated cars were allowed to pass unhindered, while white-plant and green-plated cars, ambulances included, stood waiting for hours at gunpoint.

I began to feel sick. I hadn't eaten in hours because it is impolite to eat in public during *Ramadan*, the month-long Islamic holiday of fasting that began a few weeks ago. As I grew hungrier, I stopped taking in what I was seeing. It was too disturbing, and I couldn't think about it anymore. I sat down on the curb and shoved a few bites of food into my mouth. When I emerged from my

[8] To donate money towards the education of Palestinian girls in the Tulkarem region, contact Hanan at the Palestinian Women's Developing Center. Email: *hanan716_5@hotmail.com*, Tel: (972) 92 67 58 35 or 599 675 914.

Jit checkpoint

hunger-induced daze, the scene in front of me came back into focus. I watched the Palestinians standing squeezed together like cattle in the hot sun, knowing most of them had been fasting since four in the morning. I had only been fasting since ten.

I wondered where they had learned such patience. I wondered how I would react in their shoes. If I were a Palestinian, would I resist? Would I stand up for myself? Yes, probably. And then I would be kicked down. And down, and down again until I had no more spirit. Or maybe my spirit would grow stronger with every kick. Oppression affects people differently. Some grow more and more determined; others grow weak. Perhaps a few have the lucidity to think rationally about the situation. Then again, attempting to think rationally and practically in the context of such inhumanity would probably drive most sane people crazy.

Beit Amin checkpoint

Witness in Palestine

The Wall, Munira's House, & Other Families in the Seam

© IWPS 2003

The author and Munira's son in front of the Wall that separates Munira and her family from their village and land

Friday, November 21, 2003

Today I visited a warm and soft-spoken woman named Munira who lives with her husband Hani and their six small children on the outskirts of Mas'ha village. Hani and his family came to Mas'ha as refugees from the War of 1948, known to Palestinians as the *Nakba* or "Catastrophe," because it marked the exodus of three quarters of Palestine's native population, who have never been allowed to return.[9] Hani's father was killed in the war. Left without a breadwinner, the young Hani and his family were homeless for 10 years.[10]

When Hani grew up, he built a home for himself and his family in Mas'ha. He and Munira built nurseries and greenhouses, and lived off their trees, land, and animals. Even when the nearby Elkana settlement was founded in 1978 and grew to within 20 ft of their bedroom window, the family did not move. Then, last year, another *nakba* of Palestinian recent history began: the building of Israel's "Separation Barrier," the Wall.

If you were to build a Wall to prevent two groups from hurting one another, where would you build it? Most people would build on the border between the two peoples' territories. In fact, that is where most supporters of Israel's Wall believe it to be: between Israel and the Palestinian Territories. But any map of the planned and partially completed path of the Wall—a map that you're unlikely to find in any mainstream US newspaper, even though Americans are the ones paying for it—reveals a different reality. According to the United Nations Office for the Coordination of Humanitarian Affairs (OCHA), the Western half of the Wall is expected to annex approximately 14.5% of West Bank land to Israel, a percentage OCHA estimates will at least double after completion of the projected extensions and closures on the eastern side. The barrier winds deeply into the West Bank, passing close by Palestinian built-up areas and annexing the surrounding land and water sources to Israel, along with

9 For details about the *Nakba*, see pp. 332-337.

10 Anna Weekes, "The One-Family Bantustan in Mas'ha," *Green Left Weekly* (March 10, 2004).

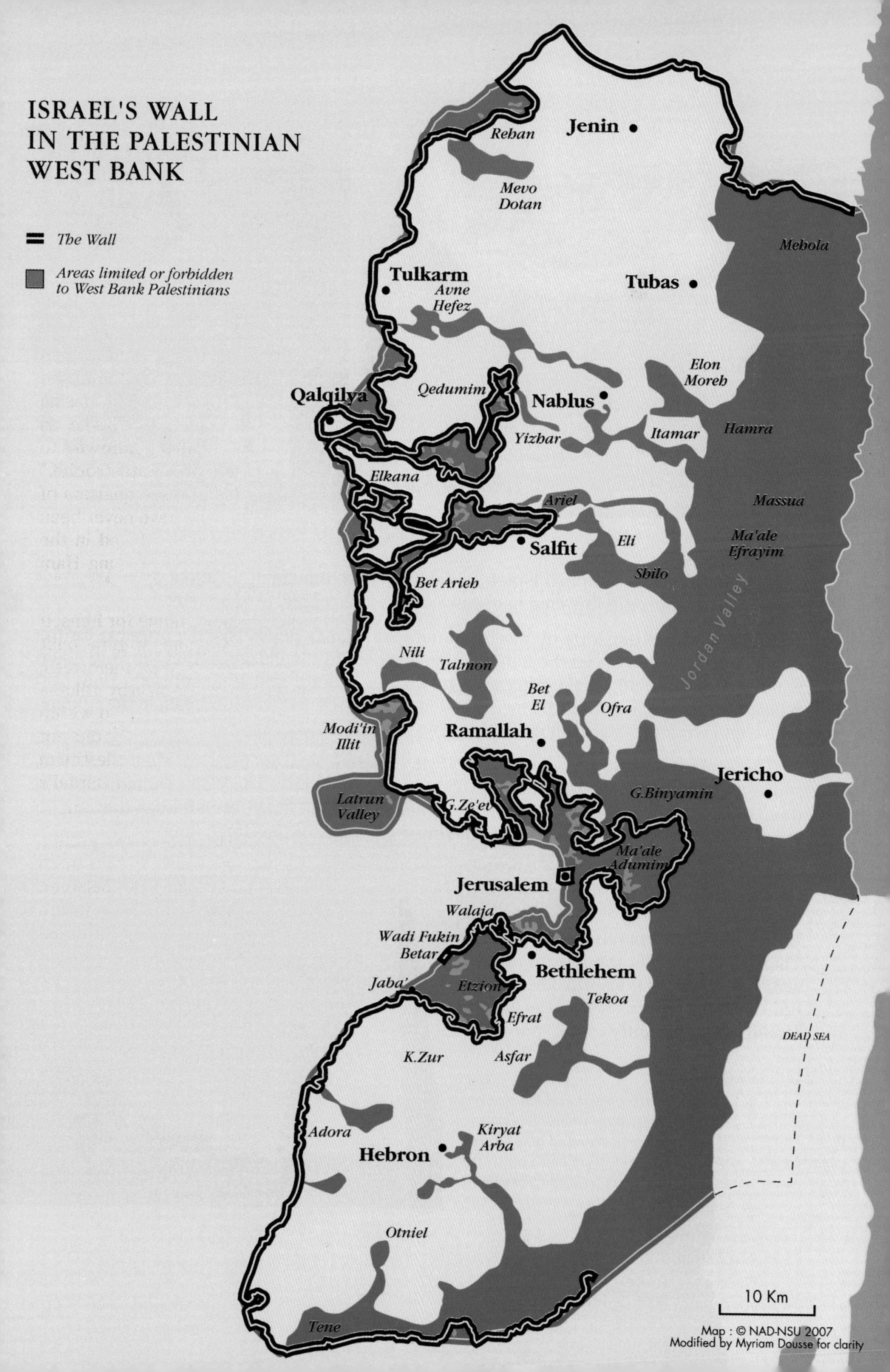

ISRAEL'S WALL IN THE PALESTINIAN WEST BANK

= *The Wall*

■ *Areas limited or forbidden to West Bank Palestinians*

Rehan
Jenin
Mevo Dotan
Mehola
Tulkarm
Avne Hefez
Tubas
Elon Moreh
Qalqilya
Qedumim
Nablus
Itamar
Hamra
Yizhar
Elkana
Ariel
Massua
Eli
Salfit
Ma'ale Efrayim
Shilo
Bet Arieh
Jordan Valley
Nili
Talmon
Bet El
Ofra
Modi'in Illit
Ramallah
Jericho
G.Binyamin
Latrun Valley
G.Ze'ev
Ma'ale Adumim
Jerusalem
Walaja
Wadi Fukin
Betar
Bethlehem
Jaba'
Etzion
Tekoa
Efrat
DEAD SEA
K.Zur
Asfar
Adora
Kiryat Arba
Hebron
Otniel
Tene

10 Km

Map : © NAD-NSU 2007
Modified by Myriam Dousse for clarity

The Wall passes close by built-up Palestinian areas, annexing all the surrounding land into Israel.

existing settlements. Although Israeli settlements have only built up about 3% of the West Bank, with the surrounding land and water sources they control about 40%.[11]

Situated on the outskirts of Mas'ha, Munira and Hani's house posed a problem for the Israeli army, who implored the family to move closer to the village so that the Wall could annex the house and neighboring area to Elkana. Munira and Hani refused. They also refused financial compensation, insisting that all they wanted was to remain in their home, to live and work on their land in peace.

The army responded by building a 25 ft concrete wall in front of Munira's house, separating the family from their land, village, and community. The Wall continues in both directions, leaving Munira's family on the Israeli side of the fence, even though they are on internationally recognized Palestinian territory, well east of the Green Line.

In Munira's backyard is another fence keeping the family out of neighboring Elkana which, like all settlements, is reserved for Jews only. There are fences on the remaining two sides of Munira's house to keep them out of Israel proper, where the family would also qualify as "potential

Munira's house: An army road and the concrete Wall stand where the family's olive groves and greenhouses once stood. Wire fence continues on the other three sides of the house, forming a complete cage.

[11] *PASSIA* 2007, p. 313.

terrorists." Surrounded on all four sides, Munira and her family live in a cage—an open-air prison.

Munira and Hani are determined to stay in their home as long as they can, but the obstacles increase every day. Because of the Wall, Hani can no longer easily reach his work in nearby Azzun Atma, and Munira can hardly leave her house for fear of it being destroyed. To reach their remaining land, Munira and Hani have to wait hours for soldiers to unlock the gate of the cage. Hani says the army initially wasn't going to build a gate, but they agreed to after the Red Cross, United Nations Relief and Works Agency, and various Israeli human rights groups interfered. Munira and Hani say they feel like foreigners on their own land. Their youngest children, on the other hand, have grown accustomed to their cage, having forgotten what life was like before the Wall. The parents worry about the children's isolation from other children, and the long-term social, economic, educational, and psychological effects that the two *nakbas* will have on future generations.

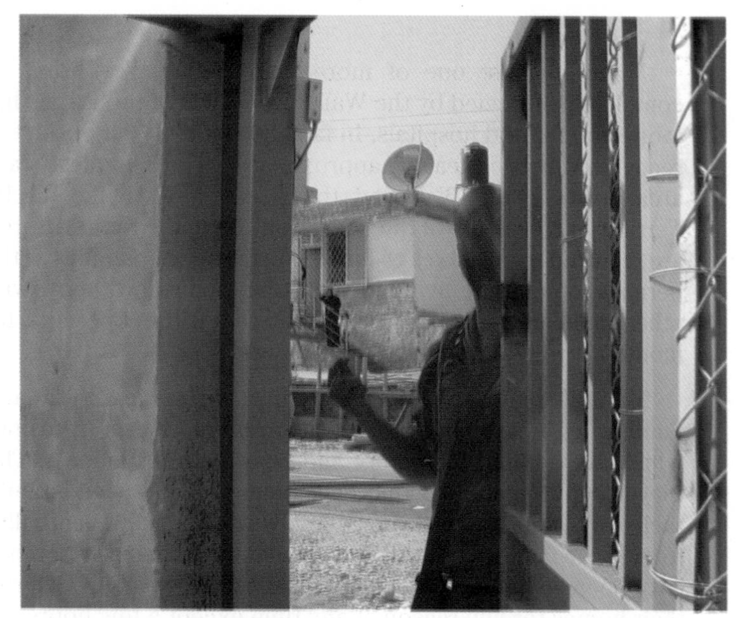

A soldier guards the gate to Munira's house.

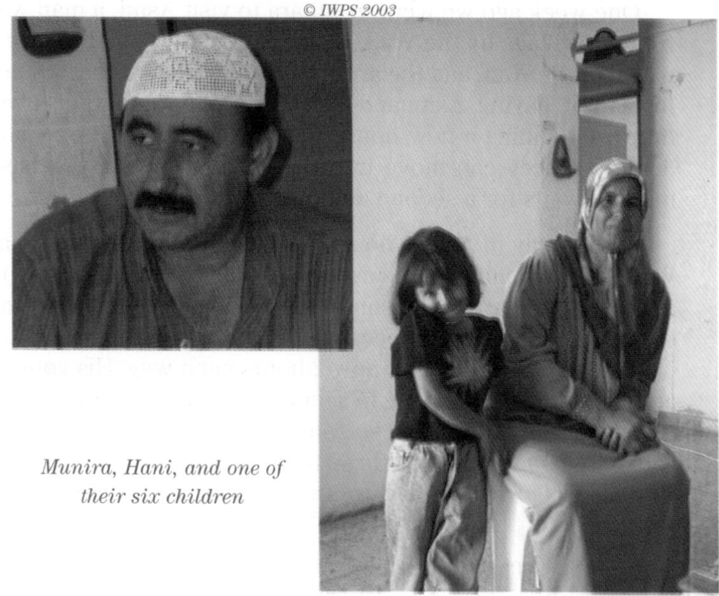

Munira, Hani, and one of their six children

Friends, family, IWPS, and delegations try to visit Munira often, but we're dependent on soldiers' schedules and whims. During Ramadan the gate to Munira's cage has been open just once a day, from four to five in the afternoon. It is well-known that this hour is reserved for cooking and the breaking of the fast, and is not a time when people can visit, particularly not women. IWPS inquired about the reasoning behind this schedule, but the army did not respond. The intention, however, seems clear: to render life so difficult that the family surrenders and leaves.

Munira is just one of more than 31,000 West Bank Palestinians who have been completely encircled by the Wall.[12] Hundreds of thousands have been separated from their jobs, schools, and hospitals. In fact, 80% of the Wall doesn't even touch the internationally recognized border, leaving approximately 375,000 Palestinians stranded in the "Seam," the area between the Wall and the Green Line.[13] Like all Palestinians in the Occupied Territories, residents of the Seam don't have the rights afforded to Israeli citizens, but they are required to pay taxes to Israel. Furthermore, families in the Seam are required to obtain permits to continue living in their own homes on their own land. Jewish Israelis, on the other hand, are free to move into the Seam without permits. In fact, I could move there next month if I wanted to, because I'm Jewish.

Munira's is not the only family that is resisting. In an act of civil disobedience, many families in Jubara village near Tulkarem have been refusing to carry the Israeli permits, which are difficult to acquire and expire after 3 months. The families are worried that if they accept the premise that Palestinians should need Israeli permits to continue living on their own land in the Seam, the government will eventually revoke them as a means of forcing the families out. As punishment for refusing to obtain permits, the people of Jubara have been kept under Israeli military curfew, during which residents are forbidden to leave their homes for any reason at any time except a few hours a week to get food. The curfew has prevented any residents from leaving their village for the past month.

One week ago we went to Jubara to visit Asmi, a man whose house has been separated from his village by the Wall. Every day, military jeeps drive through his backyard on their patrol of the Wall, and the army has informed him that his house is under demolition order. Instead of leaving, Asmi and his family have found their own unique method of resistance: they are building a new house right next to the old one, so that when their first house is destroyed they can move into the second, buying themselves more time (assuming the military waits for a second demolition order).

On the way to Asmi's house, we met another family separated from their village by the Wall. The son smiled at us as we walked by and eventually the whole family came out and invited us in for tea. The son was studying at a university in Nablus but had not been able to go to school recently because of Jubara's checkpoint and curfew. His commute, which used to be half an hour, is now 2 hours each way. His younger sister and brother came out and we asked if they were in school too. They said they were, but that their school was on the other side of the Wall, so sometimes when the gates are closed they don't make it. The gates are usually opened three times a day for an hour at a time. If they are closed, it's a 2.5-mile walk to the next gate, and another 2.5 miles to get back down to the village school.

The father of the children looked at his land and olive groves with a mixture of pride and sadness. The mother motioned towards the Wall with disgust. "Our village, our family is on the other side of that Wall!" she exclaimed. "My mother is sick but I cannot go to her when she needs me. This is what they call peace? Every day they take more. And when we fight back they take even more. But stolen territory will never bring Israel security, as they suggest. Security will come from peace, and peace will never come from a wall."

---

[12] *PASSIA* 2007.

[13] Jimmy Carter, *Palestine: Peace Not Apartheid* (New York: Simon & Schuster, 2006), p. 192.

Roadblocks & a Demonstration in Budrus

Sunday, November 23, 2003

Today we attended a demonstration against the Wall in Budrus, a Palestinian village near the Green Line west of Ramallah. Budrus is not far from where we live, but it took over 2 hours to travel there because we had to change taxis every 15 minutes or so at each roadblock along the way.

Roadblocks are concrete blocks or dirt piles installed by the Israeli military to inhibit vehicular movement on Palestinian roads. Roadblocks are not manned by soldiers and do not prevent people from crossing on foot; their sole purpose is to complicate or prevent Palestinian movement. Instead of taking their cars on the main road to work, Palestinians must take either indirect unpaved roads or taxis that shuttle back and forth between roadblocks.

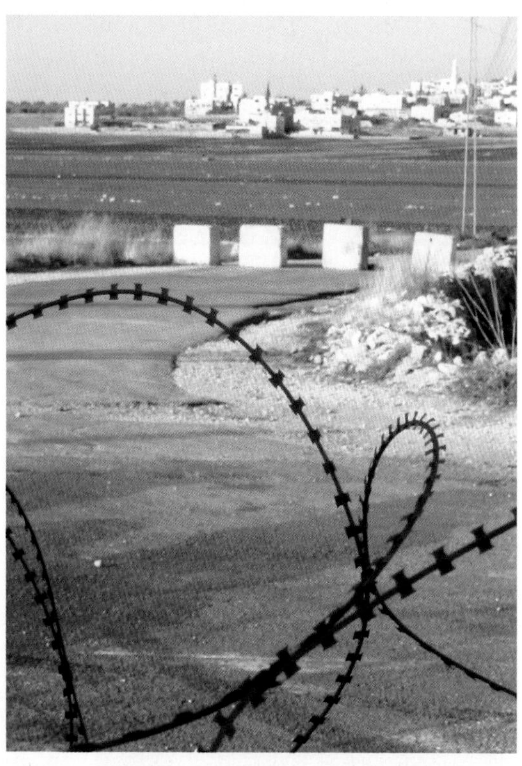

Concrete roadblocks prevent Deir Ballut villagers from using their cars on their main road.

There is a roadblock at the entrance of Haris, where we live. In order to leave Haris, we have to hike out of the village and catch transportation on the main road. Imagine if to leave your town or city you had to walk to its outskirts. Our landlord owns a car, but to use it he must take an uncomfortable unpaved detour that has already caused serious damage to the vehicle.

Like most structures of the Occupation, roadblocks are ostensibly built for Israeli security. Yet I cannot imagine how it helps Israeli citizens to prevent Palestinians from using their own cars and their own roads. More than anything else, roadblocks add stress and struggle to any movement. For instance, a commuter will drive his car every day to a roadblock obstructing his road to work, park his car at the roadblock, walk across by foot, and then take a taxi the rest of the way. He may end up paying more for taxis than he earns at his job, rendering work a waste of time. Roadblocks allows Israel to maintain a type of control over Palestinians' mobility and daily lives at little cost.

Roadblocks also affect the Palestinian economy. Transporting Palestinian products past them is a three-step process. First, a truck carrying goods must back up against the roadblocks. Then, another truck must back up to the other side of the roadblock. Finally, somebody has to manually transport the goods from the first truck to the second by lifting

A dirt roadblock prevents Yasouf villagers from driving north of their village. Commuters to nearby Nablus must drive to the roadblock, park their cars, walk across on foot, and take a taxi the rest of the way. Tapuach settlement occupies Yasouf land in the background.

the goods over the roadblocks. The added manpower, vehicles, and gas required to transport Palestinian products often renders them even more costly than their Israeli counterparts, which are quick and easy to transport on the Israeli-only roads. As a result, the Palestinian market is then flooded with Israeli products. Palestinians, many of whom struggle to make ends meet, end up buying the cheaper Israeli products rather than supporting their own economy, in effect financing the very country that is occupying them. So Israel actually profits financially from the road obstructions.

Because so many passengers and goods are forced to change vehicles at roadblocks, they have become popular gathering places and it's common to find tea vendors and falafel stands in

Roadblocks prevent the efficient transport of Palestinian products, often rendering them more costly than their Israeli counterparts.

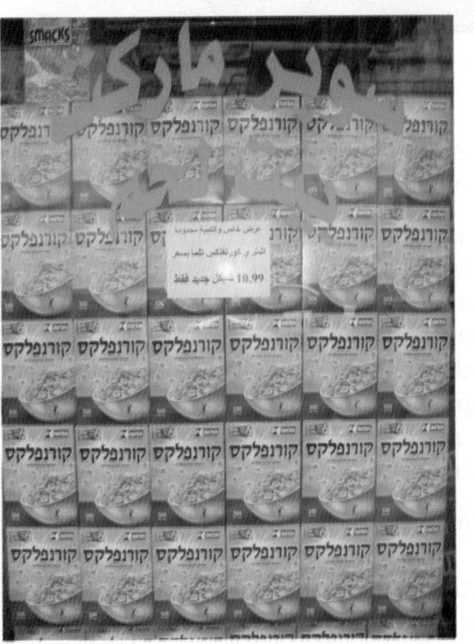

Israeli products dominate the Palestinian market.

The Qarawat Bani Hassan roadblocks are a popular meeting place where taxi drivers wait to shuttle people to and from nearby villages or roadblocks. Qiryat Netafim settlement occupies Qarawat land in the background.

addition to taxi stations. Seeing business develop from the roadblocks is both inspiring and depressing. It's inspiring to see that Palestinian enterprise and ingenuity continue to spark even in such dismal conditions; but it's depressing to see that what would normally be intolerable burdens have become normal daily life. Removing roadblocks has been a common form of nonviolent resistance during this *intifada* (Arabic for "uprising"). But such direct action invariably results in the collective punishment of the Palestinians living in the area of the action. Common punishments include the addition of new military checkpoints, the imposition of curfews, arrests and house demolitions.

On the way to the demonstration today, we passed Kfar Tapuah, an Israeli settlement near the Palestinian village of Yasouf. It is easy to distinguish the settlements from Palestinian villages. The former are usually on hilltops, for geographical advantage. With large modern houses, often identical, they look like suburban gated communities. Settlements are built rapidly, whereas Palestinian villages have usually evolved organically over time, in keeping with the topography of the landscape. Built using materials from the land, they blend naturally into the countryside.

Tapuah and the area around the settlement are home to notoriously violent ideological settlers and the army division that protects them. On weekends, settlers sometimes picnic at the natural springs and beautiful gardens of Yasouf with their children, guard dogs, and guns.

Israeli settlements are easy to distinguish from Palestinian villages.
(left: Qiryat Netafim settlement; right: Beit Furik)

The next village along our way was Qarawat Bani Zeid, where a devastatingly beautiful boy knocked on the taxi window and lifted up his shirt, revealing a massive wound that was draining into a sack strapped to his stomach. I didn't know what to do or say, but he smiled at me reassuringly as our taxi began to move. We sped off through the mountains until we arrived in Budrus and joined with locals to head towards the hills where the demonstration was taking place. As we walked, I practiced my rudimentary Arabic and the children laughed at my name. "*Ana*" means "me," "I," or "I am" in Arabic, so when I say "I'm Anna" it sounds like I'm saying "I'm me," or just stuttering: "I'm... I'm..."

The goal of the demonstration was to walk to the Budrus land that Israel is leveling for the Wall and to document and protest its destruction. As we hiked over the first hill, I made out a mass of people in the valley below. It was a moving sight: hundreds of Palestinians waving flags of pride and peace, and children running with banners that glimmered in the sunlight. At the top of the next hill, between us and the threatened land, were the soldiers standing watch. I hurried to join the crowd below.

It scared me to see the soldiers watching over us, and I fumbled with the onion I had brought in my pocket in case we were tear gassed—the strong smell of an onion is supposed to remind you that you are still breathing, countering the gas' tendency to make you believe that you are choking. I tried to be as conspicuous as possible, knowing that my purpose was not to blend in but rather to make my presence known to the soldiers in hopes that it would discourage violence. At the top of the hill, the soldiers looked ready to confront us. The crowd stopped in front of them and my colleague Jamie and the demonstration organizers stepped forward to talk to the soldiers. The soldiers had no right to be there, but I found them remarkably self-restrained given the noisy taunting from the crowd. It's astonishing to see young boys yelling at men holding machine guns, but I suspect I would yell too if I were in their shoes.

After several fruitless attempts to explain to the soldiers what the protest was about and why we should pass, the soldiers began to look bored and a few Palestinian boys started to throw rocks from

Budrus villagers gather to protest the destruction of their land.

a nearby hill. The organizers tried to encourage the crowd to disperse, and as we began walking back to the car, my colleague Dunya was hit in the head with a rock. She was bleeding heavily when I reached her and she said she was hurt and needed to leave. Our group split up: five women left and three of us stayed to make sure the demonstration ended safely.

Boys from Budrus village proudly display the Palestian flag.

I was in charge of photographic documentation so I continued taking pictures while we discussed our next steps with some other international activists and photographers. All of a sudden—and I still don't know why—the entire group of protesters turned and began to race into a field of trees. The soldiers raised their guns and fired several tear gas canisters and rubber bullets into the air. The shots were clearly over the heads of our group of internationals and landed somewhere in the trees where the Palestinians were crouched. We quickly decided to leave, since our presence was obviously not improving matters. When we left, the soldiers were still firing into the trees.

We were frustrated by the escalation of events and plan to discuss the incident at our next team meeting when Jamie and Dunya return from the hospital.[14] It is very hard to know what risks to take in such situations and how much good we can really do. It seems to vary from day to day, soldier to soldier. The demonstrators who drove us home today made it clear that they appreciated our presence immensely. One boy (with scars on his lower abdomen and lower back where a bullet went in and out 6 months ago) asked me where I was from and I told him I was Jewish-American. He looked surprised and I told him yes, I was Jewish, but that I supported Palestinians' right to a homeland and self-determination. He gave me a big smile and put out his hand for me to shake, which I did. He said I was very welcome in Palestine.

Demonstrators run away from tear gas and rubber bullets.

[14] Dunya received stitches behind her left ear.

Witness in Palestine
Jenin Camp

Monday, November 24, 2003

Today we went north to visit Jenin city and refugee camp. Jenin city has a different feel from other cities I've visited in Palestine: it is not quite broken, but it is very wounded. While the people are not unfriendly, many are suspicious after what they have experienced. We visited the ISM apartment in Jenin to look at pictures for an exhibition they were preparing. The pictures, drawn by 12-year-old Palestinian children given a free-drawing task, were of tanks and soldiers cutting down trees and shooting men, women, and children. No drawing was without violence or bloodshed. One picture showed a group of children with backpacks running from a tank. A child had fallen into a ditch behind the rest and was about to be shot. Another picture showed a pregnant woman kneeling on the floor, crying at the sight of her dead and bloodied son. Behind her, a large hole in the wall revealed the tank that had destroyed the house and killed the young man.

Above and right: Drawings by Palestinian children in Jenin given a free-drawing task

Another picture showed two soldiers standing on a tank pointing guns at two children walking to school. A friend translated the Arabic script for me. One soldier was saying, "You may not go to school," to which one of the children was responding, "We won't go home. We will go to school and we will learn and we will stay here to protect our land and Jerusalem, our capital." At the top right of the page was written "Despite the siege and handcuffs, we will stay here with our people until we achieve our goal of freedom and independence."

Jenin has a reputation for fighting back. Locals say that in April of 2002 it took 12,000 Israeli troops 8 days to capture one small section of the city because so many people fought to the death. Many residents have shown that they would rather die than surrender their homes and lives to military control. Nonetheless, Jenin is now effectively imprisoned by the Wall, which separates the city from its land and nearby villages. Most of the fertile soil for which Jenin is famous is now inaccessible. The three Palestinian villages in the Seam on the other side of the Wall are under constant pressure from the Israeli government to move. Israel frequently cuts their water and electricity off.

Two weeks ago, Palestinians and international solidarity volunteers succeeded in a direct action of cutting through a fenced section of the Wall north of Jenin. Two days later it was rebuilt even stronger, but protesters went back last Saturday to show that they would not be deterred. The second protest was successful in that it made the front page of the Israeli mainstream newspaper *Haaretz*, but it was also tragic in that a young boy was shot and killed by the army in Jenin during ISM's absence. The boy was 12 years old, a fifth-grader named Ibrahim.

Violence in Jenin is not uncommon. According to locals, Israeli Occupation forces shot seven young Palestinians in a nearby village earlier this month, two of whom died. They were dressed in their best clothes, making their way home for *iftar*, the ceremonial breaking of the Ramadan fast. Locals also recounted an incident in which three teenage boys were taken into the forest and severely beaten. Apparently, one soldier stuck a gun in a boy's face and said, "At the count of three, I will shoot you," but another soldier intervened. The boys returned to their homes with bruises all over their bodies; one boy's eye was nearly poked out. They said the soldiers had made them eat grass like animals.

The military has maintained a frequent presence in Jenin since the violent spring of 2002. That March, a deadly Palestinian suicide attack on the eve of Passover in the city of Netanya killed almost 30 Israelis. Allegedly in response to the bombing—but using an offensive planned far in advance (in part by studying German tactics in taking over the Warsaw Ghetto, according to one Israeli officer)—Israeli soldiers driving American-made bulldozers plowed through the center of Jenin refugee camp, home to 13,000 impoverished Palestinians, a handful of whom had been putting up armed resistance to the Israeli military takeover. Soldiers bulldozed homes indiscriminately, without regard to whether any civilians were still inside. According to *Amnesty International* and *Human Rights Watch* (*HRW*), Israel then prevented medical and humanitarian relief workers from entering the camp for more than 10 days, while victims perished under the rubble. Thousands of survivors were rendered homeless for the second time in recent history.

Children play among the demolished homes of Jenin refugee camp.

Amnesty and *HRW* both found that most of the destruction was carried out after clashes had ceased.[15] Israel used bulldozers to minimize soldier casualties, but no one knows how many Palestinians died in the attack. With help from the United States, Israel disbanded a UN fact-finding team investigating the attack, and simultaneously denied Palestinians access to the bodies of the dead, insisting on burying them themselves. Shortly afterward, Israel announced 46 casualties, less than a quarter of their original estimates. Israeli soldiers' and Palestinian civilians' testimonies of unarmed men being executed and bodies being crushed suggest that this number is wildly inaccurate. Israel still maintains that a massacre never happened at all, and without access to the bodies, nobody can prove that those who went missing were actually killed.[16]

Jenin camp remains a field of destroyed houses, a sort of mass grave. One Israeli soldier was quoted by locals as saying he hoped they would make it into an Israeli football field. But at present it remains empty except for a few construction workers and several children

---

[15] "Jenin: IDF Military Operations," *Human Rights Watch* (New York, 2002), pp. 2-3, Chap. 6; "Shielded from Scrutiny: IDF Violations in Jenin and Nablus," *Amnesty International* (London, 2002), pp. 14-25, 67; As cited in Norman Finkelstein, *Beyond Chutzpah: On the Misuse of Anti-Semitism and the Abuse of History* (California: Univ. of California Press, 2005), p. 52.

[16] Tanya Reinhart, *Israel/Palestine: How to End the War of 1948* (New York: Seven Stories Press, 2002), pp. 150-170.

running around playing among the ruined homes. We spoke to an old man who lived through the massacre. He told us his story:

> A young girl who wanted to walk to school asked me to walk with her for safety. My son-in-law recommended that I go to the school first to check out the situation there. As I was crossing the road, a soldier standing at the window in a house 2 meters from me lifted his rifle and shot me in the hand. I fell down clutching my wound. The soldier told me to get up but I said I couldn't get up because I was shot and bleeding. The soldier asked me, "Do you want to live or to die?" I pleaded with the soldier and then he shot me again in the foot. At that moment, I realized that the soldier wanted to kill me. I lifted myself up and started crawling down the street. I arrived at the village center where I found 10 Israeli soldiers hanging out. They told me to go away. I crawled into the yard where there were more soldiers. I was covered in blood. A few soldiers checked me for weapons and, finding none, they gave me a bandage. The next thing I knew I was in the Jenin hospital.

As the old man (pictured below) told his story, he began to cry. He looked at us and asked, "Who is the terrorist—us or Sharon?"[17] He told us that he appreciated and respected the American people, but that he could not respect the pro-Israel Jewish and Christian Zionist American lobbies and the US government, all of which continue to support America's role in sustaining the army that is committing these atrocities.

Across the street from where the old man spoke lay the wreckage of a demolished house where a mother and her paraplegic son had once lived. When soldiers came to destroy the house, she begged them to wait a moment for her to get her son out. They ignored her and bulldozed the house immediately. Several weeks later, neighbors found the flattened wheelchair of the son. His body was never recovered.

Last April, one year after Israeli troops destroyed Jenin camp, a 24-year-old American ISM volunteer named Brian Avery was coming around a corner in Jenin with several other international volunteers when an Israeli Armored Personnel Carrier (APC) opened fire at his face with a machine gun. Witnesses confirm that he posed no threat whatsoever to the soldiers. It took one hour for Brian's friends to obtain permission from the army to bring him to the hospital. He survived the attack but is permanently disfigured.

We walked the streets of Jenin with ISM volunteers who know Brian and are interviewing parents of Palestinians recently hurt or killed in similar attacks. We walked past a hospital that had been bombed during an incursion and we saw the frame of an ambulance that had exploded after soldiers opened fire on it. Three of the doctors inside made it out; one burned to death. His name was Dr. Khalil Suleyman.

---

17 Ariel Sharon was Israel's prime minister at the time of our visit to the camp.

In addition to Palestinian homes, the Israeli army has destroyed much of Palestinian society's infrastructure, such as this former Palestinian police station (left) and the façade of Nablus's main hotel (below).

We met with several doctors at the Red Crescent Society clinic to whom Dr. Suleyman had been a mentor. They said their work place had suffered repeated attacks in recent years, as had the police station down the street—now a pile of rubble. They wondered how the Israeli government could demand that the Palestinian Authority (PA) control Palestinian violence when the military systematically undermines or destroys almost every element of the PA's infrastructure. A French artist welded together pieces of Jenin's broken ambulances into a huge statue of a horse, which now stands in the square outside the clinic. The horse symbolizes the endurance of the people of Jenin.

I wish I had more heartening news to report. The end of Ramadan is approaching, so there will probably be feasting and celebrating over the next few days. I hope it inspires some much-needed (inner if not outer) peace and joy for the people here.

Huwwara Checkpoint & Nablus City

Thursday, November 27, 2003—Thanksgiving

This afternoon I observed Huwwara, the southern checkpoint into and out of Nablus city. There I met up with several Scottish volunteers from Women in Black, an international peace network opposed to war, militarism, and other forms of violence. When I arrived, the Women in Black were panicking because my colleague Kate was in danger of being arrested for arguing with soldiers at the checkpoint.

That day, the rule was that most women, old men, and young boys were allowed through, but men between 15 and 40 years of age were denied passage. Period. It didn't matter where they were going, it didn't matter where they were coming from, it didn't matter who they were. If you were a Palestinian young man, you couldn't get to work, or to school, or to the hospital, or to wherever else you were going. All the men had gathered in a ditch next to the checkpoint to wait, and hoping that the rule would change. A few men in the ditch started to pick up trash around the area and I wondered why.

The Women in Black volunteers wanted to go into Nablus to get some money, but said the soldiers had told them it was too dangerous. One soldier said, "You don't know what the Arabs are like. They don't care who they hurt. They will do anything. This is for your own protection." One Palestinian woman behind the Scots tried to get through and was also denied. She looked at the soldier pleadingly and asked, "Do you have children?" The soldier stuck the barrel of his rifle in her chest and pushed her away.

Huwwara Checkpoint

Huwwara is historically one of Palestine's most violent checkpoints and we were surprised that there weren't more international volunteers observing. The main objects of our concern were two men who had been blindfolded and handcuffed 4 hours earlier. They were both fasting for Ramadan, and we began to worry about heat exhaustion as they sat crouched in the sun.

A friend of one of the blindfolded men came and told us what had happened. He said one of the men, Wahit, was sick and had been referred by a doctor in his village to a heart specialist in Nablus. The soldiers told him he could not enter and handed him a trash bag saying he should start picking up trash around the checkpoint instead. Wahit refused, saying he needed to go to the doctor and would not pick up trash for the soldier. The soldiers insisted, and when Wahit refused and tried to push his way through the soldiers, one of them struck him twice—in the gut and in the shoulder—with the butt of his rifle. He then handcuffed Wahit, blindfolded him, and sat him down in the sun next to two large trash bags.[18]

Huwwara checkpoint: Palestinian men aged 15 to 40 are forbidden from entering or leaving Nablus city all day and wait in a ditch beside the checkpoint in hopes that the rule will change.

Palestinian men waiting at Huwwara checkpoint pick up trash for the soldiers on duty in hopes of being allowed through.

[18] Hundreds of Israeli veterans have come forward with stories of the army illegitimately detaining Palestinians. Their testimonies can be found at *www.breakingthesilence.org.il*

Nablus

I never got to hear the story of the man next to Wahit. Having avoided arrest, Kate came to say that there was nothing we could do and we hurried to another checkpoint, hoping to get into Nablus before dusk. Two Machsom Watch (Israeli Checkpoint Watch) volunteers stayed behind to work on getting the men released.

We made it through the second crossing (Awarta checkpoint) easily—evidence of how arbitrary checkpoint rules and security can be—and spent an hour in Nablus. The city was more vibrant and welcoming than I had imagined. I had expected that the Occupation would have diminished Arab hospitality in Palestine. Not so. I took a walk through the Old City to try and clear my mind of all the misconceptions about Arab culture that I'd picked up from Western media. Although Arabs are portrayed as violent fanatics opposed to any values or habits different from their own, in my experience this could not be further from the truth. All over the Middle East I have been welcomed with curiosity, tolerance, and respect, sometimes all the more because I am a woman traveling alone and an American choosing to look beyond the stereotypes about Arabs propagated in the United States.

As I walked through Nablus, children and adults came up to ask my name and where I was from. When I said I was from the US they were quick to point out that their distaste for the American president did not affect their positive feelings towards the American people. They welcomed me to Palestine. "Peace be upon you," I would say in Arabic. And their reply: "And upon you peace."

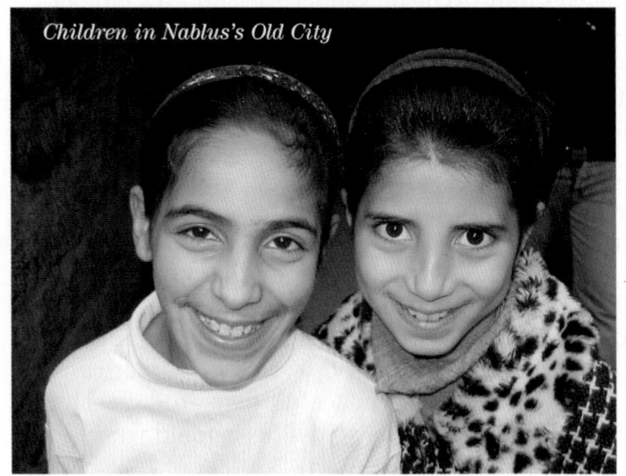
Children in Nablus's Old City

We left Nablus via the Huwwara checkpoint to see if the blindfolded men were still there. They were not; the Israeli volunteers had gotten them released. Additionally, there were several ISM volunteers on the scene. Unfortunately, the atmosphere was still tense and there were now close to a hundred young men in the ditch. One young man showed me his university card, saying he was a student in Nablus and he hadn't been able to get home to his village to see his family for an entire week. It reminded me of a man I had

A Palestinian man is detained and later arrested for yelling at soldiers who were preventing passage into and out of Nablus.

seen that morning trying to enter Nablus to see his dying mother. He was worried he wouldn't be able to reach her before she passed away.

After 15 minutes, one of the men still waiting in the ditch yelled "*Allah Hu Akbar* (God is great)" twice to signal sundown and the end of the fast, and within seconds everyone in the ditch was passing around water, dates (the traditional food for breaking fast), and cigarettes. It was a moment of peace and thanksgiving.

Just then a Palestinian boy who had walked out of the checkpoint line-up was grabbed by his collar and thrown against a concrete block. The young boy put up his arms and cooperated with the soldier who had assaulted him. A large Palestinian who had been waiting for several hours bellowed at the soldiers to let the boy go. The man's voice was strong, but he was clearly on the brink of tears. The soldiers handcuffed him for causing a ruckus. An ISM volunteer calmly tried to intervene, but the soldiers arrested her as well.

Night was falling and we were worried about making it home. One soldier motioned for us to pass ahead of all the men and we reluctantly accepted the privilege. The soldier looked at my passport and told me it was illegal for me to be in Nablus. He said, "It's violent and dangerous in Nablus." I told him it was more violent and dangerous there at the checkpoint than in Nablus. I asked him if he'd ever been to Nablus without his gun. He shook his head. I smiled and said, "It's different from what you think." He appeared to be considering my remark when I was pushed with the crowd through the line and hurried into a service taxi bound for home.

This Thanksgiving I am thankful for many things. I am thankful that I can leave my house, my town, and my country any time I want. I am thankful for options, education, medical care, money in my bank account, and food in my stomach. I am thankful that we do not have a wall outside our house in Haris, although that is likely to change soon. Most of all, I am thankful for the miracles amidst the ongoing tragedy in Palestine, and for the hope and steadfastness that remain in this war-torn land. I hope well-off Americans remember to be thankful for their relatively luxurious, peaceful lives today. The Palestinians have no trouble being thankful for what they have, so neither should we.

Witness in Palestine
Outposts, Settler Violence, & the Village of Yanoun

Friday, November 28, 2003

This morning, on our walk out of Haris, we met a farmer named Essam who said he had just been harassed by settlers from Revava settlement when he tried to reach his land between Revava and Haris. We offered to accompany Essam back to his land, and he led us to where his family was waiting with a donkey. Essam asked that just a few of us come along, including two Israeli activists. He said he was not interested in causing a scene; he just wanted to plow his land.

Revava settlement was founded in early 1991 in the face of a suggestion by world leaders that the illegal Israeli settlements be evacuated. A few dozen religious Israelis snuck onto the land at night with trailers and set up camp. They refused to move, claiming the land belonged to them.[19]

Settler trailer camps, like Revava once was, are called outposts. They are not recognized by the government, at least not at first. However, although Israeli law prohibits the government from subsidizing outposts the way it subsidizes most settlements, a majority of the 120 or so outposts in the West Bank, Gaza, and East Jerusalem are illegally funded by the Israeli state or public authorities.[20] Strengthened by the state, the outposts welcome more settlers to move in, and the illegal establishments grow.[21]

With time, the illegal cluster of trailers becomes akin to a small village or town. Soon the inhabitants need a marketplace, a road to get around, and maybe a fence to "protect" them from neighboring Palestinians. Eventually, the place is no longer an outpost; it's a settlement. Like many outposts, Revava grew into its own settlement, now recognized and financially supported by the Israeli government. This strategy has produced many of Israel's settlements.

Settlers recently set up trailers for a school in Essam's olive groves outside of Revava. One can't help but wonder why settlers who frequently complain about the threat of

---

[19] Information about the founding of Revava was collected through interviews with Revava settlers.

[20] Government participation in financing illegal outposts was confirmed by a former senior government attorney Talya Sason, who was commissioned by the Prime Minister to examine the phenomenon of illegal outposts. Her full report released in March 2005 can be found on the Israel Ministry of Foreign Affairs website. Entitled "Opinion Concerning Unauthorized Outposts," the report revealed a sizable criminal conspiracy amongst state and public authorities for whom "law violation [has become] institutionalized." The State of Israel continues to finance construction of new outposts in blatant violation of Israeli law.

[21] According to the *Alternative Information Center*, Israel will occasionally dismantle an outpost, often choosing "uninhabited structures or a few caravans," and then "advertise their symbolic [act] ... while simultaneously supporting the ongoing expansion of much larger settlements. The settlers quickly return to the outposts that were supposedly evacuated, construction (protected by the army) continues ... and the bottom line is always the steady expansion of the settlements." *AIC*, p. 27.

Palestinians would build their children's school away from the settlement itself, in the middle of Palestinian land. These trailers are not development; they are a new outpost. In another few months, the settlers will explain to the army that they need security around their children's vulnerably-located school, and they will annex the rest of Essam's and other Haris farmers' land.

But the government is one step ahead of them. If the Wall continues as projected, the villagers of Haris will lose most of their land anyway. The settlers know this, but they are impatient. While Essam and his family tried to plow, a settler drove up and asked if they would sell him their land. Essam said that this is not the first time settlers have asked. The Israeli activists told the settler in Hebrew that the farmer really was not interested in selling his land. The settler replied, "If he is smart he will sell. I will buy it now for a tenth of its value. It will belong to Revava anyway in a few months. At least this way he can make some money off it."

The settler drove away, but before the family could return to plowing, a group of schoolgirls from the new outpost began to yell across the school's fence at Essam and his family. The children were singing a song in Hebrew about "My Israel." It was disturbing to watch the youngsters, so confident in their immunity as they taunted the farmers. I waited for their teacher to come out and stop them until I realized the teacher was standing in the middle of their group, singing along.

Two Israeli activists walked towards the group of girls to talk to them, but settler security stopped them. Essam asked the activists to let it go; he and his family preferred to leave rather than risk provoking the settlers further. We walked up to Haris roadblock, where we found the army had set up a temporary checkpoint. All traffic into and out of the village was being checked. Some of my neighbors were being detained. When the soldiers realized that the activists with us were Israelis, they pulled them aside to warn them not to trust the Palestinians. "It could be very dangerous for you," they said. "We are concerned for your safety." Both activists said the only time they had ever felt threatened in the West Bank was by ideological settlers.

Indeed, the religious zealots living in illegal settlements and outposts scare me more than soldiers or Palestinians ever could, because I don't understand them. I believe the vast majority of the violence on the part of Palestinians comes from fear and trauma. The same could be said for most soldiers as well. This does not mean I condone the violence or excuse it, but on some level it does not surprise me. Ideological settlers, however, do not threaten or kill out of fear. Their actions are motivated by religious fanaticism.

Nobody has been more traumatized by ideological settlers than the villagers of Yanoun, where I headed later that day with my IWPS colleagues Jamie and Fatima. Jamie's friend Adnan picked us up from the town of Aqraba and drove us the rest of the way to the village. The road to Yanoun was bumpy and slow, but the view was spectacular: to the left we saw hill after hill of blooming olive groves, while on the right the hills dropped off into a gigantic misty abyss. It was the Jordan Valley. We could vaguely make out Jordan on the other side.

As we drove, Jamie told us about the history of Yanoun. More than 80% of the village land is olive groves that inhabitants rely on. When we remarked on the beauty of the landscape, she explained that it is in fact the richness of Yanoun's land that renders it such a target for the right-wing settlers of Itamar settlement, 4 miles away. Living in outposts

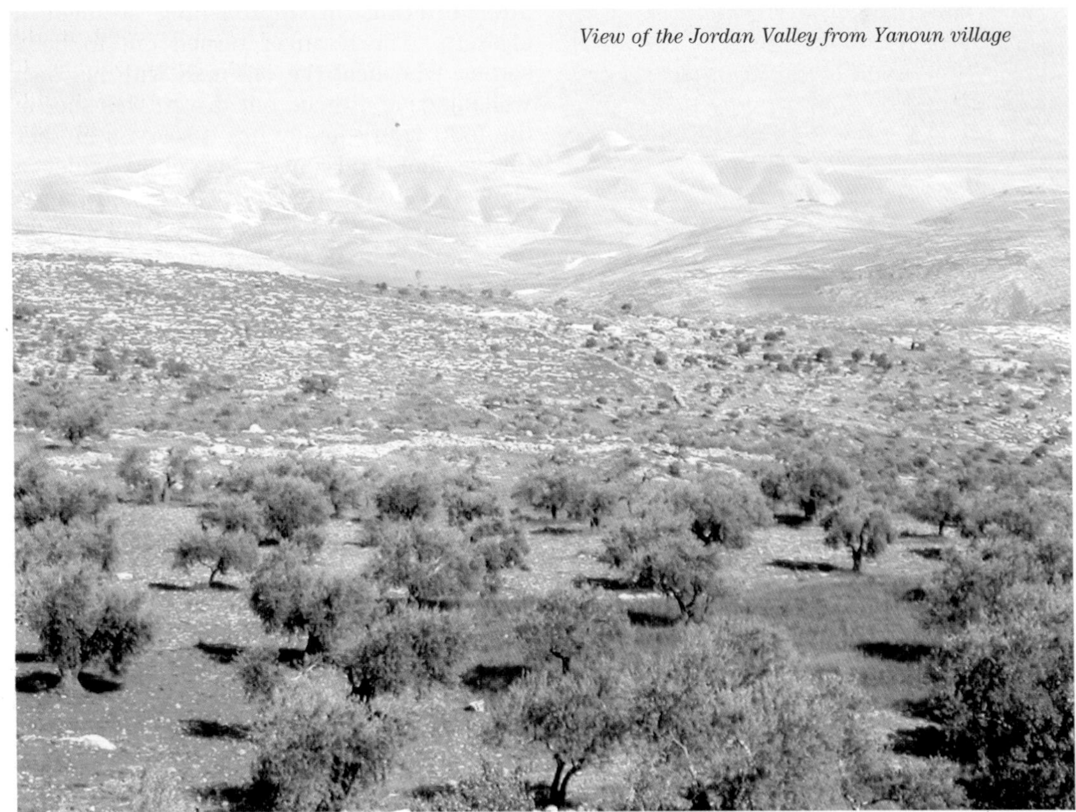

View of the Jordan Valley from Yanoun village

Lower Yanoun village

Outposts occupy the hilltops above Yanoun village.

surrounding Yanoun, Itamar settlers have been attacking and terrorizing the small village for years. They have murdered villagers who were peacefully picking their olives. They have burned the village's only generator and smashed its only water tank. They have swum in the village water supply; when villagers complained, the settlers invited their dogs in the water, too. They closed the only road into the village while shepherds were away with their goats. And the settlers have stolen 90% of the village's land, on it more than 27,000 ancient olive trees. The settlers say the olive trees were planted by Jews 2,000 years ago, and therefore they belong to the Jewish people today.

The mayor of Yanoun has been attacked by settlers seven times in the last five years and has a large scar above his eye from one incident. Another old farmer had one of his legs broken and one eye poked out by a violent settler. Another villager lost his sight after offering an approaching stranger a cigarette. The stranger turned out to be a settler, who beat the old man with his own walking cane. Adnan, our driver, was shot in the foot. Every family has a story: a mother throws her body over her child under a shower of stones from the settlers. Shepherds watch settlers poison 128 sheep but can do nothing to stop it. Even international volunteers are not immune; they have been beaten with clubs and rifle butts for accompanying farmers and shepherds to their land.

The Israeli government and army have done nothing to stop the settler attacks on Yanoun, in fact Israel continues to subsidize Itamar (in part with American tax-dollars). The Palestinian Authority couldn't do anything if it wanted to, because, like most of rural Palestine, Yanoun has so-called "Area C" status, which means that Israel is in charge of security. It also means that Palestinians are not permitted to construct any new buildings, or even to build onto their own houses.[22] Meanwhile, settlers continue to put up trailers on every hilltop around.

The violence in Yanoun climaxed in 2002, when things became so unbearable that Yanoun's residents were forced to evacuate. Fearing for their lives, the entire village packed up and left their ancestral homes and lands for nearby Aqraba. For a few days, the

[22] Descriptions and geographical specifics of Areas A, B, and C as designated by the Oslo Accords can be found on the West Bank map at the beginning of the book (pp. xii-xiii). Extensive "Area C" status is what Israel referred to as "giving the Palestinians exactly what they wanted" at Camp David II. See Appendix IV for more information on Barak's supposed "generous offer."

settlers had won. But Israeli and international activists quickly mobilized and committed themselves to maintaining a constant presence in the village if the inhabitants decided to return. About 90 of the original 300 inhabitants have now come back, but many homes remain empty.

Yanoun village's water tanks, in which settlers have swum and urinated in the past

When we arrived in Yanoun, Adnan's wife Mariam welcomed us into their home and we relaxed in the living room, drinking tea and watching the couple's 10-month-old son Rafi struggle to take his first steps. Although Jamie had been in Yanoun during the weeks before and after Rafi's birth, this was her first time seeing the baby. When Mariam went into labor, the couple took an ambulance to the nearest hospital, in Nablus. The ambulance was stopped twice along the way, at Zatara and Huwwara checkpoints. At the latter, Adnan was told he could not enter Nablus. He was forced to say goodbye to his screaming wife, who gave birth shortly afterwards while still in the ambulance. Shortly thereafter, the army closed Nablus completely, allowing nobody in or out, and Mariam waited for several days in the hospital with her newborn infant before being able to leave. Meanwhile, back in Yanoun, Adnan was beside himself with worry and frustration. When Mariam was finally allowed to return home, Rafi was 10 days old. Adnan has missed the first week and a half of his son's life.

Yanoun village's generator, burned by settlers

After we said goodbye to Adnan and his family, Jamie took us for a tour through the village. Children at every house ran outside to greet us and their parents smiled from doorways. Jamie knew everyone by name and politely played the game of refusing tea until finally there's no point and you just have to give in. In one house, there was a little curly-haired redhead named Alima. "Alima's one of my favorite kids in Yanoun," Jamie told us. "When she first saw me, she thought I was a settler coming to take her family away and started screaming hysterically. It took the family 15 minutes to calm her down and explain who I was. I've finally earned her trust."

Yanoun is divided into two parts, separated by fields and olive groves. Lower Yanoun is populated by only two families: Adnan's and Alima's. The rest of the population lives in upper Yanoun, which was built on the slope of a hill now crowned with a particularly violent outpost. On the path up to upper Yanoun, Jamie pointed out the several houses that have remained empty since the evacuation. I could hear in Jamie's voice that she regretted the families' not returning to defend their lives and land, but that she also understood why they had left. As resilient and determined as the human spirit can be, it has its limits. These families weren't willing to fight any longer.

© IWPS 2003

Armed settlers from the outposts surrounding Yanoun frequently attack villagers.

We visited house after house all the way up to the top of the village. When we arrived at the mayor's house, he welcomed us in, served us tea, and had us sign a guest book. Another family had a child anxious to learn English, so I gave her an improvised lesson. We ate dinner at the International House, where a group of Canadians had taken that week's shift as international observers in Yanoun. They were from the Ecumenical Accompaniment Programme in Palestine and Israel (EAPPI), an initiative of the World Council of Churches to work with Palestinians and Israelis towards nonviolently ending the Occupation. After dinner, we made a fire under the stars and chatted with locals who stopped by to say hello.

Sitting by the fire, I asked Dave, an EAPPI volunteer, to tell me about his experiences in Hebron. He described Hebron as a full-time war zone, with a few hundred settlers living among hundreds of thousands of Palestinians. The settlers consider their presence a sacrifice to God, calling their settlement "God's bunker." He described graffiti on the walls of the local girls' school, stars of David drawn around phrases like "Death to Arabs," and "Arabs to the gas chambers."

Dave shuddered as he spoke. "There were bars on the windows, but settlers came and stuck in pipes to break the glass. There was no money to fix them, so the girls shivered through the winter. After school, settler kids would hide and wait for the girls to walk by, throwing stones and eggs at them as they passed. The other EAPPI volunteers and I walked with them sometimes, trying to shield the attacks. Once as we were walking I saw the mother of a settler child that was throwing stones at the young girls. I pointed and said, 'Look! Look what your child is doing!' Her eyes fixed on me and her expression said clearly that she approved of her son's behavior. She hadn't come to discipline her child; she had come to watch."

I could not help but compare Dave's story with my recent experience watching the Revava teacher taunt Palestinian farmers along with her students. There's nothing more disturbing than watching adults condone or encourage inhumanity and cruelty in their children. How will settler children learn to distinguish right from wrong? Perhaps a stronger human instinct will someday surface to guide some of them towards transcending their deeply ingrained prejudices. Heroes remain to guide the way: Essam refuses to sell his land to Revava. Yanoun returnees continue to live on their remaining land. But for how long while the world stands by and does nothing?

Conversation with Omar in Balata Refugee Camp

Balata refugee camp

Saturday, November 29, 2003

I took my first days off in Balata refugee camp in Nablus. First I went to Huwwara, hoping to enter the city from the southern checkpoint, but the soldiers refused to let me through. It was getting late and I was worried about getting into Nablus before dark, but I remembered our policy of not pleading with soldiers or asking for favors. We do not ask permission for something that is our right, and we do not validate the authority of soldiers whose presence in the West Bank is to protect settlers in illegal colonies. That doesn't mean we don't treat soldiers with respect, but we are careful that respect does not appear to be consent for their illegal actions and presence. This is something we think and talk a lot about at the IWPS house, because we wish to distinguish between people and the institution that they are serving, and to recognize their humanity even amidst the inhumanity of many of their actions and the Occupation.

I asked around for a service taxi to another checkpoint, but it was too late. A young man with whom I had shared a taxi noticed I was stranded, and led me to a taxi full of other passengers who were refused entry. We set off down the highway until we reached a spot on the side of the road next to a steep hill that had clearly been trodden. Everyone hurried out of the taxi and I quickly realized that we were entering Nablus the long way, over the hills, to avoid checkpoints. We ran up to the summit and climbed over two roadblocks. There we found a taxi waiting to take us to a nearby town, where we could find transport into Nablus. By the time we reached the city it was after dark. The young man who had aided me in my journey led me to a shared taxi bound for Balata, where I was staying that night in the ISM apartment. He would not take any money for my part of the journey. I insisted, but he just put his hand on his heart and smiled to say that I was most welcome, and then walked away.

Balata sees more violence and incursions than most other places in Palestine, which is evident as you walk through the camp. There are bullet holes in every house, school, and store. The children are tougher than those in other Palestinian communities, and their parents are more suspicious. But the barrier is easily broken with a little Arabic and indication of solidarity. It was in Balata that I met Omar.

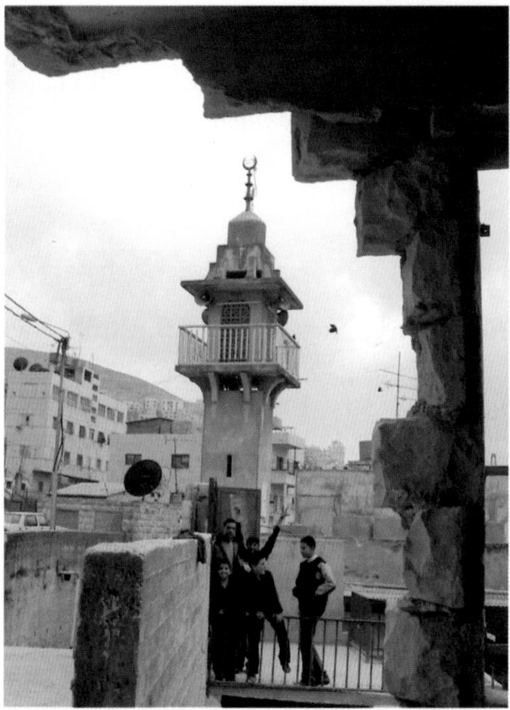

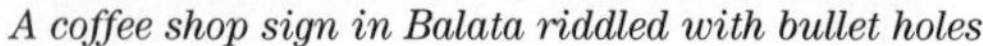

A coffee shop sign in Balata riddled with bullet holes

Children play near a demolished home in Nablus.

Omar is a sad-looking man who works with ISM. A year and a half ago, on the day I graduated from my elite university in cheerful oblivion, Omar's cousin Mahmoud was shot three times with an army tank, tearing his body into four pieces. Mahmoud belonged to Al-Aqsa Martyrs' Brigades, the military wing of the Fatah party.

Omar told me that Mahmoud had once been a Palestinian police officer but found it impossible to be effective with constant Israeli military invasions undermining all efforts towards Palestinian self-rule. One day Mahmoud confronted the raiding army with two friends; one of them was killed and the other sent to prison for over 20 years. He joined the Brigades after that.

When Omar's younger brother heard of his cousin's death, he was devastated. Five days later, he strapped a bomb to his chest and blew himself up in a city outside of Tel Aviv, killing an Israeli woman and her 18-month-old granddaughter. Omar's brother was 18 years old.

International volunteers stay at Omar's house in Balata not in support of what his brother did, but in protest of the demolition order threatening Omar's family's home, which is a form of collective punishment in retaliation for his brother's crime. There is a picture of Mahmoud and Omar's brother in the front hall of family's house. Balata camp is covered in pictures of men and women who have been killed by Israeli forces, or who have killed themselves in attacks on Israel. They are revered and mourned by the community as martyrs, regardless of how they died.

Omar and I spent the evening playing Palestinian backgammon and talking. Omar learned to play backgammon during his 7 years in and out of jail since 1985, when he was first arrested at the age of 13. He had been on his way to school when he was picked up by a jeep and put into prison for 6 months. The soldier who arrested him claimed he had thrown a stone, but Omar insists he never threw stones. Never, that is, until after he spent 6 months in jail. When he was released from prison, his attitude had changed. If Israeli soldiers were free to imprison him without trial for 6 months, he would have no qualms about throwing stones or Molotov cocktails. That was Omar's attitude until he started working with ISM.

ISM has a strict policy of nonviolence. I asked Omar what his friends and family thought of ISM's strategies and he said, "They support my nonviolent resistance work with ISM. Most of my friends do, too. Yet the Israeli media says we are animals and killers. But they are killing us!" Omar pointed to a crack in the ceiling.

> That is from a bomb that exploded the same night I stood at this window and watched my friend get shot on the street below. I wanted so desperately to go help him but I couldn't because the army was shooting. I am powerless. I am part of ISM but I cannot do Checkpoint Watch; I would have no effect. I cannot even go to an organizational meeting next week because there are three checkpoints between me and the meeting—with my last name, I will never make it. It is very frustrating, and as the Occupation policies become stricter it will become harder to find people sympathetic to ISM's strategies. Nonetheless, I believe there is still hope for nonviolence. Even with one brother paralyzed from falling debris during a raid and another one with only eight fingers, after he lost two in the same raid. Even as I watch three of my cousins and my nephew spend their lives in prison.

Omar looked at me and I saw he had tears in his eyes. When he saw my face he looked down, ashamed; "I'm sorry I make you sad. I shouldn't bother you with my problems." I encouraged him to continue. He smiled. "Thank you so much for listening to me. I have nobody left to talk to, and I'm happy to know that you are listening." I nodded. Omar was ready to tell his story. These are his words as I remember them:

> I was crossing at a checkpoint near Nablus when a soldier asked me my name. I told him and immediately he asked me about Mahmoud: "Why did your cousin die?" he asked. I said, "Because you killed him!" Then the soldier asked, "Why did your brother explode himself with bombs?" and I answered, "Why do you think?" The soldier told me I would go to jail because my family was dangerous. I said that I was different from my brother, but he said that I was Palestinian, and so I did not want peace. He called his men over to take me away.
>
> The police took me to a room where I was blindfolded and my hands were tied behind my back. Ten men beat me on and off for many hours. I remember it was raining outside. When they had finished there was blood streaming down my face so they took me to an army doctor. The doctor looked at me once and said no problem, although I was badly hurt. I waited for them to take me to my room where I could rest. Instead they took me to another room where they beat me for about one more hour.
>
> When they had finished they took me to a small, empty dark room with water on the floor. They left me there, shivering on the floor, with blood all over my body. Occasionally they would bring me food, but it was food not even fit for animals. I did not eat for 3 days. After 5 days in solitary confinement, the captain told me I would stay in jail for 6 months. When I asked why, he repeated the reasons of the first soldier: he said I was dangerous, and that even if my brother was dead the "Arab wrath" would continue in me.

The next 6 months were a living hell. If a soldier ever asks me if I prefer prison or death, I will not have to think twice. The bathrooms in jail were repulsive. Every day, we had half an hour for 30 people to use one toilet. We were all sick with not being able to go to the bathroom, and when we complained that it was not enough time the guard told us, "Don't worry, you can go tomorrow."

There were boys there only 14 years old. And there was an 80-year-old man who was very sick in bed crying. I told the guard he needed a doctor or he was going to die. The guard answered, "He is dangerous. If he dies, then the people of Israel will be safe."

One week before my prison time was finished, I could not sleep. I was tortured with fears that they would decide to keep me another 6 months, or worse, that they would deport me to Gaza so I could never see my family again.[23] And then they told me I could go. It was a wonderful feeling of freedom, until the reality sank in that I was returning to life in another cage. I had gone from one prison to another, a bigger prison, called Balata. I am still in prison. We all are.

Omar is luckier than some. He was on *Amnesty International*'s list of illegal political prisoners until he was released. Still, he remains trapped. He is desperate to leave Palestine. One international invited him recently to visit Germany. He applied for permission to leave but Israel rejected the application. Palestinians in the Occupied Territories have no citizenship and cannot travel or migrate without permission from Israel.[24] The police say Omar is dangerous, and I am reminded of how people become what people expect of them. I hope that Omar will be stronger than that. He said he hopes so too.

I asked Omar if his brother had warned him before he killed himself and others. Omar looked at me incredulously: "Are you kidding? Do you think I would have let him go?" His

---

[23] According to *Al-Haq* Palestinian human rights organization, dozens of West Bank Palestinians have been expelled to Gaza during the Second Intifada. In one instance, "[two West Bank Palestinian prisoners] were taken to the Israeli military base at Beit El in the West Bank, where they were given half an hour to say goodbye to their families before they were expelled to Gaza. They were given 1,000 shekels each, blindfolded and driven into the Gaza Strip in two armoured vehicles before being dropped off in an orchard on the edge of the Israeli settlement Netzarim. They did not know where they were, but met Gaza Palestinians who helped them." Kate Coakley and Marko Divac Öberg, "Israel's Deportations and Forcible Transfers of Palestinians Out of the West Bank During the Second Intifada, Occasional Paper 15" *Al-Haq* (April 2006).

More than 1,200 Palestinians have been deported by Israel since the Occupation began (following the initial 320,000 who were expelled during the 1967 War). According to Noam Chomsky, a program of "'invisible transfer' began under the Labor Party shortly after the 1967 conquest as one of the means to deal with the 'demographic problem' (the problem of having too many Arabs in the Jewish state).... Over 90% of the victims were women and children." Chomsky wrote in the early 1980s, "Israel appears to be the only country in the world that relies on this mode of population control as a regular practice, in violation of the Geneva Conventions [and] the Universal Declaration of Human Rights." *Fateful Triangle: The United States, Israel, and the Palestinians*, updated edition (Cambridge, MA: South End Press, 1999), p. 476-477.

[24] Israel occupies the entire border between the West Bank and Jordan, so Palestinians wishing to leave require permission first to get to the border (accessible only via Israeli roads) and then to cross it into Jordan. Permission is difficult to obtain for all Palestinians, but most of all for those whose families have had legal problems. Israel is not required to give reasons for rejecting applications beyond citing Israeli security.

Entering other countries is also complicated because Palestinians don't have any legal citizenship. Additionally, applying for visas is difficult if not impossible because most embassies and consulates are in Jerusalem, a city forbidden to the majority of Palestinians.

A poster in Balata commemorates a young man killed by soldiers.

anger turned to tears. “I would have locked him in the house and brought him food and never let him out of my sight! He was my baby brother... And if I ever meet someone who knew what he was going to do and didn’t tell me, I’ll never forgive them.”

I asked Omar if he wanted to tell me about his brother. He smiled and looked off into space. “He’s not my brother anymore. He’s a part of me, inside of me.” Omar patted his chest. “I still feel him here. He was great, very charismatic, always coming home with a new crazy hairstyle. He loved to dress up nice and wear fancy cologne and he couldn’t wait to buy a car to drive the pretty girls around.” Omar laughed for the first time that night. “He was the only person around who didn’t smoke. He hated cigarettes, and when I smoked he would yell at me that it was bad for my health. He was so smart... A year before he died he’d finished high school and wanted to study in a university, but we didn’t have the money. He had worked 3 years in a small hospital in Israel but lost his job when the Second Intifada started. After that he was working odd jobs to save up the money for school. He wanted to be a doctor.”

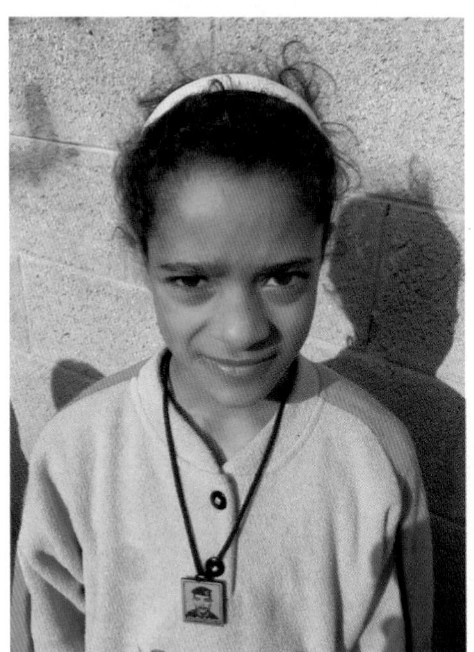
A young girl in Askar refugee camp near Balata wears a photograph of her brother, who was killed by soldiers.

Omar turned to me with a big smile, “Thank you for asking.” I smiled back, sadly. I didn’t know what to say. There were no words to comfort. How could I tell him he was not alone when so much of the world has turned their backs on people with stories just like his? He kept apologizing for troubling me, which broke my heart.

I told Omar I wanted to tell him something. He listened. I looked him in the eyes and said, “I’m Jewish.” He looked surprised, but kept listening. “My family also has a devastating history. My grandparents were refugees from the Nazi Holocaust and most of their parents, sisters, and brothers were killed by the Nazis.” Omar cocked his head and shook it slowly. A pained look had come into his eyes. He spoke. “I see Sharon as a second Hitler. I hate Sharon but I do not hate Jews, and I do not hate you. God loves everyone: Muslims, Jews, Christians, everyone. If you do good, then you go to Heaven. God doesn’t distinguish and neither do I.”

I am not writing this account to excuse what Omar's brother did. It is appalling, and likely only inspired more violence. Interactions like the one I had with Omar don't make the tragedies any more bearable, but they do remind me that Palestinians who attack Israelis or Israelis who attack Palestinians are not homicidal maniacs. Many on both sides truly believe that the other is out to destroy them, and that violence is their only hope of survival. Fear makes people do crazy things. The struggle is to revive the humanity amidst the fear.

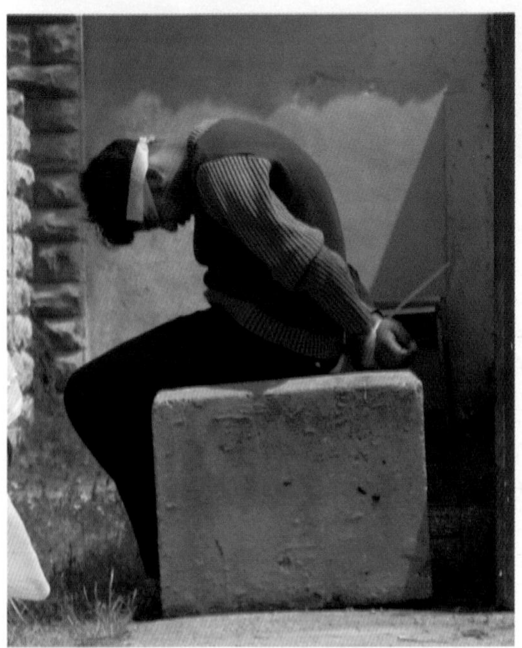
A young actor from Al-Far'a refugee camp demonstrates the way Palestinians are blindfolded and detained before being arrested.

It's hard to feel human in Palestine, with the Wall closing in and the threat of imprisonment always lurking. There are more than 8,000 Palestinian political prisoners being held in Israeli prisons today, about 10% of whom are in administrative detention,[25] meaning they can be held without charge or trial, indefinitely.[26] Approximately 40% of all Palestinian men in the Occupied Territories have been detained or imprisoned by Israel. Almost every day, I meet former prisoners. In Nablus, a young man not much older than me saw me looking confused and asked in English if he could help me. I needed a phone and he let me use his. I asked him where he had learned English and he said in prison in Israel. He had just been released the year before after 9 years in prison, from age 18 to 27.

The stories don't end; they multiply. Tonight I received a call from the father of a 23-year-old accountant named Amjad who was arrested this afternoon at Huwwara checkpoint without explanation. I tried calling the military prison where we thought he might be, but the prison operator was unwilling to talk to me. I immediately called the Israeli human rights organization Hamoked. They had more luck phoning in Hebrew and located Amjad, who is being held for inspection without charges. He has never had any problems with the army, and his family is extremely upset and worried. They are not allowed to visit him, nor can he contact them.

[25] *Addameer, Prisoners' Support and Human Rights Association* (2003). *www.addameer.org/index_eng.html*

[26] Administrative detention orders expire after 6 months but can be renewed indefinitely.

On the Way to the Samaria Ruins

Sunday, November 30, 2003

Without experiencing it first hand, it's hard to imagine what it's like to wait at a checkpoint. For most Americans, the only thing like it is security at airports, especially right after the September 11th attacks. Most of us have been through it: You arrive at the airport and wait in line to show your ID to get a boarding pass. Then you rush to another line, where you wait to go through security. Airport employees open your bags, shuffle through your belongings, ask you to take off your belt and shoes. When that's over, you rush to the gate where, often, you are checked again.

How do you feel going through this screening process? Are you annoyed that you have to wait? Are you thankful that someone is watching out for your safety? Have you ever missed a flight because of heightened security? I have, but I still comply at airports, as most of us do, because we figure it's a necessary precaution, and we know it's only once in a while.

Now imagine that you went through the airport's three-stage 80-minute security process two, four, six times *every day*, every time you went to work, to school, to the hospital, or to visit your family. Imagine that every little movement in life involved the chaos and burden of going through airport security. Imagine that instead of flights you stood to miss weddings, graduations, funerals, and other major life events. Think of how impatient many of us become waiting in line at the grocery store or the post office, and compare it to how much more Palestinians go through all day long trying to get anywhere. That gives you a small hint of how disruptive checkpoints are to Palestinian daily life.

Step 1: Palestinians wait in line to be checked.

Step 2: Palestinians get out of their vehicles.

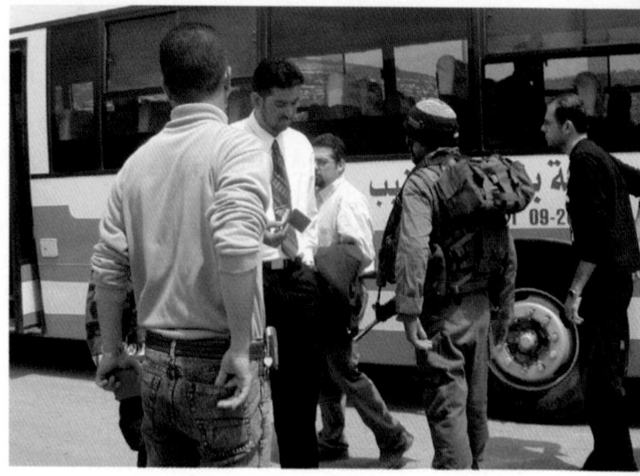

Step 3: Palestinians show their IDs to soldiers.

Step 4: Palestinians' bodies and bags are often searched.

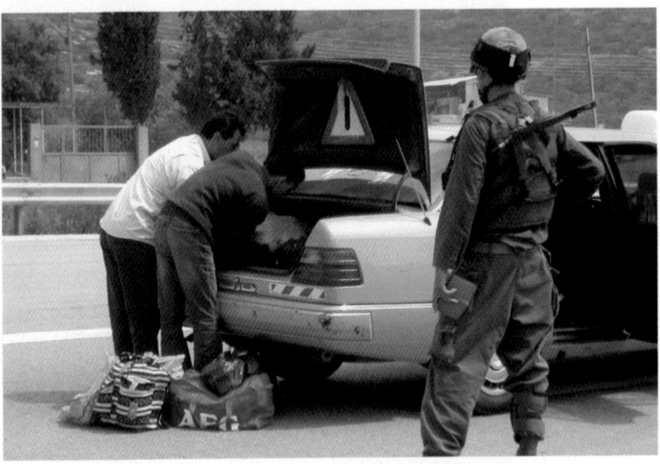

Step 5: Palestinians unload their vehicles to be searched.

Checkpoints are not just frustrating; they are debilitating. It's hard to hold a steady job if you never know whether it will take you 15 minutes or 4hours to get to work. Unless you happen to have a university in your village or the funds for a second residence, higher education is probably out of the question. And if you require urgent medical care, you're out of luck if there's a checkpoint between your home and the nearest hospital.

During my stay in Nablus, my friend Aldo and I went to visit the ancient Israelite ruins of Samaria near the Palestinian village of Sabastiya. We chose somewhere close, hoping we could relax. Our destination was just 9 miles away, but checkpoints along the way prolonged our journey to almost 2 and a half hours.

We arrived at Beit Eba, the first checkpoint, to find a group of more than 50 Palestinians waiting in the sun. They looked like they had been there for a long time, and it was another 15 minutes before the army began to show signs that they were going to start allowing people to come up and show IDs to try to get through. There was a long walkway of about 150 feet between the soldiers and the crowd of waiting Palestinians huddled around a concrete roadblock.

A soldier pointed his gun from his post to the crowd and shouted at the whole group to take a step back. All the men picked up their bags, all the women picked up the children, and everyone took one step back, so they were now 152 feet away from the soldiers. The soldier walked from one side of the post to the other and then commanded the group to take another step back. The group grumbled but obliged. The soldier began to talk to another soldier who then yelled to the group to take another step back. Finally, one soldier motioned for people to start advancing. Six women and children started towards the checkpoint window at the other end of the path. A soldier yelled something to them and the group stopped and looked confused. Then they understood. The soldier only wanted two people at a time. So four stopped to wait but another soldier yelled at them to get back to the concrete block. They turned around to walk back. When they arrived, it was their time to go up so they turned around to walk up again, two by two.

The process was painful to watch: dignified but exhausted people trying not to lose their tempers or their pride as they obeyed seemingly arbitrary commands to move to and from the window and the concrete block in the hot sun, carrying bags and babies, with flies buzzing all around. The soldiers seemed nervous and adamant about maintaining their control of the situation. Aldo and I stayed behind with the crowd to avoid the possibility of making the soldiers more nervous until we felt we could do some good.

Palestinians wait for over an hour to leave Nablus city via Beit Eba checkpoint.

We didn't have to wait long. The fourth group up was a mother, father, and young daughter holding her father's hand. When the mother handed over their ID cards, the soldier walked over to the father and yelled something very loudly and violently in his face. The little girl by his side burst into tears.

The best kind of checkpoint—an empty one

Aldo and I quickly moved down the path to the confrontation, where we quietly watched it develop. The father was trying to comfort the daughter and the mother was yelling at the soldier in Hebrew. A second soldier asked us what we were doing and we said we were watching. He said that was illegal. I told him that was not true, and that I was curious what the problem was with the family. He said that the family was Palestinian but they had Israeli passports, so they should not have been allowed into Nablus in the first place (Israelis are prohibited from entering the city). He said it didn't matter if they had relatives there. I pointed out that they were trying to leave Nablus, not enter it, but the soldier was unmoved. I told him I was concerned about the first soldier's behavior towards the family. The first soldier overheard my comment and looked noticeably embarrassed that his outburst had been witnessed by internationals.

The soldier told us to go either through the checkpoint or back to the block. About halfway down the path, back toward the crow, I turned and saw the soldiers let the family through. It was a quick, sweet moment of relief, but there were at least 40 people still waiting to get through.

Then an amazing thing happened: the line started to move quickly. An old woman was woken up from her nap in the dirt to walk the path, and the old men were let through while the luck lasted. People were called up in fives and let through with almost no hassle. Aldo and I looked at one another in wonder. Could it be that easy to make a difference?

Within 20 minutes all 50 people were through, along with another 20 or so who had arrived during the hour of waiting. After the last man passed, Aldo and I approached the window. There was a female soldier checking IDs. She was pretty, with big eyes and spiky hair. She looked at my passport for a minute and then frowned up at me. She asked, "Your name is Anna?" "Yes," I answered, and started to get nervous. Then she passed me my passport back and smiled, "So is mine."

It was a wonderful feeling to walk beyond the checkpoint. It was a relief to pass through and, although we could not be certain, it was encouraging to believe that our presence may have made a difference. The Palestinians were surer of the difference than we were: after crossing, we found several smiling and waiting to welcome us onto a bus. Kids ran up to hold our hands, and a teenage girl offered me her seat on the bus next to her mother, who invited us to her home. We didn't have the chance to accept because before we knew it, we were waiting in line again at another checkpoint.

Our bus waited 10 minutes until we reached the front of the line, where we were asked to get off the bus and show our IDs—again. The soldiers separated the men and women, and let the women back on the bus. Aldo and I stayed with the men. The soldiers then let all but two men go, but still we stayed. The soldiers asked us what we were doing and we said we were wondering what the two men had done. They said they could not tell us, but that they were being detained for security reasons. The soldiers told us it was illegal to be there and we said we would stay as long as the men were detained without charge. We said goodbye to all our new friends and the bus drove away.

We were in the middle of nowhere. The two men walked across the road to sit down. We sat down near them and leaned over to ask what was wrong. They said they had no idea. We waited. We watched the soldiers search an ambulance that had been waiting behind our bus with the emergency lights on for at least 20 minutes. The driver yelled to us that there was someone sick in the back. We all just shook our heads. The Israeli military justifies the systematic detention and holding-up of Palestinian ambulances at checkpoints by citing stories of Palestinians using ambulances to transport weapons and "wanted" people in the past. As it turns out, most of these stories are fabricated.[27] But even if the

[27] In the entire history of the conflict, there has been one single documented incident of a Palestinian ambulance *possibly* being used to transport explosives, and even this is uncertain. *Amnesty International* wrote about the case: "There are several suspicious circumstances about it. The ambulance passed through four checkpoints

accounts were true, one must remember that the soldiers are blocking ambulances traveling from one *Palestinian* town to another. How does controlling such movement enhance the security of the Israeli people as compared with the health risks to which it inevitably condemns innocent Palestinians?

Aldo and I continued to wait. Occasionally, the soldiers would look over at us to see if we really intended to stay. We pretended we had all the time in the world. After another 15 minutes the soldiers finally called up the two detained Palestinian men, gave them back their IDs, and told them to go. The two flashed us a wave and started their long walk home.

Aldo and I walked the rest of the way to Samaria and had a pleasant picnic. On our way back, we came across the same two soldiers, who were arguing with two new Palestinian men. One of the Palestinians was pointing angrily to a blocked-off parking lot full of taxis. The soldiers shooed the young men away, and when they came in our direction we asked them what was wrong. They said they were taxi drivers and that the soldiers had taken away their keys along with those of eight other drivers 3 days ago. No one had been given any explanation as to why their keys were confiscated, nor any indication of when they would be returned, if at all. They said this was not an uncommon occurrence, and that they were going to walk to the police station.[28] I remembered hearing about soldiers taking drivers' keys and either impounding their cars or making them do something humiliating like dance or bark like a dog to "earn" them back.

I asked if the taxi drivers wanted Aldo and me to come for support and they said the police station was 4 miles away. We decided against it; it was getting late. Instead I gave them a card with phone numbers of helpful Palestinian and Israeli human rights organizations. They thanked us, hailed us a service taxi, and started their long walk over the hills into the night.

---

on the way to Jerusalem without being searched (which is abnormal) and then was delayed for more than an hour before being searched to allow TV cameras to arrive (which suggests that [the army] had, at the least, prior knowledge of something hidden there)." Besides this alleged incident, the only documented ambulance abuses were by *Israel*. "Shielded from Scrutiny," *Amnesty International*, p. 35; As cited in Finkelstein, *Chutzpah*, p. 129.

During the Second Intifada, more than 150 sick or injured Palestinians died at checkpoints after they were prevented from reaching a hospital. "Report: over 5,000 Palestinians killed by the Israeli army since 2000," *Ma'an News Agency* (February 21, 2007).

[28] Dozens of Israeli veterans have come forward with stories of confiscating the keys of innocent drivers either "to teach the Palestinians a lesson" for leaving their homes, or to assert their power. *www.breakingthesilence.org.il*

Witness in Palestine
Harvesting in Ariel Settlement

Ismael

Monday, December 1, 2003

A few days ago, Ismael—the farmer I met a few weeks ago who has been denied access to his olive trees because they are on land claimed (though not yet inhabited) by Ariel settlers—finally obtained permission to finish harvesting before his crop is ruined by the rainy season. Ismael asked us to help his family pick olives today, both as protection from possible attacks from settlers or the army and as labor desperately needed to make up for lost time.

The soldier guarding Ariel was not happy to see us when my IWPS colleagues and I arrived. He told us flatly that we could not enter. We explained that we did not want to go to the settlement itself, only to pick olives with a farmer and his family on their land around the settlement. The soldier remained firm. We insisted that he call his superior, which he did. While we were waiting, my colleague Karin—who speaks and reads a little Hebrew—read out loud the first words on a big sign in front of us. She sounded them out slowly and then asked, "What does '*Bruchim habaim*' mean?" The soldier spoke under his breath; "It means 'Welcome.'" Karin laughed; "I guess this sign was not made for us or Ismael."

Having received orders to let us in, the soldier reluctantly stepped aside and we entered Ariel, where we found Ismael, his sisters, wife, and mother harvesting their trees. It had rained the week before, so many olives had to be dug out from the mud on the ground. We picked for hours, fueled by flatbread with oil and spices. Around midday, we had visitors: an army jeep came speeding down the road and two soldiers stuck their heads out the window to scream something in Hebrew, rather threateningly. We were caught off guard; I almost fell out of the tree I was picking olives in. Ismael motioned to us to move to where we were visible but to let him do the talking.

When the soldiers saw me and the other internationals, their tones softened. One soldier asked us how we were doing. The soldiers wanted Ismael to get off the land and go home, but after learning from Ismael where we were from, the soldiers themselves decided to leave. My colleagues and I offered to complain about the harassment, but Ismael said he preferred just to finish the work and avoid any more confrontations. He was not out to get apologies or compensation for his troubles; he just wanted to finish harvesting and go home.

Apart from the brief clash, the atmosphere was pleasant. Ismael sang and his wife and sister made fun of his terrible voice. Then, the women sang and I was reminded how many more tones traditional Arabic music uses compared to Western music. It's more melodic than harmonic, which is why at first it often sounds "out of tune" to Western ears. One woman stopped her singing to ask my age. I said I was 24. She told me she had a son my age and that she would like me to marry him. I smiled and told her I had come to Palestine to work for peace, not to get married.

Another woman asked my religion and I answered that I was of Jewish origin. The mother who had asked me to marry her son looked over from her picking. The woman I had just answered looked surprised. The two began to talk excitedly. Ismael and his mother came over to join the conversation. I wished more than ever that I understood Arabic.

When the conversation stopped, I felt a hand on my shoulder. I turned and one woman cupped my face in her hands and, looking into my eyes, said something utterly incomprehensible to me but no doubt very sweet. Another woman gave me a big hug, squeezing my hand as she walked away. Ismael's mother looked at me through the tree branches and nodded, "Welcome." Finally, the mother of the 24-year-old came to me and kissed both my cheeks before asking, "So will you marry my son?"

We were interrupted by a tour bus that had stopped on the road 30 ft from where Ismael stood. What were people doing touring a settlement? The passengers—perhaps Jewish Americans or Israelis interested in moving to Ariel—sat mesmerized by the sight of Ismael and his family picking olives. They moved closer to the windows and then, one by one, took out their cameras to take pictures. Ismael and his family stood bewildered. Ismael waved his arms for the bus to drive away but the passengers only took more pictures. I was nauseated. Ismael's wife looked at me hopelessly. Ismael's sister looked angry and humiliated and kept her head down as she continued to work.

The whole scene filled me with anger. For one thing, photographing without permission is something of a taboo in the Islamic tradition. But it was watching the passengers gawk at Ismael and his family as if they were animals in a zoo that angered me most. I could only assume they were surprised to see Palestinians at work on their land instead of crouched in dark caves building bombs.

The tour bus eventually left and by the end of the day the harvest was finished. Ismael had been turned away from his land for two months, but at last his trees were bare. The family rejoiced, put their olives and their eight-year-old son on the back of a donkey cart, and headed for home. My colleagues and I walked together with Ismael's wife and sisters through the Ariel gate towards Kifl Haris. On our way we passed an Israeli bus stop on the road where a young man was waiting with an M16 slung around his shoulder. He was a civilian, no more than a teenager. Suddenly, one of Ismael's sisters began to have a panic attack. She started breathing heavily and tears came to her eyes. We sat her down to rest and she tried to calm herself. When her breathing returned to normal, we walked as quickly as possible across Ariel's settler road back to the village.

I don't know why the woman panicked. I didn't want to ask. She seemed embarrassed about her emotions, and yet the more I consider the situation, the more reasonable I find her reaction. There is nothing normal about sixteen-year-olds carrying semiautomatic weapons on their way to town. There is nothing sane about breezing through security if you have a yellow license plate, but getting the third degree if you have a donkey cart. It is not for those like Ismael's sister, who get upset, that I fear most; at least they still recognize the fundamental injustice of the situation. I'm most worried about those who have adapted themselves to the Occupation so much that they aren't angry anymore, or even worse, those who simply accept life under the Occupation because they have never known anything else.

Movement Planning & Strategizing

Friday, December 12, 2003

I have been out of touch with my family and friends for the past few weeks. IWPS's computer network was down and the man who usually fixes it was put in prison.

Last weekend, I went to a meeting of ISM coordinators in Jayyous, a small village of about 3,000 inhabitants in the Qalqilya district. The Wall started in Jayyous last fall, despite resistance by villagers and internationals, who managed to prevent construction for 3 days before the army brought in more force. The Wall now winds its way through the surrounding countryside, separating a house from the village and the village from its land, all six water wells, and the Tel Aviv skyline in the distance.

Israeli activists, international volunteers, and locals from the Salfit region meet to discuss a peace camp against the impending Wall in Deir Ballut.

ISM is devoting several months to reevaluating the effectiveness of the organization and revising its mission statement. It was useful to meet the Palestinians and international volunteers who help keep the movement alive, and to hear them talk about the problems that can occur. For example, many foreign volunteers arrive in Palestine anxious to see some action and save some lives. ISM—and IWPS, for that matter—is not about "saving" anyone; it is about supporting Palestinians in building their own movement against the Occupation. It is arrogant to think that we Westerners can "educate" the Palestinians in their own resistance. The few weeks that most ISM volunteers stay for is not enough time to be properly trained and to begin to build trust within the community that could facilitate proactive collaboration in the future.

Last week, I went to a Salfit community meeting of local residents, internationals, and Israelis interested in setting up an anti-wall peace camp in Deir Ballut. A few dozen people attended the meeting, including the mayors of several villages and representatives from

Palestinian political organizations who are all interested in working nonviolently. At the meeting, people shared ideas and feelings about working together against the Wall. One Israeli woman shared her story:

> I am a Jewish Israeli. I am not here to give you an example of a good Jew, I am here to tell you how much my family hates me. I have two children almost 18 years old, and unlike most mothers who are proud to see their children grow into adults, I have a terrible feeling in the pit of my stomach because I know it is time for them to decide whether they will join the army or suffer the consequences of civil disobedience. I brought them here to the West Bank to show them the system that they could choose whether or not to be a part of, and they hate me for it; they hate me for showing them the underside of their privileged lives.
>
> There was a missile that destroyed part of the Wall recently, and although destroying the Wall is a good use of a missile, we all know that the Wall will only be built up again, even stronger, with more supporters. If we keep that in mind, whatever you decide to do I will be there in support, with friends and with the conviction that nonviolence is the bravest and most effective strategy.

Munira's husband Hani, whose family has been caged in by the Wall in Mas'ha, was also present at the meeting and spoke with conviction:

> I am not here because the Wall damaged my house and my family. I am not here because I am Palestinian. I am here because I am a human being who wants the best for humanity. I understand that nobody can stop the Wall, but at the very least let people say in the future that it did not pass without resistance. We must demonstrate to show how wrong this is, and to support the people whose lives continue to be ruined by the Wall. When the land around my house was being destroyed, there were so many people who called, who heard my story, and who stood in solidarity with me. The media was there too, and it all made a difference to me, even if it did not stop the Wall.

It was Hani's first sentences that struck me the most. When I tell people in the United States that I'm working in the West Bank, they always ask the same question: "Which side are you on, the Palestinian or the Israeli?" I never know what to answer; the question sounds so absurd to me. This is not a struggle between Palestinians and Israelis, it's a struggle for freedom and basic human rights. I would be doing the same work if the roles were reversed.

What does it even mean to be on the "Israeli side?" It's not easy to find two Israelis who agree about the situation, let alone unanimity in the whole country. There are Israelis all over the political spectrum, and to say that Israelis support the Occupation is to ignore the considerable heterogeneity of Israeli opinion.

While Palestinians agree that they want the Occupation to end, they are far less unified regarding what they would like to happen after that. A large number of Palestinians, for example, would rather see a binational secular state for both Jews and Palestinians than a country called "Palestine" for Palestinians only.

So which side am I on? I am on the side of human dignity and self-determination. I am on the side of those who seek equal rights for all, regardless of religion, nationality, or ethnicity. This is the struggle of everyone sharing those ideals, even if today the victims are Palestinian. Tomorrow they could be you. This is your struggle, too.

The solidarity that exists between Palestinians and Jewish Israelis working against the Occupation, and the common interest in peace that the majority of both groups share, demonstrate that this is not a struggle between Palestinians and Jews; this is a struggle for freedom and justice against a mutually destructive system.

Uprooting the History & Future of Palestine

Saturday, December 13, 2003

Israel's rapidly-constructed canyon outside our house in Haris is allegedly an extension of a settler road more than 15 feet above it, but locals fear the cleared land may be the beginning of the Wall.

When we look out of our window in Haris, we see parallel to the settler road a flattened dirt road that grows with time as more of our neighbors' olive trees are cut down. The army claims to be expanding the settler road; other officials claim that they are digging to build a new water system. But there is a sinking feeling of disbelief in all of us, an understanding that this is probably the beginning of the Wall in our village.

One extremely frustrating aspect of the Wall is that it's rarely clear where and when it is coming. The Israeli government and military have been reluctant to publish official maps of the planned route, so the related land confiscation often comes as a surprise. Some farmers have never even heard of the Wall that will soon separate them from their land or their communities. Occasionally the army issues demolition orders for houses, but more often the bulldozers show up unannounced and begin cutting down trees. This way, Palestinians can't organize ahead of time or ensure that media are present to document the events as they occur.

Sometimes the land-razing goes on for days, sometimes for weeks. Then suddenly it stops, and continues in another village far away. This strategy keeps the Palestinians guessing. Meanwhile the Wall is built in small pieces here and there that look harmless enough until they are connected. If this Wall were truly a legitimate construction, what would be the point of keeping it such a secret? Why doesn't the government publish the planned map in Israeli and international newspapers for all to see? Up until now, the only maps widely available are estimates from peace organizations.

A week ago, villagers of neighboring Kifl Haris called us frantically because bulldozers had appeared out of the blue and were uprooting their trees. By the time we arrived, the owners were hysterical. They kept screaming "*hamil*!" as the ancient trees were ripped from the ground by the monstrous machines. "*Hamil*" is a word that can be used to describe trees during the time that they bear fruit; it means "pregnant."

Not every olive tree can be *hamil*. It takes over 20 years for olive trees to begin to bear fruit. Until then, the owner must tend to the young tree, to assist it in the process of aging. Season after season, the farmer returns to the tree, nursing its wounds from storms,

Bulldozers uproot olive trees in Kifl Haris.

making sure it receives just the right amount of sun, trimming branches that block the light and nutrients that will help it mature. It is not an exaggeration to personify trees with the word "*hamil*"; to many families who have been with their trees for hundreds of years, generation after generation, the fruit-bearers are an integral part of the family.

I felt sick watching the trees ripped from the earth with the American-made bulldozers. Some of the trees looked thousands of years old. Their roots were so strong. By the time the Wall is completed, more than two million trees will have been uprooted since 2001.[29] Some of them may have stood during the time of the Romans, and Jesus. They are irreplaceable. Stealing them is a rape of the land, and the destruction of both the history and future of the Palestinian people.

I took pictures and had a couple of uncomfortable conversations with the construction workers, who insisted they were uprooting trees for peace. They left behind a sort of mass grave, with trampled olives and oil instead of blood. After they left, the families stood in shocked silence, except a few young boys sifting through the broken pieces of their families' livelihood, picking out branches to take home for firewood. Some electric lines and water pipes had also been destroyed by the work, so the village lost electricity and water for 3 days.

I recently returned to Kifl Haris's demolished groves to take more photographs. Beyond the recently leveled road visible from Haris is an enormous canyon. It's unlikely that the road will extend into it—as soldiers claim—because of its depth. I walked through the canyon past the bulldozers and cranes and then climbed up a side of rubble near the main

[29] *PASSIA* 2007.

road. Hidden beyond the remaining trees was another bulldozer, a smaller one. I approached and found the machine clearing out a new ditch alongside the road, this one even deeper than the canyon. I immediately thought of the Wall.

Bulldozers dig a new ditch next to the canyon near Haris, strikingly similar to the ditches lining the Wall.

The driver of the bulldozer did not yet see me, and I managed to take a few pictures before I was discovered. Within seconds two security guards appeared at my side, telling me to leave immediately. I was standing on a public street and quite sure I was doing nothing illegal so I remained. One angry guard tried to push me with his hand but I shook off his touch violently and gave him a look of warning, suprising even myself. The other guard told him not to touch me—he knew that my complaints about army abuse could reach further than those of a Palestinian. When I got tired of the guard screaming inches from my face, I began to walk away. The guards got into their truck and drove up to me. One stuck his head out the window and made kissing noises. I shivered with disgust and they drove off.

A fallen Palestinian olive tree

Witness in Palestine

Flying Checkpoints & a Demonstration in A'ram

Monday, December 15, 2003

On Saturday we went to an anti-Wall demonstration sponsored by *Ta'ayush*, an Arab and Jewish Israeli grassroots movement. The demonstration took place in A'ram, a town between Jerusalem and Ramallah, normally 90 minutes from Haris, but this time it took us that long just to get out of the Salfit region. I got my first taste of "flying checkpoints," which are like regular checkpoints but mobile, meaning they can pop up unannounced anywhere at any time. For the first hour, our bus was stopped nearly every mile by soldiers standing in the middle of the road blocking traffic and searching Palestinians. As usual, yellow-plated Israeli cars were allowed to pass unobstructed.

At the first flying checkpoint, we waited for 20 minutes until a soldier emptied us out of the bus, and checked our IDs, before letting us continue. Two minutes later, soldiers stopped our bus again, insisting that the repeated checking was a security measure due to a threat of terrorism in the area. I could think of several nearby terrorist attacks by non-Palestinians. (Our plans that day to pick olives in Deir Istiya had in fact been cancelled after an unarmed 19-year-old village boy was shot twice, in the hand and near his rectum, by the army. Deir Istiya was put under curfew to prevent retaliation. Of course, curfew also prevented the victim's parents from visiting him in the hospital, and other villagers—like

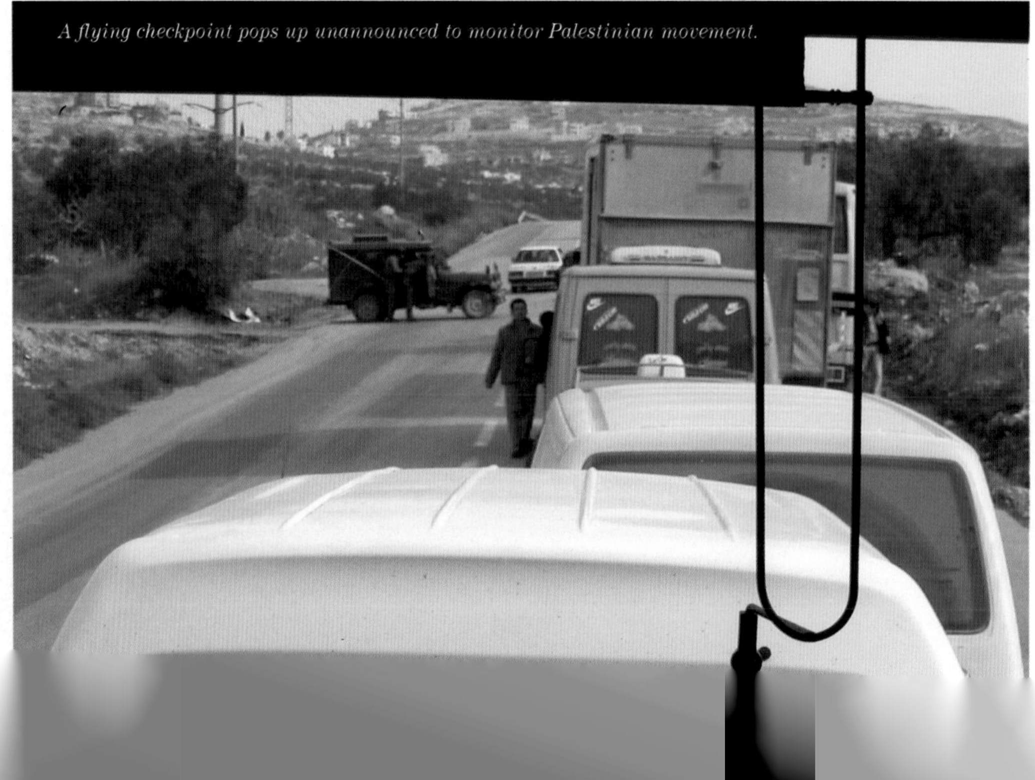

A flying checkpoint pops up unannounced to monitor Palestinian movement.

Soldiers have passing Palestinian drivers empty out their cars to be searched at a flying checkpoint.

the farmers we were to pick with—from going to work or school.) I refrained from pointing out the irony of the illegal Occupation forces punishing Palestinians for "terror." We were already late.

After getting through the second flying checkpoint, we drove all of 4 minutes before being stopped again at Zatara permanent checkpoint, where there was another line of vehicles waiting. The line was long and unlikely to move for at least 30 minutes, so my colleague and I got out to take pictures, agreeing to meet our bus when it passed the corner ahead. There were several Palestinian ambulances waiting as usual. The ambulances were told to move to the side of the road so Israeli cars could pass. Several Israeli cars were blocked for a few minutes by the commotion and they began honking impatiently. Apparently they had places to be.

Half an hour after our bus finally made it through Zatara, we arrived at the demonstration at last to find about 2,000 protesters cheering and waving flags in Hebrew, Arabic, and English. The sun was shining, the mood friendly, and the atmosphere international. There were hundreds of Israeli activists who had come to show their support.

The crowd had built a 10-foot fake wall that people were spray-painting with peace slogans as television crews filmed. Within minutes, drums began to sound and the crowd stirred with excitement. A group of protestors charged the Wall, ripping it apart, Styrofoam flying everywhere. The crowd was thrilled. Before I knew it, a cheer erupted from my throat. I was overcome with emotion as I imagined the day when Palestinians and Israelis will tear down the real Wall together, freeing themselves from the mutually destructive system of separation.

Palestinian, Israeli, and international protesters demonstrate against the Wall in A'ram.

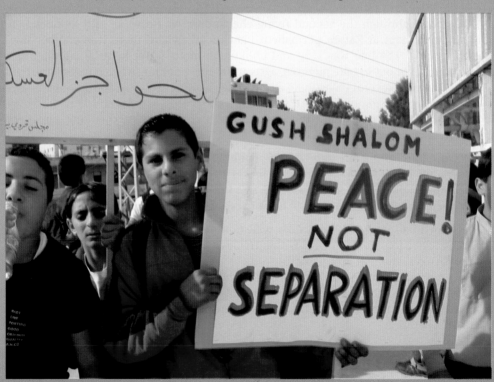

Waiting at the Gate

Tuesday, December 16, 2003

On Saturday night a friend called to say that for several weeks, many farmers in Mas'ha village have not been allowed through the Wall to reach their land. Although the Israeli government claims that permits and gates allow Palestinian farmers to access their land across the Wall, the reality is that permits can be impossible to obtain, and soldiers are rarely on hand to open the gates even when farmers have the permits. A colleague and I agreed to accompany the farmers in the hope that we would have more luck in reasoning with the soldiers.

The next morning we walked from Mas'ha village to the gate with three farmers, their donkeys, one child, and four Israeli activists who had come from Tel Aviv to help. The farmers said the army passed by about once an hour on the security road on the other side, but that they rarely stopped when there were only Palestinians waiting. We began to wait. We waited an hour with no sign of the army. Two farmers sat down on the ground beside the road. Another farmer went to fetch us food from the village. One farmer's small child walked up to the gate and started to shake it, trying to break through. He could see his family's land on the other side. After a while he sat down, playing a game of putting small stones through the holes in the fence.

In rural parts of Palestine, the Wall is composed of wire fence instead of the concrete that is used in urban areas. Nonetheless, I find references to the Wall as a "fence" very misleading. Unlike a typical fence, the Wall is armed with heavy-duty electric sensory wire, thermal imaging, video cameras, sniper towers, and razor wire.[30] The psychological and

The "fence" sections of the Wall are often reinforced with heavy-duty electric sensory wire, thermal imaging, video cameras, and razor wire.

[30] Razor wire is similar to barbed wire but with small razors instead of barbs; Wall components cited in Carter, p. 192.

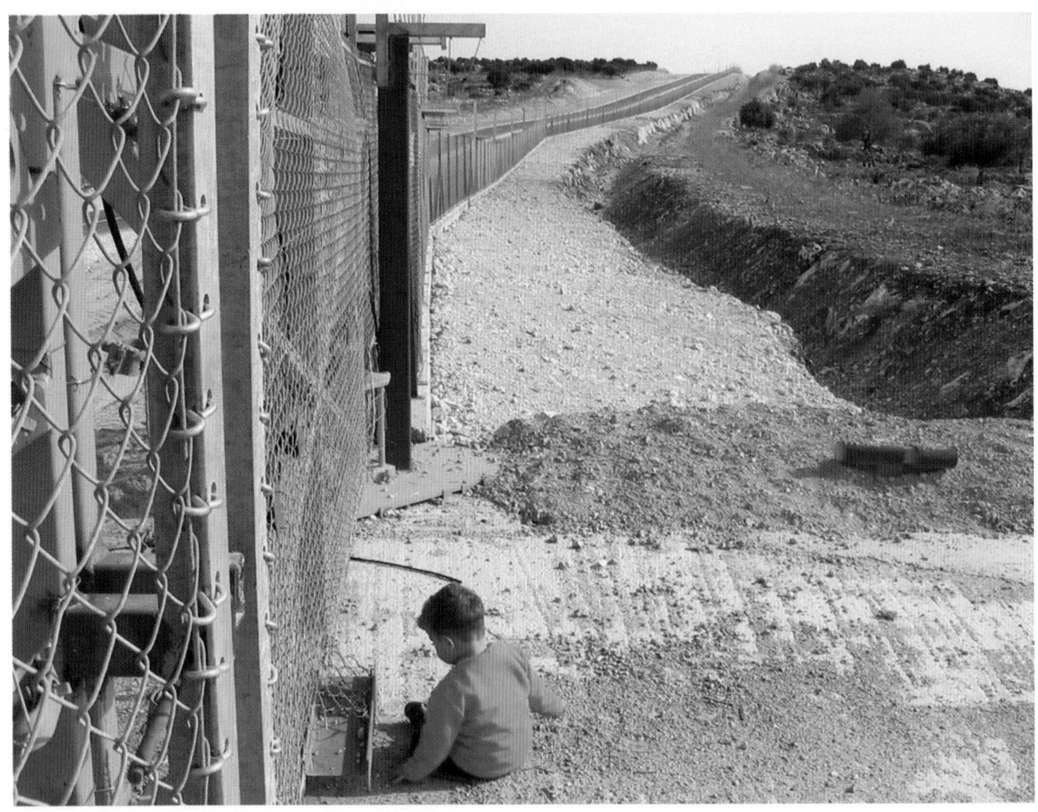

A young child waits with his family to visit their land on the other side of the Wall.

impenetrable natures of the structure are more those of a wall than of a fence. The fenced sections of the Wall are also more destructive to the landscape, since almost all trees and crops within at least 100 feet have to be cleared to make room for an army road, a 6-foot trench, and another fence—*on each side* (three fences, two trenches, and two roads in all). Some Palestinians say they prefer the concrete sections of the Wall, where they can usually at least access the land left on their side of it.

We tapped the electric wire a few times hoping it would provoke the army to come investigate. Sure enough, a jeep pulled up and three soldiers hopped out. The soldier in charge explained that something had happened and all the gates had to be closed. He apologized on behalf of the army, saying things were not run the way he would like. "Off the record," he said to an Israeli activist with us, "I'm getting out of the army in a few months and I'll come join you on the other side." The activist was unimpressed. "I'll believe it when I see it," he explained to me later. "He's one of many Israeli soldiers who tell themselves they are against the Occupation. But the Occupation would not function without them."

We called the District Coordination Office (DCO), the supposed facilitator for movement in the Occupied Territories, and were told that the gates would open an hour later, at noon. We spent the next 5 hours waiting in vain before giving up and heading home. We decided to return at 8 a.m. the next morning, when the DCO had assured us (again) that the gate would be opened.

A colleague and I arrived at the gate with the farmers around sunrise and began to wait. The army did not come. At one point a truck passed slowly along the road spraying pesticides through the fence, and we ran to avoid being sprayed. One farmer said it was plant poison to keep grass from growing near the Wall.

At last an army jeep drove down the road. We waved emphatically, but it passed without stopping. I wanted to scream. The farmers were more patient. One of them was a cheery man with short legs that bounced on his donkey when he rode it. The other farmer was older, and the entire left half of his body was paralyzed. He walked slowly with a cane, taking frequent breaks but never complaining, even after walking and standing for hours with no results. Sometimes when he found his balance he would set his cane aside and take out two sheets of paper with his functioning hand. One was a land deed that he claimed went back to Ottoman times, proving that the land belonged to his family. The other was an Israeli permit allowing him access to his land from mid-November to mid-February. He would look through the papers over and over again, reading through them to himself, as if trying to understand what he'd done wrong.

At nine o'clock, one jeep finally stopped. Two indifferent-looking soldiers leaned their heads out, listened to our story, and then drove away. They said they had no orders to open the gate and "didn't feel like" calling the DCO to check. We continued to wait. Twenty minutes later another jeep stopped and four soldiers hopped out.

A handicapped farmer waits to be allowed through the Wall to visit his land.

Soldiers hang out, deciding whether or not to allow Palestinian farmers through the Wall to reach their land.

It's amazing how diverse the soldiers can be. One soldier wearing reflecting sunglasses and a smirk yelled, "*Sabah al-kher!*" ("Good morning" in Arabic) in a sarcastic tone. Another soldier was older and quieter. The Palestinians picked him out and brought their case to him. "Look, these women came from France and America to help us," one farmer said, pointing to us. "Won't you help us?" The soldier was too distracted to answer—his partners were laughing at something funny one of them had said.

One of the soldiers eventually spoke up: "Look," he said, "we are only doing this for security. There are terrorists and that's why everything is closed." I asked him if he thought the two unarmed old men were a threat, pointing out that one of the men was half-paralyzed.

"You never know."

I asked the soldier if he thought it was right to treat everyone as a terrorist because "you never know." I pointed to his friend. "What about him?"

"No, he's not a terrorist."

"So you only suspect certain people of being terrorists. Don't you think that's a little prejudiced?"

He paused. "What are we supposed to do? We have orders not to open the gate."

"There have been some heroic people in history who were strong enough to disobey unjust orders. Alternatively, you could call the DCO that told us the gate would be open."

The soldier disappeared for 10 minutes and returned. He told the other soldiers to take away the razor wire and he opened the gate to let us through. I asked him how we would get back into the village after we were finished. He asked what time we preferred, and the farmer said noon. He agreed and we began walking to the land.

It had rained hard the night before, so the farmers could not pick or plow, but they seemed content just to be on their land. After a while the cheery farmer suggested we have a picnic and called to ask his family to bring breakfast and supplies. We watched him approach the gate and catch bread, soda, and hummus as his son threw them over, one by one. He rode back to us on his donkey, whistling an old song that bounced as he did. We feasted for an hour or so before going back to the gate to wait to be let back into the village.

Farmers wait to cross the Wall back to their village after picnicking on their land.

Deir Ballut Peace Camp Against the Wall

Friday, December 19, 2003

For the past few weeks, Palestinians from the Salfit region, Israeli activists, and volunteers from IWPS and ISM have been meeting regularly to organize a peace camp against the Wall in a half-built school at the edge of Deir Ballut, a small Palestinian village that has since grown very close to my heart. The school lies on the expected path of the Wall so it is slated for demolition, something that we hope the presence of Israeli and international activists can help prevent, or at least publicize.

The purpose of the camp is to bring activists together, to provide a space for learning and strategizing resistance to the Wall, and to publicize the Wall's destructive impact on Palestinian rural communities. Over the course of 2 weeks, the camp will host activities including nonviolence workshops, television interviews, tree-planting, and nonviolent demonstrations. The idea for a camp was inspired by last summer's peace camp in Mas'ha, where thousands of Palestinians, Israelis, and international volunteers camped out together in solidarity on land threatened by the Wall. The camp was started by Palestinian farmers and remained for over 4 months until soldiers came and arrested over 70 nonviolent activists. The Wall proceeded to take 95% of the village's land. Although Mas'ha Peace Camp didn't stop the Wall, it did make international headlines and exposed the nature of the Wall as an obstacle to peace.[31]

Israelis, internationals, and locals from Salfit commence the Deir Ballut Peace Camp Against the Wall at a half-built school on the path of the Wall.

[31] Nazeeh Sha'alabi, "The Camp in the Eyes of a Palestinian Activist," *Stop The Wall* (December 31, 2004).

Deir Ballut Peace Camp Against the Wall began yesterday. We marched from Town Hall to the abandoned school on the outskirts of the village, overlooking some of the thousands of olive trees that the village stands to lose. We marched with banners, and young boys climbed onto the roof to display welcome signs and wave to newcomers.

Within a few hours we had started settling in. The village electricians connected cables all the way from the village and set up lights in both the men's and women's rooms. Others stacked bricks in the glassless windows to keep out wind and rain. I lay down sleeping bags and hung up signs calling on Israel to clear out of Palestine and men to keep out of the women's sleeping room.

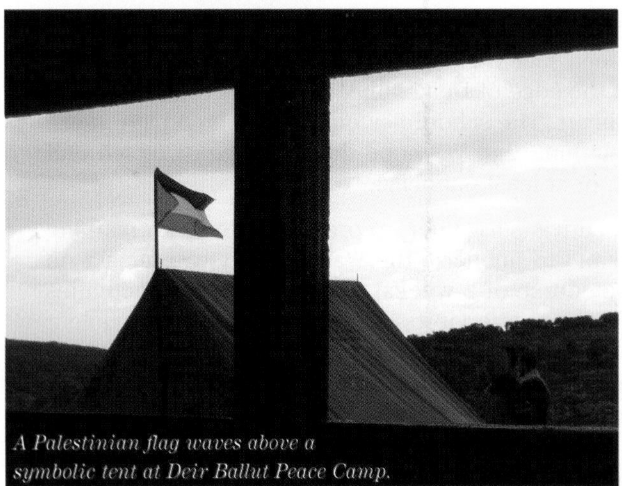
A Palestinian flag waves above a symbolic tent at Deir Ballut Peace Camp.

At night we hovered around the fire, sipping fresh sage tea and talking about justice. Some internationals played guitar and sang while three Israelis and I settled down to a game of poker. I met Gavriel, a young Israeli activist whose family moved to Israel from South Africa many years ago. "From one apartheid to another," he said, and I looked up from my cards, hoping he would tell me more.

"My uncle is a settler near Bethlehem. My cousin just founded a new outpost near Hebron. She's in *Kahane Chai*.[32] They believe God promised them this land, just like the Afrikaaner people used to say about South Africa. They feel no guilt as they literally take land from under farmers' feet. They think I'm evil for what I'm doing. They say I'm going against my country, against my people. Just like people used to say in South Africa. It's the same, really."

"So how did you turn out so great?" I asked, smiling.

"That's the funny thing," he said, smiling back. "My family raised me with good values. They just use a double standard when it comes to Israel."

That made sense to me. I can't relate when people say some settlers are just "evil." People are basically good, and most have some sense of morality and ethics; they just become blind at times from fear or brainwashing.

People like Gavriel have sacrificed a great deal. Gavriel spent 2 months in prison for refusing to join the military. Other conscientious objectors risk serving up to 3 years. But it doesn't end there. Gavriel continued:

> In Israel, being a soldier is the pride of your family. Many young Israelis are afraid their families would hate or even disown them if they refused. They say that if you're not (or weren't) a soldier, then you're not a man. It's hard to choose to be an outcast.

[32] *Kahane Chai* is a far-right Israeli political party advocating the forcible expulsion of Palestinians from Israel and the Occupied Territories. It is on both Israel's and the US State Department's lists of terrorist organizations.

Lots of my friends who are soldiers agree with me, but say they can't resist the pressure of this militarized society. We are encouraged from day one to join the army and fight for our country. In school we spend one year on world history and two years on the Nazi Holocaust. After that kind of education we all walk away thinking just two things: we're really scared, and we have to defend ourselves at all costs, because we have nowhere else to go. That's a dangerous attitude, especially when you're handing a gun to every high school graduate.

We learn that this land is ours. They call it "a land without a people for a people without a land." Never mind the hundreds of thousands of Palestinians kicked out in 1948, or the 450 villages that were destroyed. Tel Aviv University, where I study, used to be an Arab village. Does anyone know that? No. Jewish terrorists of the past are heroes. And people who refuse to fight for more land? We're traitors. It's all your classic signs of a fascist government: the economic instability, the security hysteria, the culture of fear.

I couldn't help but consider Gavriel's observations in relation to my own country. Many American liberals fall to the right on this one subject of Israel/Palestine. We, too, are taught from grade school about the Nazi Holocaust; it is at the forefront of our minds when we imagine any sort of injustice in the world. That's why, until recently, I too was ashamed to criticize Israel. Jews are supposed to be the victims—how can they be the oppressors too? Many people refuse to face the paradox. For them, Israel can do no wrong. Period.

Gavriel continued:

The worst part of all is that people really don't know what's actually going on! One of my friends lives 10 minutes away from the Qalqilya ghetto, and he couldn't tell you a thing about what life is like here. People are so removed. You feel it as you drive back into Israel, into the lights and the billboards and the traffic. You forget. And your only reminders are headlines of violent Arabs, headlines that never mention how many fewer civilians are killed by Palestinians than by the Israeli military, headlines that make you want to be more and more removed and "safe." When I tell my friends who've joined the army what I think of what they're doing, they start complaining about the unpleasant reality of their own lives. I can sympathize. I say, "Yeah, life as a soldier sucks. But have some perspective. Life 10 minutes away from here is a living hell. Compared to that, you are living in paradise. That hell is what plagues your life too. And you have the power to change it. We all do if we work together."

But nobody wants to be the one to do it. Students here aren't liberal like in other countries. They think, "Hey, after 3 years in the army I have served my country. I don't have to feel any responsibility any more." Some liberal Israelis even join the army thinking that as a 'humane' soldier they will be replacing someone who could have been even worse. There are so many excuses. The fact is, lining the Green Line with soldiers would bring Israel more security than the current policies do. But my family and people like them would never accept that. They want more than security. They want land.

I know from experience how hard it is to resist the system. But I still expect people to do it, and I don't excuse them if they don't. It's wrong. It's immoral. It's South Africa all over again, and anyone who thinks they have done no harm despite their participation in the system is fooling themselves. One of my soldier friends told me a story recently. He said he and his team were occupying a flat in Ramallah. They knew they would need the building to have ideal shooting visibility in the neighborhood, so they charged into the house and locked the family downstairs below their apartment with their hands tied behind their backs. All this in the middle of the night. Picture it: Grandma's fainting. Grandpa's shaking. Daddy's already in the slammer with almost all the other under-40-year-old men in the neighborhood. Children are clinging to their tied-up mothers as they cry. What will become of those children? What do we expect that child to become? A peace activist?

I tell my friends in the army, "Expect the bullet. Expect the rock. You are on someone else's land. If someone were on your land, you would do the same thing." And deep down they know that I'm right.

Gavriel's mention of the Qalqilya ghetto reminded me of my last trip north along Israel's Highway 6, west of the Green Line. I was stunned by the difference between the way the Wall looks from the Palestinian city of Qalqilya and the way it looked from the Israeli highway. On the Israeli side, there were grass and flower beds built up almost to the top, so it didn't even look like a wall. I realized that although Israelis are generally much better informed about the Occupation than most Americans, many of them may not necessarily know what the Wall looks like. They may see the top of it as they drive to work every morning, but do they really know what the Wall is about, where it's being built, and how it's affecting average Palestinians? Disguising the Israeli side of the Wall prevents the reality of what the Israeli government and army is doing from reaching the average Israeli citizen. That's why activists like Gavriel are so important: They bring the realities across the Green Line, and provide an alternative youth culture to the militarism that Gavriel described.

I stayed up the first night of Deir Ballut Peace Camp with activists like Gavriel, discussing our hopes of what the camp can accomplish. Two weeks of like-minded Palestinians, Israelis, and internationals coexisting in the same space with respect and companionship in the spirit of dialogue, action, and solidarity is, at the very least, a step in the right direction.

The Wall, from the Qalqilya ghetto

The Wall, from the Israeli highway

Birth & Death at Deir Ballut Checkpoint

Sunday, December 21, 2003

I woke up early on the second morning of the peace camp to observe Deir Ballut checkpoint. Deir Ballut has the misfortune of having both a checkpoint and roadblocks obstructing movement into and out of the village. The main road is obstructed by four large concrete blocks. To reach the checkpoint on the other side of the blocks, travelers must take a 2-mile, unpaved detour through the countryside, or walk on the main road past the blocks and wait for public transportation. I walked across the roadblocks to find about 30 cars waiting after they had taken the long way around. It was almost eight in the morning. The checkpoint was supposed to have opened at seven, but the soldiers were late for work. So were almost a hundred Palestinians who had to wait for them.

Deir Ballut checkpoint closes every evening at seven. Anyone who arrives any later is simply out of luck. Less than 24 hours after I left the checkpoint, at 2 a.m. the following morning, a local woman named Hessa who was 7 months pregnant with twins began having contractions. Her husband drove her quickly to the checkpoint, which they needed to cross to reach the nearest hospital in Ramallah. When they reached the checkpoint, the soldiers sleeping above it came down to meet the frantic couple. They were very polite and said: "The rule is very clear: Palestinians are not allowed through until seven in the morning. Please come back at seven."

Deir Ballut villagers walk along the main road—now blocked, preventing vehiular passage—to the checkpoint that separates their village from the nearest hospital in Ramallah. Ele Zahat and Pedu'el settlements occupy Deir Ballut village land in the background.

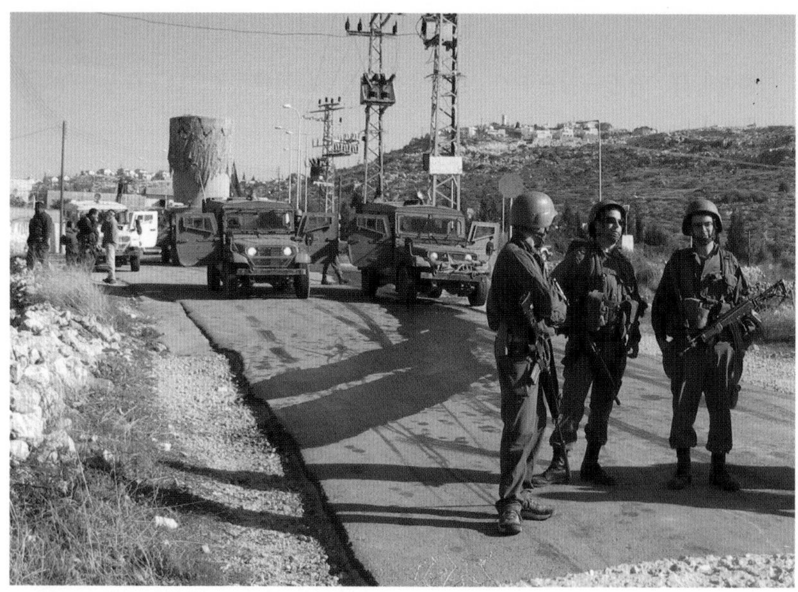

Soldiers guard the checkpoint that separates Deir Ballut villagers from the nearest hospital in Ramallah.

Deir Ballut checkpoint

Hessa clearly couldn't wait 6 hours to have her babies so they argued a bit more. Again, the soldiers were very polite, even apologetic. They just kept saying the same thing over and over: "Look, we didn't make the rules, and we don't even agree with them. We're just following orders."

Hessa's husband called an ambulance to come from Ramallah, about 25 miles away, to the other side of the checkpoint so that his wife could simply walk through on foot and be shuttled back to Ramallah. For the next hour, Hessa waited in pain with her worried family in the winter night. Hessa's pain increased dramatically waiting in the cold, and soon she was ready to give birth.

When the ambulance finally arrived, the soldiers shook their heads again, apologetically: "Look, it doesn't matter if you're crossing by foot or by car. You're still a Palestinian. It's still the middle of the night. You still can't cross." At that point Hessa's husband exploded with anger, telling the soldiers they could punish him however they wanted, but that his wife must be let through. The soldiers called their superiors, who arrived 20 minutes later. By this time the family had been waiting more than 2 hours in the cold. The army agreed to let Hessa through, but not her husband. Before letting her onto the stretcher, they examined her stomach to make sure it wasn't a bomb.

Hessa gave birth to the twins in the ambulance on the way to the hospital. But because they were premature, as twins often are, the babies required immediate hospitalization. One baby died before arriving at the hospital. The second baby died the next day.[33]

---

[33] Stories like Hessa's are not uncommon. In its "Operation Defensive Shield: Soldiers' Testimonies, Palestinian Testimonies" 2002 report, *B'tselem* tells a similar story:

If Hessa had known it would take so long to pass through the checkpoint, she could have taken a different road to Ramallah, one that is much longer and bumpier but has no checkpoint. There is only a roadblock, where the ambulance could have met her. Anyone who wants to get from Deir Ballut to Ramallah without passing through a checkpoint can do so, and the army knows that. Just like they know Deir Ballut's roadblock simply requires Palestinians to take an uncomfortable detour in their cars, meaning more money for gas, more wear-and-tear on their vehicles, and more stress overall. The primary consequence of checkpoints and roadblocks is not increased security for Israel, but strain on daily life accelerating the breakdown of Palestinian society. I wish everyone—especially the soldiers, most of whom are convinced they are following orders designed to protect their families and communities—could see that.

Palestinians wait at Deir Ballut checkpoint after taking an unpaved detour from their village since their main road is blocked by concrete roadblocks.

"On Friday, April 5, 2002, Tahani 'Ali 'Asad Fatouh, a pharmacist from Al Msakan Ash Sha'abiya in the Nablus District began having labor pains. Her husband, Dr. Ghassan 'Ali Nashat Sha'ar, called an ambulance to take his seven months pregnant wife to the hospital. Due to the curfew imposed on the area, the ambulance could not reach the house and Dr. Sha'ar had to deliver the baby with the help of his neighbor, Dr. Sulfeh. The delivery went smoothly. During the delivery, the ambulance crew tried to reach the couple's house, as the newborn would have to be placed in an incubator. All attempts failed. Some 30 minutes after the birth, the baby's health began to deteriorate. Dr. Sha'ar managed to resuscitate his son twice. On the third attempt, the baby died. Tahani Fatouh had become pregnant after four years of fertility treatments. The hospital is only two kilometers [less than a mile and a half] away from the couple's home."

During the first four years of the Second Intifada, 13 newborn infants died at checkpoints. Gideon Levy, "Killing Children is No Longer a Big Deal," *Haaretz* (October 17, 2004); When this book went to press, at least 68 Palestinian women had given birth at checkpoints since 2001. *PASSIA* 2007.

The Women & Children of Deir Ballut

Women from Deir Ballut Peace Camp visit Munira's house to plant trees in solidarity with the family's resolve to stay in their home.

Thursday, December 25, 2003

Deir Ballut Peace Camp runs the risk of excluding local women, since it would be unheard of for them to sleep overnight next door to a room full of strange men in a run-down abandoned schoolhouse. Nonetheless, we are committed to making the camp a place where everyone can participate, by offering various activities for women and children.

On Tuesday, in a show of support, a group of women planted trees in front of Munira's encaged house in Mas'ha. We brought young trees ready to be planted and volunteers eager to get their hands dirty. It was fun, despite the dreary concrete wall in the background. We managed to plant several new olive trees on the small strip of dirt in the family's yard—the only remains of their former fields and greenhouses. The army wants the family to leave now, but Munira planted trees that will only blossom in decades. The young olive trees are a symbol that Munira and her family intend to stay in their house for years to come, in spite of the dangers posed by the settlers, the army, and the Wall surrounding their home.

Women role-play at a leadership workshop at Deir Ballut Peace Camp.

Youth from Deir Ballut draw pictures expressing their feelings about the Wall.

Other recent camp activities have included discussions, women's leadership workshops, resistance films, first-aid training, and activism through art. Local young people spent Tuesday morning drawing pictures of the Wall and what it means to them. The children produced colorful and heartbreaking scenes that reminded me of the drawings I had seen in Jenin. Most portrayed the Wall as the end of their futures, an eternal prison. One young boy wrote in Arabic, "After the Wall is built, that's it. We just wait here to die."

A few children chose to illustrate the shortsighted nature of the Wall. They emphasized that it can never destroy the Palestinian people and spirit, and that one day the Wall will be destroyed. I believe them.

Many of the children's pictures and ideas became posters for a children's march today. Dozens of youth marched with their pictures through the village, their parents and older siblings cheering them on from houses as they walked by. They took turns using the microphone and holding the loudspeaker.

One of the kids in the parade was Leila, a young girl who would giggle and hide when I caught her sneaking a glance at me. Her mother invited me to dinner that night, and when I arrived Leila was too shy to come out from behind the sofa. Her family patiently asked me questions while I stammered out half-sentence answers in Arabic. Eventually Leila's vanity outweighed her bashfulness and she jumped out to greet me as soon as the conversation topic strayed to something other than her. She spent the evening by my side as I enjoyed my first meal in a real house for days.

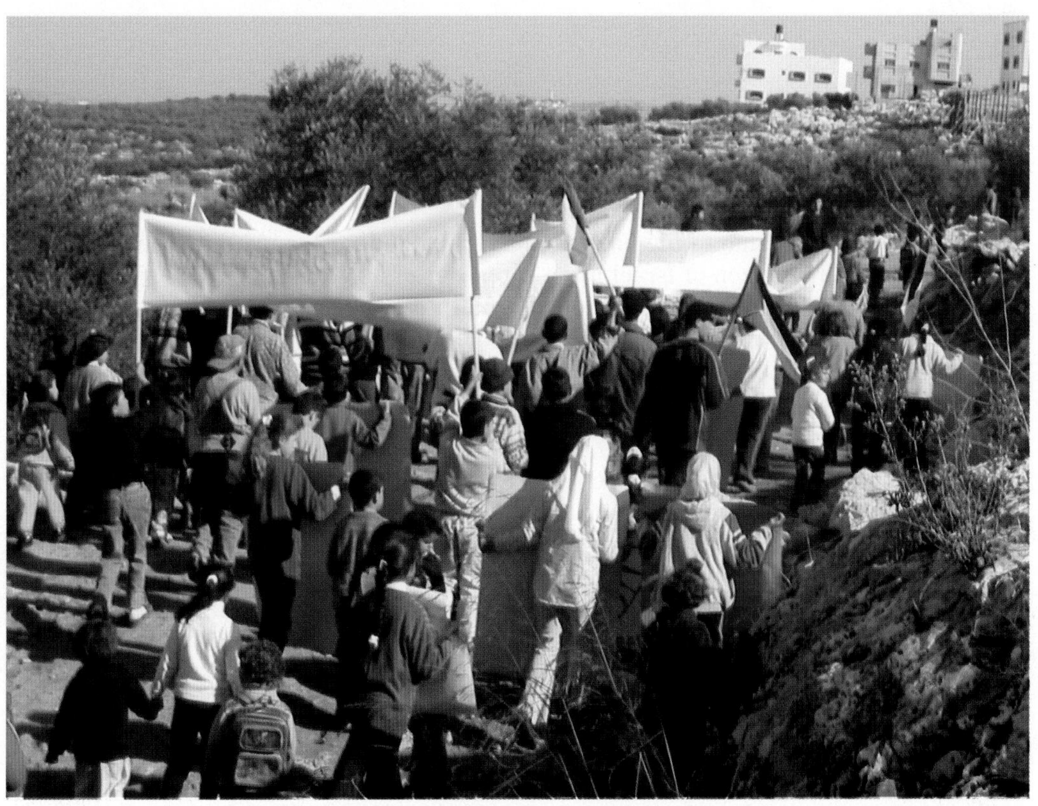

Deir Ballut children march against the Wall.

Deir Ballut children demonstrate against the Wall, which will soon surround their village and destroy their future schoolhouse.

When the subject came to my background, I repeated my standard answer, that I am Jewish but neither a citizen of Israel nor a supporter of its government. Everyone around the meal accepted the answer easily enough—except Leila. She froze as soon as she heard me say the words, "I am Jewish." I could guess the thoughts going through her head: I was one of them. I had betrayed her. Before her mother could explain the misunderstanding, Leila ran out of the room. Her mother followed her.

My spirits fell as Leila disappeared. I felt awful for upsetting her. Leila's family assured me that experience would later teach her to understand what she was too young to understand now. But her family and I had both underestimated Leila. A few minutes later, I looked up and I saw Leila waiting in the doorway next to her mother. She walked slowly up to me, reached out for me, and when my hand was in hers she lifted it, kissed it, and brought it to her forehead, repeating the last two gestures several times. This was something I had only seen a few times in Palestine and always with respected elders. Leila was apologizing without words. She was asking for forgiveness, with a gesture of respect and humility. I smiled instantly and took her onto my lap. She clung to me for the rest of the evening.

I spent the next evening in the home of Zahara, a woman who was arrested for her leadership in the women's resistance in the late 1980s during the First Intifada. Zahara was

Palestinian youth hang out with Israeli activists at Deir Ballut Peace Camp.

ıprisoned for many years with 27 other female activists held for similar reasons. In 1996 ·e army agreed to free all but five of the women, but the remaining 23 activists refused to ave. They said it was all or none of them, a nonviolent resistance technique called prison ›lidarity. The guards cut off water and electricity and brought in the army to "encourage" .em to leave. Zahara says they went through 21 days of absolute hell, but shortly after, in ›97, all 28 were freed. She believes that pressure from *Amnesty International* and other :tivists was instrumental in securing the women's release.

Zahara invited me for dinner and I met her whole family. Her 5-year-old granddaughter on't let Zahara out of her sight. The family let me use their shower and gave me some ean underwear. Families in Deir Ballut like Zahara's and Leila's have opened their homes Israelis and other foreigners who tire of the rainy nights in the camp and are looking for warm shower or bed. Local women come by the camp several times a day with large eaming plates of rice, meats, and vegetables. They always bring a meat-free and dairy-free ate on the side for the Israelis who keep kosher, and the vegetarians and vegans. There a real sense of family and solidarity building here, evident in even the smallest things. I ı excited to be a part of this creative experiment.

Witness in Palestine

Israeli Activist Shot & Reflections on Nonviolence

Tuesday, December 31, 2003

I returned to Munira's house in Mas'ha the day after Christmas for a large demonstration against the Wall. After a large meeting at the Mas'ha library to plan the action, we arrived at the Wall to find soldiers waiting on the other side of the wired fence that makes up part of the cage around Munira's house. A group of Palestinians, Israelis, and internationals—all wearing signs in Hebrew so the soldiers couldn't pick out the Palestinians—approached the fence and shook it with all their strength. A few began to cut the fence with wire-cutters. I remember the tremendous rattling and shaking, the looks on the faces of Munira's children who came outside their house to watch, and the adrenalin rush among the demonstrators, fueled by the noise. For a few moments, the people had taken back control.

The soldiers were scared. Their fear did not surprise me—they are used to being in control. One soldier fired his gun at a dark-skinned young man, hitting him twice, in the knee and in the opposite thigh. The victim was Gil Na'amati, an Israeli recently released from the army. He is one of a number of ex-soldiers who find themselves on "the other side" of the Wall, having experienced the injustice and violence of the Occupation from the inside.

Gil was shot with live ammunition from a short distance while shaking the fence, and could easily have bled to death. At first, the doctors weren't certain they could save his leg, but in the end they didn't amputate it. He will be able to walk again, but not as he did before. I remember the way two Palestinians swept him swiftly off the ground and into their arms to rush him to the nearest ambulance after he was shot. I remember the long faces of the villagers after the incident; it was as if one of their own had been hurt.

Palestinians, Israelis, and internationals shake the Wall in Mas'ha seconds before Israeli ex-soldier Gil Na'amati is shot by Israeli soldiers from close range with live ammunition.

Gil's shooting also reminded me how much more attention Israeli victims receive than Palestinian victims do. The story is all over the news, all over the world. This is not the first time a demonstrator has been shot since I arrived in November, but it's the first time friends and family in the United States and Europe are hearing about something I was involved in and writing with requests for more details. The event in Mas'ha lasted 10 minutes. What about the months of peaceful marches and olive harvesting that Palestinians have organized since I arrived? And what about the 75 Palestinians who have been killed by the army since I arrived in Palestine, many of them civilians killed with American-made weapons? Why haven't my friends and family who paid for those weapons with their tax-dollars heard about those deaths? Most have heard about the nine Israelis killed by Palestinians during the same interval.[34]

The shooting has provoked other questions for me as well. The demonstrators' actions in Mas'ha were direct and confrontational. But were they violent? The concept of "nonviolent action" turns out to be rather controversial. People around here define violence in many different ways, and I don't know exactly where I stand. This work evokes many questions for me, each with more than one possible answer:

1. What is violence? Is it measured by the amount of force exerted by the agent (the person acting)? In that case, shaking the Wall is violent but putting up the Wall itself is not.
2. Is violence measured by the damage produced upon the object? In that case, shaking the Wall is nonviolent but the existence of the Wall is violent, because it produces so much suffering and hardship in the lives of those it encloses.
3. Does it matter if the object is alive or not? Can we simultaneously call ourselves nonviolent and condone the destruction of property?
4. Can violence be verbal or emotional? Is it violent when a soldier swears at a mother who won't cooperate? Is illegitimate imprisonment violent? Is a young boy exercising violence when he yells angrily at a soldier to leave his land?
5. What about forceful self-defense—is that violent? And what qualifies as self-defense? Did the soldiers shoot Gil in self-defense? Were the protesters shaking the Wall in self-defense?

During my nonviolent direct action training with ISM, the most memorable activity was when we were asked to mentally divide the room into four quarters with the north-south axis representing violent-nonviolent respectively, and the east-west axis representing effective-ineffective. The trainers then called out scenarios and we were to respond by placing ourselves in the section of the room that we felt best corresponded to the extent to which the scenarios were or weren't violent and effective. We were then asked to justify our placement and reflect upon differences in the room, of which there were many.

The diversity of the answers was incredible. One scenario was: "A peace activist pulls a violent settler off the Palestinian whom the settler is beating up." I immediately went to nonviolent and effective, but a friend of mine went to violent-effective. His reasoning: "Physically forcing anyone to do or not do something against their will is violent."

---

[34] *Middle East Policy Council* (December 31, 2004). *www.mepc.org/resources/mrates.asp*
"Numbers *do not* include Palestinian suicide bombers (or other attackers) nor do they include Palestinians targeted for assassination, though bystanders killed during these assassinations are counted. However, [Israeli] soldiers killed during incursions into Palestinian lands *are counted*. Data collected from *B'tselem* (the Israeli Information Center for Human Rights in the Occupied Territories), the Palestinian Red Crescent Society, and the Israeli Ministry of Foreign Affairs."

When suicide bombs came up, everyone agreed that they were violent but disagreed about whether or not they were effective at ending the Occupation. That surprised me, as did the response to the next scenario: "A young boy throws a rock at a tank."

I thought it was a no-brainer: violent-ineffective. I saw a few friends at the opposite corner and assumed they were confused about the question, but they weren't. One woman spoke for the group: "A child throwing a stone a tank is nonviolent because it cannot harm the tank or anyone in it. It is effective because it allows that child to express his anger at and opposition towards his oppressor in a clear, nonviolent way."

It took me a long time to understand my friend's answer. I had always seen stone-throwing as counterproductive because it's futile in the face of a military armed with tanks and machine guns, and simply produces retaliatory violence from soldiers. Indeed, sometimes it seems like the soldiers are waiting for kids to throw stones so they can retaliate. There have been many cases of soldiers encouraging stone-throwing in order to have an excuse to single out and take action against the village "troublemakers."[35]

The words of my friend Luna helped me see stone-throwing from another perspective:

> These kids are subjected to a level of suffering and humiliation that we can't even begin to comprehend—every day, they wait in a line until the 19-year-old with the gun decides whether or not they can go to school, or get back home. Meanwhile, settler children of the same age are free to kick, punch, and sic dogs on the kids and their families. The psychological effects of such trauma are enormous. Some children are afraid to go to school. Many are chronic bedwetters.[36]
>
> People always focus on 'violence'—and violence is important—but from my experience living in Hebron, violence is not the worst thing. Think of a child, a very young child, who knows that his parents and siblings are never safe, and that none of them can keep him safe. Think of a two-year-old who shuffles his feet faster and lowers his head with fear at the sight of any settler. Think of a kid who watches his mother and father humiliated on a daily basis and can do nothing to protect them. Think about the shame, the feeling of powerlessness, the suppression of the normal, healthy instinct to fight back. These are the greatest crimes. Any day a Palestinian child dares to stand up to his oppressors is a small victory.
>
> We cannot expect young and traumatized children to respond to violence with nonviolence. If throwing a stone symbolizes that kid taking back a morsal of control over his life, who are we to judge? They never throw stones up-close—that would be a death-wish. They throw them from afar. And they throw them because they're tired of cowering or running away. Palestinians have every right to assert their anger and rejection of being treated as subhuman every day of their lives.

I'm not quite ready to embrace stone-throwing as productive, but I think Luna's points are good ones. They force me to answer important questions. Many of us know what we don't want Palestinians to do, but we are not as clear about what we expect them to do.

---

[35] Dozens of Israeli veterans have come forward with stories of soldiers and entire units intentionally provoking Palestinian children to throw stones. One example of many can be found at *www.breakingthesilence.org.il/testimony_en.asp?full=415*

[36] "Majority of Palestinian Children Suffer Chronic Psychiatric Disorders", *WAFA Palestine News Agency* (June 5, 2007).

A Palestinian boy throws a stone at army jeeps guarding the destruction and annexation of his village's land.

So I ask you the questions I ask myself daily: What would you do if the walls were closing in on you? What would you do if your brother was dead, your father was in prison, and you couldn't get a job or go to school? What would you do if your food sources were uprooted and people in neighboring settlements urinated and defecated in your water source? What would you do if working for change within the system failed you again and again? Would you bow down? Would you fight back? Would you kill yourself? Would you kill them? What would you do if you had nothing left? Remember, the walls are getting closer... What would you expect from yourself in that situation, and how does it compare with what you expect of the Palestinians today?

■ Witness in Palestine

Fire & a Demonstration in Deir Ballut

Friday, January 3, 2004

Spending more than just a few fleeting moments in Deir Ballut has allowed me to build friendships and connections with people in Palestine in a way that I hadn't before. My dearest friend of all in the village is Reem, a warm and politically active mother of four whose house has become a real haven for me. On the first night of the New Year I was sitting with Reem and her husband drinking tea when I smelled smoke. I opened the window and found the night air uncommonly foggy. It was raining ash. We could hear people yelling outside, appealing to everyone in the village to come help. We ran outside to find the streets full of women and men carrying buckets of water from their homes. They were running towards a building with a great cloud of smoke growing behind it. I saw huge flames exploding from behind the building. I asked someone near me if anyone was inside and she shook her head.

Shop owners tear down the charred walls of their store in Deir Ballut the morning after a small fire began in the shop. The fire escalated due to a lack of water and the prevention of a fire truck from passing the village checkpoint.

Reem had already run home and was carrying out buckets of water. I ran to help her. I asked why nobody had called a fire truck and a woman nearby said people had, half an hour ago, when the fire was still small. It hadn't arrived yet. I said to Reem it was crazy to try and stop the fire with small buckets of water. She nodded with agreement and said, "What choice do we have? We don't control our water supply, Israel does. We can't access the amount of water needed to stop this fire quickly."

The flames continued to grow. As women carried buckets back and forth, Hazem and others were working on connecting a series of irrigation tubes to form a hose from the nearest irrigation source to the building. Each time they turned on the source, the tubes fell apart. It would to take the entire village holding the tubes together to reach the building.

Everyone dropped their buckets and ran to hold a section of the hose. With everyone in position, the source was turned on and water began to flow through the tubes. Water sprayed out from every crack until everyone was soaked, but most of the water reached the building. We stood holding the hose for ages—shivering in the cold and slipping in the mud—and eventually the fire was put out. Smoke hung in the air as people searched around for their buckets and family members to return home. The building's facade was scorched black, and a gaping charcoal hole remained where the fire had burned for over an hour.

The next morning I returned to the scene to find a couple sifting through the remains of their furniture factory, where the fire had started. They were looking for things they could still use or sell. Everything was ruined. They said the upper floor where they lived with their family of 20 was not burned, but it had been structurally damaged. The building was no longer safe to live or work in, but the couple said they intended to stay there, seeing no other option. They estimated about US$45,000 worth of damage and losses from the factory. It was everything they had.

The couple kept repeating how small the fire had been, how easily it could have been stopped if only they could have reached the water sooner. I thought about all the water used in the West Bank to fill settlers' swimming pools and hot tubs while Palestinians struggle to find enough water to drink, let alone put out fires. One telling statistic is that in the Occupied Territories, one settler consumes as much water as 17 Palestinians.[37]

I asked the couple if they knew why no fire trucks had come. They said that firefighters from nearby towns had not been allowed to pass the checkpoint. I cursed myself for not having realized this the night before, when I could have gone to the checkpoint to try to help. I thought about all the other people from the village who had suffered that week because of the checkpoint, including Hessa and her lost twins. And then I remembered the recent news since Gil was shot: a new checkpoint was being established on the Palestinian road between Mas'ha and Deir Ballut, presumably as punishment for the demonstration in Mas'ha. The injustices aren't going to decrease—they are going to multiply.

A new checkpoint established by the army between Mas'ha and Deir Ballut controls passage to and from the peace camp.

The final event organized by Deir Ballut Peace Camp was a demonstration today against the village's checkpoint and roadblocks. I slept last night at Reem's and woke up early to help make signs and practice songs. The demonstration was scheduled to begin after the midday call to prayer, so we gathered around the mosque in anticipation. When we heard the voice of the *imam* (Muslim prayer leader) ring from the minaret above, we began to march through the village towards the checkpoint. An ambulance trailed behind the demonstration in case of any injury.

---

[37] "Israeli Settlements on Occupied Palestinian Territories," *The Palestine Monitor* (February 3, 2003). *www.palestinemonitor.org/factsheet/settlement.html*

Reem's brother-in-law had offered to stay and watch the kids while she attended the protest, but Reem insisted that the children march as well. Children were not allowed in the front of the march for safety reasons, and consequently many women ended up towards the back with their kids. I joined hands with friends and their children, and we chanted Palestinian songs and rhymes until our voices were sore. Before us marched hundreds of Palestinian men, Israelis, and internationals towards the soldiers waiting at the checkpoint. When the protesters in front arrived at the roadblocks, they sat down and began to make speeches.

I ran to take pictures in front and caught the first words of the mayor's speech. He was updating protesters on the status of hundreds of Israeli activists who were supposed to attend the demonstration but hadn't shown up. The mayor announced that 300 Israeli demonstrators on their way to Deir Ballut had been prevented from passing the new Az-Zawiya checkpoint. He added that 13 of them had been arrested when they attempted to pass in spite of the soldiers. The crowd let out a cheer when they heard how many Israelis had come to support their struggle. They were visibly moved by the gesture of solidarity and saddened by the news of their friends' arrests. One protester asked if the mayor would send a message of thanks to the Israelis on behalf of the village.

A few Israelis and internationals from the Peace Camp also said a few words. The sitting protesters watched and listened, holding a huge banner written in Hebrew, "We come in peace. Please don't shoot us." Some young

Left all: Deir Ballut villagers and their supporters march to the roadblocks and checkpoint that hinder movement into and out of Deir Ballut. Demonstrators wave flags, sing songs, and give speeches, holding signs in Hebrew that read, "We come in peace. Please don't shoot us."

men climbed atop the roadblocks to wave their flags as high as possible. Reem's husband Hazem tried to talk to the soldiers, explaining that he had many Israeli friends and he wished only to coexist in peace with them. One young boy ran away from the demonstration into a nearby field and stuck a Palestinian flag into the ground. His message was clear: this land is Palestine. The crowd was filled with enthusiasm, which quickly turned to frustration when a soldier marched onto the field, picked up the flag, dropped it onto the ground and stomped on it.

Deir Ballut villagers and their supporters march to the roadblocks and checkpoint that hinder movement into and out of Deir Ballut.

The young boy ran back into the field to retrieve his flag but at the last moment he stood it back up in the ground and left it waving in the wind again. The crowd cheered twice as loudly as before. When he returned, protesters began to head back towards the village, and the children in the back had their first chance to see the soldiers. They watched each other silently. Then, just before turning around to walk away, a group of young girls held their hands up with victory peace signs at the frowning soldiers. It was a spontaneous moment of creative nonviolence, a perfect ending to a successfully publicized and unifying demonstration.

Young girls from Deir Ballut flash victory peace signs to the soldiers guarding the roadblocks and checkpoint that control movement into and out of their village.

Witness in Palestine
Nonviolent Resistance in Budrus

Wednesday, January 8, 2004

In 1990, four brothers in the Palestinian village of Budrus put together their collective life savings and bought about 15 acres of land, planted 400 olive trees, and worked the land for 13 years. Recently, bulldozers arrived in Budrus and began their rapid destruction of everything in the path of the Wall, including the four brothers' land. Although Budrus is miles from the Green Line, Israel is using American tax-dollars to build the Wall through the village's fields, annexing some 300 acres from a community that lives primarily off its agricultural work.

The four brothers, Ayed, Na'im, Nasir, and Mohammed, have since become leaders of the growing nonviolent resistance movement in Budrus village. Every day that the bulldozers come, so do the people. There are two rules: everyone is expected to participate, and no one will throw stones. The soldiers are supposed to protect the bulldozers to ensure they level the land. They are accustomed to stones and come ready with their weapons to retaliate. But what if there are no stones? What if the soldiers come to find old men and women, mothers and fathers, and young children sitting peacefully on their land? That's what is happening in Budrus.

Budrus land and the Wall (background) threatening to annex it into Israel

According to Ayed, the first time the soldiers encountered complete nonviolence in Budrus, they turned back. They didn't know what to do. He says two sundays ago, when farmers heard the bulldozers were coming, almost the entire village went down to the fields at seven in the morning to sit on their land in protest. Israeli and international volunteers were also present. When the tractors arrived, the drivers realized they could not level the land without leveling the people too. And so they left.

But nonviolent resistance is not new to Palestine, and the Israeli army has developed strategies for this kind of situation. The next day, the army arrived shortly after six in the morning to declare the village's land a "closed military zone." In doing so, soldiers were empowered to label any villagers sitting on their own land as "criminals," and arrest or shoot them. This is a common strategy, and the resistance organizers were ready for it.

Villagers gathered en masse and walked down to their land, ready to face arrest, or worse. Seeing the group approaching, the soldiers quickly surrounded the protesters, blocking them from reaching the bulldozers. The military blockade, however, was only tight enough to prevent adults from passing; the soldiers weren't counting on the children making a move and were surprised when a group of girls squeezed through and made a dash for the bulldozers. One young teenage girl climbed into the claw of a bulldozer. As the soldiers turned to pursue her, the adult demonstrators made their own run for the fields and quickly positioned themselves in front of their trees. Unable to move forward, the soldiers drove all but one bulldozer away—the one with the girl in its claw was completely surrounded by demonstrators and could not move. The soldiers promised to leave if the villagers moved away from the tractor. The girl came down and the army left.

The girl in the claw was Ayed's daughter, an extremely bright 15-year-old who welcomed me warmly into her home when I arrived in Budrus a week later. She spoke English so well I mistook her for a Westerner at first. Ayed and his wife were equally hospitable and found time amidst their busy organizing to set up a bed for me in a guest room where five other international volunteers were staying with the family. From fellow activists and villagers I heard stories of the days following the young girl's brave act:

According to one activist, last Wednesday at 6 a.m. jeeps sped through Budrus announcing on loudspeakers a village-wide curfew. Under curfew, anyone leaving his or her home is considered a criminal. More than one hundred villagers were ready to break curfew, and mobilized with eight internationals and four Israelis to walk down to the fields. But this time, the army outnumbered the demonstrators in manpower as well as machine power. Fifteen hummers, six border police jeeps, and six police jeeps surrounded the small group. One soldier said they would not allow a repetition of the day before, to which the chanting demonstrators cried, "We can do it!"

After 10 minutes, the soldiers began making arrests. They started with Israeli demonstrators, who clawed the ground to prevent themselves from being lifted and taken away by the soldiers. The army responded with batons and shoves until they had successfully arrested three Israelis, and beaten off the 10 Palestinians who were trying to protect their Israeli colleagues.

Ten minutes later, the soldiers began arresting internationals. Knowing arrest meant almost certain deportation, Palestinians surrounded their international friends, trying to protect them with their bodies. Soldiers did not hesitate to beat villagers, and the bruised and gassed demonstrators eventually retreated. Three internationals were arrested, including Gustav Fridolin, a member of the Swedish parliament who had come to witness first-hand the situation in Palestine. Another was Kate, an active and founding member of IWPS.

An IWPS colleague called me on New Year's Eve to give me the bad news about Kate. We needed someone at the IWPS house that night to send out a call to action to inform and mobilize friends of Kate and IWPS. We hoped that with enough calls of complaint from around the world Kate might not be deported. I had hoped to spend New Year's Eve with friends in Deir Ballut, but given the circumstances I offered to spend the night at the office in Haris sending emails and answering calls from the press and Kate's supporters.

© IWPS 2004, Kate Raphael-Bender

Villagers protest the Wall and the soldiers whose presence protects its construction.

The phone rang all night long. Fellow activists, family members, journalists, and Palestinian friends were desperate for news about Kate. At 11:59 p.m. I took a break and ran upstairs to the roof to count down to the New Year. The village was peaceful and I thought about Kate in jail. She has been a major source of inspiration for me in this work, and a good friend.

I last talked with Kate on Monday when I arrived in Budrus. Villagers called her in jail constantly to make sure she was all right. I stole the phone for a minute and we exchanged a few words. She sounded fine and stressed how much better internationals are treated compared to Palestinians in Israeli prisons. I asked her what had happened and she said the soldiers had arrested her because she refused to stop filming the army beating peaceful demonstrators. I told her I was proud of what she had done. She wished me and the villagers of Budrus luck in the continuing struggle.

The past week has been a whirlwind of bureaucratic phone calls and faxes, trying to secure Kate better access to her lawyer, annul her deportation order, and release her from prison. IWPS tries to provide legal and administrative support to arrested volunteers, a luxury most imprisoned Palestinians don't have. During the month in which Kate was arrested, so were dozens of Budrus village demonstrators, including Ayed and two of his brothers. Ayed and Naim were arrested for organizing protests against the Wall, and their brother Nasir was also charged with "hosting internationals in his home." All three were released when a military court judge ruled that peaceful protests against the Wall organized by Palestinians and attended by international volunteers did not constitute a threat to Israeli security.

Far more frequent than arrest is army brutality. During the week of Kate's arrest, 80 Palestinians were beaten by soldiers, and 10 of them had to be hospitalized. Some of the most severe beatings were administered to Palestinians who were defending their Israeli and international counterparts from arrest on New Year's Eve. Ayed, for example, was beaten on the head with a baton and lost consciousness. Later he saw on video that he had

Soldiers respond to nonviolent protesters with violence.

been beaten all over his body after he passed out, as were his wife, brothers, sisters, daughters, sons, and friends. But Ayed said neither the arrests nor the beatings were the most disturbing things he saw that day:

> After our Israeli and international friends had been arrested, and more than half a dozen villagers were sent to the hospital from beatings, many boys in the village could no longer control their desire to respond with force. Several boys picked up stones and began throwing them at the soldiers and bulldozers. It was a step backwards for us. We must remain nonviolent if we are to be effective. With stones they need just a few soldiers and bullets to hold us off. With no stones, we are stronger than the soldiers.

The few days I have spent in Budrus have been calm ones. Mass demonstrations continued daily until a week ago, when bulldozers destroyed 60 of the village's olive trees in 4 hours. When I arrived on Monday, I saw that the land we wanted to protect was already lost. The trees were gone and the cement was laid down.

Although construction was suspended this week, every day I walk with Ayed, his brothers, village schoolgirls, and old farmers to the threatened land. The people of Budrus have pledged to protest the Wall until its path is changed to the Green Line, the internationally recognized border between Israel and their village. Most villagers agree that even a wall on the border is a step backwards—peace evolves naturally from justice, not separation—but they are not even asking that the Wall not exist. They are insisting that its construction adhere to international law and basic decency. Time will tell if the resistance in Budrus will achieve its goals before more land and lives are destroyed.

*Israel continued constructing the Wall in the West Bank throughout 2004,
in spite of the International Court of Justice's ruling that the barrier is illegal.
Peaceful demonstrations also continued.*

I left Palestine on January 12, 2004. Kate was deported 5 days later, after more than 2 weeks in jail. She is not the first IWPS team member to be deported by Israel, and she probably won't be the last. Although physically harming international volunteers could entail undesirable diplomatic repercussions, Israel is free to prevent internationals who admit to working with Palestinians from entering Palestine, since Israel controls all movement into, within, and out of Palestine. As a result, IWPS volunteer numbers are dwindling.

In the fall of 2004 I was informed that IWPS needed volunteers in early 2005, so in February I flew to Israel and crossed into the West Bank for 3 more months in Haris. The Wall had grown quite a bit during my absence despite the International Court of Justice's ruling in July that Israel's Wall[38] *was in breach of international law and a violation of Palestinians' human rights and right to self-determination. The court demanded that Israel cease construction of, dismantle, and make reparation for all damage caused by the Wall. Israel responded by rejecting the court's opinion and declaring its intentions to continue Wall construction. The United States continued its unwavering financial support for the Wall by increasing its billions of dollars of foreign military financing of Israel the following year.*[39]

Nonviolent resistance continued all over Palestine throughout 2004, and much of it was met with violence from the Israeli army. During the 12 months that I was gone, Palestinians killed about 110 Israelis. During that same period, Israeli Occupation Forces and settlers, killed more than 935 Palestinians.[40] *Whenever Palestinian violence against Israelis stopped, the government cited the change as proof of the Wall's efficacy. When Palestinian attacks resumed, the government cited Israeli casualties as justification for the Wall.*

One promising piece of news: continuous nonviolent demonstrations in Budrus village succeeded in getting the Wall's path near Budrus moved all the way to the Green Line, except for a dozen acres in one area that are still threatened with annexation. Villagers continue to demonstrate nonviolently for these last acres; their actions have included cutting through large chunks of the fence. In response, the army is replacing the wire-fence Wall near the village with a concrete one.

---

[38] The ICJ deliberately chose to use the term "Wall," rather than "Separation Barrier."

[39] Frida Berrigan and William D. Hartung, "U.S. Military Assistance and Arms Transfers to Israel: U.S. Aid, Companies Fuel Israeli Military," *World Policy Institute.* *www.worldpolicy.org/projects/arms/reports/israel.lebanon.FINAL2.pdf*

[40] *Middle East Policy Council* (December 31, 2004). *www.mepc.org/resources/mrates.asp*
"Numbers *do not* include Palestinian suicide bombers (or other attackers) nor do they include Palestinians targeted for assassination, though bystanders killed during these assassinations are counted. However, [Israeli] soldiers killed during incursions into Palestinian lands *are counted.* Data collected from *B'tselem,* the Palestinian Red Crescent Society, and the Israeli Ministry of Foreign Affairs."

Witness in Palestine
Boys' School Under Attack

Monday, February 14, 2005

It is difficult being back in Palestine. We are busy and freezing, and I have been fighting a cold for weeks. But I am filled with energy and excitement about being back here. The competing forces of war and peace-making all around make me feel awake and alive in a way that I rarely feel at home.

Palestine is even more beautiful than I remembered it. Every tree, grove, and field is so ancient, fertile, and cared for. I am surprised to feel a strong attachment to the land here unlike anything I've ever felt in my own country, even though I make no biblical or hereditary claim to Palestine. Feeling an attachment to land for the first time in my life helps me to understand why people would fight so hard to take or keep it.

I spent last weekend in a village called Qarawat Bani Zeid (QBZ), where locals had asked for an international presence at a boy's high school due to frequent incursions by Israeli soldiers. Two years ago, several soldiers entered the village on foot and opened fire in the school courtyard, killing two and injuring several others. The attack was retaliation for students throwing stones at army jeeps in the village. There have been dozens of Palestinians killed in the village since then, with no justification given, no investigations carried out, and no one held responsible. The jeeps continue to drive around and the boys continue to throw stones.

My colleague Fatima and I were asked to sit at a bus stop on the main road next to the school on Saturday morning, the first day of the school week. The children gathered in the courtyard at eight o'clock to sing the anthem and get organized for the day. Five minutes later, a jeep and a Humvee drove by and the students quickly picked up stones to throw. We were helpless, unable to prevent the army from coming into the village or the students from throwing stones. But we were visible in the road, watching. The Humvee drove away and the students went into the school, where they spend all morning except for one recess.

The army returned precisely at recess. This time, the teachers had received a call from a nearby village warning them of the army's approach and managed to usher all the students in before the soldiers passed. As the jeep and Humvee drove by, a soldier threw a sound bomb[41] into the empty schoolyard. Then they were gone.

I tried to imagine how the exchange would have been reported in the mainstream American press: "Angry Palestinians Shower Israeli Soldiers With Stones," with no mention of the terror the village faces each time a US-sponsored Israeli army jeep zooms through. Two days ago a young man was arrested; two weeks before, two men were killed and one house destroyed. Residents wonder what is coming next.

---

[41] Sound bombs are explosive grenades frequently used by the Israeli army to disorient or stun protesters. At close proximity, the explosions can cause burns, hearing loss, and nervous-system damage.

Students hang around QBZ boys' school, where soldiers opened fire in 2003, killing two.

The article would also not mention that the army consistently drives by during the recess period, when the boys are outside. We interviewed the headmaster, who said that the pattern had become so obvious that the school changed its recess time to avoid confrontation. He said the army now comes during the new break time with regularity that cannot be coincidental. We asked what it was like to teach under such circumstances, and he sighed. "We have to seize each day to teach them. Who knows if tomorrow we will have the chance?"

Sitting at the bus stop, we talked to passers-by about the situation, each one seeming less hopeful than the last. Some were students taking a break. One young Hemingway fan asked me if I had read *A Farewell to Arms*, his favorite book. The English teacher Dawud came out during his free hour to welcome me. He had heard that I was Jewish and told me that Jews are cousins of Arabs and the neighbors of Palestinians. But he lamented the 30,000 homeless in Gaza and the innocent people killed every day. He said he no longer wondered how people could blow themselves up: "When you've lost everything and everyone, you want to do something to make yourself feel powerful again"

One man waiting for the bus spoke excellent English and French. After shaking our hands, he said in the most respectful way possible, "Something has been troubling me." He read aloud from the IWPS card we had given him—"We support nonviolent resistance to the military occupation"—and then said, "I welcome you to our country and I thank you for the work you've done, but tell me, why do you only support nonviolence? Violence has always been an acceptable means of fighting oppression in most countries in the world... Why not here? How can you expect us to be nonviolent when we are under attack? What else can we do?"

I explained that I believe the resolution to the problem must include international pressure on Israel to stop, as it did with apartheid in South Africa. I also believe that pressure might never be realized if people in other countries continue to view Palestinians as terrorists.

Fatima, who is from South Africa, pointed out that there was also a major armed resistance to apartheid that helped end the system in her country. She said, "I believe nonviolent resistance was part of the struggle, but not all of it." Our new friend asked what she would recommend, and she suggested boycotting Israeli products.

He laughed. "Boycotting?! What can we boycott? Israel completely controls our imports and exports, so we have no choice but to buy from Israel or its trade partners, and both of those options contribute to the Israeli economy. The few products produced in Palestine, like milk and hummus, would never make a difference. Once we tried to boycott fruits and vegetables and Israel lowered its prices so low that farmers couldn't keep up. Believe me, we've tried. But it doesn't work." He smiled. "Your most important work is not boycotting; it's telling your family and friends what you see here. And our work is to resist, and to never, ever lose hope. We are not leaving."

He's half right. Most Palestinians are not leaving, despite the curfews, incursions, house demolitions, arrests, and killings. They are more determined than I could ever be, but I wish that their success matched their determination. It's unclear to me what would be most effective, and from my perspective much of the resistance seems chaotic and disorganized, with no principal strategy to guide and unify the movement. As it is now, I believe most of their nonviolent sacrifices are forgotten.

Fatima and I took an arrest report in QBZ for a young man named Hassan. We visited his family in their modest home and they welcomed us graciously, feeding us copious amounts of food. On their wall hung a poster of another son, Hassan's younger brother, who was killed at the age of 16 for throwing a stone at a jeep. He smiled handsomely in the poster and in a framed picture that they kept on the sofa next to them, as if pretending he were in the room. They bragged about another son, Rami, who was a policeman in Ramallah. I recognized Rami's name from a witness statement I had read earlier that day describing the events of a military incursion in QBZ 18 months earlier. Here is an excerpt from Rami's statement:

> Suddenly they started to fire in the air and I saw a child, Tamer Arrar (eleven years old) crying when he saw himself alone and all who were around him escaped. I approached him on the eastern hill, while down from us stood the three soldiers with [a tall] blond soldier directing his gun towards us. We both lay down on the ground. I told Tamer not to raise his head because I could see the tall soldier targeting us. But as soon as he raised his head, a bullet hit him in the head and I saw his head exploding. The soldiers were about 400 meters [1,200 ft] from us. We were not throwing stones at the soldiers and there were no clashes between them and the children....
>
> [Then] some young boys and I threw stones at the patrol cars and ran away towards the fields and they followed us shooting and firing at us until I reached a dead end. The soldiers and I came face to face and were separated by only 10 meters [30 ft]. The same

tall and blond soldier and another one insulted us and the tall one shot at me. The bullet penetrated my right thigh, where it entered from the front and exited from the back. On the same day, my brother Rafat was injured in the stomach and my friend Ghassan was also injured in the right thigh.[42]

It was not the shooting of two unarmed children that startled me most, since such stories are not uncommon. What took me off-guard was the mention of a boy injured in the stomach: I had only been to QBZ once before, and I remembered clearly a striking young boy who had come up to the window of a taxi I was in and lifted his shirt to reveal a large stomach wound from which fluids were draining into a sack. I had forgotten about him until I read Rami's statement, and I almost fainted when he walked into the room where we were eating with Hassan's family.

I told Rafat that I remembered him and he verified that he had a wound in his stomach. He was nonchalant about the injury, since his father and three older brothers have also been shot. His younger sister was also hit in the eye and disfigured with a stone thrown by her older brother at a jeep.

© IWPS 2005, Ridwana

Rafat and his cousin Rabia play chess in the QBZ International House.

Abu Hassan told me the story of his son's arrest several days before. He said soldiers woke him up at 5 a.m. and asked him to identify his son, who was wanted for being a Hamas supporter. Abu Hassan refused to go, but they threatened him with force. He was taken to a nearby village, terrified the whole time that he would be forced to identify his son's corpse. When he arrived at the village he saw three young Palestinian men standing, including his son, whose arms had been tied to a jeep. Dozens of soldiers were milling around. An Arabic-speaking officer pointed to each of the three men in succession, asking Abu Hassan each time whether the man was his son.

It is difficult to appreciate the position Abu Hassan was placed in, forced to choose between condemning his son to jail by identifying, and denying his relationship to him. He chose the latter, saying "no" to all three. But when Hassan heard his father say no, he could not help but smile. He said, "He is my father, and I am very proud of him." They shook hands, and Hassan was taken away. Hassan's friend Mohammed was also arrested for letting Hassan stay in his home.

---

[42] Lena Johansson, "Provocation to Kill: The Use of Lethal Force in Response to Provoked Stone-Throwing, A Case Study of Qarawa Bani Zeid," *Al-Haq* (2003).

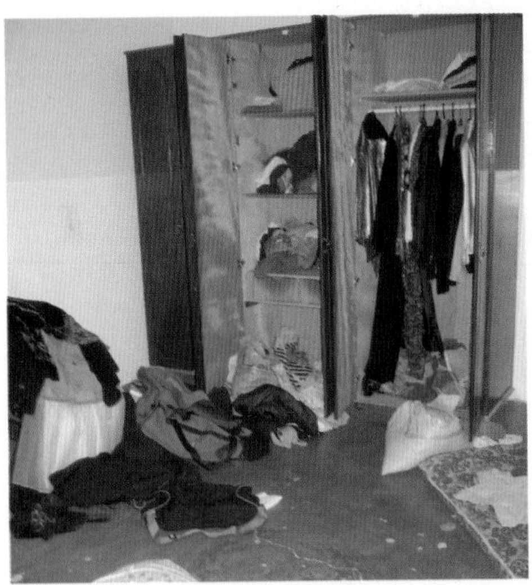

Mohammed's room after the army searched it because he had taken in his friend Hassan, a supporter of Hamas

The soldiers called Abu Hassan a liar and forced him to squat on the road for a long time. This was difficult because he has a bullet-wound in his leg. When he couldn't take it any longer he stood up, and was forced down again. Finally he was left with Mohammed's crying mother, infant daughter, and toddler son. The three had been made to wait outside in the cold as the soldiers searched the family home, which they turned upside down. Before they left, the soldiers threatened to destroy the house, but Mohammed's mother was too devastated by her son's arrest to care.

House demolitions are commonly used to punish the families of Palestinians who carry out armed attacks against Israel, even though the Fourth Geneva Convention explicitly prohibits collective punishment and the destruction of personal property by an occupying force. According to the *Alternative Information Center*,[43] "House demolitions are extra-judicial; there are no charges, no trial, and no effective way to appeal."[44] And today, a research committee commissioned by the Israeli army announced that house demolitions are also overwhelmingly *ineffective* at preventing Palestinian violence, because the anger they produce grossly outweighs any possible benefit. I can't say I'm surprised. I wonder if this means Israel will stop demolishing family homes.[45]

Mohammed's house was spared that night, but at least 10,000 Palestinian homes in the West Bank and East Jerusalem have pending demolition orders. Many will no doubt soon join the hundreds of thousands of Palestinians who have been left homeless by illegal house demolitions. Many of the demolitions date back as far as 1967, decades before suicide bombings began.[46]

[43] The *Alternative Information Center (AIC)* is a joint Palestinian-Israeli publication and advocacy group: *www.alternativenews.org*

[44] *AIC*, p. 33.

[45] This seems doubtful given that the vast majority of house demolitions are not punitive. See pp. 112-113.

[46] Israeli Committe Against House Demolitions (ICAHD). *www.icahd.org*

Discussing Faith & Peace with Old Friends

Tuesday, February 15, 2005

I recently visited my friend Reem, whose family I stayed with during last year's Deir Ballut Peace Camp Against the Wall. My fondest memory of Reem's family was the day we took two old village jeeps, overflowing with children and food, and drove to the family's land for a picnic. I remember how, as we drove, we could see the Israeli cities of Tel Aviv and Petah Tiqvah in the distance, along with closer illegal settlements, outposts, and military camps. When the jeep stopped, the children bounded out and spread across the great fertile land. Two girls gathered flowers to put in their hair, while several kids played hide-and-seek among the olive trees. When I sat down to write in my journal, a crowd of children gathered around me. I asked them to teach me their favorite song. It's a song about Palestine, about their love for their land and their capital, Jerusalem. The song's chorus goes, "We are not the terrorists."

On the way to a picnic on the threatened land of Deir Ballut

Deir Ballut land, threatened by the impending Wall

Meanwhile the adults were busy. Several men had made a fire and were balancing a teapot on uneven rocks to make tea with freshly-picked sage. Several women had unfurled blankets and spread out plates piled with pita, tomatoes, hummus, and barbequed chicken. After the

Picking flowers and playing charades with Reem's family on Deir Ballut land threatened by the Wall

meal we played charades. Reem fed her husband Hazem ideas, and everyone laughed as he made a fool of himself. It felt like a normal picnic in the park, except for one thing: the land would be gone in a matter of months. The Wall was coming and the families would lose it all. Time was short and our pleasure was bittersweet.

Hazem was so heartbroken by the idea of losing his land that he decided to leave. Last year, he went to work in Jordan for 6 months. I was disappointed when he left, thinking this meant defeat, but he told me he could see no other choice. He used to be an activist, and then his name came up on a list somewhere and he was sent to prison for 2 years. He told me he was blindfolded and handcuffed for several weeks and periodically deprived of sleep: every time he would doze off the soldiers would punch him, until he was so delirious that he thought he was going to die. They leaned their weight against his chest with their feet and made him hold himself upright on a stool despite his fatigue. He related these stories somberly and said he couldn't do it again, not to his wife and their children. He swore he would stay out of politics, because if he died or went away he couldn't imagine what would happen to them.

This year, Hazem looked even more depressed and asked what it would take to move to the United States. I told him the United States was not as generous to foreigners as people believe it to be, moreover it is extremely difficult to get a visa. He sighed; "There is no future here for my children. I want my kids to go to college, to find work to support their own families in the future." We watched together as his daughters practiced writing Arabic next to the electric heater in the living room. The oldest daughter, Athir, is first in her school.

Much of my visit was spent next to that heater, sheltered from the rain, consuming fresh persimmons and hot chocolate. Reem's sister-in-law gave me a lesson on Arabic script, and Hazem took his first beating from me in backgammon. When it stopped raining, we went back by jeep to where we'd picnicked a year ago, this time to take pictures of the bulldozers clearing away the village's land to make way for the Wall. I took photographs while Hazem walked with his youngest son on his shoulders, pointing out a gazelle racing by and the ruins of an ancient city. Hazem's friend made a fire, and one at a time the men left the circle to pray while the rest of us sipped tea together. The praying men bowed towards Mecca across the valley, with the half-constructed Wall in the distance.

Hazem asked me if I was religious. I told him I wasn't, but that I was always open to spirituality. When I admitted I didn't feel the presence of God, he shook his head and said in a low voice that that was very bad. I smiled and asked why it was so important that I believe in God if I am a good person. Several others joined into the conversation, and one asked if I believe in Heaven. I said no. They were shocked. I defended myself: "Some people do good because they want to go to Heaven. But I work for justice because it's the right thing to do." Hazem's friend Lutfi understood and nodded to himself. He said in a low voice next to me, "You have a good heart, so you will go to Heaven." "*Insha'allah* (God willing)," added Hazem, still worried.

I had spoken with Lutfi the evening before about extremists in Israel and Palestine. It was just after Sharon and Abbas's summit, and Lutfi was criticizing Sharon, saying he pretended to want peace but encouraged more suicide bombs by keeping the situation in the West Bank and Gaza so intolerable. I said that the fear generated by the suicide attacks is what drives moderates in Israel to support someone like Sharon, and without it maybe he would have no power. Lutfi reminded me that the track record of Likud, Sharon's political party, on Palestinian rights and statehood is no worse than that of the only realistic alternative, the Labor party. Although at times Likud has been more explicit about colonizing the West Bank and transferring non-Jews away from the area, even the celebrated Israeli political dove Yitzhak Rabin recognized that his party "Labor does not differ from Likud about the 'right of settlement' but only about its manner."[47] And the notion that the conflict would best be solved if all the Palestinians would leave Israel/Palestine has deep roots in the socialist and liberal Zionist philosophies on which Labor was founded.[48]

Drinking tea with Hazem and his family on a break from documenting the Wall construction (background)

---

[47] *Davar* (November 11, 1982); interview with Trialogue, journal of the Trilateral Commission (Winter, 1983); As cited in Chomsky, *Fateful*, p. 112.

[48] Chomsky, *Fateful*, p. 49.

I asked Lutfi what he thought of Sharon's idea to put the West Bank under Jordanian control. Hazem, nearby, scoffed. "The Jordanians are just as bad. We don't want a changing of the guard, we want our own country! We want freedom to move, build, study, and work as we please." That Sharon would think Palestinians would rather be occupied by Jordanians than Israelis just shows the extent to which people misrepresent or misunderstand the problem. The problem is not about Jews and Arabs; it's about oppression and freedom.

Most Israelis have learned to use the word "Arab" instead of "Palestinian." Some even say "Palestinians don't exist" because the term "Palestine" was not commonly used to refer to the area before Zionist immigration began. In actuality, "*Filistin*" (Arabic for Palestine) and its historic borders became known throughout the Islamic world as early as the end of the 7th century.[49] But regardless, it is not the word that is most important; the main point is that the majority of the people living on the land that was declared the state of the Jews were part of a non-Jewish indigenous population, the majority of which was expelled in 1948. Using the word "Arabs" to refer to all Palestinians is a way of ignoring their particular historical connection and claim to the land that is now called Israel.

The tendency of Israelis and others to group Palestinians, Jordanians, Moroccans, and Kuwaitis all into the category "Arabs" is also misleading, because it implies a camaraderie between the groups that for the most part does not exist. Under orders from King Hussein, Palestinian refugees were killed by the thousands in Jordan. In Lebanon, Palestinian refugees are an oppressed minority prohibited from holding a large majority of jobs. It is absurd to say that the Palestinian people should somehow just be absorbed into "the Arab world" when their culture, dialect, and lives had been evolving in Palestine for hundreds of years.

I also speak up at times when I hear Palestinians talking about "the Jews" in reference to violent soldiers and settlers, another attempt at clumping a large and diverse group of people into one sweeping category. I sometimes point out that I am Jewish, yet I stand in opposition to the Israeli government's policies of discrimination and colonization. While it is true that the soldiers and settlers that Palestinians complain about are probably Jewish, that has nothing to do with their crime. Such wording can also be easily misunderstood as anti-Semitic, when in my experience its source is generally not an irrational or abstract hatred of all Jews, but real grievances of discrimination and dispossession.

[49] Edward Said, *The Question of Palestine*; As cited in *The Origin of the Palestine-Israel Conflict*, published by Jews for Justice in the Middle East, third edition. *www.cactus48.com*

The Qalqilya Ghetto & the Refugees

Wednesday, February 16, 2005

A few days ago our team went down to Bethlehem to hear two South African colleagues from IWPS lecture on the similarities and differences between the current situation in Palestine and that of South Africa during apartheid. On the way down, we stopped in Abu Dis, a university neighborhood east of Jerusalem with sections of the Wall running through it. The Wall is currently made up of short, unfinished curves, but in time these curves will be connected, surrounding or isolating the Palestinian neighborhoods and villages in the area. Many homes that used to look out onto the Jerusalem hills now face a massive concrete façade.

Students from Abu Dis University have painted large murals all along the Wall—we saw pictures of doves, Che Guevara, and a screaming man in chains. But most of the Wall in the West Bank is not as colorful. I recently visited Qalqilya, a city of 45,000 completely surrounded by the 25 ft concrete Wall, complete with sniper towers. The only way into or out of the city is via one gate controlled by Israeli soldiers. The once lively Qalqilya city is now the Qalqilya ghetto. Nothing remains of the commerce and vibrancy that used to characterize the urban center, now a ghost town. Formerly prime real estate is now used to store sheep. The Wall is visible in every direction, a never-ending expanse of gray but for a few hopeful pictures of Palestinian flags, the once-forbidden symbol of Palestinian independence. But independence has never been more out of reach for the people of Qalqilya than it is today.

Abu Dis is starting to look more and more like Qalqilya. Certain neighborhoods have already been split in half, with one side in East Jerusalem and the other now considered part of the West Bank. Families are being torn apart: suddenly a father is considered a resident of the West Bank, while his wife and kids have Jerusalem IDs. He can no longer go to his house, where he lived for years with his family, because it is off-limits to people from his side of the Wall.

Qalqilya city—now known as the Qalqilya ghetto—has been completely surrounded by the Wall.

The Wall bisects Abu Dis neighborhood and university on the eastern outskirts of Jerusalem.

That night in Bethlehem, my colleagues spoke about the walls that the white Dutch colonists built in South Africa to isolate people of color into bantustans: isolated black African "homelands" lacking any real legitimacy or power. Apartheid in South Africa started with racial segregation in the 17th and 18th centuries by the Dutch, who also abused the Old Testament to justify what they called "separate development." A few of the speakers felt that Israel had perfected South African apartheid techniques while others found important differences between the two. But for those of us in the audience, the similarities were all too real. State-enforced segregation, isolated communities, curfews, imprisonment without trial, and torture—these were the realities we saw every day.

One Palestinian in the audience asked what strategy had worked to end apartheid in South Africa. The speakers agreed that Palestine currently seemed to lack the unifying leader and common strategy that was needed, and that Palestinians should focus on things like education that could strengthen their cause. They also emphasized the importance of international pressure. But the movement would have to start from within Palestine, one of the speakers explained. "Nobody will come and save you," he told the audience. A Palestinian stood up to say that he wished he'd learned that lesson years ago. In 1967, he explained, Palestinians had waited for Arab countries to save them, and then in the 1980s they pinned their hopes on the Palestine Liberation Organization (PLO). It was only in 1988, with the First Intifada, he said, that most Palestinians started to take up the fight themselves. And now Palestinians are even worse off than they were before. The man shook his head and said he couldn't expect any move from the international community if there was no clear movement within Palestine itself.

That night we stayed in Dheisheh refugee camp, a densely-populated third of a square mile that is home to 11,000 refugees from Israel's "War of Independence." Dheisheh's refugees come from 46 of the more than 500 Palestinian villages that were destroyed following the flight of more than 750,000 Palestinians from their homes by incitement or military force in 1948. After Zionists declared the establishment of the State of Israel, the refugees' homes and villages were planted over with fast-growing pine trees and all but forgotten. Ziad, who gave us a tour of the camp, said it was revolting to hear how "the Jews made the desert bloom" when much of the aggressive planting was the covering up of ancient Palestinian villages. He said his family's land is now part of Israel's US-funded "American National Park," where Israelis and tourists go to take walks with their kids and dogs, but where refugees and their families are forbidden ever to return.

Hundreds of Palestinian villages like the one above were planted over with trees after their residents were forced to flee during Israel's "War of Independence" in 1948.

As we walked through the run-down camp, children shouted hellos from the rooftops, comfortably hopping from one to the next to keep up with us. We walked by the ruins of a house, with furniture and personal belongings poking out from

All: Deheisheh refugee camp

the rubble. Ziad talked about the history of the Palestinian refugee community after the 1948 and 1967 wars, both of which created hundreds of thousands of refugees. He spoke of living in tents and caves in the cold, sharing toilets with hundreds of others, and their ever-growing dependence on the Israeli state. He recalled waiting in vain for help from the Arab states. Most of all, he talked about the curfews imposed on refugee camps: 49 days straight during the Gulf War and an average of 4 months every year. During the curfews, anyone caught outside risked being shot. He said the soldiers used to shoot warning shots in the air first, but now many are instructed to shoot to kill.[50]

From 1985 to 1995, Dheisheh also had a wall around it. The only way out was through a revolving metal turnstile controlled by Israeli soldiers. Outsiders would peek in through the fence. Now that the wall is gone, the refugees say they no longer feel like animals in a zoo—now they just feel ignored. "The 'refugee issue' is simply not an issue anymore because the government ignores it," an Israeli friend told me. "Israel accepts no responsibility for having caused the problem, or for solving it now. It's as if the problem, and the refugees, never existed. When you go to a park or natural area, they always have signs explaining the history of the land, but when they come to the era of the 'Arabs,' they skip it. The existence of Palestinians is not only being threatened in Israel today; the Palestinians are being erased from history as well."

In late 1948, the UN General Assembly resolved that "the [Palestinian] refugees wishing to return to their homes and live in peace with their neighbors should be permitted to do so at the earliest practicable date" (Resolution 194). The UN has reaffirmed Resolution 194 over 130 times in the 58 years since its introduction, but Israel has never complied. Israel was admitted to the United Nations on condition that it accept relevant resolutions (such

[50] Many Israeli army veterans have come forward with stories of being ordered "to shoot or kill unarmed people without fear of reprimand." For details, see Conal Urquhart, "Israeli Soldiers Tell of Indiscriminate Killings by Army and a Culture of Impunity," *Guardian* (September 6, 2005). *Breaking the Silence*'s testimonial booklet #2 also contains several first-hand testimonies, most notably "the Wild West at the Nablus Kasbah."

as 194), but decades later it has yet to follow through with the obligation.[51] The right of return for Palestinian refugees remains off the agendas of any significant voice in the international community and is mostly dismissed even by Israeli "leftists."

But for Ziad, the right of return for Palestinian refugees is the key to peace. That said, he makes a distinction between the *right* of return and the *actual* return of the six million or so Palestinian refugees now living in the diaspora. Thirteen million Jews worldwide have the option of living in Israel, yet almost two thirds of them are not taking advantage of the privilege. Why should the Palestinians be so different? Many of their families have now spent generations abroad and would not choose to go back. For Ziad, the point is that Palestinians should be able to make that choice for themselves. He, for example, would choose to live in a house near the home where his family grew up, where his neighbors would all be Jewish. Others would surely prefer to stay in a Muslim or Christian community. What's important is the self-determination to choose where you want to live your life, something most of us take for granted.

The refugee problem is real, and it is not going away. Although much of the world seems to have forgotten about UN Resolution 194, the millions of refugees remaining without justice or a homeland have not. Each of those six million Palestinians deserves a home, security, and self-determination as much as any Jew in the world, and neither Israel nor the international community can expect lasting peace until the refugee problem has been acknowledged and justly resolved.

[51] Qumsiyeh, p. 44.

Witness in Palestine
Israeli Activism, House Demolitions, & Jerusalem

Sunday, February 20, 2005

There is nothing that gives me hope like hanging out with Israeli peace activists. This week I went tree-planting with Rabbis for Human Rights, who have donated hundreds of young olive trees to farmers who have been separated from their land by the Wall. With the help of RHR and IWPS, the farmers planted young trees symbolizing their continued propriety over the land, despite their difficulty accessing it.

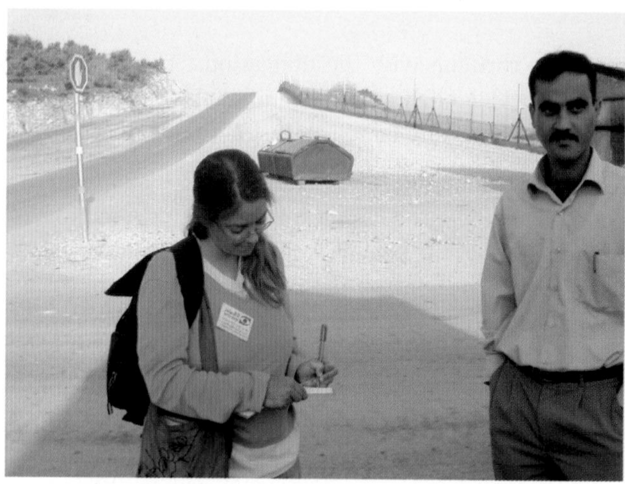

Shelly, an Israeli activist, documents human rights abuses at checkpoints with Machsom Watch.

Among my colleagues at the action was Shelly, an Israeli activist recently convicted of "obstructing the work of a police officer" for sitting in front of a bulldozer about to uproot olive trees as a means of collectively punishing an entire village. She was arrested alongside another Israeli named Neta, who had chained herself to the trees in protest. Shelly is calm and compassionate, and very dedicated to the cause. She works odd jobs to support her political work, and the rest of the time leads Israelis on tours to the Wall. Shelly said that Israelis are always shocked to see the reality of the Wall, and the tour facilitates discussions for people to process what they've seen in a productive way.

Rabbi Arik Ascherman, the director of RHR, was recently tried for standing on the roof of a Palestinian family's house about to be demolished because it did not have a building permit. Although he lost in court, Rabbi Ascherman used the lawsuit to publicize the difficulties Palestinians face in obtaining building permits. The situation is most dire in Jerusalem, where Palestinians with Israeli citizenship account for a third of the total population but have access to only 7% of urban land. According to the Israeli Committee Against House Demolitions (ICAHD), the Jerusalem Municipality has constructed 100,000 housing units in Jewish areas since 1967, compared with only 500 in Palestinian areas.

Palestinian applications to build on their own land are both extremely expensive and rarely successful. The entire application process for a modest house in East Jerusalem costs roughly US$22,000, more than most Palestinian families can afford and often higher

A Palestinian father and his sons stand in front of their home, which was demolished by Israeli soldiers because the family was unable to obtain an Israeli permit to build a house on their own land.

than the price of building itself. Application costs for larger homes are even more expensive.[52] But even those Palestinian families who can afford to apply for a building permit are rarely granted one. The Israeli Jerusalem Municipality annually issues about 100 building permits to Palestinians, compared to 1,500 to Jewish Israelis.[53] Israel maintains a perpetual shortage of around 25,000 housing units for Palestinian Jerusalemites, forcing them to either leave the city or build homes without permits. Families often save up to apply for a permit, are rejected, lose their application fees, and subsequently resort to building illegally. Many of their homes are later bulldozed as well, a loss to the family of thousands more dollars (not to mention the psychological effects of displacement and losing everything they own).

Outside of the city, Israel has declared more than half of the West Bank "state lands," annulling Palestinian land deeds going back generations and rendering thousands of Palestinian homes "illegal." Demolishing these homes allows for the construction and expansion of Israeli settlements in the West Bank, confining the remaining Palestinians into tight enclaves. In East Jerusalem, the land is more than occupied—it's annexed. Continuous expansion of so-called "Greater Jerusalem" allows Israel to control the entire

[52] Jimmy Johnson, ICAHD (March 8, 2006), personal correspondence.

[53] Jonathan Scott, "The Niggerization of Palestine" *Black Agenda Report* (November 1, 2006).

central region of the West Bank, separating Palestinians in the north West Bank from those in the south, and both communities from Jerusalem: the economic, geographic, political, and spiritual heart of Palestine.[54]

Compartmentalizing the West Bank is one of several methods used by Israel to solve the so-called "demographic problem" posed by too many Palestinians in an exclusively Jewish state. The *Law of Entry to Israel*, issued in 1952, has been used extensively to control the number of Palestinians living in Jerusalem and Israel. According to the *Palestinian Academic Society for the Study of International Affairs* (*PASSIA*),[55] "the following restrictive provisions [from the Law of Entry] do not apply to Jewish permanent residents or Israeli citizens, but only to Palestinian Jerusalemites:

1. those who wish to travel abroad must obtain an Israeli re-entry visa otherwise they lose their right of return;
2. those who hold or apply for residency/citizenship elsewhere lose their residency right in Jerusalem....;
3. those who live abroad (which since 1996 includes the West Bank and Gaza) for over seven years lose their residency rights;
4. those who want to register their children as Jerusalem residents can do so only if the father holds a valid Jerusalem ID card."

PASSIA continues: "On 31 July 2003, the Knesset [Israeli parliament] approved a bill to prevent Palestinians who marry Israeli citizens from receiving Israeli citizenship ... and [the bill] applies retroactively."[56] The so-called *Citizenship Law* also "denies citizenship to children born of an Israeli citizen and resident of the West Bank or Gaza. Via special permission from Israel's Interior Minister, children [have been] allowed to remain with their family in Israel until the age of 12, when the child [is] uprooted and forced to leave the state."[57]

According to *B'tselem*, the Israeli Information Center for Human Rights in the Occupied Territories, in the late 1990s Palestinian Jerusalemites living outside of the city's municipal borders lost their rights to live and work there or anywhere else in Israel (the equivalent to losing your citizenship for going abroad, or even to a city other than the one on your identity card). The number of Palestinian Jerusalemites living outside the city was, of course, inflated due to the housing shortage for Palestinians in East Jerusalem.[58]

Disproportionate housing allocation is but one example of the unfair division of land and resources between Palestinian and Jewish Jerusalemites. Although Palestinians in East Jerusalem pay taxes like any city resident, they do not receive equal services. According to *B'tselem*,

> The Jerusalem Municipality has continuously failed to invest significantly in Jerusalem's Palestinian neighborhoods. Since the annexation of Jerusalem [by Israel in 1967], the Municipality has built almost no new school, public building, or medical clinic for Palestinians. The lion's share of investment has been dedicated to the city's Jewish areas.

---

[54] Israeli Committe Against House Demolitions (ICAHD). *www.icahd.org*

[55] *www.passia.org*

[56] *PASSIA* 2007, p. 297.

[57] Ibid at 292.

[58] "Revocation of Residency in East Jerusalem," *B'tselem*. *www.btselem.org/english/Jerusalem/Revocation_of_Residency.asp*

> Less than 10% of the Municipality's development budget for 1999 was allocated for Palestinian neighborhoods, although the population represents a third of the city's residents.... Entire Palestinian neighborhoods are not connected to a sewage system and do not have paved roads or sidewalks; almost 90% of the sewage pipes, roads, and sidewalks are found in West Jerusalem. West Jerusalem has 1,000 public parks; East Jerusalem has 45. West Jerusalem has 26 libraries; East Jerusalem has two. West Jerusalem has 36 swimming pools; East Jerusalem does not have even one.[59]

House demolitions are the last major hallmark of discrimination targeting Palestinian Jerusalemites. One widespread misconception is that most houses destroyed belonged to the families of Palestinians who carried out armed attacks against Israel. In reality, punitive demolitions account for no more than one sixth of the Palestinian homes that have been destroyed by Israel during the Occupation.[60] The demolitions are simply another form of systematic discrimination under Israeli law, employed to encourage Palestinians to leave and thus to preserve the Jewish character of Israel.[61]

The problem is that a Jewish state cannot offer equal development opportunities to non-Jews and simultaneously ensure a Jewish majority indefinitely. That's why Palestinians with Israeli citizenship are treated as second-class citizens.

While we were planting trees, I asked Shelly what she thought about the contradiction between Zionism and democracy. Shelly agreed that it was a dilemma. "I don't have the right answer," she said. "We need a dialogue between both sides to find a solution, but that cannot occur while one side is occupying the other." In other words, two people cannot have a reasonable discussion with one person's foot on the other's neck.

Another Israeli was a little more pessimistic. He agreed that the Occupation needed to end, but he felt that the two sides could never get along and should simply be separated once and for all. A third Israeli had just been released from the army and was new to the debate. He didn't know how he felt about the dilemma, only that he felt very guilty for crimes he had committed during his service and wanted to give something back.

There have been many soldiers who, after finishing the army service, published letters describing the atrocities in which they had participated. **Refusenik** pilots and soldiers go a step further, refusing to take part in operations beyond the 1967 borders of the West Bank and Gaza. Some refuseniks even refuse to join the military at all.

---

[59] "East Jerusalem: Neglect of infrastructure and services in Palestinian neighborhoods," *B'tselem*. *www.btselem.org/english/Jerusalem/Infrastructure_and_Services.asp*

[60] This is certainly not to say that the punitive demolitions were justified. Punishing the families of attackers is collective punishment, which is illegal according to the Fourth Geneva Convention, not to mention ineffective at deterring terrorism.

[61] The Israeli government commission of inquiry established to investigate the uprising in October 2000 by Palestinians inside Israel revealed decades of systematic discrimination against Israel's Palestinian citizens. Known as the "Orr Commission," the September 2003 report's panelists wrote that "the government treatment of the Arab sector was characterized by prejudice and neglect.... [The state failed to] budget resources on an equal basis to the [Arab sector and] ... did not do enough to promote equality in the Arab sector and ... uproot the phenomenon of discrimination." "'Orr Panel' Finds Decades of Discrimination Against Palestinian Israelis," *Palestine Media Center*, *Al Jazeera* (September 2, 2003).

Israeli activists demonstrate alongside Palestinians and internationals.

Refuseniks give me great hope. Israelis have a power to affect change in a way that my international colleagues and I do not. After all, even though my country is funding Israel's Occupation, I am still an outsider. To soldiers, I'm just a naive American girl who thinks she knows everything. I don't know what it's like to live in Israel. But Israelis speak the language of soldiers and settlers and live amidst the fear and propaganda that plague Israeli life. That's why when there is a problem at a checkpoint, for example, we always try to defer to Israeli groups like Machsom Watch, which maintains a frequent presence at checkpoints to monitor human rights abuses. Machsom Watch is a small group of women trying to monitor a very large army, and sometimes at a moment's notice members leave their daily activities to rush to the West Bank, where they try to reason with the soldiers. If that doesn't work, the women appeal to higher authorities in the army, often with good results. They have a spin-off group *Yesh Din* ("There is law" in Hebrew) that accompanies Palestinians who want to file complaints regarding settler or soldier crimes.

Another key group of Israelis working against the Occupation is *Gush Shalom*. Calling itself "the hard core of the Israeli peace movement," Gush members are dedicated to exposing misinformation that fuels Israeli public support for or acceptance of the Occupation. They organize boycotts against products manufactured in settlements. (Government housing and transport subsidies encourage companies to build factories there for higher profits.) They circulate maps and facts that refute widespread propaganda regarding Barak's "generous offer" at Camp David II[62] and current myths about the Wall enhancing Israeli security. Gush Shalom advocates a two-state solution, with Jerusalem as the shared capital, a reestablishment of the 1967 borders, and an allowance for "each refugee to choose freely between compensation and repatriation to Palestine or Israel" (using annual quotas if necessary).

I always learn something new when I talk with Israeli activists. The ex-soldier we planted with said, "Often Palestinians speak to Israeli soldiers as if the soldiers were their masters." This comment scared me a lot, and I've been thinking about it since. Yes, there are people willing to use civil disobedience or even violence against an illegal or unjust oppressive force, but the majority of Palestinians just want their needs met. It's easier to smile and be submissive than to disobey. Most Palestinians cooperate and some even collaborate with soldiers, either for money or privileges, or because they are being blackmailed. It's a game: soldiers are the bosses because they have the government, the army, and the justice system on their sides. They hold the guns and the power. But the more the game is played, the more

[62] See Appendix IV for more information on Camp David II.

Israeli volunteers from Rabbis for Human Rights help Palestinians plant trees and harvest their land, much of which is annexed by the Wall or threatened by expanding outposts and violent settlers.

real it becomes. Eighteen-year-old Israelis start to feel like gods, and Palestinians become psychologically even more dependent than they already are.[63]

A few days ago, we went plowing again with RHR and a Palestinian family who had not been to their land since the beginning of the Second Intifada 5 years ago. The farmers said they were repeatedly harassed by armed settlers who threatened to shoot them if they ever returned. Because they don't dare punish the ideological settlers, a small but politically powerful minority in Israel, the army's solution to the violence is to assign soldiers to supervise farming in the area. Palestinians are now forbidden to farm alone. The trouble is, the army doesn't usually provide ample time, and soldiers frequently don't show up when they are supposed to. It is also disempowering to farmers to rely on chaperones to do the work their families have done successfully for generations.

Because the army has been so unreliable, RHR and IWPS have stepped in to observe farmers instead. As we sat in the sun watching the farmers plow, two armed settlers came walking down the road, holding large guns. Obviously surprised by the sight of the internationals and Israelis, they turned around and left.

Ten minutes later, an army jeep drove by. The soldiers yelled at the farmers that they weren't supposed to plow without army supervision. The villagers replied that the army wasn't around, and the land needed to be plowed. We explained that we had come for that purpose. Then the army ordered the farmers off their fields. They said they had orders to allow plowing on the right side of the road, but not the left. The villagers appealed by saying they didn't know if or when they would have another opportunity to plow. The soldiers replied, "We don't agree with it; we're just following orders."

I interrupted.

"So what is the reason they can't they plow on the left side? Do you think it's a security threat?"

---

[63] One Israeli ex-soldier's testimony on the "power trip" of being a soldier with often unchecked power over the lives of Palestinians can be found at *www.breakingthesilence.org.il/testimony_en.asp?full=354*

"No, I told you. I'm just following orders."

"Are you thinking about what you're saying? Do you realize how absurd and cruel the order you're following is?"

"I don't think. I'm a soldier. If every soldier thought, the army would fall apart."

"If every soldier thought, there would never have been any genocide, or the Nazi Holocaust."

"Look, I'm just doing my job. I don't have a choice."

"And what about when you're finished with the army, when you will have a choice, *then* will you make an effort to change things? Or will you just forget?"

The soldier sighed and looked at me sincerely. "I'll move on with my life and try to forget."

Soldiers come to tell farmers that they are not allowed to plow on the left side of the road that day.

One of my best Israeli friends thinks I'm wasting my time. He hates Ariel Sharon and the settlers, but he doesn't think it does any good to argue with soldiers. He says soldiers can't think for themselves, or armies would not be effective. The choice was made when that soldier joined the army, and some would argue that's hardly even a choice at all. All Jewish Israeli men and women who cannot gain exemption from military service on religious, physical, or mental health grounds must serve or face going to jail. Those who do refuse suffer consequences beyond imprisonment. Much of Israeli society looks down on them as cowards and traitors, or worse, "self-haters." Furthermore, refuseniks are ineligible for certain jobs and economic benefits reserved for ex-soldiers. Palestinian citizens of Israel, who generally do not serve in the army, are automatically excluded from these advantages and professions as well.[64]

It's a lot to ask for an 18-year-old to sacrifice acceptance and respect from his community and to risk his future in protest of his government's policies. I know a handful of refuseniks who have been disowned by their families. The Occupation has separated families in the Occupied Territories *and* in Israel. It has imprisoned the youth of Palestine, and on some level it has robbed the youth of Israel of their freedom as well.

But those are not the most frightening effects the Occupation has had on Israelis. The Nuremberg Principles—developed during the Nuremberg trials of Nazi party members

---

[64] "Israel and the occupied territories," *Bureau of Democracy, Human Rights, and Labor* (February, 28, 2005).

Israeli 18-year-olds are required to serve in the army, where they are frequently given orders that violate human rights and international law.

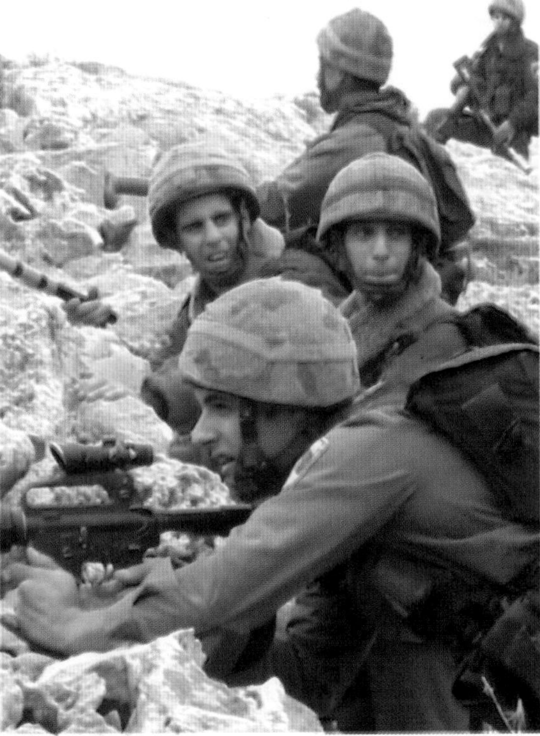

A minority of Israelis refuse to take part in the Occupation. Some end up at protests on the other side of the Wall, alongside Palestinians.

after World War II—state that any person who commits a crime under international law is responsible for his actions and subject to punishment, regardless of his country's laws at the time, and regardless of whether he was following the orders of his government or his superiors. The Occupation is not protecting the future of Israelis; it has turned Israel's youth into participants in war crimes.

Terrorist attacks are not the most common cause of death for Israeli soldiers these days—suicide is.[65] According to the Israeli newspaper *Ma'ariv*, more than 450 Israeli soldiers have killed themselves since 1992, averaging more than one every 2 weeks. The adverse effects of the Occupation on Palestinians are obvious, but what is the Occupation doing to Israelis and the traditional Jewish values of social justice?

[65] By the end of 2005, five times more Israeli soldiers had committed suicide than were killed by Palestinian violence over the course of the year: 30 to 6. *Ma'ariv* (October 10, 2005), p. 6.; As cited by *If Americans Knew*. *www.IfAmericansKnew.org/stats/deaths.html*

Witness in Palestine
X-Ray Checkpoint, Prayer on Threatened Land & an Ad-Lib Roadblock

Friday, February 25, 2005:

The most depressing part of being back in Palestine is seeing how far the Wall has come. Last summer construction started near Iskaka, a village in the *center* of the West Bank. The Wall is reaching about 15 miles east of the 1967 border, taking everything it can with it. The protests continue, but for some it's too late; the cage door has been shut. Munira and her family still live locked up in Mas'ha, while nearby Elkana settlers move freely to and from Israel. On the other side of the very same settlement is a village named Azzun Atma, now stranded between the Green Line and the Wall. Azzun villagers are cut off from most of their schools, shops, land, and loved ones, and they live in what is rapidly becoming for all intents and purposes part of Israel. However, they are denied the basic rights granted to their neighbors because they don't have Israeli citizenship.

The villagers who work or live in Azzun Atma now rely on permits for everything. They apply at Qedumim settlement and they have to renew them every 6 months. Meanwhile, Jews are encouraged to move into settlements on Azzun's land. They don't need permits.

Azzun Atma villagers who want to enter other parts of the West Bank must pass through a checkpoint in the Wall. That's the easy part—the hard part is getting back to their village. The checkpoint's westward passage involves extremely long waits and then passage through a body-screening device rumored to be an x-ray machine, like those installed by Israel at the Rafah international crossing from Gaza.[66] According to the *Palestinian Centre for Human Rights*, the x-raying has raised serious concerns about adverse health effects and violations of privacy.[67]

Shelly and I went to Azzun Atma to do Checkpoint Watch. When we arrived at 7 a.m., there were 25 people waiting to go through, either in cars or standing in line to show their IDs. I asked a man at the front of the line how long he'd been waiting and he said 2 hours. He said one has to get there between 4 and 5 a.m. to avoid the lines. Security going into Azzun is strict because you are effectively entering Israel. The thing is, the people waiting in line don't want to go to Israel. They want to go to their homes and jobs in Azzun village. Israel unilaterally built the Wall inside the West Bank, but the Palestinians are the ones who have to come before dawn to get somewhere that used to be as close as their backyards.

---

[66] "Gaza Strip: Access Report" *UN OCHA* (July, 2005).

[67] The x-ray machines have allowed Israeli soldiers to view civilians completely naked, and the x-ray ionisation process is considered particularly harmful to pregnant women (many of whom have to leave through the crossing to pursue health care that is unavailable in Gaza) and people with heart conditions. "Israel's Peeping Tom in Rafah still operational," *PCHR* (April 7, 2005). *www.pchrgaza.ps*

Every day Palestinians wait several hours and endure rigorous screening to pass through the Wall to reach their land or jobs in Azzun Atma, a Palestinian village in the Seam.

More than half a million Palestinians live less than a mile east of the Wall, and need to cross it to maintain land, jobs, and family connections.[68]

The soldiers aren't making it any easier. The morning I came to the checkpoint with Shelly, four soldiers were manning it, two of whom were exceptionally rude. One, who looked barely 18, kept yelling at people who advanced too slowly or quickly when he waved his hand to make them come. He looked very scared. He even seemed threatened by a farmer who rode up on his donkey. The old man had nothing but an empty, rickety cart and a tired old animal, but the soldier insisted that he stand in line, where he waited an hour to pass through the machine.

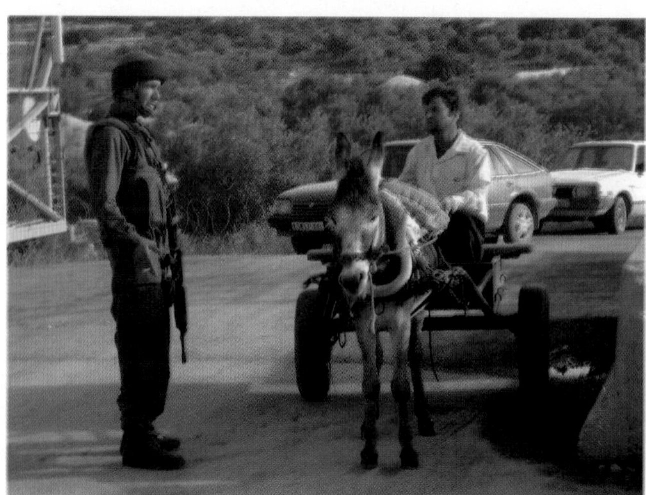

A soldier insists that a farmer on his donkey-cart be rigorously searched before he can reach his land.

I asked the soldier whether he was really suspicious of the farmer and his donkey and he replied sharply, "We need to maintain order! No exceptions for anyone."

Exceptions are not uncommon at checkpoints. That day at Azzun Atma, for example, most women and children were not being searched. The old man on the empty cart was clearly not carrying any explosives, but the young soldier's fear had made him either delusional or just plain mean.

The screening process was painfully slow. I watched a man go through the steps and break down. He looked like he was in a hurry, but he wanted to pass through, not make a scene. First he parked his car in line and went to wait in a line of about eight people. It took a full 10 minutes to scan every ID—how long does it take to enter a number?—so he waited well over an hour. Then he pressed his ID up against a window and waited for a soldier inside to check it in the system. After a while, he was told to walk through the machine and came out carrying his belt and coat (which everyone must remove during the scan). Then he went back to his car and waited another 20 minutes before being allowed to turn on his engine and advance forward. When he did come forward, the soldier started yelling at him for passing the line on the road that he should have stopped at before getting another signal to come forward.

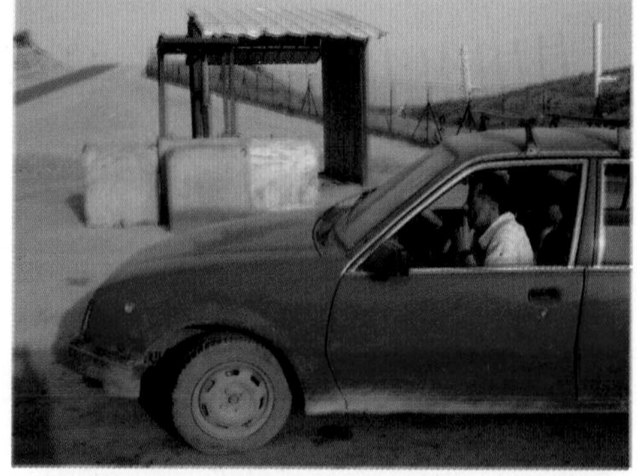

A Palestinian man tries to be patient as he waits for young soldiers to allow him go to his village.

[68] John Dugard, "Implementation of General Assembly Resolution 60/251 of 15 March 2006 Entitled 'Human Rights Council,' Report of the Special Rapporteur on the situation of human rights in the Palestinian territories occupied since 1967," United Nations Human Rights Council, A/HRC/4/17 (January 29, 2007).

He sighed and backed up his car, waiting for the signal from the 18-year-old. But the soldier decided to punish him by making him wait longer.

The man in the car put his face in his hands and then banged his head against the steering wheel. When he was finally motioned through, his car screeched forward in an explosion of his pent-up emotions. Fifty feet later he was told to stop the car and turn off the engine again. Two soldiers had him empty everything out of his car and wait while they went through his belongings.

I wondered how this man could contain his frustration. I don't think most people in the United States would be so restrained if their ten-minute commute to work was turned into a humiliating two-hour ordeal. Just watching the man, I felt the urge to lash out, to express my aggravation with the system.

I got a chance to vent a few days later at a demonstration in Rafat village, where Wall construction threatens the olive trees that local families have lived off for generations. We were marching to the groves when army jeeps revved their engines behind us, anxious to pass. Several protesters stood in the road to block the jeeps but soon gave way as their friends talked them out of it. As the jeeps passed, they sprayed tear gas on the demonstrators, most of whom had done nothing more than walk with signs and sing liberation songs.

© IWPS 2005, Ridwana

Villagers of Rafat and their supporters walk together to the village's threatened land to protest the construction of the Wall.

Once in front of us, the army stopped the march in its tracks. We could see the land being destroyed ahead of us, and it made us feel powerless and angry. The organizers encouraged demonstrators to sit down, which can be a good strategy to make your point without being threatening. As we sat, village representatives stood up to make speeches. Some soldiers listened. Others laughed.

Then a special thing happened. A village imam began to sing a call to prayer, his voice loud and strong, even over the drone of the bulldozers. The protestors, who just moments ago had been waving banners and chanting, became silent. I realized it was Friday, the Muslim holy day. The villagers began to rub their hands in the dirt and symbolically "wash" their faces with it (in the absence of water, Muslims can use earth to clean themselves before prayer). After they had each said their individual prayers, they stood up, facing east, shoulder to shoulder, and began to pray together. I stood captivated next to the soldiers as hundreds of men, women, and children for a moment seemed to forget about everything—the bulldozers, the Wall, the Occupation—as they bowed their bodies and touched their heads to the land. What a simple but precious luxury to be able to worship with your hands in the soil that you've nurtured for generations. But for many it may have been the last time. Bulldozers rip through the precious soil with every passing day.

© IWPS 2005, Ridwana

Left and right pages: Muslim demonstrators pray together on their razed land, knowing it may be their last time before Israel confiscates it with the Wall.

© IWPS 2005, Ridwana

After prayers, demonstrators began walking back to the village. A few protesters dropped rocks in the path to delay the jeeps. Others caught on and dropped larger stones. Pretty soon people were working together to move large boulders into the road, not because anyone thought it would actually prevent the jeeps from passing, but to give the soldiers a taste of the roadblocks they install to block Palestinians every day.

I didn't know what to think. Putting rocks in the road seemed like provocation for the soldiers to retaliate. On the other hand, it was a nonviolent act of civil disobedience, and isn't that what I'm here to support? I didn't join in, but I started to cheer. Why shouldn't soldiers get a taste of the frustration that Palestinians suffer as a result of the Occupation that those same soldiers are upholding?

The soldiers patiently moved the stones out of the way by hand so that they could pass. They didn't retaliate. I was relieved. We left with a feeling of having made a point, despite the fact that the land destruction we had come to protest had continued unabated.

Witness in Palestine

Reflections on Armed Attacks Against Israel

Saturday, February 26, 2005

Last night as my colleague Renée and I were finishing up our work at midnight we received a phone text message that read, "Have you heard the news?" We called the sender and a woman explained frantically that there had just been a bombing in Tel Aviv. She was terrified of how the army would react the next day, and she prayed that the perpetrator was not from Nablus, where she lived.

As we hung up, a silence fell over us. We checked online and learned that at least four Israelis had been killed and many more injured by the attack as they waited in line to dance in a nightclub. We could no longer concentrate, so we climbed to the roof of our apartment to get some fresh air.

Outside, the night was quiet and peaceful, nothing like the chaos only 30 minutes away in downtown Tel Aviv. I felt overcome with sadness for all the Israelis who had lost someone dear to them. The silence was striking in comparison to the violent collective punishment that we knew from experience was to come over the next days in retaliation. I was filled with fear for all the innocent Palestinians whose lives would be made even harder. There would be new checkpoints, longer lines, imposed curfews. For some families, there would be state-sponsored incursions and searches, detention and interrogation, and perhaps torture and murder.

We thought about what it must have been like to witness the explosion, the terror and fear it must have evoked. We also thought about the young man who had killed himself, what he was thinking as he walked through downtown Tel Aviv, and whether he saw the faces of those he was about to kill. We thought about the anger and despair it must have taken to push that button and end his life and the lives of those around him.

It seems odd to me that the question of where and how this anger and despair originate never seems to be addressed in the media. Perpetrators of suicide attacks on Israel aren't even considered people anymore. First they're "bombers," and then simply "the terrorists." But these people, these humans of flesh and blood that once felt joy and pain, why did they choose to leave their families and lives and blow themselves into bits and pieces on a downtown sidewalk? Even if we avidly oppose what they did, we cannot ignore these questions.

Renée stayed up all night writing about her reaction to the bombing, in light of a Checkpoint Watch incident 2 days ago at Huwwara checkpoint, where metal turnstiles have been installed to keep waiting Palestinians in a controlled line. I find her words poignant and illuminating:

> We stood for an hour in a mass of waiting people, slowly edging our way forward towards four turnstiles activated by a button which the soldiers controlled.... When the soldiers

Metal turnstiles at Huwwara checkpoint keep Palestinians waiting in a controlled line.

pressed the button, the metal doors turned and there was a sudden push forward to allow the next person through. The turnstiles would stop at a half-turn and someone would be left stranded between two doors and the side, completely encaged. There he or she would wait patiently until a soldier turned his or her attention back to the gate again. Sometimes the soldiers went for cigarette breaks and left people stranded. One woman holding a baby was stuck between the bars for 30 minutes....

The young boys were undaunted as ever by the humiliating situation and passed the time talking and laughing, but I sensed that their bravado was tinged with anxiety and anger, anger at the humiliation and the injustice of their position. Many of them ended up in the "pen" to wait for their ID to be checked and when I asked the officer why he kept them so long when it only took a moment to ring up about each, he said "They jumped the line, they must learn to wait." I asked "Is this your purpose, to teach the boys to be patient?" and he replied with a sentence that has puzzled me ever since: "If women holding babies can wait for an hour, then the young boys can too."

I wondered how he could recognize the patience of the women and yet remain an instrument in their daily suffering. I was frightened by his reasoning... Of course the mothers will cradle their babies! They will wait forever if need be, but that is not going to stop the young boys from continuing to test the boundaries, and from trying to establish their right to live as equals with the young soldiers who are occupying their country.

For some, perhaps this means having to fight with force, stones or otherwise. But when we see how they live and how they are daily humiliated and threatened by Israeli forces, who are we to condemn them for taking up the only weapon that they have left—their bodies? It is their way of telling the world that the ceasefire had no effect on the lives of people it was supposed to help. The tragedy in Tel Aviv didn't end a "time of calm" at all! There hasn't been a moment of calm in the West Bank since the summit. Nearly every other day a Palestinian has been killed by the Israeli army. There have been internationals beaten by settlers, Palestinians beaten by soldiers at peaceful demonstrations, and old men overcome by tear gas. This has been daily life for the Palestinians… How long must Palestinians continue to be subjected to daily humiliation and injustice without retaliating?

I accept that it has been quiet in Israel, but only for those who choose not to listen to and look at what their government is doing to Palestinians. Officials can talk about "reining in the terrorists" but nothing will change unless the fundamental issues of inequality are addressed.

A Palestinian man shows his ID through a glass window to young soldiers and waits to see if he will be allowed to earn a living or reach his family that day.

Checkpoints are only one element of the injustice. Renée's journal doesn't even touch upon the arrests and deaths that follow when people stand up to authority by organizing protests or refusing to treat soldiers as a legitimate authority. The systematic imprisonment or assassination of anyone actively involved in resisting the Occupation, even nonviolently, makes it a wonder that resistance continues at all.

Many people say that the entire Palestinian population should join together to denounce last night's attack as violent and cruel. Violent and cruel it certainly is; but is it surprising? How far must people be pushed before they lose it? Can we really expect the entire Palestinian population to mobilize against their extremists and make apologies to their oppressor as the grip around their necks tightens? It is delusional to expect Palestinians to devote their dwindling energy and resources towards fighting other Palestinians in an effort to ensure the security of a nation that has been collectively humiliating, robbing, imprisoning, and killing them for 40+ years.[69]

The past week has been very hard for me. I feel tired. I feel frustrated. I feel disgusted. I've become cranky and rude, and sometimes I wish I could spend the whole day in my room under the covers, pretending that none of this is happening. It never lets up. How can I expect Palestinians to act reasonably when I, a foreigner who has been here for less than one month, cannot even keep it together?

It's true that strapping a bomb to my body is the furthest thing from my mind. So why shouldn't I expect the same of all Palestinians? The answer is simple: I have a choice. I can leave. This isn't my life, and anytime I want to, I can go back to my comfortable home in the United States. But for Palestinians, there is no light at the end of the tunnel.

[69] Palestinian-American Dr. Mazin Qumsiyeh articulates the crookedness of such expectations in his book *Sharing the Land of Canaan*, p. 107:

"Such is the matrix of logic of the outside world in this day that the onus always falls on the oppressed to explain his position, to prove his sincerity, to justify his platform, to articulate his vision of the future and to truly, truly convince his oppressor (whose napalm and military occupation, whose racist excesses and sadistic regressions have crushed his very soul and reduced him to a fragment) that he is motivated by love and not hate."

Settler Violence in Kafr Thulth & Yasouf

Friday, March 4, 2005

Recently, I have been working closely with a woman from *Amnesty International*, interviewing victims of settler attacks in our region of Salfit. I have been trying to find a way to give each story the mention it deserves without becoming tiresome or repetitive. These reports are just one blow after another, and I know it must be hard to keep reading, and to keep feeling. As I write, I try to remember that Palestinians don't have the luxury that I have of getting bored or jaded. Day after day, year after year, this is their life. The least we can do is to hear their voices and stories.

Hameed is a sweet elderly farmer from the village of Kafr Thulth. Near his village is the settlement of Ma'ale Shomeron. Settlers arrived more than 20 years ago and have been setting up outposts ever since. Hameed woke up one morning to find a group of trailers on his land. Not long after that, he discovered a small road leading from the new outpost to Ma'ale Shomeron. Next, the settlers brought 10 more trailers, installed water pipes underground, and built an asphalt road.

Hameed took me to his land one day and pointed out stump after stump of trees cut down near the outpost. As we toured the damage, Hameed continued to work, pulling out

Hameed, an elderly farmer from Kfar Thulth, takes a break from tending his land, much of which has been occupied or destroyed by an outpost (background) of Ma'ale Shomeron.

Hameed goes to fetch water from a well near Ma'ale Shomeron settlement, which occupies his village's land.

Hameed's calloused hands are testimony to years of hard work on his land in spite of settler attacks on him and his olive trees.

weeds and throwing away stray stones that he saw. He had to sit down every 10 minutes or so to catch his breath, but still he worked. I struggle to find the words to describe the love exuded by this man for his land. His deep connection to and complete knowledge of each tree and stone wall were evident from every gesture, and from the bruises and cuts all over his rough hands, scars of his endless work as a farmer. He pointed out a little clearing next to an old tree guarded from the wind and said he likes to sleep there in the summer, all by himself.

It's hard to imagine why anyone would want to hurt Hameed, but last Tuesday he was thrown off his donkey cart by three armed settlers who hit him in the head. He showed us the wound. Hameed's friends came up to us as we walked, trying to get their stories heard at last. One 72-year-old farmer with heart problems said settlers cut down 235 of his trees 6 months ago. Another friend said 150 of his trees were cut down by someone in uniform, not a settler. "This is a war of attrition," he said. "Not day by day—hour by hour!"

Tapuah settlement was built above Yasouf on the village's land.

The settlers surrounding Hameed's land are moderates compared to those living in Kfar Tapuah, home to many supporters of the settler extremist group *Kahane Chai* (meaning "high priests of life" in Hebrew), which favors the expulsion of all Arabs from Israel and the Occupied Territories. The Israeli government declared *Kahane Chai* a terrorist organization over 10 years ago but still facilitates their attacks on Palestinians by financing settlements and providing army protection to violent settlers. Kfar Tapuah is built on land belonging to Yasouf village in Salfit. I took stories from three Yasouf farmers—Suleiman, Wasfiyah, and Marouf—about their encounters with their settler neighbors.

Suleiman was harvesting olives with his wife last November when three settlers—two carrying guns and wearing masks—began throwing stones at his wife. Suleiman was on a ladder at the time. They ordered him to come down, and when he did they beat him with an iron bar, breaking his arm. Then they stole his olives and two donkeys. The couple appealed to soldiers in the area for help, but the army responded, "We are in charge of protecting the settlers from you, not the other way around."

Wasfiyah was walking to a bus stop on her way to Nablus to see her sister in the hospital less than a year ago when a gang from Tapuah attacked her with stones. She escaped and ran to the police, who said they would help. But nothing was ever done, despite a history of complaints against one of the perpetrators. Her husband recently found the family's crops poisoned as well.

Two villagers from Yasouf point out the section of their village land past which they are not allowed to go.

Marouf is a sweet old man who wouldn't tell us his story until we were served tea and introduced to the whole family. He said that just last week seven soldiers approached him while he was working alone on his land, and without saying a word began to beat him. He said one grabbed his hands and pinned them behind his back while another picked up a large stone and beat him in the head with it. Marouf paused to show us the deep gash along the left side of his face, above his forehead and near his temple.

Marouf explained that the attacks continue on his family and community. His granddaughters have been intimidated by settlers, and his village is surrounded by expanding outposts. Much of Yasouf's land lies far beyond the outposts, but the owners can no longer go to it because that would require crossing a road linking the outposts back to Tapuah. The outposts themselves—not to mention their roads on Palestinian land—are illegal, but the only rule enforced by soldiers is the one barring Palestinians from crossing the outpost road to reach their land.

Yasouf's gardens, where Tapuah settlers sometimes picnic with their children, guard dogs, and guns

Are Things Getting Better?

Wednesday, March 9, 2005

Today a few of us went to visit a Bosnian woman whom my colleague had picked up from the Tel Aviv airport a few days ago. The woman's husband, a Palestinian businessman, was not allowed to pick up his wife himself because he lacks the correct Israeli-issued ID. On our way home, we met our neighbor Ayman, who operates a modest gas service shop on the road near our house. Ayman said the army had come one week ago to tell him he had one week to obtain proper papers for his shop from Qedumim settlement or they would take it away. But a few days later—well before the one-week deadline—the army arrived unannounced and destroyed the shop. Ayman said he had every intention of going to get the paperwork by the given deadline, but the soldiers were not interested. We can see the remains of Ayman's shop from our office window—nothing but a tired metal frame and a small handwritten sign now crumpled and torn on the ground. Ayman still sits there every day with his dog the way he used to, but his means of supporting himself are now gone.

Many people have written me recently wondering if things are getting better here, if the mood in Palestine is as positive as it looks from the outside. Everyone is talking about Sharon's planned disengagement from Gaza, and the new hope and potential for peace that Mahmoud Abbas—or Abu Mazen, as he is known in these parts—could bring. Are we finally moving towards peace?

Evacuating the settlers from Gaza is certainly not a bad thing, but it should be put into perspective:

Ayman's modest gas shop near Haris was taken away by soldiers because he didn't have a permit for it.

Settlement and outpost construction and expansion are ongoing.

For every settler in Gaza, there are at least 50 more in the West Bank. While Israel prepares to pull 8,000 settlers out of Gaza, Israel is building houses for more than 8,000 *new* settlers in the West Bank, which is far richer in land, water, and other resources. Yet we don't hear about the new settlers in the news. Israel is milking the pre-evacuation hype for more than it is worth, enjoying a collective pat on the back from the international community, while US-sponsored settlement expansion accelerates in the more crucial West Bank.

As for Mahmoud Abbas, the people most optimistic about his power to bring peace seem to be Israeli. Even those Palestinians who support Abbas have no illusions about his ability to change the situation in Palestine as long as every aspect of Palestinian life, government, and security is subject to the will of the Israeli army. Just last week I documented an army raid on the local Palestinian police station in the village of Kafr 'Ain. The soldiers said they were looking for weapons they had seen in a picture taken from the sky. They found nothing. Some of the Palestinian policemen were beaten by the Israeli army, and one claimed that soldiers stole 1,000 shekels (US$240) from his bag, in addition to trashing the police headquarters and breaking a ceiling fan.

Palestinian policemen in Kafr 'Ain are prevented from carrying weapons and are just as vulnerable to the Occupation as civilians are. A weakened and routinely undermined Palestinian Authority is helpless to control Palestinian attacks on Israelis as long as Israeli attacks on Palestinians continue with such regularity.

So my answer is no: things in Palestine have not improved. Not yet. Life here is more or less the same: farmers are beaten by settlers, young men are arrested en masse, resistance leaders are imprisoned or assassinated, and the checkpoints, roadblocks, and Wall prevent people from making a living or getting an education. Sharon's disengagement plan and Abbas' election don't make an ounce of difference in the daily life of average Palestinians like Ayman, and they are not likely to for awhile. So while Bush and Sharon congratulate themselves on their "Roadmap to Peace" and Israelis enjoy a time of relative calm, nobody in Palestine is sleeping easily.

Witness in Palestine
From Jericho to Hebron

Saturday, March 12, 2005

I took a short day trip to Jericho several days ago; it was love at first sight. My friend and I were welcomed to the city with free bananas by friendly merchants who sold us fresh fruit from orchards within walking distance. Jericho is more like a big farm than a city. I had never been to a desert with so much green (it turns out Jews aren't the only ones who can make a desert bloom). The air smelled like citrus and flowers; and in the late afternoon, a family sitting in their garden invited my friend and me for tea. We accepted after the requisite three refusals, and soon tea turned into supper, which turned into an invitation to stay the night that we couldn't refuse.

The evening air was warm, and from the garden I watched the local children riding their small bicycles home from school and the well-dressed adults riding their bigger bicycles home from work, past the palm trees and setting sun. Behind the orchards we could see the mountains, dusty and still, peaceful.

The next morning I took a walk to the ruins of Hisham's Palace, one of the city's biggest attractions. The archeological site is beautiful, and the mosaics are extraordinary. I received a personal tour from a 1948 refugee working there, who said "the pleasure of my company" would be his payment.

I wondered why Jericho felt like such a different world from the rest of the West Bank, so relaxed, spontaneous, and open. Then it hit me: I hadn't seen a jeep or heard a sound bomb my entire time there. There were no Humvees zooming past in the middle of the night, no soldiers demanding who I was and where I was going. Jericho is—almost—Palestine without the Occupation. And it is beautiful. It's a vibrant reminder of what Palestine could—and hopefully someday will—be. Who says all Palestinians would rally against Israel if left alone? Nobody I met talked much about Israel while I was there. They were too busy living their daily lives, like most people in the world.

It takes just 2 hours to get from Heaven to Hell. At least, that's how long it took for me to go the next morning from the paradise of Jericho to the nightmare of Hebron. Until recently, Hebron was the only city in the West Bank besides East Jerusalem suffering from settlements within its city limits. Usually settlers establish themselves on hills surrounding villages or cities, but many of the settlers in Hebron have moved into the second floors of Palestinian homes in the Old City, always by force and sometimes with the help of the army.

Hebron's were the first settlers in the West Bank after Israel occupied the area in 1967, when the Old City's Palestinian population was around 7,500. Twenty-five years later, that population had shrunk by 80% to 1,500, a mass exodus provoked by Israeli settler and state violence and dispossession. The wealth left with the refugees; only the poorest residents remain, those with nowhere else to go. Today the old market, which used to be bustling and

Jericho

Hebron

vibrant, is run-down and abandoned. Unemployment hovers around 80%. The local economy is in shambles, as are the hopes of many Hebron residents.

I took a tour of the city led by Christian Peacemaker Teams (CPT), a faith-based organization that witnesses and intervenes nonviolently to prevent violence in Hebron and other hotspots around the world. We walked through the market area, where the few remaining Palestinian merchants have hung netting above their shops to catch trash that the settlers throw down from their apartments onto the Palestinians' streets and rooftops. Said one merchant, "I'm not here to make money anymore. I just sit here because there's nothing else for me to do. I'm waiting to die." Even if his old customers had the money to spend, the merchant couldn't get to his shop because it's in the Old City, which is now cut off from the rest of the holy city of Hebron by a checkpoint. The people of Hebron can no longer go freely to their city center, nor to their main place of worship. I wonder how Israel would react if Palestinians started moving into the Jewish section of old Jerusalem by force, and then cut everyone off from it but themselves.

It doesn't make sense. In a city of more than 120,000 Palestinians, there are about 600 settlers calling the shots, and about 2,000 soldiers and police stationed to protect them. In 1994, Baruch Goldstein, a local settler from New York affiliated with the Kach Israeli extremist political party, opened fire on a mosque full of praying Palestinians. He waited until they were bent over with their heads to the floor in worship before shooting 29 men to death, injuring about 100 more.

According to the imam who was present during the shooting, when the soldiers heard the shots they assumed they were from "Arab terrorists" and began to target Palestinian residents in retaliation, including one in the process of evacuating the body of a friend who had just been slaughtered. Riots following the massacre left 9 Israelis and 26 more Palestinians dead. Since the massacre, Hebron settlers have built a monument in Goldstein's honor and make pilgrimages to his tomb.

The 1994 massacre was not the first Hebron has seen. In 1929, some 30 Jews were brutally murdered by Palestinians who resented their growing presence in Hebron. A native from Hebron named Hisham sometimes gives tours of the city, sharing little-known details about the time of the 1929 massacre, which he himself witnessed as a young boy. According to Hisham, before the massacre there was a large population of Jews in Hebron who considered themselves Arabs. They were well-integrated and respected in the community. As the Zionist movement gained ground, some people began to resent the huge influx of Jews flooding to Hebron with hopes of establishing an exclusivist Jewish state. Hisham said the vast majority of Jews killed in the massacre were recent immigrants from Europe, because most of the native Hebron Jews were saved by their Muslim neighbors who hid them in their homes.

Hisham's family members, for example, were "*shabbes goys*" (non-Jews whom Jews hire to perform work that is forbidden for observant Jews on the Sabbath, such as switching lights on and off and cooking) for a Jewish family next door, whom they took in during the massacre. Hisham added that the majority of perpetrators of the massacre were not from Hebron.

It's disappointing that these stories of Jewish and Palestinian solidarity are not more well-known. People remember the non-Jews who risked their lives to help Jews escape the Nazi Holocaust, but those who sheltered Jewish Hebron residents in 1929 are mostly forgotten. Similarly, the Arab media doesn't go out of its way to talk about Israeli activists

Soldiers control the Palestinian entrance to Hebron's main mosque, where settler Baruch Goldstein massacred 29 praying Palestinians in 1994. The sign behind them reads, "Tomb of Abner: Kindly show respect for the sanctity of this site."

who risk attack and arrest every day for standing in solidarity with Palestinians against the Occupation. It seems the media on both sides have an interest in perpetuating fear and racism rather than taking advantage of the solidarity that has always existed here, albeit limited.

Although the native Palestinians in Hebron can be blamed for neither Goldstein's massacre nor the one of 1929, they continue to pay the price for both. The earlier massacre is still used to justify excessive security measures at the expense of Palestinian freedom of movement and self-determination in Hebron. Ironically, Goldstein's crimes are used to justify the same security measures. After he opened fire in the mosque, Palestinians in Hebron were put under curfew for a month (presumably to prevent retaliation), while the settlers were allowed to roam freely shortly afterwards. The Palestinians, who had been the target of the massacre, were shut in their homes for 30 days, unable to go to work or school, let alone visit one another and pay their respects to the dead.

Another result of the Goldstein massacre was that the site of the massacres—the Cave of the Patriarchs, where Hebron's main mosque, the Ibrahimi Mosque, sits—was split into two, with one side for Muslims and one side for Jews. Both the curfew and the division were allegedly to prevent further confrontation, but in reality they served to further curtail the rights of the very population that had been attacked. The Israeli army and government call Goldstein's gang terrorists, but in practice they are the group's most crucial suppliers of security and impunity.

Witness in Palestine
Conversation with Hamas Supporters

Hebron's Old City and the biblical Cave of the Patriarchs, segregated since the 1994 massacre of 29 praying Palestinians

Sunday, March 13, 2005

While wandering around the Hebron Old City a week ago I met a young boy who told me not to take pictures of his younger siblings. He seemed suspicious of me, so I put my camera away and smiled, turning to walk away. The boy's father, a blacksmith, was working in his shop nearby with his brother and invited me to chat. When the son saw me interacting so comfortably with his father and uncle he came over and apologized. Soon he wanted me to meet the rest of his family. After the requisite three invitations, I climbed with him through the twisted stairs and alleys of the ancient city up to his home, where his mother and sisters welcomed me warmly and forced heaps of food upon me; luckily I was famished. I ate and the family asked me questions about my work and my family, and invited me to stay the night.

The 13-year-old boy who had led me in turned out to be quite a Casanova. Not long after we arrived he asked me to marry him. I referred him to Turkey, where he could find many beautiful women who, unlike me, could also cook. Then the subject turned to an incident a few weeks ago in which the army came in the middle of the night and handcuffed and blindfolded the 13-year-old boy's older brother, terrifying their sister's 15-day-old son in the process. The family said they didn't know why the army had come. The mother asked me if I knew about Ahmed Yassin. I didn't know what she was talking about until she took out a poster of a man I recognized as the spiritual leader of Hamas.

I asked if the family supported Hamas. They did. I told them I didn't know very much about Hamas, but that I would like to learn from them. I said that in the United States, we are told that Hamas is dangerous because it supports armed Palestinian attacks on Israel. I asked the family if they supported such attacks and they said they did. They were not altogether surprised to hear that in mainstream American media, Palestinian armed attacks on Israelis are called "terrorism," while Israeli armed attacks on Palestinian civilians are often called "defense" or are simply not covered by the media at all. I asked them what they would say to a person who condemns suicide bombs because they are meant to kill civilians. They said that Israel has killed more than four times more Palestinian civilians than Palestinians have killed Israeli civilians, but it's easy to criticize guerilla warfare when you have the luxury of an army doing your fighting for you.

My colleague Hannah said something similar once: "If you're a pacifist, you have every right to express objections to Palestinian violence against Israelis (although you'd be a hypocrite if you weren't also equally or more concerned about Israeli violence against Palestinians). If, however, you do believe there is a place for armed struggle, it is unfair to refer only to the oppressed Palestinians targeting their oppressors as terrorists when their actions are no more fear-inducing, politically-motivated, or inhumane than those employed by almost any country at war."

The family also reminded me that the first people to use terrorism in Palestine were the Zionists in their own struggle against the indigenous Palestinians and the British occupiers before 1948. Zionists were the first to plant bombs in crowded market places, such as the electrically timed mines used against Palestinians in Haifa in July 1938.[70] Zionists planted grenades in cafes and booby-trapped cars. They were the first to kill with letter bombs and parcel-post bombs. In July 1938 alone, Zionists murdered 76 Palestinians in terrorist attacks.[71] Zionists sanctioned the first plane highjacking[72] and not only took hostages but whipped and murdered them. Zionists blew up ships and government offices with civilians inside,[73] and introduced the political extra-judicial assassinations that continue today.[74] Not only did early Zionists use terrorism, but they lauded it as a moral imperative in their struggle; after all, violence is a standard feature of nationalist movements, and Israel's was no exception.[75]

I asked the family if they hated the Zionists for what they'd done. The family said they did, not for what the Zionists had done but for what they continued to do. Then I asked if they would be willing to live in a Palestinian state with a Jewish state next door. The mother asked what kind of a Palestinian state it would be: "What about the settlers? What about the checkpoints, the roadblocks, the road permit system? What about the Wall?"

She pointed out the window to the house next door: "What about them?" Next door we could see a soldier occupying the neighbors' house, using it to patrol the area. She shook her head. "We cannot allow a Jewish state that imprisons our own."

---

[70] Bombs in crowded marketplaces cited in *Sefer Toldat Ha Haganah*, Tel Aviv; Zionist Library and Marakot, 1954-1972; Grenades in cafes cited in *Colonial 146*, HM Stationary Office, London, 1938; Booby-trapped cars cited in R.D. Wilson, *Cordon and Search* (Aldershot: Gale and Polden, 1949), p. 259; Letter bombs cited in *The Times* (June 5-7 & 10, 1947); Parcel-post bombs cited also in *The Sunday Times of London* (September 24, 1972); As cited in materials provided by the Interfaith Community for Palestinian Rights (ICPR) in Austin, TX; *www.icpr-austin.org*

[71] Simha Flapan, *Zionism and the Palestinians* (New York: St. Martin's Press, 1977); As cited in Qumsiyeh, p. 101.

[72] Qumsiyeh, p. 101.

[73] Wilson, pp. 55, 87, & 132; see also Nicholas Bethel, *The Palestine Triangle* (London: Andre Deutsch, 1979), pp. 191 & 338; Blowing up government offices also described in Thurston Clarke, *By Blood and Fire* (London: Hutchinson, 1981); As cited in materials provided by ICPR, Austin, TX.

[74] One of the first Zionist assassination victims was Count Folke Bernadotte, appointed Special UN Mediator to the Middle East after he successfully challenged Nazi plans to deport 20,000 Swedish Jews to concentration camps during World War II. Bernadotte said that "it would be an offense against the principles of elemental justice if these innocent victims of the conflict [the Palestinian refugees] were denied the right to return to their homes, while Jewish immigrants flow into Palestine. Zionists assassinated Bernadotte 4 months after the state of Israel was declared; Qumsiyeh, pp. 44-45 & 101.

[75] Chomsky, *Fateful*, pp. 485-486; See Appendix V for quotations from early Zionist terrorists.

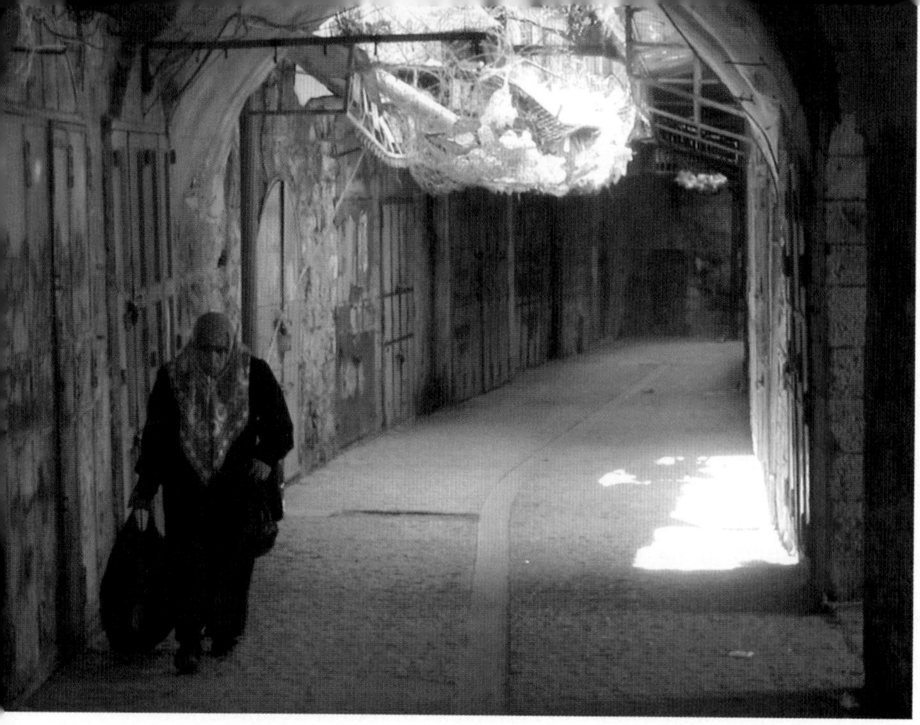

Netting hangs over the Hebron Old City to catch trash thrown down into the abandoned market by settlers occupying the top floors of Palestinian homes.

I understood the mother's hesitation. She—like most Palestinians—has learned to be cautious of tricky wording. "Palestinian state" can mean very different things. Israel's various two-state proposals have always stipulated the continuation of many existing settlements, along with control over borders and most key water sources. Palestinians want a Palestine with viable borders, and a chance at real independence from Israel. No "peace" proposal has ever come close to that.[76] I clarified what I had meant:

"No, I mean what if all that was gone. What if the settlers were gone, the political prisoners were freed, the checkpoints and roadblocks were dismantled, and the Wall was torn down? What if you never had to let another soldier into your house, or show them another permit?"

She continued, "And my family could work and study freely? We could go to our mosques and to our land and nobody would stop us?" I nodded. She looked at me with wariness and a little hope in her eyes: "That would be wonderful." I asked if she would still support killing Israeli civilians in that case and she thought for a moment and answered, "No. I want my children to live in peace, not war."

We all went up to the roof to gaze down at the beautiful abandoned Old City. I told the family that I had something to tell them, and they instantly became silent. I was scared, but I knew it was something I had to do, to make a point and to know the answer myself. I spoke:

"I'm Jewish. My mother's Jewish, and her mother's Jewish, and so on, and that makes me a Jew. But I don't support the Israeli government and I hate what it's doing to your people. I love your country and people deeply, but I'm afraid that now you will hate me. Everyone told me you would."

---

[76] For details on Camp David II, which many believe produced the most generous peace proposal to the Palestinians, see Appendix IV.

It took a moment to sink in. The family didn't understand at first how I could be Jewish but not support Israel or believe in the religion. I tried to explain, and they tried to understand. I think they did, and they began talking amongst themselves too quickly for me to interpret. I interrupted (jokingly, but also a tad serious), "You don't want to kill me, do you?" The mother broke into a smile and threw her arms around me. "Of course not! We were just discussing in whose room you will sleep tonight. You'll stay, won't you?"

Unfortunately, I couldn't stay the night, and Casanova walked me back to the CPT house, where I was staying. On the way we passed the abandoned shops in the Old City and I asked him if he remembered the time when they were open. He began to tell me what it used to be like, with lots of people crowding by, children playing next to stands heaped with vegetables. I asked him what happened. He said the soldiers came and took everything away.

Now the old shops are covered with settler graffiti, spray-painted stars of David and the words, "Get out!" I peered into one shop whose windows were smashed, and a man's voice behind me said, "I used to sell clothes there." I turned to see a man pointing opposite the alley. "And my brother used to sell groceries over there. The settlers would parade through and take stuff from his shop without paying, just to show their power. Now they've taken everything."

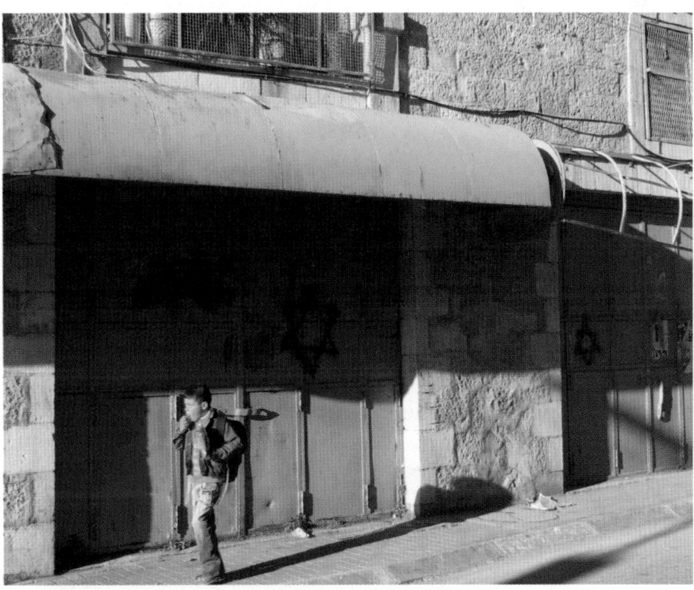

A Palestinian child walks past settler graffiti on his way to and from school

The young man's name was Zafer. He showed me around the neighborhood and we snuck up to where we could see the bulldozers working to expand a new settlement next door to his house. He told me that the place where we were standing used to be a mechanic's shop, but now it's too close to the settler "security fence" to be safe. There was a run-over kid's backpack on the ground and I wondered who had carried it, and what had happened to him or her. Just then Zafer's brother, a toddler, ran up and hugged Zafer around the leg. Zafer picked him up and held him in the air above his head. The child squealed with joy. Zafer brought the boy close against his chest and declared to the world, "This kid makes me sooo happy!!" They both glowed. The settlers and soldiers have taken a lot, but I guess there are some joys that persist in spite of just about anything.

Witness in Palestine

Environmental Destruction & a Stolen Road

Saturday, March 19, 2005

One of IWPS's projects is organizing opportunities for people unfamiliar with the situation in Palestine to visit and see it for themselves. Last year, IWPS took Israeli activists into the West Bank on a ten-day tour called *Mikarov*. Two of my colleagues are currently developing a project to give West Bank tours to non-Israeli Jews, including those who have just participated in the "Birthright Israel" program, which sends young Western Jewish adults on a 10-day tour of Israel. My colleagues' program is called "Birthright Unplugged."[77]

A few weeks ago, IWPS led a delegation of journalists, embassy officers, and ambassadors' wives on a one-day tour of several villages in Salfit. The tour started in Deir Istiya, where the mayor and a villager reviewed the multitude of occupations that have plagued their families and land for centuries, the Israeli military Occupation being only the most recent. The villager told us about an old Ottoman law proclaiming that "land-owners who do not tend their land for 3 years or more lose their ownership rights." Israel has adopted that law with regard to the West Bank and uses it frequently to justify mass settlement expansion and land confiscation. I thought of the family I had recently accompanied to plow their land for the first time in 5 years. Settlers, having prevented the family from tilling their land by force, can now lawfully claim that the land no longer belongs to the family. I also pondered the irony of such a law from a country founded on the idea that the Jewish people have claim to land that their ancestors may have fled 2000 years ago.

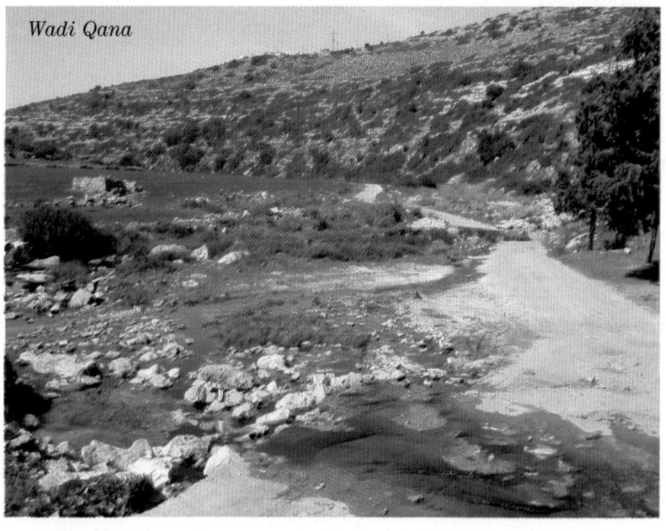
Wadi Qana

Once one of the largest villages in the West Bank, Deir Istiya has lost more than two-thirds of its land and population. Some of the remaining inhabitants are from nearby Wadi Qana (or "valley of canals"), a small village that was evacuated in 1986 when life there became unbearable. The idyllic valley of Wadi Qana has been slowly surrounded by illegal settlements, subsidized by the Israeli and US governments. Years ago, several of the hilltop settlements started to send their sewage pouring into the valley, either

[77] For more information about Birthright Unplugged, visit *www.birthrightunplugged.org*

Wadi Qana has been abandoned due to sewage from surrounding settlements that flooded the idyllic valley, transforming its fresh water river into a river of human waste.

down the land or through pipes. Ironically, the area is classified as a nature reserve by Israel. But the nearby springs that used to provide towns all the way to Nablus with precious drinking water now run brown with urine and feces: a river of human waste. You can smell noxious fumes from the highway, and the surrounding vegetation is long since dead. Settlers occasionally come down with guns to walk by the abandoned homes and picnic near the only remaining fresh water source.

Our delegation proceeded north from Wadi Qana to Kafr Qaddum, a friendly village that became stranded when two illegal settlements established themselves on either side of the village's main road. Now the settlers claim that the road is theirs, and Palestinians must make a long detour on several unpaved roads to leave their village. The rockiness of the detour road renders it next to impassable for some cars, and those taxis that can make the trip charge a premium. The village is just 7 miles from the city of Nablus where many inhabitants work, but what used to be a 15-minute commute is now at least a 2-hour journey.

I met two young women from Kafr Qaddum who were studying in Nablus, both of whom spoke

Isra and Samea, two engineering students from Kafr Qaddum, can no longer reliably travel to and from their classes in Nablus without taking an expensive detour or hiking several hours through the countryside.

excellent English. They said they could hardly afford the commute anymore (now US$6 instead of US$1.50) and missed many classes. The girls said they were determined to continue studying and sometimes hiked over the hills to reach their university. Said one, "Without education, we can never overcome our poverty and the Occupation. Education is our best weapon, and it has always been very important to our people." She's right: Palestinians' traditional focus on education is well-known in the Middle East. For example, more than 90% of Palestinian children continue from primary school to secondary school, and more than 56% of them go on to a university. Despite tremendous obstacles to education presented by the Occupation, Palestine still maintains literacy rates of at least 90% for both men and women.[78] Palestine is also the first Arab land where students learn English from the first grade on.[79]

After recent rains, Kafr Qaddum's detour road became positively unusable, and locals insisted on getting access to the main road again to avoid being completely trapped in their village. The army agreed to limited use for Palestinians: five minutes every hour. (These kinds of arbitrary concessions unmask the false pretext of security—is it really safer for settlers to share a road with Palestinians 8% of the time rather than 100%, or are these restrictions about separation and control?) Soon the army sent a bulldozer to remove a few rocks from the detour road and closed the good road again to Palestinians. The villagers were not about to lose their road for a second time, so they organized a demonstration to raise awareness and solidarity surrounding the unjust road closure.

Two weeks ago, villagers, internationals, and Israelis gathered in the village to march together to the forbidden road. The army was waiting when we arrived, and they prevented us from reaching even the road closure, so we stopped to cheer and listen to speeches. One old woman approached the army as a representative of the village; as she spoke, the soldiers stood stone-faced, except for one who was smiling as he filmed the woman with a video camera. I wondered what he intended to do with the footage. Watch it at home with his friends and family? Submit it to the authorities so the protesters could be identified and perhaps punished? Or perhaps he just thought it was funny to film the same people filming the soldiers. If he was trying to convey apathy towards the villagers' grievances, then he succeeded.

After an hour, organizers intent on keeping the demonstration nonviolent asked people to go back to the village before tear gas, sound bombs, or stones might begin to fly. Demonstrators gathered with translators in the Town Hall to get acquainted and exchange ideas about continuing resistance. It was then that a village representative invited IWPS to bring our delegation to Kafr Qaddum, an offer we accepted a few weeks later.

The delegation was greeted with endless bowls of hummus, falafel, salad, and roasted meats. After eating our fill, we headed to the road closure where a settler with a shotgun and an army officer told us we could go no further. We explained that we were Israeli and international journalists, ambassadors, and human rights workers, but the officer said it was a closed military zone. I looked at the supposed "military zone": a quiet gated neighborhood with white picket fences, sun umbrellas, barbecue grills, and SUVs. I commented that it looked more like an American suburb than a military zone, but he wasn't listening. He was on the phone with the army and soon a backup jeep had arrived.

---

[78] Palestinian literacy rates were at 90% for women and 97% for men when this book went to press. *PASSIA* 2007, p. 328.

[79] Ibid.

esidents of Kafr Qaddum attempt to reclaim their main road. Armed settlers and soldiers have orbidden villagers from using the road, effectively trapping them in their village unless they take a long and unpaved detour through the rural untryside. The farmer below, in the keffiyeh, owns the land occupied by one of the settlements.

Kafr Qaddum villagers protest the occupation of their main road by settlers.

Meanwhile, the villagers remained stuck behind the metal road gate. An old man broke past and started shouting at the soldiers that this "closed military zone" was his land. His voice grew tired, and he sat down miserably. Settlers drove by, bemused by the scene. They spoke English with American accents, probably Brooklynites from New York. Many ideological Jewish settlers in Palestine are immigrants from the United States.

Eventually we gave up arguing with the soldiers and drove (the long way around) to our delegation's final stop, the village of Marda. Marda is easily recognizable from the road by the massive heaps of trash tumbling down behind the village from the hilltop above. The village has the misfortune of being situated directly below Ariel settlement, an Israeli city in the middle of rural Palestine. I once overslept on a bus from Israel and ended up inside the settlement, amidst the city's strip malls, carefully manicured children's parks, and opulent one-family three-story houses. Subsidized by the Israeli government, the illegal settlement offers residents a state-of-the-art recreation center and luxurious swimming pools, while Marda villagers below struggle to make ends meet. The irony is that Ariel was built on land belonging to Marda farmers; the settlement alone has annexed more than 1,000 acres of village land. To add insult to injury, Ariel dumps its trash down the hills onto Marda, enlarging the already massive pile of noxious waste that has forced several families to move.

Ariel settlement: a suburban heaven complete with strip malls and swimming pools

When we arrived in Marda, a village representative welcomed the delegation and introduced us to five of the seven local youths, aged 14 to 16, who had been arrested by Israeli forces in November and imprisoned for several months without charge. The remaining two were still in jail. Israel has no juvenile courts for Palestinian children, whom they hold as young as 12 years old and try as adults after age 14 in violation of international law.[80] The kids stood up, clinging to each other, embarrassed to be at the center of attention. They looked like kids you'd see anywhere, still full of life and excitement. But they were also worn, with scars on their faces and a little more experience in their eyes than their peers have.

The representative told us of the distress the young prisoners' parents had gone through while their children were gone, wondering if they would ever see them again. According to *Addameer* Prisoners' Support and Human Rights Association, over 2,500 Palestinian children[81] have been arrested since September 2000, and at least 340 are currently being held in Israeli prisons.

---

[80] *Addameer* Fact Sheet: Palestinians detained by Israel. *www.addameer.org/addameer/campaigns/manal/factsheet.html*

[81] *Addameer* defines "children" as youth under the age of 18.

Ariel settlement, built on land from Marda village, where settlers dump their trash

Five young boys from Marda village were imprisoned for throwing stones at army jeeps.

The prospects look grim for the children of Marda and their families. Unemployment plagues the village. Marda used to have a farming cooperative called the Unity Development Center where many villagers worked until soldiers raided the cooperative 4 years ago, destroying its computers and files. The village has not had the money or infrastructure to start over, especially as the land they are allowed to farm continues to shrink. According to village officials, the Wall is expected to result in the uprooting or confiscation of a full 20,000 olive trees from the district, in addition to everything that has already been annexed by the ever-expanding Ariel settlement.

Barqan Israeli industrial center

Marda families struggle to survive in the face of plans to cut the village in half with the Wall (apparently the people of Ariel don't want the Wall too close to their homes) and a disturbing prominence of cancer in the area. The latter could be due to air and water pollution from the nearby Barqan industrial center. Barqan's aluminum, fiberglass, plastics, electroplating, and military industries pollute the groundwater of our area with heavy metals. Israel offers tax incentives to Israeli industries and fewer restrictions on pollution in the Occupied Territories. Consequently, many of the most environmentally destructive companies move to the West Bank,[82] and are conveniently situated far enough from Israel proper to avoid potentially causing health problems to Israeli citizens living there.

There is, however, one bit of good news: due to persistent court appeals, the planned route of the Wall has been moved several hundred yards to the south so that it will no longer bisect Marda. The village of Deir Ballut also recently won a court case, and some of the land on which I enjoyed that memorable picnic and charades game will now stay with its owners.

It's hard to celebrate these victories, though, when the villages have "won" but a small part of what was already theirs. Why should they be joyous or grateful? Small bits of progress against the Occupation are often misleading. For example, when things feel permanent, a spontaneously disabled roadblock feels like an act of charity by the army. Palestinians feel lucky when they encounter a lenient soldier, or the Wall is pushed back a few feet. But the roadblock, soldier, and Wall should never have been there in the first place, and the concessions are not privileges, they are rights. I suspect the token gifts are more a way to pacify Palestinians than to help them.

Ultimately, those farmers who "won" back their land have still lost. The Wall's construction—or rather "de-struction"—has already begun. The damage is done: the trees are gone; the soil is ruined. The disastrous long-term environmental destruction brought by Israel's Wall, highways, and settlements is likely to outlive the Occupation itself. Settlers and soldiers can be removed, but the air of Barqan may never be clean, nor the rivers of Wadi Qana. On the day that peace finally comes, we pray the Palestinian and Israeli victims will begin to move on and let go. The ecological victims, however, may not be so forgiving.

[82] "Question of the Violation of Human Rights in the Occupied Arab Territories, Including Palestine," *UN Commission of Human Rights*. As cited in Qumsiyeh, pp. 140-141.

Thieves in the Night

Wednesday, March 23, 2005

Last night at 10 p.m. a friend in Marda called to say the army was uprooting trees near the road. My colleague Hannah and I rushed to the scene where we found two jeeps and a van patrolling the area as an American-made bulldozer dug out tree after tree. The soldiers were not pleased to see us and tried to make us leave. We asked them why they were uprooting trees in the middle of the night and they said, "This is no place for two girls at night." Each time we repeated our question the soldiers would answer, "All we want is for you to be safe. Now go home." Finally one soldier answered us. He said some boys from the village had put rocks in the road, causing a car accident between a Palestinian and a settler. Hannah said to me that she recognized the story and had heard it used before to justify collective punishment. We wondered whether or not it was true.

My phone rang. An Israeli friend had learned that the uprootings were unauthorized by the army and that it would be stopped. But 10 minutes later the same source told my friend a different story. Now the soldiers were uprooting trees because Palestinian boys had hidden behind the trees as they threw Molotov cocktails onto the settler highway running through their village land.

So many stories. Were the uprootings because of a car crash, or Molotov cocktails, or something else? Or was it for nothing at all? Did it matter? Regardless, it was collective punishment. Those trees didn't belong to the boys, if there were boys at all. The soldiers were stealing the livelihoods of several families right before our eyes, like thieves in the night. But they had nothing to fear: There is no regulated accounting for the actions of the military. Meanwhile, actions taken by Palestinians are retaliated against ten-fold.

Hannah said she once talked to an army official who explained the army's policy of collectively punishing Palestinians. They acknowledge that the vast majority of civilians want peace, but they harass entire cities and villages to encourage the majority to convince the minority to stop getting in the army's way. Of course, the more people suffer, the angrier and more vengeful they become.

The soldiers eventually left with their two jeeps, Humvee, bulldozer, and van, but not before throwing two sound bombs in the village to wake everyone up. I was glad to see them go. We returned this morning to find the shattered trunks and branches of 17 olive trees scattered around the leveled landscape like broken bones. We wondered if there had been more; sometimes the army removes entire trees and replants them in Jewish settlements or inside Israel for the charming ambiance that the old trees bring. We looked for whole trees that the farmers might replant, but the army had taken the time to chop up each individual tree that they left. It felt like a burial ground, and I thought about all the families that had nurtured and cared for those trees over hundreds of years. Perhaps their owners didn't even know yet of their demise.

Sometimes the army uproots Palestinian olive trees and replants them in Jewish settlements or inside Israel.

Marda's uprooted olive trees were chopped up by the Army.

This evening we received a call that the army was in Marda again. Our friend in the village said the soldiers were driving around in jeeps and throwing sound bombs, forbidding people to come out of their houses to see what was happening or to look after their children, and simultaneously preventing villagers outside from going into their homes. Our friend told us the soldiers were going into people's houses and that one person was arrested. When we arrived the soldiers had left, but then one army jeep came back and detained five young men while checking their IDs. We asked what was going on, and the soldiers said someone had thrown a stone that broke a car window.

I noticed that the license plate of the jeep was the same as the one we'd seen the night before. I asked the soldiers if they knew anything about the uprooted trees, and one replied, "Someone threw a stone. That's always the reason." I said that was the third story I'd heard. I continued:

"So when was the court hearing for this stone-thrower?"

They looked at me like I was crazy.

"Where I come from, people aren't punished for rumors. People suffer penalties if they are proven guilty, but not before, at least not in theory. What you're doing here and what the army did last night is extra-judicial collective punishment. And it's illegal."

The soldiers didn't seem to be listening, but I continued, perhaps more for my sake than theirs.

"Let's say I threw a rock at you. Would you attack America?" This made them laugh. We asked them if they would be back there tonight and they laughed again, avoiding the question. Soon they left and we walked to the roadblock on the village outskirts to catch a shared taxi home.

Two of Marda's three entrances are obstructed by dirt roadblocks. People can go around them, but cars can't. Yesterday, the army opened one previously-closed road and closed the previously-open one. It makes no sense. It can't be for security, because cars can still use the now-open entrance.

Same with the checkpoints: No one personally familiar with the situation could believe that checkpoints keep Israel more secure. Anyone who wants to get into Jerusalem or Nablus can; there are roundabout mountain roads everywhere. Twice I "snuck" into Nablus, once over a mountain and once through a family's field. When the roadblock in Haris was up, villagers drove their cars through rocky fields into other villages to get to the main road to drive to work. When Zatara checkpoint closed after the bomb attack in Tel Aviv, passengers pushed their taxis up rocky hills around the Yasouf roadblock nearby to drive to work via a long detour.

I once stayed with a woman near Bethlehem who wakes up every morning at 3 a.m. to get to work by 6 a.m. at a place 15 minutes away. The sole income-earner in a family of six, she has worked for several years as a nurse in West Jerusalem, illegally because people with her type of ID aren't legally allowed to go to Jerusalem. Every morning and afternoon she takes an elaborate roundabout route to and from work that involves switching vehicles, walking a long time, and changing the shape of her headscarf at one point to make herself look like a religious settler. The commute is absurd and costs her 40% of her income, but it's reliable. Again, *anyone* who wants to get from the West Bank into Israel can.

The army surely knows about all the alternative routes, so why do they bother making roadblocks and manning checkpoints? I believe the answer is control. The status quo keeps Palestinians guessing and running around, like mice in a maze. One week an obstacle goes up and another goes down. This happens so often that it seems there is no point to the restrictions other than to assert power and slowly break the will of the Palestinian people until they eventually give up their claim to the land and leave.

It is midnight and we have just learned that the soldiers are back in Marda. I'm so tired of this. Apparently they are driving around the village throwing sound bombs again, and this time they're also banging on people's doors. If that's not terrorizing, I don't know what is. If there was ever any doubt in my mind, it is gone. The soldiers are not preventing terror; they are provoking it. The Israeli military is informed enough to know that, but most of the Israeli and American public are not. And so the violence continues.

A broken stone wall in Marda's olive groves, left by bulldozers that uprooted 17 olive trees next to a settler highway in the middle of the night

Marda Farmers Refuse Compensation

Thursday, March 24, 2005

Today the verdict arrived: the Israeli army has confirmed that the uprooting of Marda's trees Tuesday night was unauthorized and illegal. The soldiers uprooted the trees on a whim. Will the perpetrators be prosecuted? Doubtful. It's a lawless land for some.

I returned to Marda to interview the owners of the uprooted trees to give them the news and to find out if they wanted to try appealing for compensation. A young woman greeted me warmly when I came to the first family's door. She said her father, Talad, would be delighted to meet me, but that I must talk loudly because he is almost deaf. The family welcomed me into the living room where we drank tea and ate cookies for breakfast. Talad was old, cross-eyed, and very kind. He kept interrupting the conversation to tell me to eat more cookies, even as I was eating them.

I asked Talad and his wife if they wanted to try to sue the army for compensation. They said they didn't want money, they wanted their trees back (now firewood in the front yard after the army cut them up). I went to see the other owners, and they said the same thing: "You can't put a price on trees. Trees are our past and our future. We would be ashamed to make any deal that might normalize or excuse Israel's disregard for our human rights. We don't want money, or anything that could be mistaken for what we really need—freedom."

I was humbled by their answers. I had assumed they would be happy to get some money as a result of the army's admission of guilt. But Palestinians don't want compensation; they want their lives back. Unfortunately, like the thousands of uprooted trees and the hundreds of destroyed villages, many of those lives don't exist anymore.

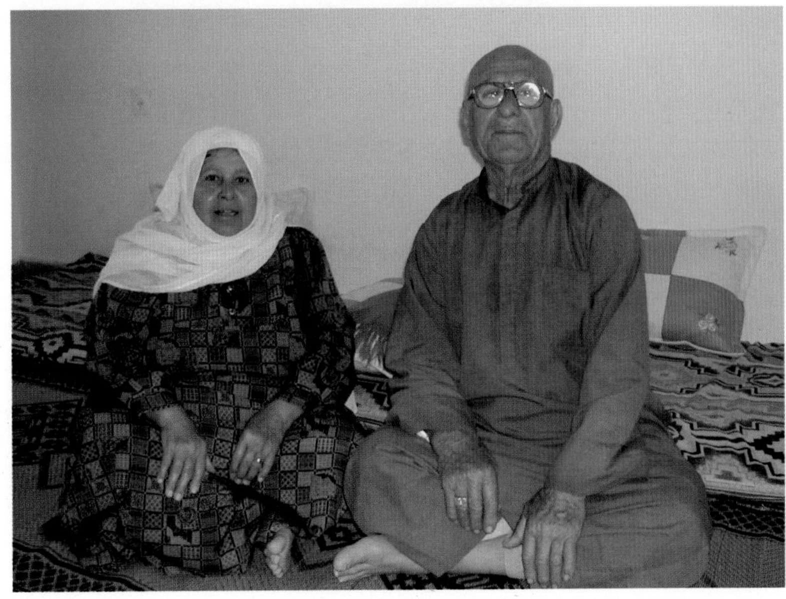

Farmers whose olive trees were uprooted in the middle of night as collective punishment on the village of Marda. When asked if they wanted compensation, they refused, saying that nobody can put a price on the ancient olive trees that their family has lived off for generations.

This month is the 2-year anniversary of both the current war on Iraq and the brutal killing of Rachel Corrie, an American activist my age who came to Palestine with the International Solidarity Movement. Two years ago, Rachel stood between an American-made Caterpillar bulldozer and the house that the Israeli military was about to demolish with it, in Rafah, Gaza. The threatened house was the home of a Palestinian doctor and his family. Rachel wore a neon vest and spoke with a bullhorn so that she would be seen and heard, but the bulldozer operators did not stop. The bulldozer ran over Rachel, then backed up, and then ran over her again.

Caterpillar continues to sell machinery to Israel, despite consistent proof that Israel uses these machines to violate international law and human rights. Caterpillar even custom-designs certain products according to the occupier's needs, be they demolishing houses, uprooting trees, or building the Wall. Caterpillar is just one of many US companies profiting off the Occupation.

Although she will never get to see the day when Palestinians will be free, Rachel remains an inspiration for many international activists and Palestinians here to continue the struggle.

Rachel Corrie was killed by the Israeli army with an American-made Caterpillar bulldozer. Caterpillar is just one of many US companies profiting off the Occupation.

Palestinian Christians March Towards Forbidden Jerusalem

March 25, 2005—Good Friday

When people call the conflict here a religious war between Muslims and Jews, I am always quick to point out that more than 10% of Palestinians are Christian (many of them in the diaspora), and the approximately 175,000 Christian Palestinians remaining in Palestine suffer from the same human rights violations and obstacles to education, employment, medical care, and proper housing as their Muslim counterparts.

Most Christian Palestinians living in the Occupied Territories reside in the Bethlehem area, just a few miles from Jerusalem. Like almost all West Bank Palestinians, they are consistently denied access into the holy city by a fortified military checkpoint. Now the Wall is further sealing off the thousands of Christians from their places of worship and religious sites. In Bethlehem the biblical Rachel's Tomb, which had remained undamaged for millennia, was seized by Israel and transformed into an army camp, off-limits to all non-Jews.[83] In response to what they see as both religious and racial persecution, the Palestinians of Bethlehem organized a demonstration in honor of Good Friday, with the goal of marching past the soldiers at the Bethlehem checkpoint all the way to Jerusalem.

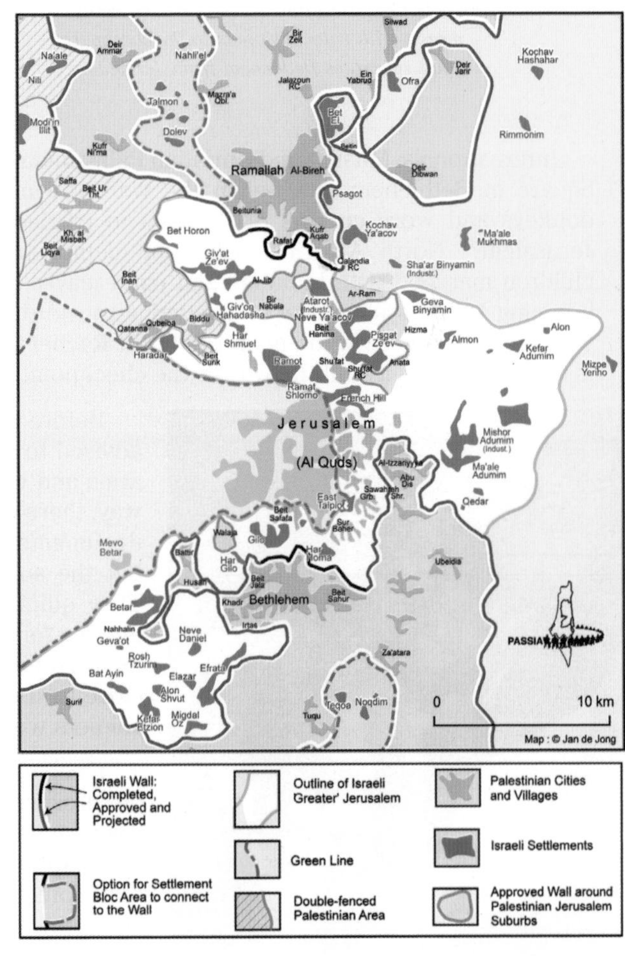

The Wall in Jerusalem & Bethlehem

[83] Joseph's Tomb near Nablus was also taken over by the Israeli army. Qumsiyeh, p. 65.

All: Christian and Muslim Palestinians march with internationals to the checkpoint that separates Bethlehem from Jerusalem.

Internationals, Muslim and Christian Palestinians, and gathered with donkeys at Manger Square in Bethlehem and began the walk towards Jerusalem. Palestinian youth rode donkeys and wore crowns of thorns and carried signs reading, "Why can't we go to Jerusalem?" North American Christian demonstrators sang songs about Jesus while children marched with balloons and palm leaves. The march was led by a truck with a booming sound system that rang stirring music throughout the city. The group paraded with enthusiasm down the main road past Rachel's Tomb, past the half-finished Wall that is to enclose the city, all the way to the checkpoint.

Before reaching the checkpoint, children were advised to leave, and the remaining adults linked arms and walked towards the checkpoint. On the way, there was a sign that read, "Stop, and prepare documents for inspection." We ignored the sign, but the soldiers were waiting for us beyond it. They quickly formed a line to prevent us from moving forward, and one soldier started yelling at us to go back. We had succeeded in getting quite close to the checkpoint, so I was scared that the soldiers would begin using physical force.

I separated myself from the group to take pictures from a stone wall nearby. One soldier had drawn a picture on the back of his army vest that was captioned "Freedom," and protesters found that ironic from someone manning a checkpoint. One protester had brought his daughter and was being interviewed by a news station. As time passed, it seemed the demonstration was achieving one of its intended objectives: media

Palm Sunday: Protesters march with flags and palm leaves from Bethlehem towards forbidden Jerusalem.

attention. Passing through the checkpoint, however, seemed to be out of the question. So the demonstrators did the next best thing: they sat down.

Our collective squat told the soldiers that we were not going anywhere. This could be seen as a small victory since it seemed we were already holding up the Israeli cars coming from Jerusalem into Bethlehem. The soldiers brought out metal barriers, which they lined up in front of us.

One Palestinian woman began to sing "We Shall Overcome." It was a wonderful moment, and everyone who knew the words joined in. When we finished singing, a representative of Holy Land Trust (a non-profit humanitarian organization based in Bethlehem dedicated to strengthening and improving the lives of communities in the Middle East) stood up to give a speech that the organizers had prepared. The soldiers and demonstrators became quiet as he began to read.

Bethlehem Palestinians present olive branches and a message of peace to the soldiers that guard the chekpoint separating Bethlehem from Jerusalem.

As-Salaamu 'alaikum (Peace be upon you),

We in the Bethlehem community have come to you today with a message on behalf of our people. We represent the families and friends who are imprisoned by these concrete walls and wire fences that now create the Bethlehem open-air prison. You, like prison guards, control our freedom and ability to live as human beings with dignity in this holy land.

Our strong delegation of civilians comes to you without weapons but with great strength and commitment to deliver the message of just peace. In the name of security, you do not permit us to travel, to [go to] school and to worship in our holy sites in the city of Jerusalem. Your government deprives us each day of basic human rights to self-determination. Each day you keep us from being with our families at weddings, funerals, graduations, birthdays, and religious holidays. Although Jerusalem is only 20 minutes from Bethlehem, we have not been allowed to pray and worship at our holy sites.

Each day as you come to our city, you serve the system of violence that keeps our people imprisoned and without the ability to live a life of a normal human being. With your guns, tanks, and insults, you teach our children to hate.

However, we believe each of you has the power and choice to choose a different ending to this story. We appeal to your conscience and humanity as individuals and as soldiers who may feel there is no way out of this system. Put your guns away—I repeat, *put your guns away*—and join us in the fight for peace and freedom.

The People of Bethlehem[84]

It was hard to know if any of the soldiers were listening. Several seemed bored and uninterested, but at least one or two must have let the words sink in. I found the speech powerful and made a mental note to suggest using group letters as a tool in other protests as well. Although we hadn't made it through the checkpoint, the symbols, words, and music of the demonstration had made it one of the best protests I had ever been to. Having made our point, we rose, as a group, and began the long walk back to Bethlehem.

[84] Speech written by Husam Jubram and Jennifer Kuiper of Holy Land Trust: *www.holylandtrust.org*

The Twisted Easter-Egg Hunt

Sunday, March 27, 2005—Easter

Yesterday I left Bethlehem and continued south past Hebron to the village of At-Tawani, whose residents had appealed to IWPS for help with an action. Like Yanoun, At-Tawani has been repeatedly threatened and attacked by violent ideological settlers. Villagers' tractors have been ruined, their olives stolen, their wells poisoned with dead chickens, their sheep stabbed, and their children stoned. The Israeli government silently supports the settlers by subsidizing their settlements and by not condemning their illegal attacks on Palestinians. But the people of At-Tawani remain, in silent but determined resistance.

At-Tawani village

The illegal settlement of Ma'on is just over the hill from At-Tawani. Closer still is a small forest occupied by a new outpost. The children of At-Tawani and surrounding villages are frequently stoned by settlers as they pass the forest on their way to school. The youngsters now take a long detour road to avoid confrontation, but the settlers have started coming to the new road to harass the students. Instead of confronting the settlers and forcing them to stop, the army provides jeeps to ride alongside the children as they walk. The children have to run to keep up. They have learned that the army will protect them. They are too young to understand that these same people are also their oppressors.

The action that I participated in was not against the stoning of children but something even more shocking: In an effort to expel the villagers, settlers recently scattered the fields with poison to kill the sheep grazing there. They boiled barley seeds in anti-coagulant rat poison designed to spread through the body and cause excessive internal bleeding. According to *Amnesty International*, the particular poison that they used is illegal in Israel, except for government use.

The settlers know that villagers depend on their animals for food, and this is one more attempt to starve them out. Dozens of sheep are already dead or dying, along with other wildlife in the area. The ecologically disastrous nature of the settlers' action is testimony to their ignorance of the fragility of the land they claim is theirs.

I traveled to At-Tawani with a large group of Israelis and Palestinians from *Ta'ayush* to attempt the impossible: to remove every poisonous seed left by the settlers. We put on plastic gloves and masks and walked in a line across the landscape. The pellets were intentionally hidden under prickly shrubs where sheep graze, and we sat patiently, picking out the tiny pieces of death. It was an awful, endless job. Someone called it a "twisted Easter-egg hunt," since the next day was Easter Sunday and the poisonous seeds were egg-shaped and turquoise.

Israeli activists, international volunteers, and Palestinian villagers work together to remove poison from At-Tawani's land. Settlers placed barley seeds boiled in rat poison under shrubs with the intention of killing village sheep to discourage farmers from going to their land.

The army was stationed in At-Tawani yesterday to "protect" our official action from the settlers, but instead they only made our job harder. First they threatened the shepherds who were grazing sheep on a nearby hill. Although the land belongs to the villages, settlers have claimed it, rendering it a "disputed area." So the army has taken control and pronounced it a "closed military zone." The action was intentionally planned on a Saturday because on weekends the area is officially supposed to be open. But the soldiers told them to go to another area, where we were picking out poison. We insisted that the sheep couldn't graze there or they could be poisoned, but the soldiers didn't seem to care. They were worried about a confrontation between us and the settlers who had started to come out from the trees. Atop the hill where we were working, more and more settlers emerged, watching and waiting.

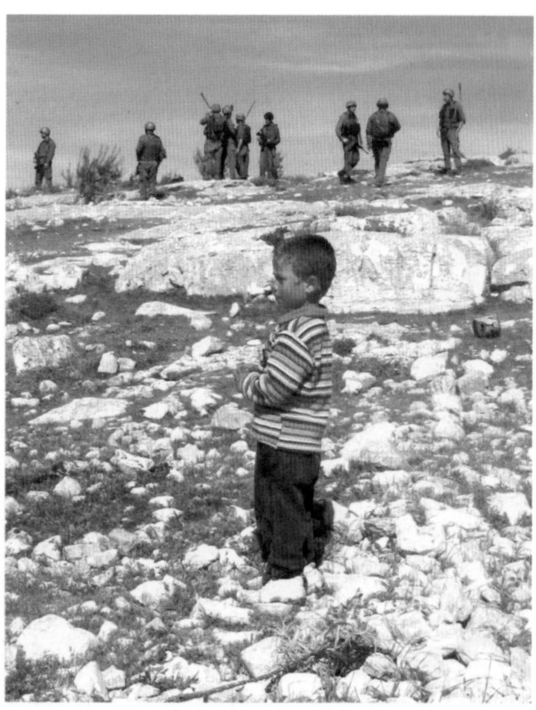

Soldiers prevent villagers from going to their land, forcing shepherd familes to graze their sheep on the poisoned land below.

The shepherds tried to protect their sheep, refusing to go down into the poisoned valley. The army grabbed one villager and arrested him. We were too far away to help him, but a member of *Ta'ayush* yelled for us to make groups around other shepherds and "hug them" if the army came close. I thought he was joking, but he wasn't. We surrounded the remaining shepherds, standing between them and the officers every time they tried to arrest another one. It worked! We used our bodies as shields, knowing that the soldiers would be more reluctant to use force against us than against the shepherds. The soldiers became tired of the game and grabbed a young boy. They held him, saying that he would only be released if we moved down. This time the shepherds were scared. They were willing to risk their own lives, but not that of a child. The whole group moved down and started to pick out poison frantically where the sheep were eating.

This wasn't enough for the settlers. They wanted us out altogether. The watching settlers formed a line, and for a moment we thought they were going to come down towards us. But they were smart; they knew our real weak spot.

The settlers turned and began to walk down the road towards the village, now lacking any international presence or army "protection." We yelled at the soldiers to do something but they were clearly reluctant to confront the settlers. We began walking quickly towards the village, worried that we would not reach it before the settlers did. One settler left his group to walk down towards us, but the army stopped him. They didn't want a confrontation, at least not between the settlers and other Israelis. They seemed more worried about us than about the Palestinians.

The settler seemed annoyed that he had been stopped but cheered up when his comrades applauded as he returned to the group. He gave a little bow and they all laughed. Even the soldier was amused, and put his arm around the joker as if they were old friends. Meanwhile we hurried towards the village, having gained the lead during the interlude.

Once we were positioned between the settlers and the village, we sat down in a small group on the road. There were no more than 10 of us and at least 20 of them. The soldiers were anxious to avoid a confrontation, so they stood in front of us as if we were going to attack. We asked why they didn't stand in the way of the settlers, but we already knew the answer: this was easier.

When the settlers came close, my heart began to pound. They were singing a song for Purim, laughing and dancing in the street. Many of them were children. The Palestinian

Soldiers wishing to prevent a confrontation between violent settlers and Palestinian villagers or internationals often restrict the latter groups in order to avoid standing up to the settlers.

youth, on the other hand, were terrified. A woman from Operation Dove, an Italian peace team stationed in At-Tawani, began to sing "Old MacDonald Had a Farm" in Italian with the children to distract them. It was very effective, and I felt inspired by her creativity in making the situation less tense. The soldiers stood over us and sent the approaching settlers off to the side. Fortunately, they complied. They held hands and skipped off towards Ma'on settlement, leaving us all to catch our breath—soldiers included.

I tried to take photographs of the settlers but a soldier prevented me from doing so. I told him I thought it was important to document the situation, and I asked him what he was afraid of. I pointed out that he was the one with the gun, not me. He wasn't listening. He just repeated "Go away" again and again, unwilling to even look at me. I was exasperated. I pleaded with him to look into my eyes so we could talk. I didn't want to believe that someone could follow orders so blindly, so inhumanely. But he was lost in his world of "duty" and my words were in vain.

A filmmaker started to record my interaction with the soldier, and the soldier stopped him, too. The filmmaker asked why the soldier didn't want him to film, and the soldier just kept his head down, repeating the same "Go away." So I answered for him: "People who don't want to be recorded are often ashamed on some level of what they're doing." I don't know if he heard me or not.

We spent the rest of the afternoon sitting with the children from the village, hoping the settlers would not come back. They didn't. At least not that day. But they've been back since, and they will be back again. The pellets we removed have been replaced by new poison, and either the villagers will give up their land or their sheep will continue to die. Of course, our action was less about removing the poison than attracting media attention to the incident. It was also about taking a stand; it was a symbol to the settlers that their actions are opposed and documented, and a symbol to the shepherds that we stand in solidarity with their fight to preserve their land and their lives.

Palestinian Land Day

Wednesday, March 30, 2005

Today is Palestinian Land Day. There have been demonstrations all over the West Bank in every major city and many towns and villages, from Hebron to Jenin, commemorating the killing of six unarmed Palestinian citizens of Israel more than 30 years go while they were protesting the expropriation of their land. IWPS spent Land Day in Wadi Qana[85] at a demonstration organized by the local group Women for Life. The action was short but to the point: women chanted and marched with anti-Occupation signs that reflected in the masses of sewage that flood the would-be paradise.

Women and children demonstrate in Wadi Qana in honor of Palestine Land Day.

Every day feels like Palestinian Land Day. The demonstrations are nonstop. I went to two in Deir Ballut village just this month, both planned with the intention of praying on land soon to be taken by the Wall. The first was relatively successful: international and Israeli activists joined Palestinians in a spirited march to the threatened land. When the call

[85] For more information on Wadi Qana, see pp. 144-145

to prayer sounded from a village in the distance, villagers were reminded of something stronger than their individual pain, and they lined up to worship. After prayers, several demonstrators began the long walk home. Some young boys stayed to throw stones at the bulldozers, and for the first time I saw a boy pick up a tear gas bomb and throw it back towards the soldiers. One young protester had climbed a tree on a nearby hill and stuck a Palestinian flag at the top. All around us were small signs of children taking back power.

Left and above: Deir Ballut villagers protest the annexation and destruction of their land.

Below: Soldiers retaliate for a spontaneous and nonviolent roadblock.

At Deir Ballut's second March demonstration, the army parked at the village outskirts to prevent demonstrators from reaching their land. Protesters piled up near the jeeps, and in broken English the mayor struggled to convey to the soldiers how unjust their blockade was. After 20 minutes, most protesters were either injured from beatings or sound bombs or back in the village strategizing. I saw a group begin walking towards a broken truck on the side of the road. Moments later there were dozens of villagers pushing it towards the road. Before long, protesters had blocked the road with the huge truck and set it on fire. Now we weren't the only ones trapped—the soldiers were, too.

Protesters walked back to the village, and the soldiers spent more than an hour trying to clear the road so they could leave the village. In the meantime I chatted with villagers and met their families. Occasionally a tear gas canister would fly onto a residential street and children would begin to cry. I escaped onto the roof of a tall house and watched as the soldiers slowly made their way back through the village. It was payback time. Everyone vanished into their homes. Soldiers jumped out of their jeeps one by one and ran through the streets. They were like characters in a video game, ready to snipe anything that moved. The village stayed quiet for hours until the soldiers finally got bored and left.

Witness in Palestine
Reflections on Zionism

Monday, April 4, 2005

Four days ago a man in a village near here was shot in the face while he was sleeping by an army sniper. The bullet pierced his right cheek and exited through his left cheek, knocking out most of his teeth and shattering his jaw. His brother came to help him get to the hospital. While the brother was carrying the victim to the car, the sniper shot him, too. Then, while they both lay helpless, the sniper got closer to the first victim and shot him in the chest. Miraculously they both survived, but they remain in critical condition. The end of the story is that it turns out it was a mistake. They got the wrong guys.

It is unlikely that anyone in the army will be prosecuted for the incident. What is so frustrating is that I could describe such an incident to friends and family in the United States and many would refuse to criticize Israel. Perhaps they would see this as an isolated incident, which it is not. But more likely, they would feel that any criticism of Israel is either anti-Semitic or anti-Zionist. Mass propaganda has succeeded in equating the Israeli government and army with the Jewish people: a criticism of one has become a criticism of the other. The Israeli government has hijacked the Jewish identity in the same way that George W. Bush has hijacked American identity during the Iraq War: "If you're not with us, you're against us." But occupying Arab populations has nothing to do with Judaism or Americanism. Being Jewish or Israeli doesn't have to mean unconditionally supporting the actions of the Israeli government any more than being American means unconditionally supporting the actions of the United States government.

People who consider themselves Zionists feel especially uncomfortable with my work, even though my principal writing topic is not whether or not there should be a Jewish state, but rather how such a state should comport itself. Just because one supports the idea of a Jewish state does not mean that one must also support all that Jewish state's actions. In fact, I would argue that Zionists *should* be against the Occupation, as the current situation is putting the Jewish state at greater risk than ever. Israel's Occupation of the Palestinian Territories is protecting Israel about as much as the United States' occupation of Iraq is protecting the United States. The Occupation has produced resentment and disapproval towards Israel from people and governments around the world. It has undermined the Jewish tradition of humanitarianism and social justice and created a dependence on US military aid that cannot be sustained indefinitely. Israel, as an occupying power, is doomed. Those who love it can help it most by working for justice and peace, not power.

People differ in their definitions of Zionism, but I use the term in reference to the political philosophy that supports a Jewish state in historic Palestine. Unlike a Jewish homeland, which could be a homeland for others as well, Israel is a Jewish state in the exclusive sense, i.e. the state of the Jewish people and only the Jewish people. Israel is not the state of its citizens. Israel is the self-proclaimed state of *all* Jewish people, even those in the diaspora. In other words, Israel is the state of a group of people who are *not* its citizens, and not the state of a group of people who *are* its citizens. Israel is my state, but it is not the state of the Palestinians with Israeli citizenship, including families that have lived in Palestine for hundreds or even thousands of years. They can never be nationals of their own country, because there is no Israeli nationality. You are either Jewish or Arab—this is specified on your ID card.[86] Jews are allowed the privileges of a national, such as owning or leasing state land. Jews can come and go as they please and never lose their rights to live in Israel. Palestinians in Israel, on the other hand, are treated like foreigners, even those whose families have been here since long before Zionist immigration began. They receive far fewer services from the government than do their Jewish counterparts (even though they pay the same taxes) and they are the targets of deliberate policies to condense or minimize the Palestinian population in order to ensure maximum space and resources for Jews.

There are many Jewish Israelis working for minority rights in Israel. Many of them believe that you *could* have a Jewish democracy in Israel if you just fixed all the laws to give equal rights to all. But even if the law dictated equality, Palestinians could still not expect any more inclusion than, say, Jewish Americans or African Americans could expect if the United States suddenly became the sovereign state of the Christian White people.[87] How would Jewish Americans feel about the US flag being replaced by a flag with a giant cross on it? Palestinian citizens of Israel live under a flag that doesn't represent them, a flag that symbolizes a religion that they are not even invited to become a part of.

Israel's discriminatory laws are not a perversion of Zionism—they are an inevitability of it. The exclusivist framework of an ethnically Jewish state is inherently anti-democratic and has given rise to animosity and resistance that have haunted Israel since its inception. How can you have a democratic Jewish state when the majority of people with legal claim to the country are not Jewish? Non-Jews make up a significant minority within Israel today, and that minority is growing. What happens when they get to be too many? Another *nakba*? Israel either has to push out and keep out the non-Jews, or somehow convince millions more Jews in the Diaspora to come live in Israel.

This second possibility deserves a closer look. Jews in Israel would not risk being outnumbered so dramatically if only the millions of Jews outside Israel *wanted* to leave their lives at home and

The Israeli flag, bearing the Star of David, does not just represent a nation; it represents the Jewish people, a group to which many of Israel's citizens do not belong.

[86] When this book went to press, Israel was no longer listing nationality on ID cards. Ethnic "Jewishness" is, however, still distinguished in the date of birth section.

[87] Noam Chomsky makes this analogy at the end of his book, *The Fateful Triangle*, p. 565.

move to a Jewish state. But here's the thing: for once most Jews don't seem to be desperate to flee lives of persecution. Perhaps they don't see themselves as victims anymore. What a wonderful thing! Shouldn't we rejoice that most Jews left in the Diaspora are not desperate to come to a place where they will surely live freely as Jews? The fact is that most people taking advantage of the Jewish "Law of Return" to Israel are Eastern Europeans and Ethiopians fleeing economic poverty more than religious or ethnic persecution. Meanwhile, millions of Palestinians with nowhere else to go are prevented from returning to their homes purely on the basis of *their* ethnic and religious backgrounds.

Given the current demographic realities, I cannot support the existence of an exclusively Jewish state any more than I can support its policies in the Occupied Territories. I cannot believe it has taken me so long to admit this to myself. I felt guilty before, as if criticism was somehow a disservice to my grandparents, great uncles, aunts, and cousins who perished during the Nazi Holocaust. But now it is clear to me. I cannot change the world if old wounds blind me into making or condoning new mistakes. There is no reasonable justification for reserving a country for people of one ethnicity—many of whom, like me, although born with the privilege have never needed it—while millions of people from another background with legal and historical claim to the land suffer desperately next door.

Certain early Zionists envisioned a Jewish homeland rather than a Jewish state, somewhere always open to Jews but not exclusive to them. I have met many Palestinians who would be willing to explore this and many other options that would respect international law and the human rights of everyone in the region. I personally believe the path to a lasting peace in the Middle East lies in creating a single homeland for both Jews and Palestinians, with equal rights for all regardless of ethnicity. It has been done before: consider blacks and whites in the United States and South Africa. Desegregation is not easy, and it takes a long time, but most would agree that the two-state alternative—i.e. separate states for blacks and whites—would only have perpetuated the racism and injustice. Peace founded on segregation is not real peace, and it won't last. Coexistence, equality, and justice eventually heal wounds that separation never can.

My personal realization that I oppose Zionism will make for interesting debates with friends and colleagues, but ultimately I know that my opinion is not important. The decision whether to pursue a binational homeland or a two-state solution lies with Israelis and Palestinians. If the majority of Israelis and Palestinians prefer two independent states side by side—which, according to polls, seems to be the case—then it is not my place to interfere. My role goes only as far as a brutal occupation is being carried out in my name as a Jew and with my tax dollars as an American. Once the political stranglehold of the Occupation is lifted, both sides can sit down at the negotiating table as human beings and decide how to ensure peace, security, and self-determination for both peoples.

Prayer on Deir Ballut's Blood-Stained Land

Friday, April 8, 2005

Wednesday morning I received the type of news I have been dreading: "Four people were shot in Deir Ballut." Four people shot anywhere is a tragedy, but I have a special affection for Deir Ballut and the people in it. My colleague and I rushed to the village, my heart pounding the whole way, wondering which of my dear friends I might never see again. Two friends directed us to the village land, where the shootings had occurred. One of my friends could hardly hold back her tears. We were stopped halfway there by a familiar sight: the soldiers had declared the area a "closed military zone" and nobody was allowed any further, except of course the Wall workers and bulldozers which continued their land-razing in the background. A group of women sat crying at the soldiers' knees. One grabbed me and told me that her brother had been shot in the gut. She begged me to do something, to tell the world. I was paralyzed, not knowing how I could ease her pain.

A woman of Deir Ballut picks through leaves stained with the blood of a loved one.

Above and right: Deir Ballut women mourn the shooting of their loved ones.

Two men stepped forward and negotiated with the soldiers to be allowed down to the land, where some people had remained after the shootings. I walked behind them, explaining to the soldiers that I felt there should be an international observer as I passed by. They didn't stop me. They did, however, stop a professional journalist and photographer working for the French press because he was Palestinian. Their reasoning: "First you are an Arab, then a journalist." For a while, I was the only "reporter" at the scene.

We walked quickly down to the land near the Wall construction, where we found the mothers of two of the victims. They wailed when they saw me, holding up the bloody clothing for me to photograph. One jacket had a bullet hole in the shoulder and the back. I wondered whose son had been wearing it just a few hours before. I sat with the women as they cried, and I asked them to tell me the story when they were ready.

They recounted that the Abdillah family had come down to their land to work that morning, as they had been doing for several weeks. Each day they worked their land on one side of the valley while the bulldozers destroyed it on the other. They were tortured by the injustice but felt they could do nothing. I asked if they sometimes threw stones at the bulldozers out of anger, but they shook their heads. What would be the point? Plus, they knew the Israeli security guards at the Wall and had even drunk tea with them once.

"But today that changed," said a man nearby who had heard me speaking to the women. His name was Marwan. He explained that he and four friends had walked a few meters towards the security guards that day to appeal to them to stop the destruction of their land.

They then yelled at the people building the Wall to leave. According to Marwan, the security guards then opened fire on the group, hitting his four friends almost simultaneously. He moved his hands past his head to convey the feeling of bullets flying past his ears, and thanked God that he had been spared. The closest shooter, he explained, had been 30 ft away while the rest were much further. He confirmed the women's claim that no stone had been thrown.

Marwan led me around the area of the shootings. He pointed out drops of blood on a few rocks, and then I began to notice the stains myself. They were everywhere. There were pools of blood thinning to trickles where the victims had struggled to walk away. I learned that one young man named Samir, who was my age (25), was shot in the leg and struggled the 2 miles back to the village with help from his friend and a donkey. His injury seemed less serious than those of the others, who had to wait for ambulances to arrive, ironically via the path of the Wall. Majid, Samir's 30-year-old brother, was shot in the shoulder and the bullet exited his back. Hamada, his cousin of 24, was shot in the chest. The oldest victim Khalil, 58, was shot near his groin and the bullet exited his backside. His 75-year-old mother was by my side the whole time until she found the blood of her son on the leaves of a plant near where he'd been shot. She held up the bloody leaves helplessly. I didn't know whether to take a photograph or cry. I did both.

As we mourned, a nearby soldier pointed me out to his partner and grinned. I wanted to throw up. How could he be so inhumane? He was not the only chipper soldier, and I was reminded of all the innocent young men and women of Israel who have been dehumanized by their military training. How far this is from the traditional compassion of Judaism! This Occupation is destroying us all.

But it wasn't soldiers who shot Samir, Majid, Hamada, and Khalil. It was guards from a private security company hired to protect the bulldozers working on the Wall. If it were the army, I could almost guarantee there would be no investigation. Does that go for private guards too? I couldn't understand it; what could those guards have been thinking? Were they so threatened by the five familiar unarmed men yelling at a distance from them? Surely they aimed to kill if they hit one in the chest and another in the shoulder. These guards are contracted by the Israeli government to ensure the safety of the Jewish people of Israel. What about the safety of the Palestinians?

At first I found Marwan's story unbelievable; I couldn't imagine why the guards would have done such a thing with so little provocation. But my skepticism vanished when I went to visit Samir and Hamada in the hospital yesterday, and they both told exactly the same story. Hamada greeted me with a big dazed smile and a weak handshake. He had been shot in the chest, but thankfully the bullet went through his left breast from side to side, not front to back. His heart remained untouched and it looks like he will be fine.

Samir, a few doors down, was in far worse shape. After his long struggle back to the village, he was turned back at Deir Ballut checkpoint.[88] Samir was forced to take a long and bumpy detour to the town of Biddya, where he was told that they didn't have the proper equipment to treat his serious injuries. Only then was he permitted to reach Ramallah, taking two different ambulances because he had to be manually carried over a roadblock in the middle of the trip.

Samir lost critical time and a lot of blood during the ordeal and remains in a great deal of pain. When I entered he recognized me but could hardly speak. He just kept biting his lower lip, looking up at the ceiling with tears in his eyes. The bullet had severed the source of blood to his feet, and at this stage even the doctors in Ramallah feel helpless. He is hoping to receive permission from Israel to travel to a better-equipped hospital in Jordan. Nobody knows how his family will pay for his care there.

I didn't have the opportunity to see Majid or Khalil because they are being treated in a different hospital, but I did go to visit their families in Deir Ballut. Majid's wife welcomed me warmly and explained how attached her husband was to the land they were losing. For him and many other Palestinians, land is like a child, connected to you in that deep inexplicable way through interdependence and dedication. Majid had taken the kids to work the fields with him that day, saying, "If they take our land, they might as well take us too." The kids apparently watched the bullet fly through their father and they gathered around him screaming "*Baba! Baba!* (Daddy! Daddy!)"

Khalil's children are my age and have children of their own. They appreciated my visit and told me what a serious condition their father was in because of his age and the proximity of the bullet to his groin. We sat in silence until the children started to goof around and break the somber mood, as children do so skillfully. They asked me about my family and invited me to marry someone in Deir Ballut and settle down there. I smiled and tried to change the subject.

Today, the village of Deir Ballut held a demonstration in protest of the Wall construction and the shootings. Their plan was to pray on the rocks stained with the blood of their loved ones. Hundreds of villagers and many internationals and Israelis gathered and marched towards the symbolic land. The soldiers were waiting for us along the way and formed a line across our path with their bodies to prevent protestors from advancing.

---

[88] This is the same checkpoint where a pregnant woman lost her twin babies last year (See pp. 77-79). Clearly things haven't gotten better. My good friend Sofia waited 3 painful hours at the checkpoint in the middle of the night 6 months ago, before she was permitted to pass to have her baby in Ramallah.

Demonstrators responded to the obstacle in different ways. One group of men started talking to the soldiers in Hebrew, explaining why it was important for them to pass. A group of women from Women for Life began singing a traditional Palestinian folk song to invigorate the demonstrators. A few children climbed the rocks above the path, holding flags in silence as photographers documented the scene. But the soldiers were unmoved; nobody could pass. And so the resistance stepped up a notch.

Deir Ballut women pray on the blood-stained land of their loved ones.

An old woman stopped yelling and started pushing. She pushed her way through the crowd and then through the line of soldiers, who hardly knew what had hit them. Then came another woman, whom they tried to stop, but by the time she'd passed a certain point they could no longer attend to her because that would weaken their barrier. And so, one by one, several brave individuals broke through the line of soldiers. After each successful passage, the group cheered with renewed energy and determination. The group of people who had made it through encouraged others to join them.

I saw my friend Reem trying to get around the side of a soldier, and I rushed to help pull her through. I put out my hand, and a soldier scooted between us. Still I pulled, and the soldier pushed her back, and before I knew it Reem's husband had jumped in the middle to help his wife. He was angry with the soldier for touching her forcefully. Then his brother

Women of Deir Ballut demonstrate against the shootings of four local farmers.

joined in to help separate the soldier and Reem. Within seconds, things had escalated and everyone was pushing and shoving. I saw Reem's brother-in-law being dragged along the ground by his neck. Then the soldiers began to throw sound bombs one after another to scatter the crowd. Reem and I watched from the side, paralyzed and clutching one another, the sound bombs exploding in our ears and faces. We closed our eyes and waited for it to be over. When we opened our eyes, we were relieved to see that Reem's husband had emerged from the conflict unscathed. His brother's arm, however, had been sprained. I was thankful that the soldiers could not use tear gas because they were so close that they would be gassed themselves.

The demonstrators were not deterred. It seemed those most affected by the confrontation had been the soldiers, who were visibly shaken. They agreed to let the protesters through, but only in groups of five. They seemed very pleased with themselves for their generosity. An Israeli activist friend and I watched them work, wondering how it was that they saw it as their authority to give Palestinians the red or green light to go to their own land. We couldn't understand the five-person rule, except that perhaps it served to reaffirm that things were being done on the soldiers' terms, even though most would say that the soldiers had been defeated this time.

The demonstration proceeded quickly to the land where the shootings had taken place. It was almost time to pray. Parents, siblings, children, and friends of the victims lined up to worship together. There were drops of blood visible everywhere, and a young girl wore her uncle's jacket with the blood and bullet holes. On a loudspeaker, the imam called a prayer that echoed across the valley to where the bulldozers continued their razing. The villagers prayed in unison, in solidarity, each connecting to the land individually for a moment. When they finished, they began their long walk home. It was a small victory in a long fight, but there was a feeling of empowerment and hope within us as we walked, an encouragement to those still nursing wounds from a few days before.

Deir Yassin & the Modern Victims of Extremism

Saturday, April 9, 2005

With every passing day in the West Bank, more and more of the "facts" of history that I learned growing up the United States as a Jewish-American dissolve into myths as I hear first-hand stories about the past and present of Israel and Palestine. I recently learned that 57 years ago today, members of the Irgun and Stern gangs, two armed underground Zionist militias, broke into homes in the Palestinian village of Deir Yassin in the middle of the night and systematically murdered between 110 and 140 peaceful inhabitants. The village lay outside the area recommended by the United Nations to be included in a future Jewish state, but within the area coveted by Zionist forces and eventually declared part of Israel.

Deir Yassin is now in ruins, wiped off the map and forgotten by most. The modern Jewish neighborhood of Har Nof now stands where the village used to be, and remaining buildings have become part of a local hospital. My colleague Hannah attended an anniversary memorial service in Deir Yassin and wrote the following in her journal:

> One survivor of the massacre was there, and she began to tell stories, personal stories about many of the killings. She talked about the good relations the Palestinians and Jews had previously enjoyed, how they had been friends, how she doesn't know what the Palestinians could have done to the Jews to make them do this to her family. She talked about pregnant women being sliced through the stomach and killed, old men thrown off the roofs of houses, seven young boys sleeping in bed who were rounded up, taken outside, lined up, and shot. A few members of her family (herself included) were given the choice of whether they wanted to be shot or stabbed to death, only to be saved at the last minute by one gang member who said, "Don't kill them, let them go." This is how she survived, along with the other families that were put on a truck and shipped out, away from their village where they'd been for so many centuries. Still they cannot go back.

According to witnesses, Jewish commanders took 25 male villagers, paraded them through the Jewish quarter in Jerusalem, and then shot them dead in a stone quarry along the road from Givat Shaul to Deir Yassin. The leader of one of the gangs, Menachem Begin of Irgun, was later elected Prime Minister of Israel. In his own words, "Arabs throughout the country" were "seized with limitless panic and started to flee for their lives; this mass flight soon developed into a maddened, uncontrollable stampede. The political and economic significance of this development can hardly be overestimated."[89]

The version of history that I heard growing up was that the Palestinians fled in 1948 following radio broadcasts urging them to get out of the way, so that the surrounding Arab armies could drive the Jews into the sea. This is the same story that my mother was told,

---

[89] Noam Chomsky, *Peace in the Middle East? Reflections on Justice and Nationhood* (New York: Vintage Books, 1969), p. 170.

and Hannah, and millions of other American or Israeli Jews. Yet numerous Israeli scholars and others have examined the archive of Arab 1948 radio broadcasts and found virtually no evidence to support the claim that Arab leaders incited Palestinians to leave their homes as part of a tactical maneuver.[90]

This should come as no surprise: what population in history has ever voluntarily left its ancestral homeland to facilitate a military maneuver led by a foreign power? People don't just uproot their families because some foreign leader tells them to. Would you? The vast majority of Palestinians who fled in 1948 were forced out or left out of fear induced by stories like that of Deir Yassin and the many other Palestinian villages that suffered similar fates at the hands of radical Zionists.

In 1948, Israeli militants wanted the land of Deir Yassin to build a small airfield for the Jewish residents of Jerusalem. Today they want a parking lot, or a highway, or a garbage dump. The evacuation and destruction of Palestinian communities with the goal of Jewish purity and privilege is far from over. The massacres continue, at a slower pace but on a greater scale. So today, while many Palestinians honored the lives lost in Deir Yassin, I conducted interviews with some of the modern victims of Zionist extremism.

I interviewed victims of settler violence in As-Sawiya, the hometown of a good friend of mine who had invited me many times to visit. He showed us around the ancient village, introducing us to friends and family. His mother welcomed us emphatically and wouldn't stop feeding us, even as she told a story of being attacked by settlers during the 2002 olive harvest. The old woman explained that two men from the nearby settlement of Eli approached her, kicked her until she fell down, and then stole her donkey and olives. (She recovered the donkey 2 days later.) She's a tough old lady and continues to work on her land every day, but some of her friends are not so resilient. Down the street lives a carpenter whose house was broken into by settlers one night that same fall. The intruders reportedly broke his windows and doors, damaged his carpentry tools, and burned his wood. Journalists documented the incident, but no arrests were made nor was compensation offered. Traumatized, the old carpenter is now too frightened to return to his land near Eli, even though his carpentry work alone is insufficient to provide for his large family.

Built on a slope, As-Sawiya looks across a small valley at five vast hills of land belonging to the village, each one now topped with a settlement or outpost. The settlers have seized far more land than they actually use and have established a seemingly arbitrary "safety line" far below their houses, above which the villagers are prohibited to farm. Even below the

[90] See Shlomo Ben-Ami, *Scars of War, Wounds of Peace* (Oxford Univ. Press, 2006), p. 43; See also Simha Flapan, *The Birth of Israel: Myths and Realities* (New York: Pantheon, 1987), p. 86; See also Erskine Childers, *The Spectator* (London, May 12, 1961); As cited in personal correspondence with Jason Weeks (November 19, 2006); For more sources and information on the myth of voluntary exodus see Appendix IV.

"safety line," villagers frequently report attacks by settlers with guns, sticks, chains, and guard dogs that they sic on children from the village.

Many villagers have appealed to the Israeli army for protection. The army grants the village 2 days of protection per year—one during the olive harvest and the other during plowing season—an impossibly short period of time to tend to their 15,000 acres of land. The rest of the year seems to be a free-for-all. According to witnesses, soldiers have stood by as settlers bathed in the village's precious water source, as they built a road without government permission through Palestinian land, and as they poisoned 40 of the village's trees. One villager reported being shot in the foot by a settler while a soldier looked on.

A shepherd (left) who was attacked by settlers during the 2002 olive harvest stands beside her daughter.

Then there are the schools. Eli settlers have organized repeated nightly raids on the local girls' school, presumably because of its proximity to a main settler highway. One night, locals witnessed 45 settlers enter the premises and set fire to classrooms, books, computers, files, and furniture. After the incident, the village worked together to refurbish the school and raise money for new computers and other lost property. But just one year later, the settlers returned to steal the new computers and further damage the buildings. Now the school must hire guards, but its financial situation is already so dire that it has had to lay off desperately-needed teachers and staff in order to do so.

The settlers enter the girls' school through a gate less than one hundred yards away from a village house occupied by soldiers, yet the army has never attempted to prevent or stop an attack. At the boys' school, settlers broke in and damaged the gate, windows, chalkboards, walls, and the pole where they hang their Palestinian flag.

The settler attacks on As-Sawiya are not anomalies. Neither was the massacre in Deir Yassin. The assault on Palestinian life has never ended; worse than that, it has never really been acknowledged. We don't want to believe that Jewish people are capable of abusing power and privilege or inflicting horrors reminiscent of those suffered by their parents and grandparents. It is always easier to believe you are the victim, not the oppressor. But people are responsible for their actions regardless of their past. When the United Nations calls upon Israel to withdraw from the West Bank and to allow for the return or compensation of refugees who fled in 1948, the international community is holding Israel to the same standard as any other country in the world. That is not anti-Semitism, or insensitivity to the plight of the Jewish people; it is equal treatment, which persecuted Jews yearned for before Israel existed. Today Israel ranks among the richest countries in the world; it is time to learn that with equal treatment comes equal responsibility.

Witness in Palestine
Punishing the Victims

Sunday, April 10, 2005

April 9th is no longer only the anniversary of Deir Yassin. Yesterday, three boys aged 14 and 15 were shot dead by soldiers in Gaza when they ran towards the "security fence" to fetch a soccer ball. They were unarmed.

Yesterday was the 74th day since Sharon and Abbas began ceasefire talks in January. Since the talks began, five Israelis have been killed, four in the last suicide attack in February. During that same period 30 Palestinians have been killed by settlers or soldiers.[91] Another Palestinian minor was killed today. His name was Nasser. He was 17 years old.

Yesterday was also the day extremist settlers announced they would bomb Al-Aqsa mosque (Temple Mount), the holiest site in Palestine for Muslims. Such an attack would provoke a violent reaction from Palestinians that would destroy any hope for peace in the near future, effectively sabotaging Sharon's plan to forcefully evacuate all the settlers from Gaza this summer. Some settlers don't want peace; they don't want any compromise at all, because they believe that they are doing God's work and that He will protect them.

The Dome of the Rock on the Temple Mount in East Jerusalem, one of Islam's holiest sites. The Temple Mount was the target of threats from Israeli settlers wishing to provoke retaliation in order to sabotage Israel's planned disengagement from Gaza.

[91] *Middle East Policy Council* (December 31, 2004). *www.mepc.org/resources/mrates.asp*
"Numbers *do not* include Palestinian suicide bombers (or other attackers) nor do they include Palestinians targeted for assassination, though bystanders killed during these assassinations are counted. However, [Israeli] soldiers killed during incursions into Palestinian lands *are counted.* Data collected from *B'tselem*, the Palestinian Red Crescent Society, and the Israeli Ministry of Foreign Affairs."

In response to the bomb threat, the army set up temporary "flying" checkpoints for Palestinians all over the West Bank. Let me repeat: the army set up checkpoints for Palestinians because *settlers* threatened to incite violence. It's the same logic by which Hebron was put under curfew after Goldstein's massacre and farmers are forbidden from plowing their land and grazing their sheep when settlers might attack. It is easier to restrict Palestinians—who aren't allowed guns or political representation—than to stand up to the fundamentalist settlers.

Soldiers set up a flying checkpoint to restrict Palestinian movement on the day when Israeli settlers threatened to attack Al-Aqsa mosque.

I encountered a flying checkpoint on my way to As-Sawiya yesterday. Some Palestinians said they had been waiting in their cars for nearly 4 hours. They told me that earlier that day the line had stretched all the way up to Zatara checkpoint, more than a mile away, which itself had a one-hour wait for Palestinians. Most travelers probably had to wait at both.

I walked to the front of the checkpoint where I found four soldiers who were supposed to be checking IDs. One was talking on the phone and laughing and another was taking pictures of Palestinians waiting. I asked the two young soldiers why they were fooling around, keeping hundreds of people waiting.

Soldiers set up a flying checkpoint to restrict Palestinian movement on the day when Israeli settlers threatened to attack Al-Aqsa mosque.

They nonchalantly went back to work. They seemed bored and apathetic. I watched them angrily and took pictures. They were very curious about me and kept asking me questions. I told them I would tell them about myself and my work as soon as it wasn't at the expense of Palestinians' time. They were game. Suddenly they started letting cars go through quickly, hardly checking any IDs.

The soldiers made a kind of game out of letting the cars through, teasing Palestinians with their pointing, summoning (with a wave of their hands), and stopping (with a flat hand). They often kept cars waiting a few seconds before letting them through, even if they didn't check them. They occasionally took breaks to smoke and chat but grew weary of my glares. Once the last few cars were finally through, the soldiers turned to me and asked what I was doing. I told them I lived in a nearby Palestinian village. One said, "You're lucky you're not Jewish or the Arabs would kill you." I thought that was funny, and informed them that I was in fact Jewish. They told me I was nuts and I told them they were brainwashed and that I didn't appreciate them calling my neighbors and friends dangerous. That was the end of our conversation.

We have an ongoing debate in the IWPS house about whether or not settlers and soldiers "choose" to commit their crimes or whether they are simply unaware of what they're doing. Some believe that people who are blind from propaganda and fear are not making a choice because the alternatives have never occurred to them. Others believe that they are ignoring the truth, choosing not to register the fundamental injustice of being able to pass freely on roads where people with a different ethnic background wait for hours or aren't even allowed. What about all the Israelis who have no idea about what is going on in the West Bank and Gaza, just a few miles away? Is their ignorance excusable? Even most so-called "leftist" Israelis who oppose settlements don't know the extent of the situation, despite the abundance of information available—even in mainstream Israeli newspapers like *Haaretz*. For many, the Occupation is just too depressing to think about. And like everywhere in the world, people are preoccupied with their own lives and families.

Whether Israeli public ignorance is involuntary or intentional, I suspect that when the Occupation ends and the injustices are exposed and condemned—and I do believe they will be some day—most Israelis will say they had no idea what was happening and how bad it really was. I guess the worst part is that for the most part, it will be the truth.

Saffa Demonstration I

Tuesday, April 12, 2005

There is something special about Saffa. I first traveled to the village 2 months ago for a demonstration, and I arrived to find a group of farmers squatting on their threatened land refusing to be moved. Saffa has not received much attention for its nonviolent demonstrations because its activities are dwarfed by the now-legendary resistance in the nearby village of Bil'in. Nonetheless, the village council calls IWPS every few weeks and asks us to join them in their fight to save their land.

It was the mayor who called us the first time, and I traveled to the village with my colleague Amy. We were late and had to trek through endless olive groves to find the demonstration. It wasn't difficult—we followed the sound of the bulldozers until we stumbled upon soldiers "guarding" the groves from their owners. The villagers were scattered around the land, some sitting in groups, others standing and strategizing. A large group of boys had been separated from the other villagers and were under the guard of soldiers. They were sitting quietly, watching the bulldozers uproot village trees in preparation for the Wall.

A woman in the front who was speaking with a soldier caught my eye. She saw me approaching and grabbed my arm, pulling me with her to meet the other women who had

Soldiers round up young protesters from Saffa and survey them during a peaceful demonstration against the Wall.

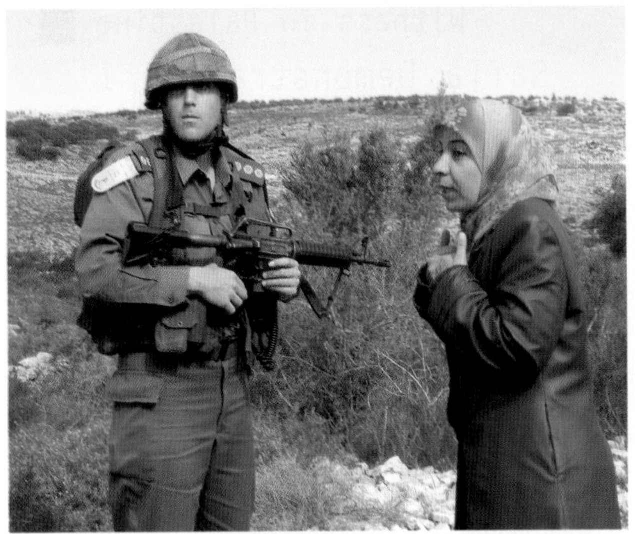

Inaam attempts to reason with a soldier who is guarding the razing of her village's land.

come out to demonstrate. The woman's name was Inaam, and she introduced Amy and me to a small but very determined group of women. They wanted to go down into the valley to get closer to the bulldozers, but they didn't want to go alone. Amy and I were happy to accompany the women, and we stood up slowly, trying to sneak away amidst the trees, out of view of the soldiers. The soldiers had not thought to closely monitor the women, and before long we were deep in the valley, halfway between the demonstration we had just left and another protest building on the opposite side coming from Bil'in. I recognized several Israeli friends in the second group.

Israeli soldiers guard the illegal construction of the Wall on Palestinian land.

I wondered how we could unite the two demonstrations and villages to increase our impact. One of the soldiers guarding the Bil'in side to prevent just that spotted our small group and pushed us up the hill into the second demonstration, away from Inaam's village. Luckily, our distraction had allowed demonstrators to advance slightly down the hill. It's a power game in which soldiers assert authority—in our view illegitimate—and protesters struggle to assert their power, often symbolic. Advancing a step at a time whenever the soldiers turned their heads was not likely to get us all the way down to the bulldozers, but it was a way of showing soldiers that they could not totally control us, in spite of their guns.

Realizing that we were advancing, the soldiers started yelling aggressively in Hebrew. They tried to push us up the hill, and when we would not move they began to throw sound bombs. The explosions broke my focus and filled me with fear. I walked up the hill slowly trying not to give the soldiers the satisfaction of knowing how scared I was. I told myself that this is what nonviolent resistance involves—responding bravely and peacefully in the face of violence.

Once the soldiers had re-established themselves in a line, we stood there for a long time, face to face, neither side willing to budge. I watched the soldier in front of me—he looked like he was uncomfortable but trying not to show it. He clutched a sound bomb in his hand just in case, and looked away when I caught his eye. I recognized him from a demonstration in Bil'in. I tried to engage with the soldier, with questions and simple eye contact. He seemed to be getting uncomfortable.

Saffa villagers protest the illegal destruction and confiscation of their land and resources.

The soldier's commander told him to ignore me. I recognized the commander from Bil'in as well: a stern-faced, determined man. I turned my attention to him, concentrating on his face for a long time until I was sure he knew I was watching him. He tried not to show it, but I knew he was uncomfortable, too. One brilliant thing about nonviolent resistance is its power to embarrass. Sometimes it's enough to simply watch and not fight back.

Inaam was anxious to reach the bulldozers, so I took advantage of the commander's nervousness and began walking past him with her. He yelled at us to stop and I told him that she was from the other side of the valley. We continued walking despite his commands.

I was inspired by Inaam's bravery. Coming from a culture with a profound respect for the rule of law, I have difficulty directly disobeying soldiers, policemen, or anyone in official uniform. An old Christian Canadian woman living in Bethlehem was the first to clarify my handicap to me. She said,

> We North Americans have learned from a young age that policemen are our friends. Our parents and schools told us that these men in uniform were the people to turn to if we were ever lost or in trouble, that they could be trusted and their rules should be followed. We are inclined to trust and obey them, because we assume their rules are fair. But here this respect imprisons us. The rules are not fair, and they are not legal—you don't have to follow them.

She was right, and with time I am becoming more skilled at dismissing illegal Occupation forces just as I would the Mafia, a terrorist organization, or any other illegal institution attempting to subjugate a population. My new skill is empowering, and soldiers sense my confidence. I know my rights, and that affords me some control in my interactions with the army.

The Israeli commander in Saffa was too worried about other activists to come chasing after Inaam and the rest of us, so we made it into the valley where the bulldozers were working. We found a few farmers talking to TV cameramen, and there were a number of soldiers hanging around. Inaam sat down to think. Amy and I followed her lead. We

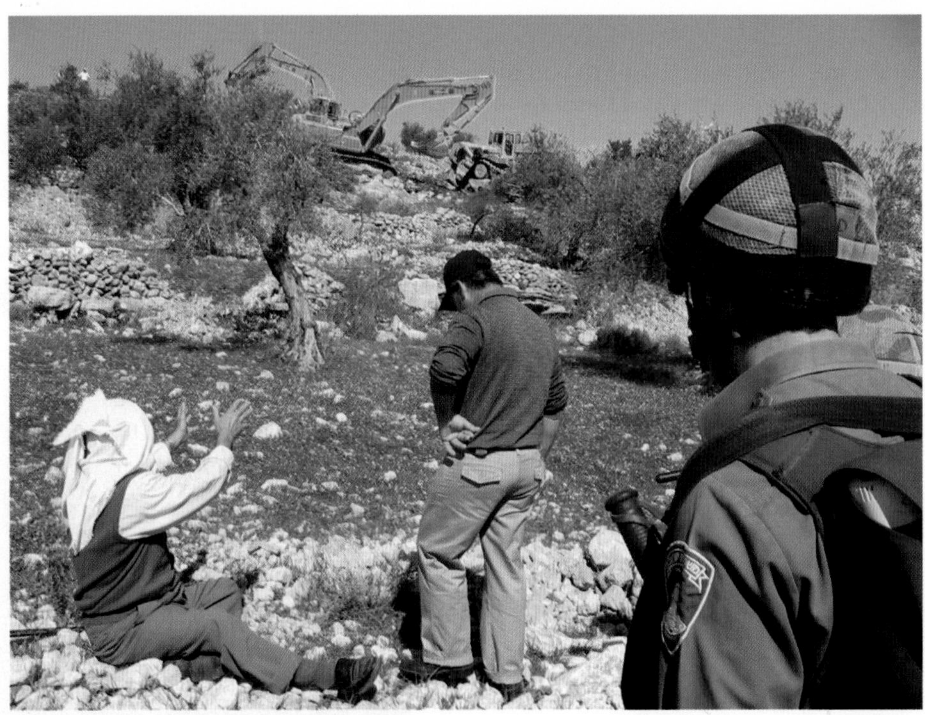

A farmer watches as his trees and livelihood are uprooted.

watched a calm old farmer finally lose his composure as he watched his livelihood uprooted. Sobbing, he got down onto his knees in front of the soldiers and begged them to stop the bulldozers. When his tears were met with stone faces he began moaning and swaying until the *keffiyeh*[92] on his head began to fall off. His friend tried to calm him down, but he was past control. He lifted his arms up towards the sky and cried, "*Allah Hu Akbar!*"[93] Then he fell to the ground and started crawling around grabbing handfuls of dirt, letting it run through his fingers. He watched it fall, and then looked up at the soldiers, imploring them to stop his misery.

I cried as I filmed the desperate man and the seemingly unmoved soldiers. He sobbed until his throat was sore and his eyes dry. Finally he collapsed, silent——defeated. Others were moved to speak and distracted the media and soldiers, but I kept watching the man. He was gone, in another world, staring into space. His land, his love, everything was lost. His heart was broken.

Inaam was a woman of action, not tears. She and her friends decided to approach the bulldozers and stop them with their bodies. We began climbing a small hill above the valley towards where the machines were working. We were spotted, and three soldiers hurriedly ran ahead and forced themselves in front of us. Inaam kept climbing, so I did too. One soldier grabbed my arm and pushed me to the side. For Inaam, he had other plans. He shoved her harshly down the hill, and she fell about 5 feet off a small cliff onto her hip. I screamed at the soldier that we were peaceful demonstrators, and I rushed to Inaam's side.

---

92 *Keffiyehs* are the traditional cloth headdresses warn by Arab men, usually white, red, or black.

93 Arabic for "God is great."

She was badly bruised, but she managed to stand up and walk again. By then the other women had been forced to retreat, so we were back down in the valley.

But the soldiers wanted us off the land altogether. They rounded us into a group and began pushing us towards Saffa. This was it: these villagers might never reach their land again. We couldn't let that happen. I braced myself to stay in place, and then a soldier grabbed my arm and shoved me towards the other demonstrators. I lost it. I spun around and began screaming at the soldiers, tears running down my face: "How can you force these people to abandon their land when it's the only thing they have left? Are you even thinking about what you're doing?"

The soldiers were shocked to see me crying. It was different from watching the Palestinians farmer break down—I was someone they could relate to more easily, from a culture and language more familiar to them. The soldiers eased their grip on me, but they continued to push. I hoped my outburst had affected at least one of them. I knew it had meant something to the Palestinians there.

We were rounded into a group and made to sit down. We were surrounded, but we were together. A few Palestinians were permitted to stand and talk to the soldiers, and with time more people were allowed up. We took every opportunity we could get. Slowly, as more of us stood, we began to prepare to approach the bulldozers again. We moved quickly and some of us made it out of the group that the soldiers were trying to contain. The army closed in violently on those who remained. I began to run with Inaam and the others, and when I looked back I saw the soldiers with raised batons, beating the villagers who hadn't left. I froze. What could I do? Inaam yelled at me to continue running, and we hid among the trees.

I heard popping noises and suddenly my eyes began to sting. We were being tear-gassed. I heard Amy calling out that she was in pain, and I grabbed her arm to pull her away from the thick of the gas. Outside of the cloud the stinging began to subside, and we tried to tend to others still recovering. Some people had thrown up. Others were hit with tear gas canisters, which can cause serious burns and blisters. I asked if anyone had been seriously beaten, and some other protesters motioned to an ambulance that had recently filled up. They told me that one demonstrator had been badly hit in the head and another in the leg.

Inaam and her friends were ready to return to the village. Amy and I felt drained, and the only demonstrators left were young boys throwing stones. We decided to leave with Inaam, who led us on the long hike uphill to the village. She invited us in for bread with olive oil and spices and introduced us to the children she takes care of, children of her siblings who have been killed, arrested, or sent abroad. She took our phone numbers and promised to call the next time Saffa held a demonstration.

Witness in Palestine
Saffa Demonstration II & Reflections on Symbolism

Saffa villagers march peacefully towards the Wall construction on their land.

Saffa villagers refuse to move from the path of bulldozers razing their land.

Friday, April 15, 2005

Inaam kept her promise. She called me a few weeks later to request IWPS presence at another protest in Saffa. This time we were fewer but better prepared. We reached the bulldozers before the soldiers did and sat down in front of the machines, hoping their drivers would stop out of fear of hurting someone. When we refused to move, soldiers threw sound bombs and we sprang up out of fear. One bomb exploded in my face, ricocheting off my neck and blasting my eardrum. For a moment I was sure I'd lost hearing in my right ear.

My ear was still ringing when the explosions stopped. The protesters were scattered. An old man had fallen and slashed his hand and was being carried away. We regrouped and walked back together towards the machines, resolved not to stop until we were physically beaten down. The soldiers drew their batons and began beating demonstrators left and right. I fumbled with my camera to catch the violence on film. It was mostly an excuse not to move forward with the others—I was paralyzed with fear of being beaten.

Our numbers were too few to move past the soldiers' batons,

so we sat down again, as close to the bulldozers as possible to prevent them from working. The bulldozer operator saw us and decided to teach us a lesson. Using the bulldozer's claw he gathered hundreds of pounds of rocks and dirt and began moving towards us. The soldiers yelled at us to move, and we scurried away just before the claw covered our ground with rubble.

Soldiers respond to demonstrators with tear gas and sound bombs.

The bulldozer operator's manifest indifference to us was disheartening, to say the least. Much of nonviolent resistance relies on the awakening of people's consciences. We sat down away from the bulldozers to observe and film; if we couldn't stop the destruction, at least we would document it. Everyone remained seated except a few children who sprang up to place a Palestinian flag above the growing pile of rubble formed by the bulldozer. Each time the machine knocked it over with more rubble, they would dig it up and put it back.

One old farmer had somehow reached his land during the chaos of sound bombs and tear gas, perhaps because the soldiers were distracted. The soldiers spotted him a few minutes after I did and told him to leave. Sitting peacefully on a rock, he declared that they would have to kill him first. They left him alone—he wasn't worth their trouble. He sat among his trees all afternoon. He had no M16 and no army, but like the children raising the flag, his peaceful determination was stronger than any gun.

The Israeli army has wreaked continuous havoc on Palestinian land and life, but it has never succeeded in destroying the Palestinian spirit. Nothing will stop humans from seeking freedom, least of all guns. Firearms don't bring security or peace to anyone. I watch soldiers clutch the massive things and I see that they are so scared, so completely terrified. And next to them are the unarmed activists, so free because they have neither a heavy gun nor a heavy conscience weighing them down.

I have started using a new strategy for talking to soldiers. At first I ignore them because they don't have any legitimate authority over me or anyone else in the area. But if they engage with me and begin to ask me questions, I politely tell them that I don't feel comfortable talking to someone with a big gun in his hands. I invite them to put down their guns and talk, but they never do.

Israeli soldiers aren't the only ones attached to their guns. One of the first things I noticed in Palestine was the prevalence of toy guns in the hands of children in the street. It didn't surprise me that they would want to play with guns—after all, the people they see in power every day, the soldiers and settlers, all have guns—but it surprised me that their parents would allow it, since most families I meet are basically peaceful. For example, a friend of mine who advocates nonviolent resistance won't let his sons throw stones at demonstrations but he lets them pose with guns in pictures. It seems crazy to me. Aren't guns about killing?

The Palestinian flag, formerly forbidden, represents freedom and independence for many Palestinians.

I don't like guns. I hate seeing them everywhere here, on posters of people killed by soldiers and in plastic replicas in corner stores. But I have struggled to understand their presence instead of just reacting to it. To me, guns symbolize violence and fear. But to many Palestinians, they symbolize strength. For a Palestinian to have a gun on his or her death poster means that he or she was brave instead of submissive, no matter what the cause of death. Guns aren't a Palestinian tradition any more than they are a Jewish one. The Zapatistas in Mexico carved out wooden guns as symbols of their struggle too. It's about honor, not killing. And honor is very important to people here. It's what they have left, as their rights and land slip away.

It's interesting how symbols begin to mean different things to me here. On my wrist I wear a wristband that says "Palestine" with a Palestinian flag in the background. It was a gift, and I like the way it looks. I like wearing it, because it shows clearly my solidarity with Palestinians when I'm in the West Bank, and it sparks interesting conversations with Israelis in Israel. But it has a flag on it, and I've always avoided flags and other symbols of nationalism. Is this one any different?

I struggle to justify this contradiction. The Palestinian flag is different from most: it was illegal for many years, and to me represents more the struggle for freedom and nationhood than the nation itself. I don't think I would wear the wristband if the state of Palestine already existed.

A flower spray-painted by IWPS over offensive graffiti on a roadblock in Haris

Hebrew graffiti near Zatara checkpoint reads "Death to Arabs" on the curb and "Revenge" on the bus stop.

Being in Palestine is a lesson in maturity and flexibility for me. On the one hand, I am learning to make judgements and take sides on issues I used to dismiss as "complicated." On the other hand, issues like stone-throwing, flag-waving, and gun-toting are not as black and white as they used to be. There have always been clear categories and rules in my life—suddenly there are none. For the first time in my life, I have to decide for myself what is right and what is wrong.

The other night a colleague and I snuck out to spray-paint over anti-Arab graffiti that settlers had sprayed in Hebrew on an old roadblock near Haris. I used to dislike vandalism, but I had no trouble spraying a big flower around the words, rendering them illegible—yet another lesson of wrong becoming right. Besides, we have to do *something* for fun around here.

Witness in Palestine

Israeli Attacked by Settlers

Monday, April 18, 2005

Yesterday I made the mistake of going to the dentist, one of my phobias. The fear aroused in me released a flood of emotions that had been building over the last few months. Out came feelings of anger and sorrow that I had been suppressing for fear that they might interfere with my work here. Out came uncertainties about my work based on reactions I've received from friends back home who feel my writing has become extremist, one-sided, and offensive. Criticism from friends is always hard for me to hear and has made me question what I'm doing here and whether my steps towards forming a more concrete and perhaps radical opinion about the situation here are doing more harm than good.

My worries and emotions have put me in somewhat of a daze, but today woke me up. I went to accompany farmers plowing in As-Sawiya with Rabbis for Human Rights. Yesterday several farmers were attacked on the village's land below the outpost. One of the victims was my friend's mother, the one who had welcomed me warmly, fed me, and told me her story. Hannah was present during the yesterday's incident and wrote about how the villagers, many of them back to plow on their land for the first time in 4 years, had gathered the courage to go that day because the army had promised them protection from settlers. But the soldiers came several hours late, by which time settlers had already come down, shoved and threatened the family, and kicked their donkey.

Today was calmer than yesterday; we didn't see any settlers, which was not surprising since there weren't many Palestinians either. Either the absent farmers had managed to finish their plowing already, or they were too scared to come back. We split up to accompany the few farmers who were present, but my group had little to do, so we sat under a tree to talk, rest, and wait. It was an interesting group: an elderly British man named John from Christian Peacemaker Teams, an Israeli activist in his forties named David, my friend Luna, and me. I began telling Luna about my recent insecurities about what I was doing, and pretty soon the four of us were engaged in a discussion about Zionism and the past 80 years of Israel/Palestine's history. John offered what struck me as a balanced account of the violence committed on both sides between the 1920s and 1970s, while David and Luna felt it was unproductive to focus on Arab violence because it was a reaction to the far greater crimes committed

A villager from As-Sawiya village points out Eli settlement across the valley. Settlers of Eli have raided the As-Sawiya's children's schools and physically attacked village farmers.

by early Zionists and the Israeli governments that followed. I found myself on John's side, saying that a massacre is a massacre, regardless of what was done to provoke it, and it's important to acknowledge the suffering on both sides, even if they are not equal.

We all agreed, though, that it was not useful to see the past and present as just "a complicated and ancient problem" that can only be resolved through mutual respect and understanding. Israel is a superpower, using the fourth strongest military in the world[94] and billions of American tax-dollars a year to occupy and colonize Palestinian land while denying Palestinians basic human rights and civil liberties. Israelis are certainly also suffering to the extent that they fear terrorist attacks, but their fear is incomparable to the suffering of those living under the constant threat of death, imprisonment, and losing their homes or livelihoods. I don't think it is useful or fair to equate the two, or to be "balanced" in speaking of the violence committed on both sides.

I used to take every opportunity to tell Palestinians that most soldiers are committing crimes because they are afraid, not because they are evil. I wanted Palestinians to understand the soldiers and other Israelis, to feel their pain and respect it. But I no longer believe that peace will come simply from mutual understanding and friendship. There's no harm in introducing Palestinians to sympathetic Jews and Israelis, but the burden is not on them to make peace and open their hearts. Peace and reconciliation will begin when the forgotten or ignored injustices and atrocities are acknowledged and dealt with justly.

At one point during our discussion under the olive tree, I realized that I had read about David before—he had been attacked in Yanoun village, the site of frequent settler violence and the place where I am headed tomorrow. David told me his story:

> After October 2002, it was clear that Yanoun needed a constant presence of internationals or Israelis. I stayed in the village with other Israeli activists for a whole month, and then some internationals came in our stead and we came up occasionally on Shabbat when settlers were most known to attack. One Saturday I learned that the two internationals in the village had been kidnapped by Avri Ran—an extremely dangerous and influential local settler with an almost cult following—and one of his followers. The internationals were stripped of their shoes and jackets in the pouring rain and made to march through the outpost on plant needles and rocks. They were then forced to lie on the ground face down in the mud for a long time before Avri finally let them go. When I met them 2 days later I learned that Avri had taken the camera of one international and thrown it on the ground near where they lay. It was a very expensive camera and I suggested that we go up to the outpost to try and find it. The army agreed to accompany us.
>
> We combed the area, but there was no sign of the camera. As we were leaving, I saw Avri and his friend approaching. I immediately stood between them and the internationals, thinking they might be more reluctant to hit me, a Jew, than the others. I was wrong. They beat me repeatedly with the butts of their rifles all over my body. The four soldiers who had accompanied us were a few meters away; they watched in silence. I tried to defend myself and remain standing but at one point Avri got me full on in the face, tearing my nose and crushing part of my skull. I cried out for the soldiers to help me but they were afraid. I was bleeding profusely.

---

[94] The International Institute of Strategic Studies estimated Israel's military strength to surpass that of all other countries except the US, the USSR, and China, *Time* (October 11, 1982); Some Israelis rank themselves third; As cited in Chomsky, *Fateful*, p. 6.

When Avri finally let me go the soldiers walked with me down to the village. The settlers continued to throw stones at me, and I tried to dodge them. I was in the hospital for some time and the next time I saw Avri and the soldiers was in court. The state was supposedly prosecuting Avri, but it didn't feel that way. Avri spoke with big eyes and words in a way that almost entranced the court. He is truly psychotic. He also must have amazing connections, because when I asked the prosecution about the photographs the army had taken of me and the other internationals after the incident he didn't know what I was talking about; apparently the army had lost the photos. One of the international witnesses had written a sworn affidavit about the incident, which was also mysteriously dismissed. The only witnesses were me and the soldiers. Three soldiers flat out lied, denying that Avri had done anything. Only one soldier corroborated my story, but the judge didn't believe him and let Avri off. Avri has killed people in the past and is likely to do it again. He is very dangerous, but the justice system and army are protecting him and his followers. Sometimes I think he'll come to Tel Aviv and kill me or my son because I have tried to expose him.

I watched David as he spoke, calmly and gently, smiling occasionally as he sat with his face in the sun. I couldn't imagine how anyone could ever want to hurt such a person. His scar is still visible along the left side of his nose, but he's otherwise fine and sound. I don't think I could recover from such a traumatic experience with the patience and courage that he has exhibited.

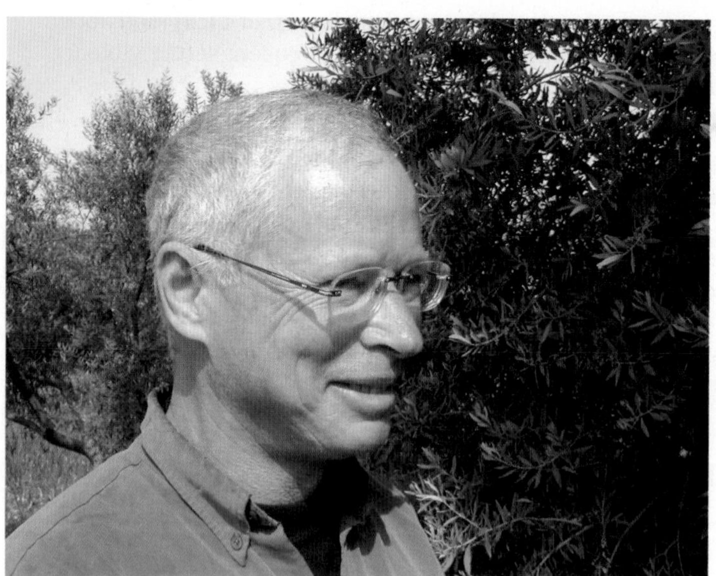

David, an Israeli activist who was beaten up by Israeli settlers in Yanoun village

David maintains close friendships with many of the villagers in Yanoun and was one of the first to hear about the most recent settler attack in Yanoun 5 days ago. According to David's sources, as night was falling four Palestinian men on a tractor were surrounded by six armed settlers who had dug a large hole and piled up the extra dirt next to it. The settlers asked the villagers if they had cell phones, and they said no. The settlers then made the Palestinians stand behind the dirt pile so that they would be invisible from the road. Night fell. Suddenly, one Palestinian's phone rang—he had lied—and he went to answer it. A settler charged him and destroyed the phone, but could not be sure if the caller had heard anything or not. The settler called another group and told them not to come to do what they had planned—he wanted to abort the mission. The four Palestinians ran off into the darkness as fast as possible, back to their village. They—and David—suspect the settlers intended to kill and bury them in the darkness, leaving no trace of what had happened. Maybe that phone call saved their lives.

© IWPS

A fundamentalist settler threatens a Palestinian farmer harvesting her olives.

It was horrible to hear David and his friends' stories, but it brought things into focus: my writing is extreme because what is going on around me is extreme. My opinions cannot remain uninfluenced by what I've seen—anyone who could remain neutral while witnessing such discrimination and injustice would have to be either amoral or insane. So I will admit to becoming increasingly radical, but I will not apologize for it. The nature of my writing is due to the reality it relates, not the way I wrote it.

Witness in Palestine
Back in Yanoun

Tuesday, April 19, 2005

I have just returned to Yanoun. I was here once before, and I would have liked it to be different this time, but it's not. Settler trailers still tower above the village in all directions, forming an almost unbroken chain that continues to choke the dwindling community of Palestinian farmers and shepherds. The nearest settlement, Itamar, is a full 4 miles away, but several of its illegal outposts are within a stone's throw of tiny Yanoun. Settlers in the area are known for their support for Kach, a Jewish extremist group sharing its origins with *Kahane Chai*. Illegal and underground since 1994 when member Baruch Goldstein massacred 29 Palestinians in Hebron, Kach advocates creating "conditions of a negative magnet that will bring the Arab population to prefer to emigrate." Translation: They'll do what they can to get the Palestinians out.

Sponsored by Israeli and US tax dollars, settlers have been coming down the hills into Yanoun for several years, terrorizing the local population in unimaginable ways.[95] Since a series of particularly violent attacks on farmers and their land forced inhabitants to flee in late 2002, there has been a constant international and/or Israeli activist presence in Yanoun. While the presence may be psychologically comforting to the families who have returned to their homes, it has not been fully effective at preventing settler raids and attacks, which continue to this day.

At night the bright lights of the outposts shine down on the quiet village. I am watching them glare down now, so harsh in the rural setting. I have just returned from dinner with old friends whom I remembered from last year: a young girl and her niece, both 11 years old. I recognized one immediately and they welcomed me into the house. Their mother, Um Hani, immediately invited me to stay for dinner and scolded me for buying vegetables in Aqraba that day when I should have known her home and food were mine as well. We took a walk around the house towards the fields, and the girls competed to see who could pick me the largest and juiciest cactus stem, a delicacy I had never tried before. They labored over the prickly skin and left me with the fruit.

Um Hani offered me a cup of tea. I asked that she make it without sugar, to which she replied, "Are you sick, too?" Um Hani, like many Palestinians, is diabetic. But she continues to cater to the sweet tooths of her husband and children. She eventually returned to cooking while I hung out with the girls outside. Suddenly an army jeep drove by with its lights on. My heart skipped a beat, but the girls remained unfazed. I guess children around here either live in constant fear, or become fearless.

Back at the International House, I have been reading letters and literature written by the settlers of Itamar and its outposts. It seems the settlers around here are nothing short of

---

[95] See pp. 43-46 for more information on the village's situation and history.

fanatics carrying out a violent campaign to ethnically cleanse the area of Palestinians. They believe that this land belongs to the Jews and always has, and that future generations of Israelis will look back on the settlers' sacrifices and struggles to "save their promised land" with pride and honor.

The villagers of Yanoun are also thinking about future generations. Many families have come back because they fear that if they leave now, neither they nor their children will ever be able to return. They do not want to repeat the mistake of their elders in 1948, many of whom evacuated for fear of being attacked, expecting to return home shortly. They were never allowed back, however, and now their homes lie buried under the state of Israel.

The settlers around Yanoun are something else. They are currently aiming to raise more than US$3.5 million for settlement "needs," such as bullet-proof cars, trained guard dogs, and a petting zoo. They have sent out appeals on the web; all donations to the settlement are tax-deductible for US tax-payers, another testimony to the marriage between right-wing settlers and the Israeli and American governments. The illegal outposts around Yanoun have already gone from nothing to being equipped with a water tower, a fish farm, concrete buildings, and electricity. Avri Ran, the infamous settler terrorist who beat up my Israeli friend David, has built an extensive free-range chicken farm and organic farm on the land he stole from villagers of Yanoun. He sells the chickens' eggs throughout Israeli with the "free-range" label. What a predicament for conscientious Israeli consumers: Should they support free-range chickens or free-range Palestinians?

I was supposed to come to Yanoun with a colleague, but a last-minute emergency kept her in Haris. So I am the only foreigner in the village. Normally this would not bother me; on the contrary, I enjoy being the only foreigner. But here, it means that I will be much less effective should anything happen, and I am also more vulnerable. If they would rip a fellow Israeli's nose apart, what would they do to me?

I am afraid. I am afraid that the settlers will come down to the village tonight and I will not be able to prevent or deter them. I am afraid they will beat me if I try to stop them, and I am afraid I will not be able to keep myself from confronting them. I am afraid, and yet I'm glad that I am here, and not safe at home watching television. I know I am where I am supposed to be, and something about the fear makes me feel present and alive.

Still, I am taking a gamble: I could get hurt, but I could also mean the difference between a situation escalating and calming down. Is this a gamble worth taking? Or am I as crazy as some people say I am? My friend Luna helped me answer these questions by setting me straight:

> Don't overestimate your importance in this struggle. Your presence is not helping end the Occupation in any significant way. But, here's my perspective: I gave up on world peace a long time ago. Humanity is doomed, one way or another. The question is, where do I want to be on the sinking ship? I can't live a normal life knowing that this injustice is going on and I could have been here as a witness and a worker, small as my role may be. So that's my answer: I hate this, but I'm so grateful to be here.

I have a bit more optimism left in me than Luna, but otherwise her words echo my sentiments. I'm here because I could not stand to be anywhere else.

Witness in Palestine
Young Men Targeted for Arrest

Bulldozers raze Saffa and Bil'in land in preparation for the Wall.

Thursday, April 21, 2005

Well, I made it back from Yanoun and then through my toughest day yet in Palestine alive—just barely. Yesterday I went down to Saffa, where the village council had invited internationals and Israelis to document recent destruction in the area. Our small group walked the short way from the village to the bulldozers and then along the path, commenting on the irony of our privilege to approach the threatened trees, while their owners would risk being shot or arrested if they came half as close. We stopped to rest in an olive grove along our hike, and three soldiers approached us to ask what we were doing. Actually, they wanted to know what the two Palestinians with us were doing and demanded to see their IDs. They wrote down the ID numbers. I asked if our friends would be punished for going to their land; the soldier ignored me.

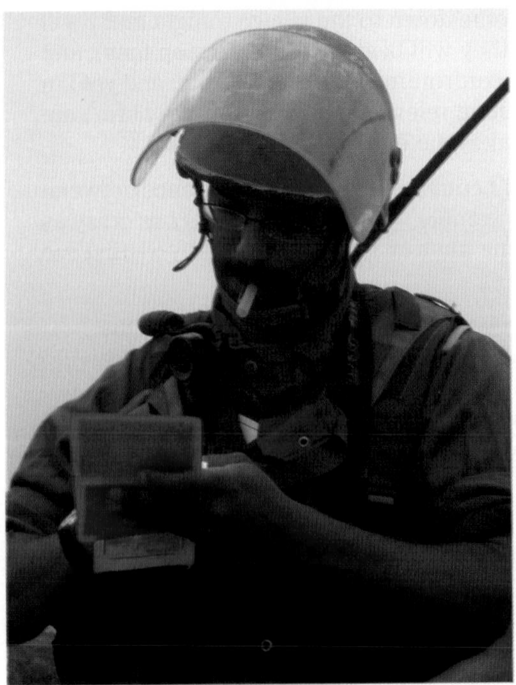

A soldier takes note of which Palestinians were showing internationals around the Wall construction in the village. Sometimes being on a list is all it takes to be harassed, interrogated, or imprisoned.

Our group walked solemnly back to the village where we found a standoff between the young boys throwing stones and the army shooting rubber bullets and tear gas into the village. We didn't know how it had started, but it was clear that neither side wanted to back down. The young boys wanted the soldiers out of their village, and the soldiers wanted the boys to stop throwing stones towards the army.[96] I understood the village boys' dilemma: if they were the first to back down, the army would have succeeded in declaring their land a "closed military zone," that is, off-limits to Palestinians.

I found it harder to understand the soldiers who kept yelling at me and my Israeli friends to move out of the way so they could shoot at the boys. Obviously, if the soldiers really wanted the kids to stop throwing stones, they would just leave the village. This wasn't a demonstration; these were kids who ran out of their houses when they saw the soldiers coming. The soldiers were trying to show the boys who was in charge.

Things started to become very heated, and two Israeli activists stepped out into the path of crossfire to deter the soldiers from shooting. The young soldiers were noticeably annoyed. The village boys stopped throwing stones so that the two Israelis would not be hurt. After a brief conversation with the activists, the soldiers turned to leave, and the village youth let out a great cheer. They felt they had won (they've got some macho in them, too). Several young boys began to throw stones as the soldiers left, until they were out of sight. But they never got out of sight. They got mad. The soldiers ran back towards the village and started shooting wildly. I instinctively ran into the area of crossfire and began waving my hands in the air and screaming as loud as I could, "Don't shoot!" A bullet flew over my head and hit a branch above me. Several leaves fell on my head. My heart skipped a beat and I choked back a sob.

Most of the young men ran away as the soldiers approached, except for a gutsy few who continued throwing stones. One waited too long, and a soldier jumped out from the side and grabbed him around his neck, pulling him away. His face turned bright red and I was afraid he would choke. The soldiers then left quickly with the young man, having gotten what they wanted; now *they* had won.

As soon as villagers realized what had happened, they started to scream, running after the soldiers en masse. A woman who had been watching from her house ran out onto the balcony and began to wail. It was her nephew who had been led away by the soldiers. The woman, her sister, and all the young men ran after the captured villager until another group of soldiers stopped them from going any further. The group watched, horrified, as their friend stumbled to keep up with the soldier dragging him by his neck, until he was behind the trees and out of sight.

The crying women would not be held back. They pushed their way past the soldiers—who are in general far more tolerant of aggressive women than confrontational men—and I followed. We ran down a steep path and slid off a steep drop onto the path of the Wall, where the young man was being held on the ground with his hands tied behind his back. His name was Mohammed. The women ran to him, and began prying the soldiers' hands off him, trying to free him from their grip. The soldier in charge told the women to leave, and one woman responded by kissing his hand and begging him to let Mohammed go. Mohammed yelled at his aunt to leave. I didn't know why until he turned his head and I saw

[96] I use the word "towards" instead of "at" because, as I've mentioned before, stone throwers rarely get close enough to soldiers to actually hit them.

Saffa villagers and an Israeli activist appeal to an Israeli soldier to free Mohammed, a villager who was captured for throwing stones at the army when jeeps drove into his village.

that he could not bear to hear her cry. His strong face had broken into tears at the sight of her.

I asked the soldiers what they were doing, and they said Mohammed was being arrested. I asked why, and they said "for throwing stones." I saw one sensitive-looking soldier and pulled him aside. "Look, I know this young man was throwing stones, and I know that's scary for you, but you have to understand that you are invaders in his village, protecting the people stealing his land. How would you react if someone came into your house with a gun and started carrying out your TV, and then your stereo, and then your bed? Wouldn't you throw a lamp at him or something?"

The soldier listened to me, and I appreciated that. But then another soldier told him to stop talking to me and to take Mohammed into the jeep. I stood in front of the jeep doors, holding on to them to physically prevent the soldier and captured villager from entering. I continued speaking: "Please think about what you're doing. You have the power to let him go or to ruin his life. Do you really think imprisoning him is going to prevent the boys from throwing stones in the future? What are you trying to accomplish?" The more aggressive soldier came from the side and yanked me out of the way. The soldier and Mohammed got into the jeep.

I went around to the side to keep talking and I saw Mohammed's face. He was covered in sweat, miserable, hopeless. I asked him what his full name was, and wrote it down for the arrest report. Then I asked him if he wanted me to deliver any message to his parents, and he just looked down. I felt like a jerk. Just for being there, for witnessing his humiliation and despair.

Several more Israeli activists began to approach, and I asked one of them to translate for me because two of the soldiers said they didn't speak any English. The activist said it wasn't any use, but I insisted, perhaps more for my sake than anyone else's. I turned to the soldier in the passenger's seat: "Do you think this young man is a threat to Israeli security?" He nodded.

"So you think that imprisoning this young man will secure Israel?" He nodded again.

I pointed towards his family sitting and crying nearby: "How do you think this will affect them? Do you think his brothers and cousins will grow up to be suicide bombers or peacemakers?"

The soldier understood my point, but he didn't want to hear it or respond. As he shut the door in my face, I hurried, "You've got one guy, but you're making 1,000 more enemies—." The driver started the engine of the jeep, and my friend and I ran in front of it, refusing to move. I gave my card of digital photographs from that day to another friend in

Saffa villagers watch as soldiers prepare to take away a young man from their community.

case I was arrested. We agreed we weren't moving until Mohammed was released. The driver stopped the engine, annoyed, and got out. I could see Mohammed's family watching. I could see the sensitive soldier reflecting. Several soldiers were discussing something.

After several minutes, my Israeli friend Kobi called me over away from the soldiers and we turned around to watch together. The soldiers were opening the back door and out came Mohammed. A soldier untied his hands and handed him back his ID. The women watching behind me stood up slowly with joy and amazement. Mohammed walked quickly and calmly back to his family who smothered him with kisses. On the way he looked over to me and mouthed the word, "*Toda*," meaning "Thank you" in Hebrew—He thought I was Israeli. We both smiled.

Appeals by villagers, Israeli activists, and internationals succeed in getting Mohammed released.

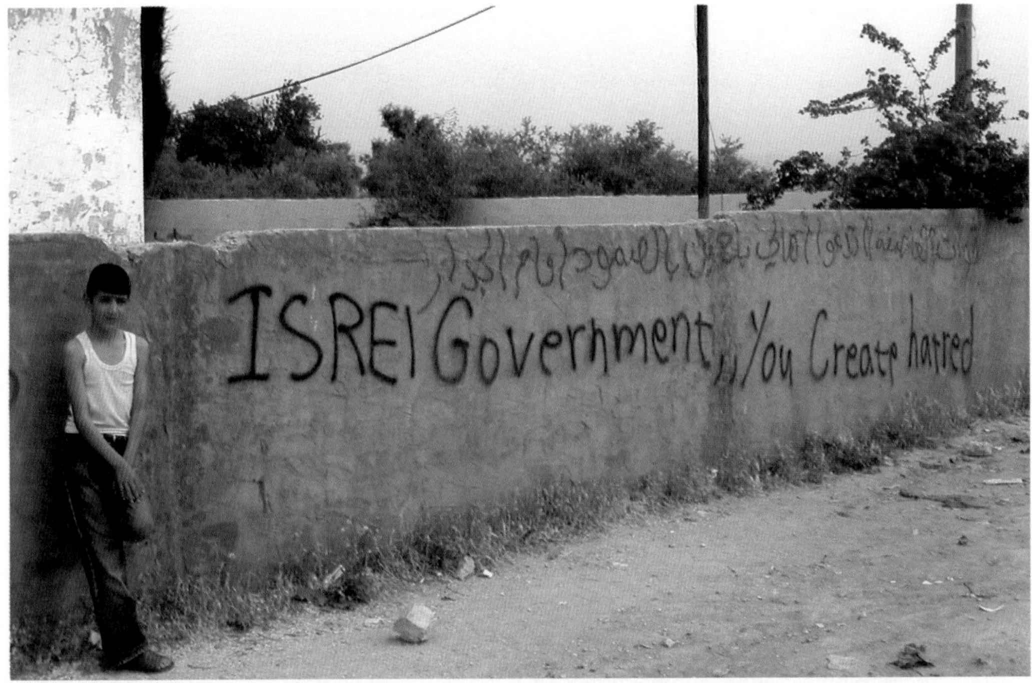

Graffiti in Bil'in village, a center of popular nonviolent resistance against the Occupation

Mohammed walked up to the village ahead of us, and before long I heard an incredible cheer erupt in the village. He was home. I allowed myself a moment of happiness at the drop of victory amidst an ocean of defeats, but I was sobered up soon enough.

After a cup of tea, we were on the way to a demonstration in nearby Bil'in, where eight people had already been shot with rubber bullets,[97] including one Israeli and one journalist. Nobody was seriously injured, but then the protest was still young.

The demonstration had started out as a children's parade of young girls and boys marching with banners, but by the time we arrived only one young boy remained. He was building a roadblock by himself out of odds and ends in the village, hoping it would prevent the army from raiding his village that night. He was too young to realize it, but he was practicing creative nonviolent resistance.

As I watched the boy, my eyes began to sting. Tear gas. I squatted down, covering my face. A man nearby yelled at me not to touch my eyes with my fingers—he said I was only pushing it in further. He was more experienced than I at being gassed. And he was right. I recovered and decided I was ready to go home.

Then suddenly a jeep pulled up in front of us and out jumped two soldiers who ran into the forest where the young boys had regrouped. Within seconds, the soldiers re-emerged pulling another young man, this one bigger and more resistant than the boy in Saffa. I rushed towards them, and the man began to tell me that he didn't know what was happening, that he hadn't done anything wrong. He asked me to help him. I recognized the soldiers from Saffa and suspected that this was another attempt at "winning" the game—if

---

97 Rubber bullets are normal bullets with a thin coat of rubber around them. They are easily capable of killing someone, despite their name.

Soldiers drag away Fadi to be arrested.

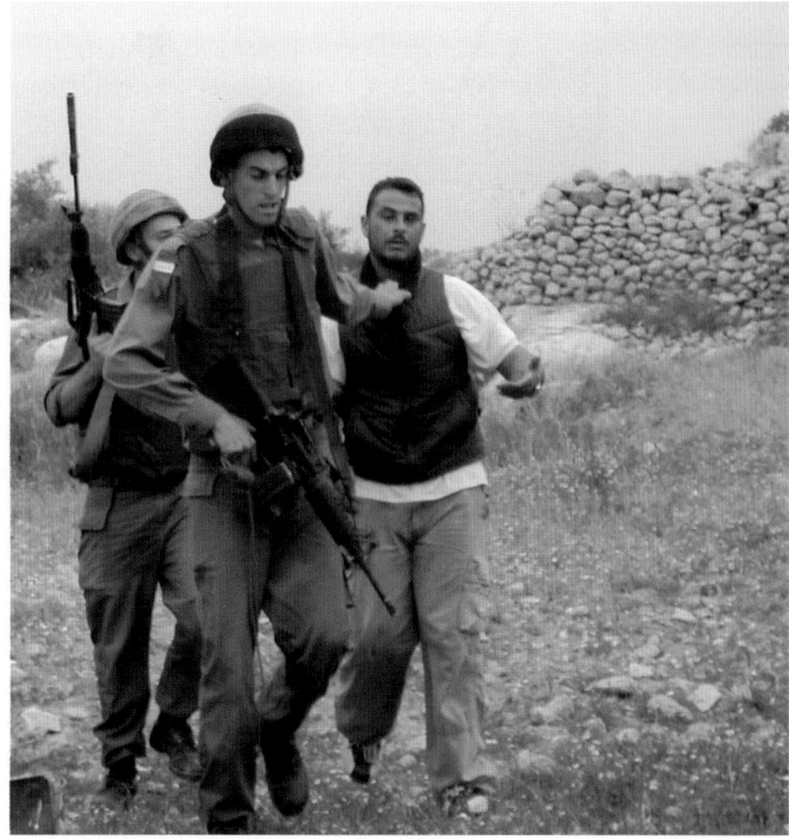

the young man had been "wanted," they wouldn't be hunting him during a stone-throwing standoff.

I instinctively threw myself between the young man and the soldier who was holding him by his neck. I tried to position myself in such an awkward way that the soldier would have to stop walking or it would hurt me. It worked. Kobi came next to me and began to use his body to separate the young man from the standing soldiers, meanwhile talking to them in Hebrew. The soldiers held on tight, and the man's face turned redder as the grip around his neck tightened. He yelled out, and in a burst of energy somehow ripped himself away, freed for a few seconds. This was his chance.

A soldier was about to lunge for him so I grabbed the soldier's arm and screamed, "Run!" I don't know what came over me. But the young man ran. The soldier shook me loose after a few moments and began to chase the young man, who was running like crazy, so scared that he didn't look where he was going.

In his path lay a cliff several meters high, separating one terrace of olive trees from another. In his frenzy, he didn't realize the depth of the cliff and ran off it, knocking his head against a sharp branch and falling—hard, on his back, onto a huge rock. Everyone froze.

The young man began to release an almost inhuman moan. I ran to the cliff's edge and looked over to find him lying spread eagle with blood all over his face. I turned around and scaled down the cliff and knelt in front of him. I heard his friend say that everything was going to be okay. I repeated the encouragement, although I was not so optimistic. I asked the injured young man his name, and he responded, "Fadi." I sat with him until a medical team arrived and took him away on a stretcher with the help of several villagers and Israeli activists. When he was gone I realized that the army was gone, too. One look at him over the cliff's edge and they had left, as stunned as the rest of us.

Fadi is taken away on a stretcher after falling from a cliff while attempting to flee soldiers.

I was sure Fadi would be paralyzed, if not worse. I looked down at my hand that he had grabbed in desperation. Now would he spend the rest of his life in a wheelchair? I tried to remember the feeling of joy I had experienced just a few hours before, but it was gone. I needed to see Fadi, to make sure he was all right. I hitched a ride with Fadi's cousin to the hospital in Ramallah, and 30 minutes later we were rushing into the emergency room. We found Fadi all bandaged up, but conscious and standing with help. He smiled when he saw me come in. I asked how he was and he closed his eyes, "*Alhamdulillah*," implying that he was all right.

I asked his father standing near his bedside what the doctors had said, and he repeated, "*Alhamdulillah.*" Fadi was pretty banged up but he was going to be okay. I asked where it hurt and he pointed to his leg. I asked about his back and head, and he pointed to an open wound on the latter where he said a bullet had grazed the bridge between his eyebrows. Had I missed a gunshot in the chaos or was he embellishing the tale? My answer was the same regardless, "*Alhamdulillah*": "Thank God." He smiled again.

Sick Man Detained at Huwwara Checkpoint

Friday, April 22, 2005

After saying goodbye to Fadi and his family yesterday, I took a shared taxi to Zatara checkpoint where I received a call that a sick man named Jaber was being held at Huwwara checkpoint a few miles north. When I arrived I found Jaber and his wife waiting in the dark in a detention area next to the checkpoint. Jaber was clutching his stomach and coughing violently. When Jaber's wife saw me, she sprang up and called out that her husband was very sick. I learned that he had been hospitalized in Nablus for over a week for serious chest and stomach problems, and he was on his way home to his village shortly after noon when the soldiers stopped them at the checkpoint. It was past 10 p.m. when I arrived. The couple had been held waiting for 9 and a half hours

Jaber looked like he was ready to pass out. The soldiers manning the checkpoint yelled at me to stop talking to the detainees, but I ignored them. One soldier came over and asked who I was. I answered that I was a friend of the wife's uncle (which is true) and that I had come when I heard her sick husband had been held without explanation or charge for more than 9 hours. I asked the soldier why they were holding him so long, and he said he'd tell me alone, away from Jaber and his family.

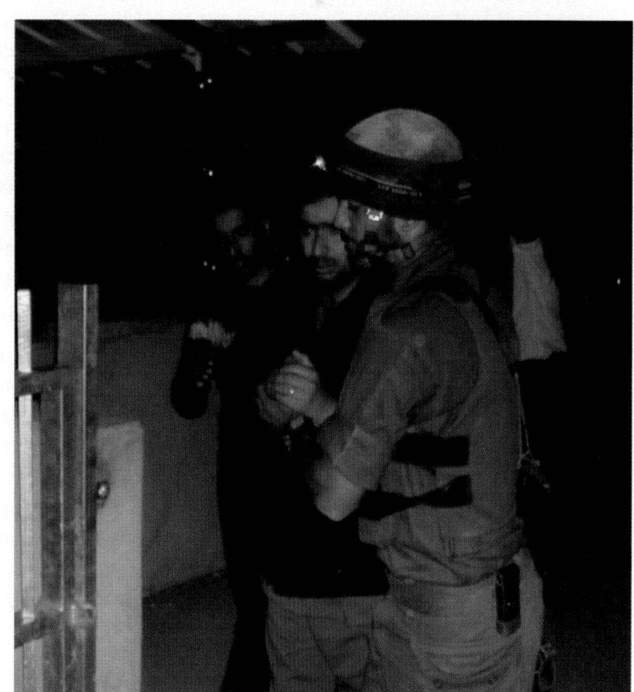

Jaber is arrested after being detained for 10 hours at Huwwara checkpoint.

I told the soldier that I would not leave my friends and that I was afraid to talk to him alone. I said his gun and illegitimate power in the situation made me uncomfortable. I think it's not a bad idea to remind soldiers that they are the biggest threat to my safety in the West Bank, after the settlers. They commit far more crimes in the area than Palestinians and have caused more serious injury to internationals than anyone else

The soldier said he didn't know why Jaber was being held but he was sure it was for a good reason. I was unconvinced. Meanwhile, Jaber had keeled over and was coughing. His wife was near hysterics. I told the soldiers that Jaber needed a doctor, and they responded by saying they were taking him away. Jaber's wife began to cry. I stepped in front of Jaber and his wife to block the soldiers, who were coming with handcuffs. A relative asked if it was really necessary to handcuff a man in such agony, and they agreed not to. They pushed me and Jaber's wife aside and threw him into a jeep. Jaber's brother, who was standing with us, told me to let it go, that it was too late now. We all walked back to the car in silence except for Jaber's wife, who continued to sob.

As we were walking away, two soldiers started chuckling and I turned to them, "Don't tell me you think this is funny." One soldier yelled out to me, "You're just a little girl. You can't do anything." I turned and yelled, "I'm older than you, asshole" and felt ashamed immediately. It was the first time I had sworn in front of Palestinian friends. I apologized and they forgave me instantly. They thanked me repeatedly, which made me feel uncomfortable; this time I hadn't been able to help, and for all we knew Jaber was on his way to interrogation.

I called the army's humanitarian office for information, but as usual their "army" side was more pronounced than their "humanitarian" one. They would not tell us why Jaber was arrested, nor why he had been held at Huwwara for so long, nor when he would be able to contact his family. They knew, but they wouldn't tell. I told them that where I come from you aren't supposed to hold people without charge. I asked if Jaber had a lawyer and they didn't understand the question. Most Palestinians don't get lawyers or a fair trial; the army rules according to its best interests.

Jaber's family and I drove together to the home of Jaber's parents-in-law in Marda, where we drank tea under the moon. After perhaps the longest day of my life, it was finally time to go to sleep, but somehow I wasn't tired anymore. I just sat there, thinking, watching the tired but resilient faces around me. One belonged to a good friend who invited me to stay the night with his family. I accepted. When I woke up the next morning, he announced that the family was throwing me a going-away party. I refused, but he insisted.

It is moving to know that I will be missed, and I am already wondering not if but when I will be back here. The truth is, I may be leaving Palestine in a week, but mentally I won't be leaving Palestine for a long time. I know how hard it will be to readjust to "normal" life and social interactions—most people don't want to talk or think about the atrocities that are being supported by their own government and permitted by their own apathy or inaction. Politically straightforward dialogue can be very socially awkward, and I know it will be a while before I can relate to most Western people of privilege in a normal way.

But the readjustment is not what scares me most. What I dread above all lies after I adjust, when I begin to—forget. I know it will happen. Of course I will keep Palestine in the back of my mind, but at the forefront will be my job, my boyfriend, and all the daily trivia that prevents most people from doing more to help those in need. And once I've slipped back into my ordinary way of doing things, what will make me different from the Israeli soldiers who serve because refusing would be too costly? I find inaction appalling in others, but most of all in myself. After all, like those Israeli soldiers and inactive citizens, or the Germans who remained silent during the atrocities in World War II, those with power and privilege are always, to some degree, responsible for that which they could help prevent but choose not to.

Jewish Emancipation & Palestinian Imprisonment

Sunday, April 24, 2005

Friday night we hosted our first official IWPS Passover *seder*[98] in Palestine. Passover, a Jewish holiday celebrating self-determination and freedom from oppression, never meant much to me in the past, but this time was different. We invited Palestinian neighbors, Israeli activists, and other internationals to celebrate with us, and also to mourn the brutal oppression that continues today. Hannah handed out copies of an alternative *Haggadah*,[99] including the "10 plagues of the Occupation" in addition to the traditionally-referenced ten plagues inflicted upon the Egyptians by God.[100]

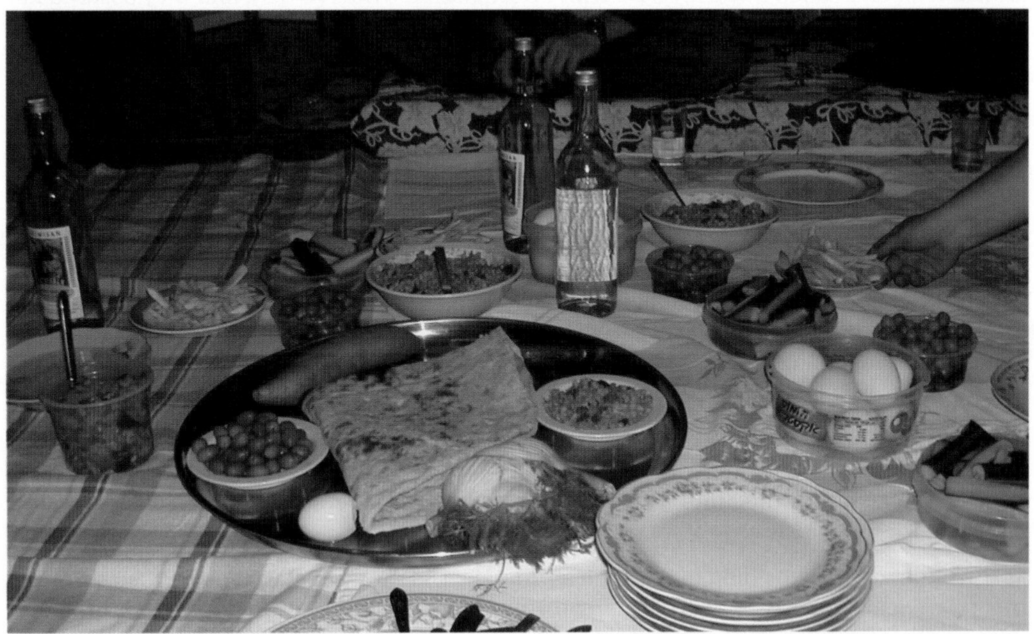

IWPS's Passover Seder plate included a Palestinian twist: taboun (Palestinian flatbread) instead of matzoh, fennel instead of maror, and olives to symbolize freedom, peace, and economic security.

[98] A *seder* is a Jewish ritural feast on the first evening of Passover.

[99] The *Haggadah* is the book traditionally read aloud during the first nights of Passover. It recounts the story of Jews enslaved by Egypt's Pharoah and then liberated following a series of plagues inflicted upon the Egyptians by God. The alternative *Haggadah* we used was based on the "Love and Justice in Times of War *Haggadah* Zine" by Micah Bazant and Dara Silverman, available at *colours.mahost.org/events/haggadah.html*

[100] The 10 plagues of the Occupation of Palestine: Home Demolitions, Uprooting Olive Trees, Blockades and Checkpoints, Destruction of Villages, Administrative Detention, the Wall, Theft of Resources, False Democracy, Erasing Histories, and War Crimes.

It was hard for our Palestinian friends to understand how any Jews could justify oppressing another people when they have suffered so much in the past. My friends knew the biblical story of Exodus better than I did—it's in the Koran—and we enjoyed comparing stories and interpretations. We talked about the past and the future, we sang songs about freedom, and we ate a lot of good food. The meal had a Palestinian twist to it: taboun (Palestinian flatbread) instead of matzoh, fennel instead of maror, and olives on the Seder plate to symbolize freedom, peace, and economic security.

Shortly after the Seder ended, there was a knock at the door. It was the sister and cousin of Jaber, the sick man whose arrest I had witnessed the night before. They were in tears, desperate to know of his condition. I had called the army's "humanitarian" office earlier that day to learn that Jaber had been seen by one of the army doctors, who are infamous for ignoring injuries and illnesses if doing so protects or facilitates the work of the army. The doctor's diagnosis: "sensitivity in the chest and heart pain, but medical condition does not bar arrest." That was all.

I called Physicians for Human Rights, who had already heard of the case. They said the doctor's diagnosis was bogus, and when pushed, the doctor admitted that Jaber had a stomach ulcer. I called the army's District Coordination Office (DCO), and they assured me that Jaber was receiving the proper medication: ulcer pills and lots of water. They said they were positive he was being properly cared for and told me to stop calling them. They even had someone from the prison call me to say Jaber was fine and well. I asked to talk to him and was told that that was out of the question.

When I told Jaber's family that he had an ulcer, they were very confused. This was not at all the diagnosis given by the Nablus doctor in whose care Jaber had been during the past week in the hospital. We called the Nablus doctor, who informed us that Jaber didn't have a stomach ulcer at all; he had meningitis.

We began to make phone calls. The DCO was annoyed to hear from us again and assured me that the army knew of Jaber's meningitis and was caring for him accordingly. "That's the same thing you said about him being treated for an ulcer," I replied. "Meningitis is a lot more serious. And it's contagious. Have they been giving him ulcer pills? He should be in a hospital, not a prison. The doctor in Nablus had released him only because he thought he could heal at home in bed—"

The official interrupted me. "He's fine! I promise. I have personally verified it. Now stop calling us!"

I wondered how he could make such a promise. Did he really know? This was too much of a risk. "Security threats" were usually tortured under interrogation during their first few days under custody, not nursed in bed.

Jaber's sister Samea was also suspicious. She said he had been arrested over 10 years ago and thrown into jail for 9 months. He had been a student at Bir Zeit University at the time, the most prestigious university in Palestine, and noted Palestinian scholar Edward Said's alma mater. She said young Jaber had been innocent, but they had tortured him until he confessed to something. His crime: they said "he was nationalistic and had the intention to do nationalistic actions." What does that even mean? Apparently it meant they could keep him as long as they wanted.

Samea asked if she could see the pictures of his arrest. When I showed her the first one on my computer screen, she began to cry. In it, you could see Jaber's face, on the verge of tears and passing out as the soldier dragged him to the jeep. I closed the picture quickly, regretting having opened it.

Palestinian actors in Al-Far'a refugee camp role-play the interrogation frequently accompanied by torture in Israeli prisons.

Samea said she had lost many people in her life but nothing this painful or out of the blue. She said she couldn't understand it. He had no political ties. He passed through many checkpoints every day to get to work at the Ministry of Finance in Ramallah, and he had never been stopped before. But Jaber's wife said a soldier had Jaber's number written on his hand when the couple arrived at Huwwara checkpoint—they were waiting for him. Someone, somewhere, must have given his name. That's all the army needs to hold people indefinitely.

Hannah and I decided to put out a call to action, asking Israelis to call the prison or DCO to demand that Jaber see a real doctor and receive genuine medical care. Israeli groups forwarded the appeal to their mailing lists around the world. The result was amazing: people began to call *en masse*. Since the prison didn't pick up, the DCO's phone line was flooded with calls from over 10 different countries. Each caller demanded that the prisoner named Jaber who was suffering from meningitis receive proper medical attention. The DCO staff was irate, but they were left with no choice. With the spotlight on them from around the world they couldn't afford to risk Jaber's life. Jaber was finally transferred to an Israeli hospital, and as luck would have it, the Jewish doctors were all on leave for Passover so his physician was a Palestinian with Israeli citizenship. That meant Jaber not only had a doctor, but one he could communicate with!

My colleague Hannah went to visit Jaber in the hospital. Here is an excerpt from her report:

> His room was not difficult to find, since it was the only one with a closed door and two armed soldiers sitting outside.... They would not let us enter, but we were able to talk to the doctor, who had not yet received any information about Jaber's prior medical situation. He seemed frustrated with the army's reluctance to share information. The doctor told us he had just done a spinal tap and would soon determine Jaber's illness.... The viral meningitis diagnosis was confirmed an hour later...
>
> When we entered [his room] Jaber was sleeping. I said his name softly and he opened his eyes and gave a little moan. I introduced myself, and he greeted me with the customary, "*Ahlan w'sahlan* (Welcome)." He started to come to his senses [and said he was] tired,

> and sick.... He kept saying "*Biddi amoot*," which could be translated as "I want to die" or "I'm going to die." I'm not sure which he meant. Maybe both.
>
> He said the doctor was good, but [that] if he's taken back to Salem detention center they might as well shoot him. He was in tears as he told us he hadn't eaten, drunk, or slept in 3 days. In Salem, he said, they threw him in a small cell with nine other people, and did not let anyone out to go to the bathroom from nine at night until nine in the morning. He spent the next 2 days on the floor in pain (there were no beds), where he said it was extremely cold at night. He told us he lost consciousness four times, but didn't sleep at all. Nobody spoke with him while he was there, so if there is to be any interrogation, it has not yet begun.
>
> He told us to lift up the blanket covering his feet, and we saw the metal cuffs on his ankles.... He was too weak to sit up or feed himself, and two armed guards sat outside his room, but he had to be shackled?! While Susy spoke to the soldier [about the shackles], I dialed Jaber's wife's number. She picked up and I quickly said, "Hi Khulud, I'm with Jaber, hold on..." and handed him the phone. They talked for a few minutes before the soldiers [forced him to hang up].... Jaber handed me the phone, thanked me, and smiled for the only time all day.

So the DCO was lying after all. They never personally verified Jaber's condition, and Jaber wasn't even given the water that the army was told was most crucial to his recovery. Now Jaber is getting food, but it's only a matter of time before he's taken back into custody at Salem.

Jaber's story is tragic, but far from unique. According to *Amnesty International*, Israel violates international human rights standards in its treatment of Palestinian prisoners in various ways, including police brutality, denial of access to a lawyer,[101] and refusal of bail.[102] Perhaps most serious is Israel's torture of Palestinian prisoners, a practice that *Human Rights Watch* found so widespread that "Israel's political leadership cannot claim ignorance that ill-treatment is the norm in interrogation centers. The number of victims is too large, and the abuses are too systematic."[103] Tens of thousands of Palestinians were "tortured or severely ill-treated while under interrogation" during the First Intifada alone.[104] About 20 Palestinian detainees mysteriously died under interrogation and detention during the same period.[105] According to *B'tselem*, "nearly 50% of interrogations end up with no charges being pressed, or any other steps taken against the detainee."

Methods of torture include covering prisoners' faces with hoods or blindfolds, hanging them by their wrists for long periods, sexual assault, electric shock, and "binding the detainee's hands to his legs so that his body is bent backward ... exposed and vulnerable to

---

[101] Attorney of Law Jonathan Kuttab reports that "in 98% of the cases, lawyers cannot see Palestinian clients until after they 'confess,' and judges will accept the 'confession' at face value," even if the confession is written in Hebrew, a language unknown to the suspect, and elicited after threats, psychological pressure, and torture; *Associated Press* (February 28, 1988); As cited in Chomsky, *Fateful*, p. 484.

[102] "Israel and the Occupied Territories: Mass Arrests and Police Brutality," *Amnesty International* (2000).

[103] "Torture and Ill-Treatment: Isreal's Interrogation of Palestinians from the Occupied Territories," *Human Rights Watch* (1994); As cited in *The Origin of the Palestine-Israel Conflict, published by Jews for Justice in the Middle East*, third edition, p. 28. *www.cactus48.com*

[104] "Israel's Interrogation of Palestinians from the Occupied Territories," *Human Rights Watch* (New York, 1994), pp. x, 4; As cited in Finkelstein, *Chutzpah*, p. 156.

[105] Finkelstein, *Chutzpah*, p. 161.

© Morshid Graib

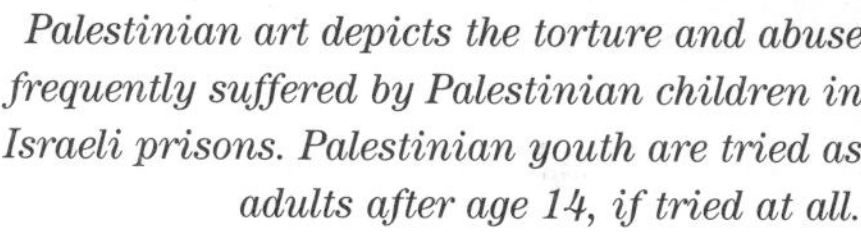

Palestinian art depicts the torture and abuse frequently suffered by Palestinian children in Israeli prisons. Palestinian youth are tried as adults after age 14, if tried at all.

the blows of the interrogators ... on the face, the chest, the testicles, the stomach, in fact on all parts of the body."[106] The *San Francisco Chronicle* reported one case in which the Israeli abusers "took photographs of themselves with their victims, holding their heads by the hair like hunting trophies," just one of many such incidents according to Israeli human rights workers.[107]

Female prisoners report additional kinds of abuse. Pregnant inmates have been forced to give birth with handcuffs on.[108] Some female prisoners are arrested, humiliated, and photographed as a means of putting pressure on their husbands.[109]

Palestinian child prisoners also consistently report being tortured, as well as intimidated, insulted, sexually harassed, and deprived of education and family visits.[110] Just a few weeks ago, a 16-year-old Palestinian from Jerusalem who was released from detention said that "Israeli investigators tied his testicles to a thread and pulled it strongly,

---

[106] "The Interrogation of Palestinians during the Intifada: Ill-treatment, "Moderate Physical Pressure" or Torture?" *B'tselem* (Jerusalem, March 1991), pp. 27-32.; As cited in Finkelstein, *Chutzpah*, pp. 142-146.

[107] Rachelle Marshall, "The Peace Process Ends in Protests and Blood," *Washington Report on Middle East Affairs* (December, 2000); As cited in *The Origin of the Palestine-Israel Conflict*, published by Jews for Justice in the Middle East, third edition, p. 32. *www.cactus48.com*

[108] Their newborns become the youngest Palestinian child prisoners, some going years never having seen the outside of a prison.

[109] "Palestinian Women Political Prisoners," *Addameer* (2005). *www.addameer.org/detention/women.html*

[110] "Palestinian Children Political Prisoners," *Addameer* (2005). *www.addameer.org/detention/children.html*

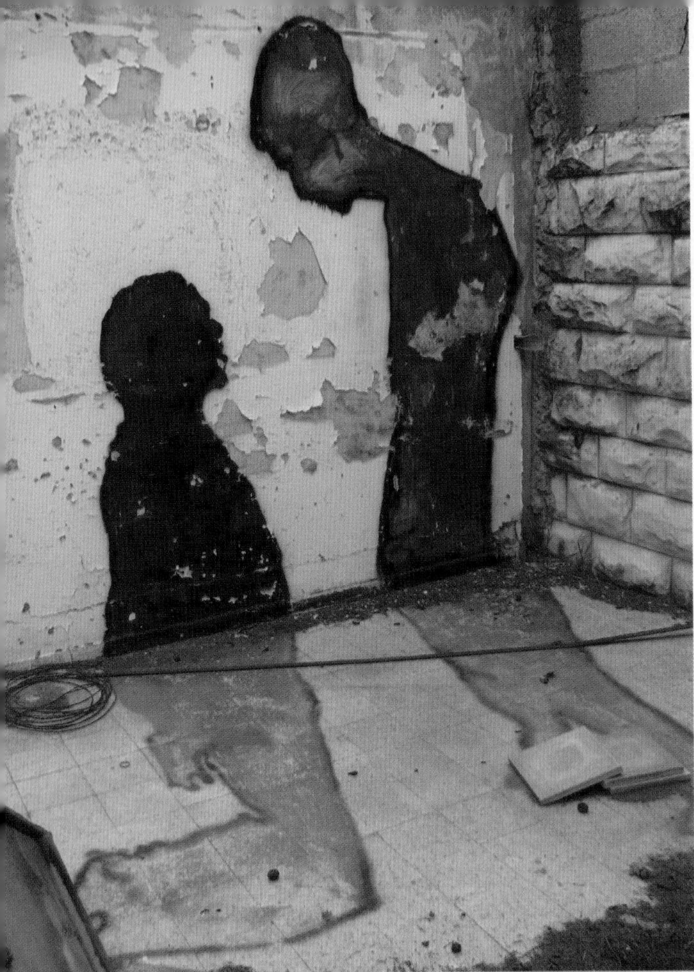

Shadows painted by Palestinians on an old prison wall portray the abuse of Palestinian inmates that is commonplace in Israeli prisons.

causing severe pains. He added that they used him as an ashtray, putting [out] their cigarettes on his skin, and that he was deprived of sleep, movement and using the toilet." The testimony came after three Israeli border guards confessed to forcing a group of Palestinian minors to eat sand and kiss their boots after being detained for not carrying their IDs.[111]

Amnesty also cites Israel's lack of effective investigation following incidents of torture of abuse by soldiers: "More than 80% of investigations of [Palestinians'] complaints relating to [Israeli] police violence are closed." The power to close investigations lies with the army, the very organization being investigated.[112] In a 2001 report, *B'tselem* put the percentage of Palestinian complaints effectively ignored higher at 100%: "All the investigation files were closed with no action taken."[113]

There are soldiers in every army who abuse their power; I don't say that Israelis are worse than most (although rarely are the abusers lauded abroad as "the most moral army in the world"). The first problem is that Israeli soldiers have no right to be in the West Bank and Gaza, yet the armed 18-year-olds enjoy virtually unchecked power over millions of people. The second problem is that Israel has institutionalized these abuses and failed to investigate complaints or allow impartial observers.

Luckily, people are watching. Each person who called the DCO on Jaber's behalf last week made an appeal on behalf of justice for prisoners—and it worked! The abuses are many, but so are we.

---

[111] "Israeli soldiers force Palestinian minors to eat sand," *Al Jazeera Magazine Online Edition* (April 7, 2005).

[112] "Israel and the Occupied Territories: Mass Arrests and Police Brutality," *Amnesty International* (November 2000).

[113] "Standard Routine: Beatings and Abuse of Palestinians by Israeli Security Forces during the Al-Aqsa Intifada," *B'tselem* (Jerusalem, 2001); As cited in Finkelstein, *Chutzpah*, p. 166.

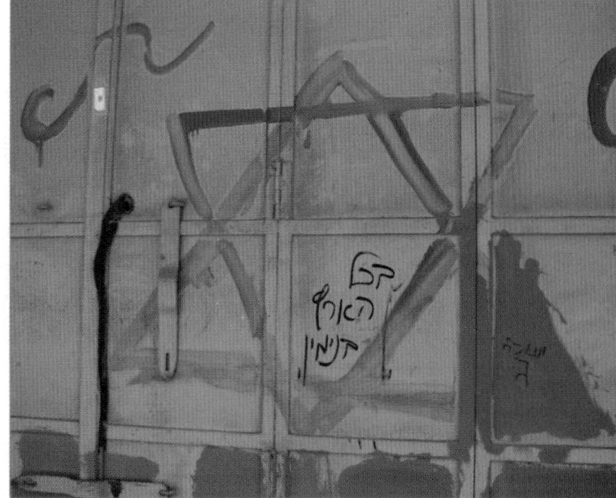

Star of David: Settlers and soldiers frequently exploit the traditional symbol of Judaism as they violate Palestinians' rights, making it remarkable how many Palestinians retain positive feelings towards the Jewish people and Judaism.

Monday, April 25, 2005

This week the army has imposed closure for Palestinians all over the West Bank so that soldiers can go home to celebrate Passover with their families. This means that Muslim and Christian Palestinians, who don't celebrate the holiday, are generally unable to get to work, school, the hospital, or to visit their own families. Settlers, however, are exempt from the closure and are allowed to travel as before.

It is often the case that restrictions on Palestinians heighten during Jewish holidays. Last fall, the army cancelled (not postponed) two of its three designated days to "guard" farmers picking olives in As-Sawiya village because the days that the army had chosen overlapped with *Sukkot*, the Jewish festival celebrating—ironically—the harvest. Settler attacks are also more common on Shabbat, when religious settlers don't work or go to school.

It's so tragic that Jewish days of celebration and rest have translated into extra hardship for Palestinians. Israel's lack of accommodation for people with other beliefs certainly does not raise respect for Judaism in the eyes of people whose exposure to Jews already consists almost entirely of soldiers and settlers upholding an unjust system. Faced with persistent human rights violations and land confiscation by self-proclaimed Jewish representatives flaunting the Star of David,[114] and branded as anti-Semitic as soon as they attempt to speak out against these legitimate grievances, it is surprising how many Palestinians retain positive feelings towards Jews. Some older Palestinians recall the peaceful relations between Jews and

[114] The Star of David is a six-pointed star like the one featured on the Israeli flag. The star is a symbol of Judaism and the Jewish people.

Arabs in Palestine before Zionist immigration. Even today, whenever there is a bombing in Israel, Palestinians who used to work in Israel call their Israeli friends to make sure that no one was hurt. Younger Palestinians, however, have few opportunities to meet Israeli Jews who aren't a part of the Occupation. This is yet another reason why the Jewish Israelis coming into the Occupied Territories to support Palestinians are so important.

The other day, 10 Israelis and I made our way to the Palestinian village of Deir Sharaf for a demonstration. Settlers from the surrounding settlements had decided to build a dump at the village's doorstep a few years ago. The settlers brought in a crusher and dug out a huge landfill some 300 meters from Deir Sharaf, where they now throw all their waste. What's worse, as a way to make money, the settlements have advertised the dump for people in Israel proper to use. Trash from Israel and West Bank settlements is now threatening the area's air, animals, communities, and most importantly, its water. Less than 300 meters from the dump is the largest fresh water source in the region.

The villagers of Deir Sharaf are upset about the noxious fumes and health threats created by the dump, and they recently organized a march from the Town Hall to the dump. IWPS took part in the event. When we arrived, the mayor welcomed us and said he wished we could be meeting under better circumstances. He gave us a brief history of the issue and said the village didn't know what else to do other than to try and tell the world about their crisis, through activism and the media.

More land from Deir Sharaf has been cleared to make way for more trash from settlements.

We walked down to the landfill, where noxious fumes forced us to cover our faces. Before us stood a city of trash with a freshly cleared area the size of a football field—room for more garbage to come. The setting could have been beautiful; cliffs towered above and the weather was perfect. But the place was revolting.

A nearby stream flowed urine and feces instead of water. I asked a villager whether the pollution came from settlements, as in Wadi Qana, but he said the sewage came from other Palestinian villages. He told me the community had sought permission to build a water purification facility, but the Israeli government rejected the request. And so yet another hydration source was lost, in a desert land where water is critical.

This demonstration was different than any I'd seen before. There were no chants, hardly any signs, no rocks or tear gas or sound bombs. We just walked through the destruction in silence. The setting told more than any slogans could have.

Having accomplished our objectives of involving the media and bearing witness to the destruction, we were ready to turn back. The mayor of Deir Sharaf wanted to arrange rides for the Israelis and me, but we said we were happy to walk with the other demonstrators. Within minutes we regretted our decision.

An army jeep happened to drive by and stopped when the soldiers inside saw us. They were worried about our safety. They told us it wasn't safe to walk with Palestinians without

Deir Sharaf villagers demonstrate peacefully against the settler dump that pollutes their land and air.

army protection. The Israelis argued with them in Hebrew, but the army insisted on driving alongside us. Soon they called for backup. Eventually, a jeep and a Humvee were escorting us into the village, scaring everyone in sight. People came out of their shops and houses, children left school out of fear or curiosity. Some began to whistle.

We had been heading for Town Hall to have a discussion on the dump, but now it seemed we were causing more harm than good. And so we did what we should have done at the entrance of the village: we stood in front of the army vehicles. We used our bodies to prevent the jeeps from intruding further. The soldiers had no choice but to stop since the village streets were too narrow for them to drive around us. I felt the villagers watching and supporting us. I could sense their appreciation when they caught my eye. This was probably the first time many people in Deir Sharaf had seen foreigners and Israelis standing up for them.

Jeeps follow Israeli and international activists into Deir Sharaf to "protect" them, provoking fear and commotion in the village.

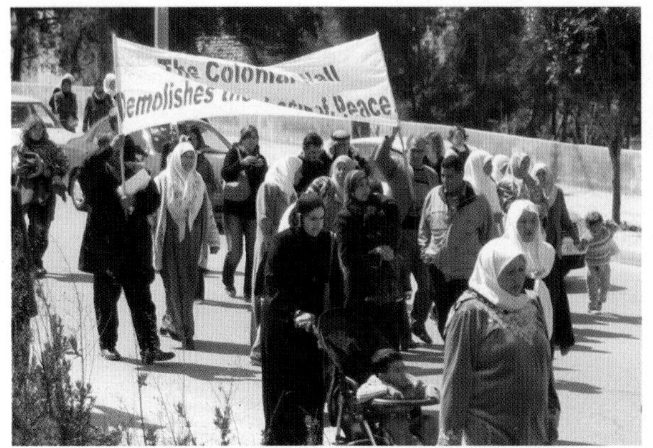

Demonstrators protest UN Secretary General Kofi Annan's avoidance of the Wall during his visit.

I felt good about our use of privilege in the situation. Palestinians couldn't have stood in front of the jeep—they would have been mowed down or arrested. But we were relatively safe, and pretty soon the Israeli activists convinced the driver to leave. The village cheered, and the protesters met as planned. We reflected on the march and generated ideas for the next step. One was from one of the Israeli anarchists, who said we should take a truckload of trash left by settlers and return it to them, on their front lawns or in their parks. I thought it was a creative idea, but several villagers were sharply opposed to it. They said it was hypocritical to complain about trash in their community and then put it in someone else's. They said everyone deserves to live with clean air and water, including Israelis.

The story of Deir Sharaf illustrates what a difference the presence or absence of soldiers can make at a demonstration. Before the soldiers arrived, protesters were focused on making their statement; when the soldiers arrived, protesters became anxious and angry. I cannot know whether or not provocation was the army's intention in Deir Sharaf, but that has certainly been the case for other incidents in the past. Ex-soldiers tell stories of deliberately egging young boys on to throw stones so that they can pick out the "troublemakers."[115] Undercover Israeli police once joined a Bil'in demonstration and started a round of stone-throwing before turning around to arrest those who followed suit.[116]

So what would happen at a Palestinian demonstration completely free of Israeli soldiers? I found out at a demonstration last month in Ramallah at the Palestinian Authority Headquarters where UN Secretary General Kofi Annan was meeting with Mahmoud Abbas. The event was planned to protest the fact that during his visit, the Secretary General was avoiding the Wall being constructed only a couple miles away. He had flown the 10 miles from Jerusalem to Ramallah, avoiding the land travel hassles of checkpoints and roadblocks that Palestinians face every day.

The protest began with a silent procession of women carrying portraits of their loved ones who are being held as political prisoners in Israeli jails. Shortly thereafter, demonstrators of all ages, backgrounds, and political alliances joined in waving flags and banners proclaiming things like "The Colonial Wall Demolishes the Basis of Peace" and "The Wall and Settlements are Another Form of Terror." Protesters' signs appealed to the United Nations: "Implement the International Court of Justice Ruling Now" and "Stop Ignoring International Law!" Several demonstrators gave speeches while others banged on the compound doors in hopes that Annan might hear. Palestinian policemen watched from the sides as demonstrators spoke their hearts and minds. Instead of degenerating into tear gas, sound bombs, rubber bullets, and stones, the demonstration culminated in a peaceful group visit to Yasser Arafat's tomb, after which protesters returned to their homes.

---

[115] "Trigger Happy: Unjustified Shooting and Violation of the Open-Fire Regulations during the al-Aqsa Intifada," *B'tselem*, p. 17; As cited in Finkelstein, *Chutzpah*, p. 114.

[116] Meron Rapaport, "Bil'in residents: Undercover troops provoked stone-throwing," *Haaretz* (October 14, 2005).

Silent demonstrators carry photographs of their family members who are being held as political prisoners in Israeli prisons.

Witness in Palestine
Nonviolent Resistance & the Future

Friday, April 29, 2005

I have now spent a total of 5 months in Palestine. With time, I discover new and horrifying ways that the Occupation disturbs life and happiness here. The issue isn't just that Palestinians lack employment, education, or any real control over their lives. Some of the worst effects of the Occupation are psychological, the type of things that you might hear from shell-shocked war veterans. Many here live in a constant state of anxiety and depression. I feel the difference in myself, the way I'm nervous where I used to be relaxed, the way I'm cautious where I used to be open.

It's the feeling of constant pressure and danger. It's not knowing whom to trust, who's being blackmailed, and who's a collaborator. It's my heart skipping a beat each time I hear a loud noise. It's starting to shake each time I see someone in uniform, knowing that they can do as they please and are not accountable for their actions. How much worse must it be for Palestinians, never knowing whether or when they will see their friends and loved ones again, or if they will be the next ones taken away? How much worse still for those no longer afraid, those believing they have nothing left to lose?

I have a way out. But most people here don't. This maddening state of mind is their life, and I marvel at most Palestinians' ability to live through it with grace and hope for a better future. Their resilience is extraordinary; their generosity even greater. I left my wallet in a shared taxi once and found the driver keeping it safe for me the next time we met. Twice I've lost my camera. The first time was a month ago, and dozens of villagers from Qarawat Bani Zeid worked to find the foreign car where my camera had fallen out of my pocket. I got it back, and lost it again today.

Last time I lost my camera I was upset. This time I'm calmer. I'm humbled by the patience of the people around me in the face of great tragedies. A friend drove me around today to look for the camera. I learned that his father has been held prisoner in an Israeli jail for 24 years because of his political affiliation. I felt petty worrying so much about an object that I can easily replace. He was focused and said he would continue to search tomorrow in the light again. He refused to take any money for gas or his time and said he was very sorry for my loss. I feel unworthy of his sympathy.

Someone just knocked at our door. Sajid, the young boy living downstairs, has brought us some fresh bread with olive oil and spinach wrapped inside it that his mother made. Sajid's father, our landlord Abu Rabia, is a longtime activist and one of the people who invited international women to form IWPS in the Salfit region. Sixteen years separate Sajid from his older brother Rabia, who was just 2 years old when his father was taken away for 13 and a half years. Abu Rabia was imprisoned for being a leader in nonviolent resistance to the Occupation. "The army was afraid of my ability to organize against them," he told me. "It didn't matter that my position was nonviolence." Abu Rabia is a warm and well-respected man who doesn't volunteer the horror stories (most Palestinians don't) of prison, but when I asked he told me about not being allowed to sleep for 8 days, and about prisoners soiling themselves tied up in chairs and left for days. He said it's unbelievable how much humans can endure, how strong we really are.

Indeed, the family remains strong and full of readiness to keep fighting and living. The first time I came to Haris in 2003, Um Rabia (Abu Rabia's wife) was pregnant with their third child Hudda, who was born just over a year ago. We all prayed Hudda would never be deprived of her father's presence the way her eldest brother Rabia was, and so far she hasn't. But something worse has happened: six months ago, Rabia was arrested on the charge of introducing two people who were later suspected of planning an armed attack against Israel. Rabia has been sentenced to 5 years in prison, and the family is once again torn apart.

Um Rabia wants us to go downstairs for tea. She is lonely without Rabia. Sajid opens the door for us when we knock. He has seemed so sad since his brother disappeared (the family still hasn't told him why and where). The house is cozy, and we are greeted warmly. Um Rabia puts some tea on the stove, and Sajid leads us into the living room where his father is comforting a woman from the village. She is crying. She has come to Abu Rabia for help and advice, but when we enter she tries to hide her weeping.

I can see that the woman has a slight mental disability, and I immediately make the connection. She is the mother of Mohammed, who was 16 years old, mentally retarded, and fatherless when he was shot for throwing a stone at a soldier a few hundred feet from

Um Rabia relaxes with her two sons Rabia (left) and Sajid (right), and nephew (foreground). This photo was taken during the 4 years between the time Um Rabia's husband returned from 13 and a half years in prison and her eldest son Rabia was sentenced to 5 years in prison.

our house. Witnesses say he was calling to the soldiers in a high-pitched voice (unable to speak normally due to his disability), but committed no crime and posed no real threat to anyone. That was 5 years ago.

Mohammed's mother is crying now because her only remaining son Manadel—now 16 and also mentally disabled—has just lost a finger to a small explosive. The weapon blew up when Manadel touched it while placing a flower in memory of his older brother on the site where Mohammed was killed. Probably leftover from an army raid, the explosive sent shrapnel flying into Manadel's two hands and right knee. Now he is unable to walk normally, and his mother is left alone with a medical bill she cannot pay.

Abu Rabia is no stranger to disability and health problems. Mohammed was killed during a period when soldiers came into Haris frequently and threatened villagers. Um Rabia was one victim—she had a miscarriage at 8 months, which she attributes to the constant attacks and anxiety associated with living in a war zone. Abu Rabia's brother, Issa, once a healthy and active strength-trainer in his twenties, was condemned to spend the rest of his life in a wheelchair after a bullet passed through his shoulder and out his neck. He was shot shortly after Abu Rabia was released from prison, and Abu Rabia suspects it was him they were after.

Issa and his wife have been good friends to IWPS. They have twin babies, one girl and one boy, and an older son. When we visited them a few weeks ago, Issa told us he was okay and started to talk of bigger things, as he usually does. He doesn't like to concentrate on his personal tragedy, as it is only one of so many in Palestine. For him, the greater tragedy is the Occupation.

While we visited, Issa looked down at his daughter and wondered, "What will happen to her? Will her situation be better or worse than ours?" We talked about the possibility of peace but quickly moved on to the seeming inevitability of the Wall. Issa said peace would never come from a wall, because you cannot squeeze a people into being peaceful. People must work to transform their anger into nonviolent work for justice, the only thing that will bring true peace. He quoted an Arabic saying, "You can't clap with one hand" and explained that Jews, Palestinians, and the world must work together if we are to successfully fight injustice. Issa said it's especially important that Jews speak out against human rights violations, since others are easily dismissed as anti-Semitic terrorists. He said he respects Judaism but cannot respect a country that discriminates against people based on ethnicity. He said he respects the America of Martin Luther King, Jr., but not of the current Bush administration, which finances Israel's atrocities unhesitatingly and prioritizes imperial goals over human dignity.

I marveled at Issa's resemblance to his brother—so committed to nonviolence despite personal tragedies. He shared with us his vision of a one-state solution in which Jews and Palestinians would coexist with equal rights in one country in spite of their tumultuous past. Issa spoke of the similarities between European colonialism in the US, South Africa, and Palestine. He said that although achieving true democracy and desegregation in the United States and South Africa continue to be great struggles, most people would agree that their solutions of coexistence are preferable to racial division. Why shouldn't this also be true for Israel/Palestine? The non-Zionist non-ethnocentric option in the Middle East seems so far from the spectrum of current thought that for most people it's not even an option at all. But there is a growing minority of Jews and Palestinians who now believe that only a truly democratic and open state could sustain itself and peace in the region.

The diversity of opinions among Palestinians regarding the future is remarkable. Hannah and I recently went up to Jenin to visit the Arab American University (AAU) there. We presented photos and statistics about the Wall and resistance, and afterwards one student volunteered to lead a discussion. He started with an open question to everyone: "Could you coexist peacefully in a shared nation alongside the Jewish people?"

A young man from Jerusalem spoke up first: "Of course we can. We just need to respect each other." Another student interrupted: "Maybe that would have worked in the past, but now too many people have died on both sides. It's too late."

A third student offered his opinion: "Peace cannot happen with the Wall and so many of our loved ones in jail for bogus reasons. Stopping the Wall and freeing the prisoners is the essential first step. Then we could live side by side." A fourth student said something that everyone agreed with: "Of course we want to live with them in peace. But they don't want it. They say they do, but they don't. Actions speak louder than words."

There is a new group at AAU called "Green Resistance." A few dozen students gather weekly to discuss nonviolent resistance tactics. The group's current project is organizing a campus-wide boycott of Israeli *Tapuzina* fruit juice, a product that not only supports Israel's economy (and hence, the Wall) but also contains very harmful preservatives. IWPS also tries to avoid purchasing Israeli products, but few Palestinians are so conscientious, perhaps because they don't realize the consequences of their consumption. According to Green Resistance, Palestinians in the Occupied Territories contribute US$84 million a year to Israel's economy. (Of course, that's still nothing compared to the more than US$10 million dollars *a day* that the US provides to Israel, most of it earmarked for military use.)

Green Resistance also gives talks on the history of nonviolent protest in Palestine. Many people assume that such tactics are foreign to Palestine because anything short of a bomb goes largely unreported in the Western media. I can't count the times I've been asked, "Why are Palestinians always blowing themselves up? Why can't they learn to use *nonviolent* resistance?"

The fact is that Palestinians *do* use nonviolent resistance. In fact, they use it *constantly*, almost every moment of every day. For many Palestinians, simply staying in their homes on their land and not emigrating is resistance. Farmers walk miles to harvest their trees because the old Palestinian roads have been demolished, blocked, or paved over with settler roads that Palestinians are not allowed to use. The farmers persist because they refuse to give up their right to go to their land. This is nonviolent resistance.

Nonviolent resistance is everywhere. Children wait for hours at checkpoints on the way to and from school every day because they are determined to get an education despite the obstacles; Palestinians and Israelis camp out together as partners for peace in spite of widespread attempts to turn the war into one of Jews versus Muslims; a movement leader returns from prison after 13 years and goes back to the nonviolent resistance he was arrested for; an old woman, armed with only her voice and determination, confronts a bulldozer uprooting her trees and the fourth strongest military in the world protecting it; a shepherd grazes her sheep despite threats of poison and settler attacks; a young boy constructs a roadblock all by himself with rocks and wire in an attempt to prevent army jeeps from entering his village that night; students paint murals on the Wall and young children dig tunnels to pass under it. Palestinians are not strangers to nonviolent resistance; they are champions of it.

High school girls endure long waits and rigorous screening at checkpoints on the way to and from school but they persist, determined to get an education.

Palestinian Everyda

A shepherd grazes her sheep despite threats of poison and settler attacks.

Farmers walk miles to continue to harvest their trees despite the roadblocks and forbidden settlers roads that block their old roads

Women in rural Salfit organize against the Wall that threatens to annex much of the region's land.

A farmer plows his land after being denied access to it for 4 years. He doesn't know if or when he will be allowed to return, but he refuses to stop caring for it.

Nonviolent Resistance

A young boy constructs a roadblock by himself in an attempt to prevent army jeeps from entering his village that night.

Jerusalem Palestinians climb the Wall, which imprisons them.

Palestinians organize demonstrations against their oppression and dispossession.

There are, of course, other options. Palestinians can join the movement advocating armed resistance. But in my experience, most Palestinians refuse to resort to violence, even though it's the only resistance that consistently receives attention from the media. Palestinians could also give up and accept the loss of their land and freedom. But I see no signs that this will happen, at least within the general population. To this day, farmers still refuse to sell their land even though they know they are likely to lose it soon anyway. Families plant young olive trees where old ones have been uprooted. They build new homes where old ones have been demolished. Palestinians persist in the most widespread nonviolent resistance of all: simply living under the Occupation. Existence is resistance.

Unfortunately, the most widespread resistance happening in Palestine is also the least widely reported. For as long as I can remember, the Western press has been calling on Palestinians to "choose peace," promising that if Palestinians would just work towards justice without harming Israelis, they could "earn" back their freedom and human rights, as if these rights were privileges. Given the prevalence of nonviolent resistance in Palestine and the deterioration of the situation in the Occupied Territories, one cannot help but wonder what is meant by "choosing peace."

One student in Jenin said he was tired of the false promises and wearied by the everyday resistance required to survive life under the Occupation. He wanted to go to the United States, or to Europe. But then he stopped himself: "I want to leave. But then I remember that if everyone thought that way we would lose everything. We should be allowed to live here because it's our land, and our history. It's that simple."

Resistance takes great courage, but without it Palestine would be long gone. The struggle must continue.

Even after the departure of Israeli settlers and soldiers, Gaza remained under Israeli control, while settlement expansion continued unabated in the West Bank.

It was only after I left Palestine for the second time, in late April 2005, that I finally felt ready to write and speak publicly about my experiences in the West Bank. I had never considered myself a writer, public speaker, or photographer before, but witnessing the Occupation has a way of making people feel the need to speak out. After publishing the first edition of Witness in Palestine in January of 2006, I set off on a 16,000-mile journey around the United States, speaking at universities, high schools, churches, community centers, and synagogues in more than 30 states across the country. I also presented abroad in Europe and in the Near East. I was generally well received in every city that I visited, and I saw firsthand that the movement to end the Occupation is developing not just in Palestine, but around the world.

There were a number of significant developments in Israel/Palestine during my absence. In August 2005, the Israeli settlers were evacuated from the Gaza Strip. The army left the next month. Israel's departure from Gaza was by no means a bad thing for Palestinians, but the amount of relief it provided them should not be exaggerated. Israel maintained control of Gaza's airspace, waters, and crossings, and the army declared much of northern Gaza a "free-fire zone," meaning that anyone entering it risked being killed. Israeli snipers remained stationed outside the wall surrounding Gaza which, like its West Bank counterpart, does not follow the internationally recognized border. With the soldiers and settlers gone, Israel was able to control Gaza from afar while minimizing Israeli casualties.

In early January 2006, Israeli Prime Minister Ariel Sharon suffered a serious stroke, effectively ending his political career. He was succeeded by Ehud Olmert, who promised that the Wall would be Israel's new border and not simply a temporary solution, as Sharon's government had always claimed.[117] *The construction of the Wall, along with previous annexation, has rendered more than 50% of the West Bank Israeli "state lands." And the Qadima party, which both Sharon and Olmert represent, still maintains the "historic right [of Jews] to live anywhere in the [so-called] Land of Israel," which includes all of the West Bank and Gaza.*[118]

Just weeks after Sharon's stroke, Palestinian democratic legislative elections produced a significant victory for Hamas over the ruling Fatah party. In the past, Hamas's military wing had claimed responsibility for terrorist attacks on Israelis. At the time of the election, however, Hamas had held to a unilateral ceasefire for one year as part of a transition from armed to political struggle. Hamas won on a platform calling for economic reform and an end to corruption in the longtime ruling Fatah party.

Israel and the US responded to Hamas's victory by severing ties with the new government. Israel stopped handing over taxes collected on behalf of the Palestinian Authority, and the US and the European Union cut off all aid to Palestinian civil society, plunging the already devastated population into unprecedented levels of poverty.[119] *The UN Special Rapporteur on the Right to Food cited acute malnutrition in Gaza as being*

---

[117] Carter, p. 10.

[118] Ibid, at 178.

[119] By the end of 2006, 43% of Palestinians in the Occupied Territories were living in poverty, while Israel withheld half a billion Palestinian tax-dollars. *PASSIA* 2007. For more details on the embargo and its affects, see p. 329.

on the scale of poorer countries in southern Sahara, with the majority of Palestinians eating just one meal a day.[120] *Under the pressure of economic strangulation, Palestinian civil society began to break down, and by May of 2006, interfactional violence had broken out between Hamas and Fatah.*

In June 2006, 2 days after Israeli soldiers arrested two Palestinian soldiers in Gaza,[121] *Palestinian militants attacked an Israeli outpost, killing two soldiers and capturing one. Three days later, Israel launched a 5-month attack on Gaza that left 400 Palestinian civilians and 8 Israelis (6 soldiers and 2 civilians) dead.*[122] *Meanwhile, Israel and the West continued to criticize Hamas for not denouncing violence altogether. The group eventually broke their longstanding one-sided ceasefire after the shelling of a Gaza beach left an entire family dead save one 7-year-old girl, whose parents and siblings perished around her.*[123]

Even when Hamas resumed its ceasefire, it continued to face economic sanctions for not officially recognizing the state of Israel's right to exist. A few months later, Avigdor Lieberman, an Israeli politician and advocate of transferring the Palestinians out of the West Bank, Gaza, and Israel, was invited into an Israeli government coalition as Minister of Strategic Affairs.[124] *Although Lieberman has explicitly advocated violence against Palestinians*[125] *and does not recognize the right of Palestinians to exist in the region, there was no talk about the US boycotting the Israeli government.*

One month into Israel's incursion into Gaza, Hezbollah, a political and paramilitary organization in Lebanon, launched Katyusha rockets across the Lebanese border and captured two Israeli soldiers.[126] *Hezbollah and the militants in Gaza both agreed to release the captured soldiers if Israel would release some of the Palestinian and Lebanese prisoners that it held illegally.*[127] *Several such prisoner exchanges had occurred in the past, but Israeli leaders declared the capture by Hezbollah an "act of war" and promised a "very painful and far-reaching response" that would "turn Lebanon's clock back 20*

---

[120] Carter, p. 176.

[121] Avi Issacharoff and Amos Harel, "For the first time since the disengagement, suspects are arrested inside Gaza" [Hebrew translation], *Haaretz* (June 25, 2006).

[122] Middle East Policy Council. www.mepc.org/resources/mrates.asp

"Numbers do not include Palestinian suicide bombers (or other attackers) nor do they include Palestinians targeted for assassination, though bystanders killed during these assassinations are counted. However, [Israeli] soldiers killed during incursions into Palestinian lands are counted.

[123] "Funerals for Gaza beach victims," BBC News (June 10, 2006).

[124] Jonathan Cook, "Lieberman," ZNet (January 22, 2007).

[125] As Israeli Minister of Transport, Lieberman proposed driving Palestinian prisoners into the sea, and offered to provide the buses to do so. He has also called for the execution of Palestinian members of the Israeli Knesset who have had contact with Hamas or do not celebrate Israeli Independence Day. Gideon Alon, "Lieberman blasted for suggesting drowning Palestinian prisoners," *Haaretz* (July 11, 2002); Gideon Alon, "PM defends Arab MKs after Lieberman calls for execution," *Haaretz* (May 5, 2006).

[126] "Day-by-day: Lebanon crisis - week one," BBC News (July 19, 2006).

[127] Hezbollah also demanded Israel's withdrawal from the illegally-occupied Shebaa Farms near the Israeli-Lebanese border.

years" if the soldiers were not immediately released.[128] *Israel launched a 34-day bombardment of Lebanon, by the end of which 162 Israelis were dead (most of them soldiers) and more than 1,000 had been killed in Lebanon (most of them civilians). More than 300,000 Israelis were displaced during the conflict due to ongoing rocket attacks on the northern border by Hezbollah, although displaced Israelis were able to return home when a cease-fire was declared in mid-August. Almost one million people in Lebanon were also displaced—about one quarter of the country's population*[129]*—and much of the south remained uninhabitable even after the cease-fire, due to unexploded cluster bombs.*[130]

As violence in the Middle East intensified, so did determination in Israel/Palestine and abroad for a just resolution to the conflict. It was with stronger conviction than ever that I returned to Palestine for my third stint with IWPS.

A West Bank child says goodbye to her land: Israel continued aggressive settlement construction and confiscation of West Bank land and water during its celebrated "withdrawal" from Gaza.

[128] Carter, pp. 196-198; Conal Urquhart and Chris McGreal, "Israelis invade Lebanon after soldiers are seized," Guardian Unlimited (July 12, 2006); Martin Fletcher, "Regional tensions fuel Lebanon-Israel clashes," MSNBC (July 12, 2006); "Israel authorizes 'severe' response to abductions," CNN.com (July 12, 2006).

[129] Carter, p. 199.

[130] The head of an Israel army rocket unit in Lebanon said, "What we did was insane and monstrous, we covered entire towns in cluster bombs." Meron Rappaport, "IDF commander: We fired more than a million cluster bombs in Lebanon," *Haaretz* (September 12, 2006).

PART II

2007

Palestine for Non-Palestinians Only?

Friday, January 26, 2007:

After almost 2 years of book production, touring, organizing, and advocacy work, I'm back in the chilly IWPS apartment in Haris. I flew into Tel Aviv's Ben Gurion airport yesterday afternoon. As usual, there were smiling faces and big signs at the airport welcoming me to Israel, until I reached passport control. After she'd entered my identity information and agreed not to stamp my passport (an Israeli stamp can keep you out of several Middle Eastern countries), the passport controller began to make small talk and I looked around, knowing what was coming.

Within 30 seconds there were three security guards around me, asking me how many bags I had under the plane and what color, and radioing the information out as we hustled to the security area. (Only in Israel do I never have to retrieve my own baggage!) There they left me in a waiting room, where I exchanged smiles with the other half dozen or so people waiting to be screened, most with skin color darker than my own. Eventually the guards came back with my bag and we were off to the next security area. I could have led the group myself I've been there so many times. "They must think I'm very important!" I commented cheerfully to one of the five guards carrying my bags and escorting me as we passed the 50 or so people waiting in line.

The search itself was better than usual—a female guard patted me down gently but did not ask me to remove any clothing. My bags suffered a more thorough search as the guards examined seemingly every inch of every item I'd brought. I was expecting this, of course, and had deleted any photographs, details, or contact information about my work, IWPS, or any Palestinians from my computer, iPod, and telephone; although the guards are only supposed to be looking for weapons, implicating any Palestinians in resistance work could make them a target, even if they are committed to nonviolence. Deleting the information is not only a big hassle—I have to reprogram dozens of numbers into my cell phone every time I go, and transfer practically everything I've created off my computer—but also completely absurd. Why dissect every mechanical pencil and cassette tape that I've carried in, when to my knowledge there is no precedent for international human rights workers carrying out or aiding in violent attacks against Israel? Do they really believe that I will be the first international peace activist to bring in explosives (in my mechanical pencil), or are they screening for something else—information perhaps? Or is it simply a kind of harassment to establish their authority or make me think twice about coming?

Of course, I do pose a kind of threat: a threat to the status quo. Israel could not continue its occupation and settlement of Palestine if people everywhere—particularly in the United States—knew the details of such policies and spoke out. There is a lot of information out there, and awareness is increasing as more Palestinians' voices and stories are heard. But Israel's international claim to be the only democracy and peace-seeking state in the Middle East depends on suppressing those reports.

Reports about the Occupation have become such a problem for Israel that last June border security denied entry to my friend and colleague Paul Larudee, a 60-year-old piano tuner, Fulbright lecturer, and former contract US government advisor to Saudi Arabia who volunteers with ISM. On the plane I had read a printout of Paul's story of being refused, resisting involuntary deportation, making friends in detention, and eventually losing his court case, all in the spirit of compassionate nonviolence.[1]

Ironically, Paul and I aren't even trying to enter Israeli territory. We're trying to reach the West Bank, on internationally-recognized Palestinian land where Israel has no legal authority according to international consensus and dozens of UN resolutions. Yet Israel prevents Palestinians' only airport—in Gaza—from functioning and controls all the borders, so solidarity and humanitarian workers have to pass through Israeli border police even if they have no intention of going into Israel. Of course, as foreigners, Paul and I shouldn't necessarily be allowed into Palestine—but that should be Palestinians' decision, not Israel's.

Another irony is that Paul and I work exclusively in support of *non*violent resistance, which is precisely what Israel faults Palestinians for failing to develop. Paul noted the incongruity: "Israel's repression of human rights workers is a cynical contradiction of their oft-stated wish that Palestinians and their supporters should use nonviolent tactics.... to those who in ignorance of the persistent and pervasive Palestinian nonviolent movement continue to ask, 'Where is the Palestinian Gandhi?' it is instructive to consider the lengths to which Israel will go to assure that dissent and nonviolent resistance are eliminated.... If Israel chooses to treat these movements [with such aggression], it should come as no surprise if the victims of its repression resort to more violent means of expressing their grievances."

Inspired by Paul's jailhouse anecdotes on creative resistance, I was ready for anything yesterday, but at the end of my search and a series of repetitive questions a security guard handed me my passport and told me, "Okay, you can go now. Have a nice day." Inside my passport was a prominent stamp of Ben Gurion Airport. I looked up and the guard and said, "Did you forget?"

"No," he said, "we knew you didn't want it stamped, but we stamped it anyway."

"To be mean?" I asked, incredulously. He shrugged. I guessed again. "So that I won't visit other countries in the Middle East?"

"No, you can get a new passport."

I've got it, I thought: "Spite?"

He smiled and turned around to return to his work. I had to smile too. At least I was in!

I was obviously happy not to be turned away, but as I took the train into central Tel Aviv I thought about all the people who haven't been so lucky in past years. More than 15,000 foreign passport holders have been denied entry into the Palestinian territories by Israel in the last 5 years, many of them Palestinians and their spouses with homes, children, land, and jobs in Palestine. Many of those denied had been living in Palestine for decades on permits expiring every 3 months, which they would perpetually renew. Israel has begun

---

1 "Detention Diary," July 10, 2006. *www.hurriyya.blogspot.com*

issuing "last permits," forcing people to leave or continue living there illegally. Here's an example scenario:

Children's art: Israel has begun issuing "last permits" to Palestinians in the West Bank, forcing many families to either move or be separated.

A Palestinian couple moves to the United States. They have two children there, both American. They decide to move back to Palestine, where Israel refuses to issue their American children residency (on Palestinian land, mind you; American-Israeli dual citizenship, on the other hand, is common in Israel and West Bank settlements). For 5 years the parents renew their children's permits every 3 months, until one day Israel says their children (ages, say, 6 and 8) aren't allowed to live there anymore. The couple is forced to leave Palestine. This is just one example of Israel's new practice, which legal experts say could empty the West Bank of over half a million Palestinians in a short time as Palestinian residents leave to keep their families together. According to Palestinian-American businessman Sam Bahour, "Israel has managed to destroy every Palestinian institution except the family; now they're targeting that."

Among those targeted have also been foreign academics and lecturers working at Palestinian universities, medical teams, musical groups, journalists, and human rights lawyers. Many of these so-called "foreigners" are Palestinian natives who don't have Israeli-issued IDs.[2] The Arab-American University of Jenin, which deliberately tries to hire Palestinian-Americans, has lost almost their entire foreign faculty. Israel's policy of denying entry to academics and human rights researchers, combined with the US-led international embargo on the Palestinian government, has left the Palestinians more isolated than ever from international assistance.

About five million Palestinian refugees around the world can never visit Palestine, their homeland. But I, Anna—white, American, Jewish—got in yesterday, and I'll try my hardest to do what those refugees cannot: support Palestinians' rights to freedom and their own land. Of course they are the experts, not me, but privilege is what it is. It got me in yesterday, and it surrounded me like a bubble today as I breezed through security at the bus station in Tel Aviv with three huge bags (two bag-free Palestinians behind me were patted down) and as I was whisked through the Palestinian West Bank by a settler bus on Israeli-only roads. Privilege is everywhere, but maybe it doesn't always have to be that way.

[2] Danny Rubinstein, *Davar* (November 19, 1982); As cited in Chomsky, *Fateful*, p. 177.

Back to "Normal" Life in Palestine

Thursday, February 1, 2007

I've hardly written since I arrived in Palestine. We've been running around busily as usual, trying to keep our spirits up. Much of our time is spent just trying to stay warm and maintain the house—gathering firewood and lugging gas cylinders up and down the stairs. The schizophrenic antics of the oven and washing machine seem almost endearing to me now, and I'm quickly getting re-accustomed to living without luxuries I take for granted in the United States like hot water and reliable electricity.

Zatara checkpoint in 2005

Zatara checkpoint in 2007

Palestine is as beautiful as ever—what's left of it. Settlements continue to spread across seemingly every hilltop, and we can now see the Wall between Marda village and Ariel settlement from our balcony. The Occupation feels even more entrenched than last time I was here. The nearby checkpoint at Zatara intersection between Haris and Nablus has been remodeled so that settler cars can easily bypass the soldier stations, which are also new. Israel installed a huge menorah, a seven-branched candle holder and one of the oldest symbols of the Jewish people, in the center of the prominent West Bank intersection. In

Haris, the army built a lofty army watchtower on my good friend Um Fadi's land, and its watch light shines through our kitchen window every night. There is also a small new fence around our village, and we wonder if that will be one layer of the Wall here.

A new army watchtower overlooks Haris.

It's quieter in the house than in the past. The phone only rings a couple times a day and we spend a lot of time on administrative work and organizing. We wonder if our presence here continues to be useful. Has the situation on the ground improved such that there is less demand for international solidarity workers? Or has it worsened so people have switched from resistance mode to survival mode? Have people forgotten we're here, or do they know we're here but no longer think we can help them?

We were discussing our ability to be effective last night at dinner when Amy received a phone call that three army jeeps had entered Marda and were throwing sound bombs and shooting live ammunition into the air. Amy and I agreed that we would go while our colleague Gemma would stay behind to send out reports should anything happen. We grabbed our cameras, notebooks, and vests and caught a taxi to the village, where an army jeep had blocked all local traffic (people and vehicles). Armed with white privilege and neon vests, we hopped out and began walking into the forbidden area. Soldiers shined heavy lights into our faces and yelled but we looked down and walked steadily towards what appeared to be the targeted house. Surrounded by soldiers with their guns pointed and ready, the house was easy to spot.

Israel recently installed a large menorah—one of the oldest symbols of the Jewish people—in the center of Zatara junction between Ramallah and Nablus.

Our friend Nasfat greeted us and thanked us for coming. He explained that there had been a death in the village, and as per tradition locals were gathering in the village community center to mourn after the funeral. He said that the soldiers had come to the door where the mourners were sitting and demanded that everyone leave. The mourners refused, and Nasfat—who speaks Hebrew—explained to the soldiers the purpose of the gathering. Suddenly, five of the soldiers began walking towards us quickly. I lifted my camera to photograph their approach, and they stopped as soon as they saw the flash. One soldier was visibly angry with me, but the soldier in charge was calmer. He asked us what we were doing there and we said that our friends had called to ask us to document the army's incursion. The soldier asked to see our IDs and we explained that we didn't feel comfortable handing them over to an illegal occupying army.

The soldier was polite, "I don't want to bother you; I just want to make sure you have permission to be here."

"But we don't need permission to visit our friends. We come here all the time."

The soldiers began talking amongst themselves in Hebrew. Nasfat mumbled quietly so that only I could hear: "They are talking about taking your camera." I slipped my hand under my jacket and carefully removed my flash card, and then slipped it into my back pocket.

The head soldier turned to me and said, "We have to remove your photos." I told him there was no law against photographing such incidents. When he insisted, I pretended to delete the photos, but they were clued in by the "No Memory Card" display. I shrugged, "I guess I forgot my card." Annoyed, but not prepared to search me, they eventually returned to their jeeps, leaving shortly thereafter. As usual, it wasn't clear why they were leaving—nor if it had anything to do with us—but we suspected they would be back.

We decided to stick around for another hour in case anything should happen, but things remained calm. Nasfat drove us to a house in the village that I immediately recognized. I'd been there once before after documenting the arrest of Jaber, a Palestinian accountant with meningitis. This was the family home of Jaber's wife, and we immediately began talking excitedly about the big news: Jaber had been released! After almost 2 years in prison on unsubstantiated charges and with insufficient medical care, Jaber is back with his family in Qira village. Hannah and I went to visit him today.

When I saw Jaber waiting outside his house for us, I hardly recognized him. He was radiant. He welcomed us enthusiastically onto their sunny terrace and encouraged his children to shake our hands, but they hid shyly behind their father. Only the youngest stood aside: Jaber said that Ahmed, born less than a month after his father's arrest, is still getting accustomed to him. He'd never seen his father out of prison until 2 weeks ago.

Soldiers surround a house in Marda where villagers are mourning a death in the community.

Jaber's wife and mother smothered us with hugs and kisses, and fed us Hannah's favorite Palestinian dish, *maqlouba*. Jaber began speaking to us in English, and I remembered that he had studied at Bir Zeit, the most prestigious university in

Palestine, where all classes are in English. He was embarrassed that he'd forgotten some of his English, and explained that he'd been learning another language in prison: Hebrew.

Jaber told us that in addition to learning to read and write Hebrew in jail, he'd also written a book on Palestinian history. I told him I'd written a book about Palestine too, and we agreed to trade. I couldn't get over the difference in Jaber—he could hardly stop smiling. His countenance changed only when we asked about his treatment at the hospital. He said the army had shackled him to the hospital bed and beat him behind closed doors. Nonetheless, he said, he'd recovered, and that was all behind him now.

Reconnecting with the community here is important for maintaining people's awareness of and trust in IWPS. As outsiders, we depend on having contacts who will be honest with us about what they need and what they don't need from internationals. We must be ready to adapt accordingly to the worsening situation.

I've already begun a number of human rights reports documenting the ongoing atrocities, but on some level I'm most surprised and saddened by how quickly life under occupation has begun to seem normal to me again: the checkpoints and roadblocks; the families and villages separated by the Wall; person after person who's lost a mother or a son, an eye or a leg, a house or olive groves to the Occupation. It's so familiar it hardly seems worth writing about anymore. But once people accept life under oppression, the Occupation has succeeded in the most tragic dispossession of all: taking away people's ability to imagine something better.

Witness in Palestine

Palestinian Women & the Struggle for Real Peace

Monday, February 5, 2007

Before each of my trips to the Middle East, friends back home are always concerned for my safety and comfort as a woman. When I answer that my greatest threat comes from Israeli soldiers and settlers, people are often taken aback—what they are really wondering is what life is like for women living in a predominantly Muslim community. As an outsider, however, that is not a question I can answer. I can never know what my female Palestinian neighbors experience because foreign women have a sort of special status in Palestine: we enjoy many of the privileges of being female without the same restrictions imposed on local women. What I *can* say, however, is that some of the most inspiring and independent women I've ever met have been Palestinian. Each one has a story of struggle—as a woman and as a Palestinian—and also of survival. Take, for example, my friend Fatima.

The daughter of refugees from 'Ager village (in present-day Israel), Fatima Khaldi spent her early years in Rafah camp in the Gaza Strip until her family moved to Saudi Arabia in search of a better life. An outsider in both places, Fatima's already difficult life became even harder when she was once beaten with a metal skewer in the left leg, which permanently stunted its growth. After Fatima's father died, the family was left without a breadwinner and returned to Gaza. When it came time for college, Fatima was instead sent to work in a sewing factory to support her younger siblings. But she had bigger dreams.

Determined, Fatima took two jobs to put herself through school, studying during the day and splitting her free time between caring for orphans and caring for the elderly. She founded the first campus group at Jerusalem Open University, a club for female social work students like herself. After graduation, she worked as everything from a political organizer to a nurse for drug addicts. While taking care of disabled people, she met the man she would later marry, a blind musician, and, when the young couple moved to his village of Qarawat Bani Hassan near Haris, Fatima started the village's first kindergarten. Meanwhile, she began working at the Working Women's Society in Nablus, raising awareness among women about human, social, and worker's rights.

Life in Qarawat was never easy. Fatima's husband was controlling, unsupportive, and physically and emotionally abusive. Then, after the Second Intifada began, checkpoints consistently disrupted Fatima's commute to work, and she was forced to leave her job in Nablus. Shortly thereafter, her husband left her for another woman. Alone with five small children in conservative Qarawat, Fatima longed for the support of her own family, whom she hadn't seen in over a decade. But because Israel does not allow free travel between the West Bank and Gaza, Fatima knew that if she left the West Bank—even just for a visit—she might never be allowed to return to her children.

Always a survivor, Fatima overcame her daunting obstacles with strength and perseverance, and that same year joined with two other Salfit women to form Women for

Life (WFL), an organization dedicated to empowering local women in their struggle "to live in a free, just, and democratic society." I met Fatima the year after WFL began, and she has since become one of my closest friends here. I've watched her organization grow from 3 to more than 200 members, meeting regularly to participate in, among other things, legal and leadership workshops, job training, domestic violence awareness, and creative nonviolent resistance to the Occupation.

Fatima Khaldi

Over the years, I have come to see Fatima's life as a microcosm of the story of Palestinian women today: fighting a battle on multiple fronts. Fatima's leg is the least of her handicaps; she is also a woman living in a traditional, patriarchial society, and a Palestinian living under a brutal military occupation. But in spite of the obstacles, women have long been prominent in the Palestinian struggle for peace—real peace, not simply the absence of war.

Women from areas of conflict have found the conventional description of peace—the opposite of violent force—insufficient. According to PeaceWomen Across the Globe:

> Peace is best understood in terms of "human security," [which is] the combination of:
>
> 1. Economic security (having an assured basic income)
> 2. Food security (physical and economic access to food)
> 3. Health security (access to basic healthcare)
> 4. Environmental security (access to clean water, clean air, ecological integrity)
> 5. Personal security (freedom from physical violence and threats, right to human dignity and freedom of person)
> 6. Community security (cultural integrity)
> 7. Political security (protection of civil rights and freedoms and responsibilities)[3]

Each component of human security is threatened in Palestine, but groups like Women for Life address these issues along with the injustice of the Occupation. Palestinian women have been crucial in the struggle to overcome the devastation that remains even throughout

---

[3] PeaceWomen Across the Globe is a project born of the 1,000 Women for the Nobel Peace Prize 2005 campaign. *www.1000peacewomen.org*

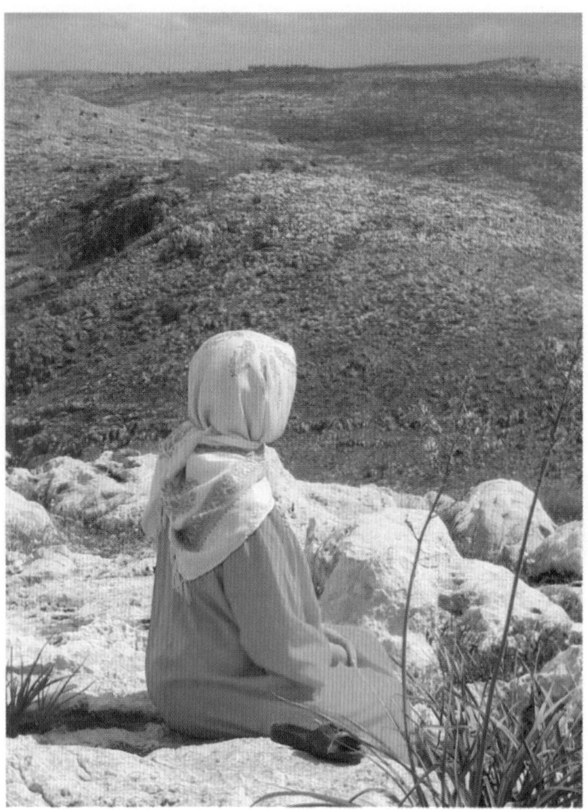

Palestinian women struggle against not only the violence of the Occupation, but also the emotional, economic, and cultural devastation that it has brought.

ceasefires and peace talks: the emotional trauma, the destruction of culture, domestic violence, economic hardship, disease, and other issues rarely addressed by heads of state at the bargaining table.

The prominence of Palestinian women outside of the traditional role of homemaking is also growing. The percentage of Palestinian parliamentary seats held by women is quickly approaching that of Israel and the United States (although still far from Europe and various African countries),[4] in part due to successful lobbying for election quotas by Palestinian women's organizations.[5] With 40% of adult Palestinian men in the Occupied Territories having spent some time in Israeli prisons or detention centers, women have often had to become the primary breadwinners for their families. They are also more able to move around to work than their husbands, since screenings of women at checkpoints tend to be less thorough. The transition from homemaking to the labor force by Palestinian women is made easier by their traditionally high levels of education. Palestinian society was the first in the Arab world to offer female students equal education opportunities,[6] and women are now in the majority at Palestinian universities.[7]

Many other women working against injustice in Israel/Palestine are located west of the Green Line. Israel-based groups like New Profile,[8] Machsom Watch, and ASWAT (a Palestinian lesbian group based in Haifa)[9] work tirelessly alongside women in the Occupied Territories in the struggle for real peace and human security for all people in the region: women and men, Palestinians and Jewish Israelis.

---

[4] "Women politicians 'making gains,'" *BBC News* (February 28, 2006).

[5] "The Question of Security: Violence against Palestinian women and girls," *Human Rights Watch* (November 2006), Volume 18, No. 7.

[6] Peter Hansen, Commissioner-General of the United Nations Relief and Works Agency (UNWRA).

[7] "General Education Statistics 2005/6" and "Higher Education Statistics 2004-05," Minister of Education and Higher Education; As cited in *PASSIA* 2007, p. 329.

[8] Information about New Profile and other women's groups based in Israel is available from the Coalition of Women for Peace. *coalitionofwomen.org/home/english*

[9] More information on ASWAT can be found at *www.aswatgroup.org/english*

Witness in Palestine
Assassination in Bizarro World

Wednesday, February 7, 2007

Several days ago while attending a Women for Life embroidery workshop for local women, we received a frantic call from the north about the killing of a Palestinian man named William. We called around to see if any other human rights groups had internationals in Jenin, but it seemed everyone had headed south to document settler violence around Hebron. The next day, we traveled to Rumani, a village on the northwestern edge of the West Bank. We brought along Ashraf, a soft-spoken Palestinian nonviolent activist studying at the American University in Jenin, to translate for us. When we arrived in the village, we were told that William's family was very religious, so Ashraf would have to stay with the men while we took the report from William's wife, the only adult witness. My colleagues and I were guided into a room full of women from the village, sitting in somber silence around William's mother and wife. I realized that this was the Palestinian equivalent of "sitting *shiva*" in the Jewish tradition, when family and friends gather right after a death to mourn and comfort the next of kin.

William's mother was expecting us and made room on both sides of her for us to sit down, spreading her blanket across us when we did. Not knowing what to do, I whispered "thank you" and sat with the women in silence for a while. Eventually I cleared my throat and explained who we were and why we'd come. Several women smiled weakly and thanked us. One who was holding a baby stood up and brought the baby over to me to hold. It was a tiny 30-day-old girl who breathed deeply as she slept in my arms. William's brother Saber, who had just arrived to translate, motioned to his brother's wife before speaking up: "This is their first, and last, child."

Saber invited us to move next door to take the report from his sister-in-law in private. There she began to tell her story, which Saber translated:

> Three nights ago, William and I were walking home from this house after visiting with family. Since there is no electricity in the village, we could not see that there were people hiding in the bushes outside our home. When we reached our door, three men in civilian clothes jumped out and demanded to see William's ID. They were speaking to each other in Hebrew. William showed them his ID and they took out a gun and shot him in the chest. He fell to the ground and then they shot him twice more in the head.
>
> Then they took our child from my arms and lay her next to William's body. They took off my headscarf and pulled me by my hair away from my child. They told me that if I cried out they would kill me and my baby too. Then they walked away and I could see the army jeeps on the main road turn on their headlights to light the way through the forest that surrounds our house. I was so scared that I did not scream.

I asked Saber if they knew why William was targeted. Saber explained that their other brother, Uday, had been arrested exactly one year before for his support of Islamic Jihad.

A poster of William hangs in his village after his assassination (extrajudicial execution) by Israeli soldiers.

William had been accused of having hidden his brother when the army came to capture him. Israeli Intelligence had tried everything—undercover salespeople, women visitors in civilian clothes, etc—and blamed William for making Uday's capture so difficult. Israel claims that "liquidations" are for security,[10] but Saber said there could be only one explanation for his brother's assassination: "Revenge."

We asked the family if they had contacted a lawyer and they said they were afraid it would only make things worse. Uday had a lawyer, but he felt that the more publicity his case received, the worse his treatment became in jail. He had been tortured until he couldn't see straight, and continues to suffer from health problems after spending more than 4 months in interrogation.

Since stories like Uday's are so common, I hardly took notice of the torture accounts. My colleagues and I call this the "Bizarro World Syndrome,"[11] where outrageous policies suddenly become unremarkable. Since 2000, Israel has killed more than 500 people, many of them innocent civilians, in extrajudicial assassinations.[12] How has anyone come to see as normal assassinating a man accused of protecting his brother?[13] Even if he were guilty of harboring a threat, or even if he were a threat himself, since when is it acceptable to hunt a suspect down and murder him? If someone in the US were planning an attack against civilians, would we advocate the government going to his home and shooting him in cold blood? Or would we advocate arrest and a fair trial to determine whether or not he's guilty beyond a reasonable doubt? Concepts like "due process" and "innocent until proven guilty" do not apply to Palestinians in the Occupied Territories.[14] Even if spared assassination, Palestinian prisoners are rarely given a fair trial, and some are not even tried at all.

---

[10] Israel provides no evidence to support this claim. In fact, in his book, *Beyond Chutzpah: On the Misuse of Anti-Semitism and the Abuse of History*, historian Norman Finkelstein concludes from *B'tselem* reports that "the main, anticipated, and intended effect of political liquidations has been to stimulate terrorist attacks" (p. 140).

[11] "Bizarro" has become a term in American popular culture to describe something with twisted logic.

[12] John Dugard, "Implementation of General Assembly Resolution 60/251 of 15 March 2006 Entitled 'Human Rights Council,' Report of the Special Rapporteur on the situation of human rights in the Palestinian territories occupied since 1967," *United Nations Human Rights Council*, A/HRC/4/17 (January 29, 2007).

[13] In fact, most targets of Israel's "liquidation" policy do not classify as "combatants" under international law. "State Assassinations and Other Unlawful Killings," *Amnesty International* (London, 2001), p. 20; "Assassination Policy," *Public Committee Against Torture in Israel (PCATI)* and *LAW*, pp. 69-70; As cited in Finkelstein, *Chutzpah*, p. 134.

[14] According to *B'tselem*, "The decision to assassinate is made in back rooms with no judicial process to examine the intelligence information on which it is based. The target of assassination is not given a chance to present evidence in his defense or to refute the allegations against him." "Position Paper: Israel's Assassination Policy," *B'tselem*, p. 8; "Assassination Policy," *PCATI* and *LAW*, p. 61; As cited in Finkelstein, *Chutzpah*, p. 135.

Israeli-occupied Palestine is a bizarro world indeed. Since when—outside of Guantanamo, lest we forget—is it normal to torture prisoners, many of them never even told what they are being held for? Last summer, Israeli soldiers kidnapped a third of Palestine's democratically-elected parliament and put the leaders in prison, where they remain today.[15] What would we do if Iran's army came in and captured a third of our government, claiming—rightfully, perhaps—that our representatives were a threat to their safety? Let us also not forget that according to the Israeli military practices that govern the West Bank and Gaza, it's dangerous to be a member of not only Hamas but just about *any* major Palestinian political movement, including Fatah, PFLP (the Marxist-Leninist Communist Party), and others. The Israeli Minister of Defense has the unchecked power to declare any organization illegal,[16] so really anyone who adopts an opinion on the political issues that govern his or her life can be a target for arrest, house demolition, or assassination. In the past, Israel also imposed harsh punishments for social organizing and the possession of a Palestinian flag, a photograph of a Palestinian leader, or other symbols of nationalist aspirations. Israeli leaders realized long ago that Palestinian nationalism, like Palestinian political organization, poses a greater threat to Israeli expansion than Palestinian terrorism does.

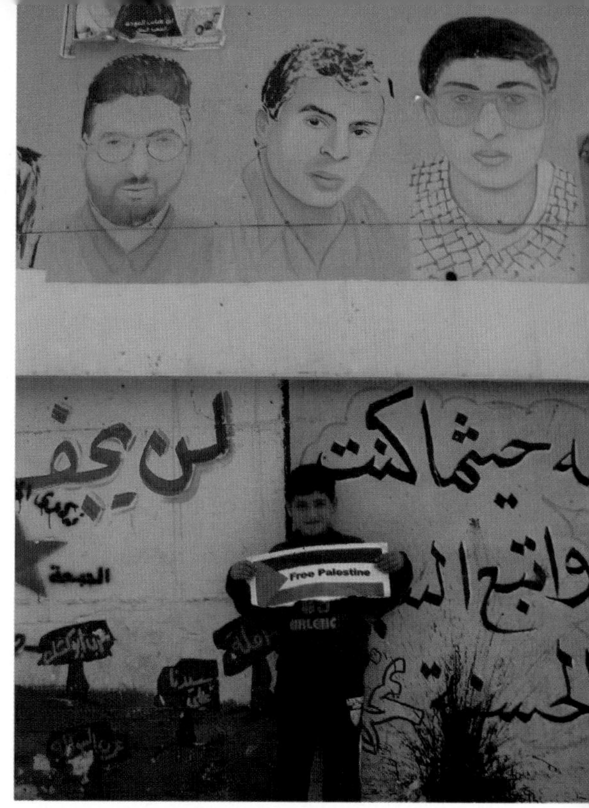

A boy stands below a painting of his father, killed by Israeli forces

This morning we received a call from the Israeli Committee Against House Demolitions (ICAHD) that two Palestinian homes were being destroyed in East Jerusalem. We were too far to make it in time, but it's not hard to guess the reason—either the family did not have a building permit, or the demolition was punitive. Although 2 years ago the army declared it would halt punitive demolitions since they are ineffective at deterring attacks (other good reasons could have included that they are illegal, unethical, and a form of collective punishment), such demolitions continue in Gaza, and I can only assume that goes for East Jerusalem as well.

One punitive demolition attempt in Gaza recently received widespread media attention: a man, upon hearing that the army would demolish his home, quickly gathered friends and family to flood his home so that demolition would require running over hundreds of people as well. Their organized direct action was successful and the bulldozers eventually retreated.[17] Who says there is no nonviolent resistance in Palestine?

---

[15] Israel also routinely denies travel permits to Palestinian elected officials, preventing them from participating in parliamentary affairs. Carter, p. 210.

[16] Ministry of Defense Declaration of terrorist organizations, illegal associations, and confiscation orders. *www.mod.gov.il/pages/general/teror.asp*

[17] "Human shield deters Israeli strike," *BBC News* (November 19, 2006).

The Israeli army said that the man was involved in shooting Qassam rockets at Israeli towns, threatening Israeli civilians. Hearing this, some people I know have sympathized with Israel. Bizarro World Syndrome. Yes, any country has a right to defend its own citizens. But Israel's punitive demolitions aren't just of the homes of suspects or confirmed criminals themselves; Israel targets the homes of their families. After the Oklahoma City bombing, did the FBI bulldoze Timothy McVeigh's home? Did they bulldoze the home of his parents, and his siblings, and his cousins? Should they have? Does Israel demolish the homes of Jewish murderers or their families?[18] It's astounding the way Israeli security hysteria—most of it understandable, in my opinion—has warped many people's senses of what is acceptable and what isn't. It doesn't take more than switching the names and ethnicities around to expose the underlying inconsistencies. Israel is one of just two countries in the world that have "punished the families of suspected offenders by demolishing their homes." The other was Iraq under Saddam Hussein.[19]

The settlements complete the bizarro world. I think my colleague Amy articulated it best in her blog when she wrote:

> Pretend you are Canadian and you went to Sweden. Maybe you bought some land there and built some houses and sold them to your Canadian friends. Maybe you even built a little fence around your compound. But is it okay to raise the Canadian flag, impose immigrant restrictions, have the Canadian military protect you, and announce it to be part of Canada? The same thing is happening here and some people think it's just fine.[20]

Amy's analogy assumes that settlers are even buying land in the Occupied Territories, which they are not, at least not from the land's rightful owners. They are stealing it, or more accurately, their government is stealing it and encouraging citizens to move onto it. The irony is that although Israeli flags, soldiers, and families are ubiquitous in the West Bank, Israel is careful not to officially claim the West Bank to be a part of Israel, because then it would have to extend rights to the people living there. Giving Palestinians in the coveted West Bank equal rights to the people who live all around them in Jewish-only towns and cities would eventually render Palestinians a majority in Israel, and Jews a minority. If it wanted to be a democracy, Israel would have to evolve from being the state only of the Jews to being a state of its citizens and occupants. But that remains a radical idea for most.

Occupation is not a transitional stage; it's a strategic limbo between annexation and withdrawal in which the occupier enjoys control over territory and its resources without having to grant inhabitants equal rights and freedoms. But although the economics of the Occupation are sustainable (as long as US aid continues),[21] the injustice is not; oppressed people will always resist. Territorially, it is not in Israel's interest to end the Occupation, but in terms of security and basic decency, I believe it is. Time will tell which interest will ultimately prevail.

---

[18] The answer is no. According to *B'tselem*, "[House demolitions have] never been used against Israeli civilians who committed acts similar to those for which Palestinian houses are demolished." "Through No Fault of Their Own: Punitive House Demolitions during the al-Aqsa Intifada," *B'tselem* (Jerusalem, 2004), p. 4; As cited in Finkelstein, *Chutzpah*, p. 169.

[19] *Human Rights Watch World Report* 1992; As cited in Finkelstein, *Chutzpah*, p. 169.

[20] January 16, 2006. *www.travelingamy.blogspot.com*

[21] For a discussion of the economics of the Occupation, see pp. 349-350.

Planting Trees with the "Palestinian Gandhi"

Sunday, February 11, 2007

Two winters ago I attended a demonstration in Bil'in village to protest the Wall, which Israel was in the process of building between the village and more than half of its land. It was the second Friday in a row that the community had come together to protest their collective imprisonment and dispossession. Now, 2 years later, the Wall is complete around Bil'in. Yet the village continues, week after week, to come together to demonstrate in new and creative ways, in spite of the obstacles.

Bil'in has paid a price for its determination. Villagers have withstood rubber bullets, sound bombs, tear gas, beatings, live ammunition, arrests, kidnappings, arson, threats of deportation, and more, yet they continue to demonstrate. When the army declared an overnight curfew on Bil'in, villagers held a volleyball tournament from midnight to 3 a.m. between teams of Israelis, internationals, and Palestinians. When the army declared that internationals were forbidden from entering Bil'in, villagers invited foreign musical groups to sing and dance on their land with them. When a nearby settlement continued expansion on Bil'in land, villagers built their own outpost! It is a fort resembling the trailers used by ideological settlers to illegally squat Palestinian land, but this one open to internationals, Israelis, and villagers to affirm Palestinians' right to live on their land. They call it the "Center for Joint Struggle," and although the original was destroyed, another towed, and yet another burned, the villagers return each time to reassert their rights and build a new community home on their stolen groves.

I visited the Bil'in outpost for the first time today. I arrived with a caravan of Israeli activists from Tel Aviv early in the morning, and was embarrassed to realize we had woken two villagers sleeping inside. One, named Ashraf, insisted he was already awake as he rubbed his eyes, and shuffled around to prepare tea and drag out mattresses for us to sit on under the olive trees. It was a beautiful day, and I admired the fort held together in part by sheets and

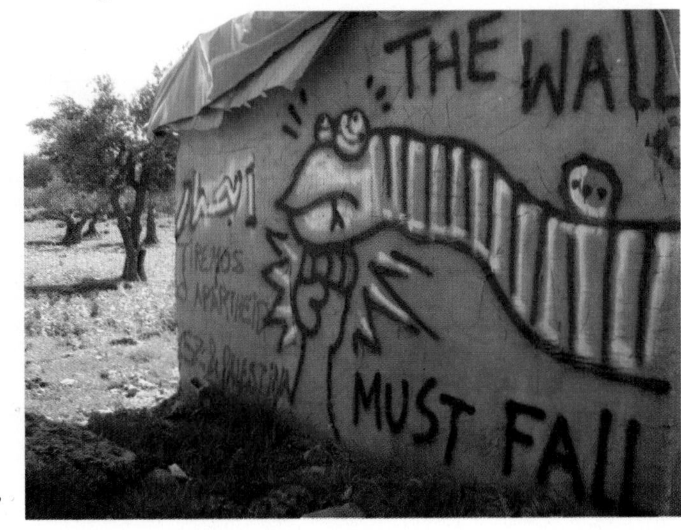

The "Center for Joint Struggle"

A friend of Bil'in documents the ongoing nonviolent resistance for which the village has become famous.

tree trunks, and the organic garden they had created next to it. We chatted and munched on chocolate wafers as we waited for other villagers to arrive for the planned action. Ashraf was disappointed when his friend Yonatan—an Israeli vegan—declined each round of cookies, and squinted through the ingredients on everything in his snack stash desperate to find something without milk. Eventually the others arrived and we began walking towards the nearby settlement of Modi'in Ilit.

I had forgotten how quickly settlements can grow. Modi'in Ilit is a large Jewish-only colony built on Bil'in village land. The settlement is home to more than 33,000 Israelis and about twice as many houses, according to an Israeli activist who drove me through it on our way to Bil'in. In spite of generous financial packages, the Israeli government has not succeeded in transferring as many Israeli families as they have made room for, yet construction continues aggressively.

Modi'in Ilit is also known as Kiryat Sefer, and its extensions are sometimes called Matityahu East or Green Park. According to my friend Kobi, an Israeli mathematician and activist, "Giving settlements different names is part of a general strategy of obstruction and disinformation by developers and the Civil Administration. Master plans are not available, construction is not announced, the planning laws are alternatively Ottoman, British, Jordanian, or Israeli, whichever suits the settlers' or contractors' purposes at any particular moment. This makes it harder for opponents to know what they're up against and to monitor it." If the court rules something illegal for one settlement, contractors will continue activity under a different name. Although the court recently required developers to cease all activity in certain areas annexed from Bil'in, we saw cranes working as we drove through.

Modi'in Ilit contractors continue aggressive construction of new housing units on Bil'in village's land even though half of the 60,000 or so current units in the settlement remain empty.

Bil'in villagers have filed a number of lawsuits against Modi'in Ilit. Today they were planting olive trees on two fenced-in enclaves that the Israeli court had confirmed do indeed belong to Bil'in

Above: Ashraf follows a fellow Bil'in resident to the village's encaged land to plant olive trees. Right: Villagers uncover illegal underground settlement infrastructure on their land.

villagers. Contractors were required to remove all infrastructure from the enclaves and to restore the land to its previous state. But as we dug holes for the trees, we uncovered all kinds of illegal activity. In the first enclave, we found water pipes, telephone lines, and remnants of an old concrete settler road. In the second enclave we found parts of a building foundation that had been simply covered up with mounds of dirt. As we dug, we were approached by settler security and eventually the contractor himself, who was visibly nervous. Half a dozen Israelis and internationals were extensively documenting his illegal work, and he was likely to get into a lot of trouble. After we finished planting, the Israelis scooted back under the fence to the settlement where they'd parked, and we began the walk back to Bil'in, where we hoped to catch transport back to our home in the West Bank.

Soldiers block Bil'in villagers from bringing international friends to their village.

It was upsetting to see the Wall complete in Bil'in, knowing all the village had done to try and prevent it, or at least change its path. Now it separates the villagers from their land, including the outpost and enclaves where we'd been. The soldiers holding the key to the gate met us along the way and declared that only village residents could pass to Bil'in.

Soldiers block Bil'in villagers from bringing international friends to their village.

Abdallah, one of the villagers, explained in Hebrew that we are his friends and he was inviting us to his village. He did not ask for permission, he stated clearly that this was his and our right and that we had come in peace. Then he began walking forward and motioned for us to come along.

The soldiers immediately began yelling and formed a line to prevent us from passing. One soldier removed a tear gas canister from his belt. Abdallah sat down in the road in protest, and invited us to sit with him. He explained once again that there is no law against us passing, and made it clear that we would not cause the soldiers any harm or use violence.

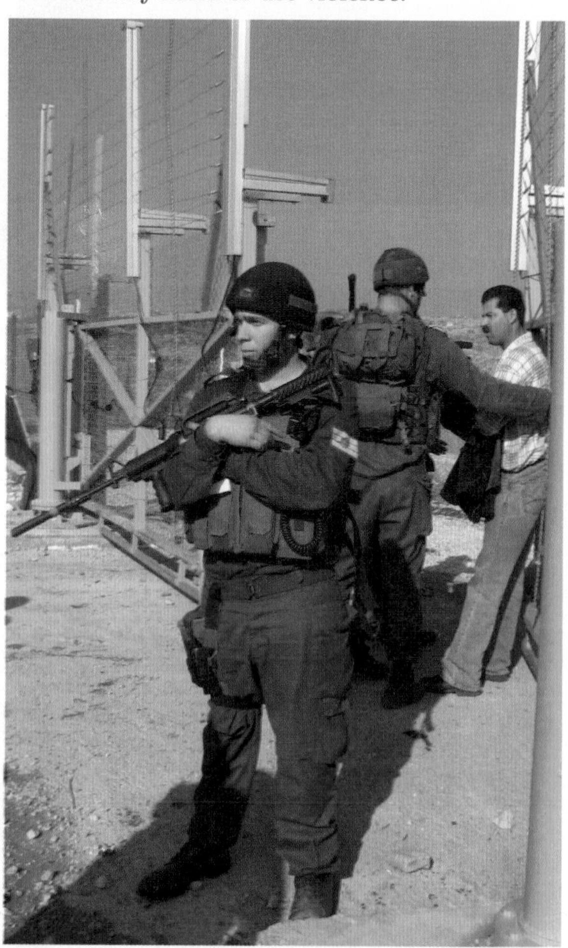

Having come between Abdallah and his friends, the soldiers edge Abdallah onto the other side of the Wall.

Abdallah is an active member of Bil'in's Popular Committee Against the Wall. He's been called the "Palestinian Gandhi" and he remains committed to nonviolent resistance, no matter how many times the army beats or imprisons him. Abdallah has been arrested several times: Once he was forcibly removed from a bridge that the village had built bearing the words, "Peace Needs Bridges Not Walls." Another time he was taken while holding a tombstone. During our confrontation with the army, Abdallah was calm and composed; I could tell that the soldiers were not accustomed to Palestinians neither submitting to them nor becoming upset.

After calling a number of army hotlines for help (in vain), we resolved to try again to walk peacefully through the line of soldiers towards the village. Abdallah led the group, with his hands up in the air. As soon as he'd passed the soldiers, they began pushing my colleagues and me back, separating us from Abdallah. They pushed him against the gate, quickly opened it, pushed him onto the other side, and closed it. He did not resist. He just kept asking, "*Lamma? Lamma?*" ("Why? Why?" in Hebrew). Another villager approached the soldiers, holding the hand of his young daughter. He asked me, "Shall we go to my village?" and I said, "*Yalla*" ("Let's go" in Arabic). He stuck out his elbow for me to link arms with him, and we began to walk towards the soldiers. They immediately broke between us and shoved the man and his daughter through the opened gate before closing it. They threatened to arrest me. I said I hadn't done anything illegal.

The only Palestinian remaining on our side of the Wall was Ashraf, who would probably stay in the Palestinian outpost "fort" again. By this time I realized he was slightly mentally disabled, and I hoped he would make it back okay. Abdallah called to us through the fence that he would meet us at the checkpoint a couple miles away if we could hitch a ride there with a settler security man who had recently arrived, curious about the commotion. The man agreed—if only to get us out of there—and half an hour later we were in Abdallah's car on the detour road back to Bil'in. On the way Abdallah told us the bad news: Ashraf, whom we'd left at the scene, had been detained. We drove quickly from the village to the gate of the Wall, now opposite the soldiers we'd confronted earlier. We could see Ashraf sitting in a military tent, handcuffed and blindfolded. Abdallah called some Israeli friends

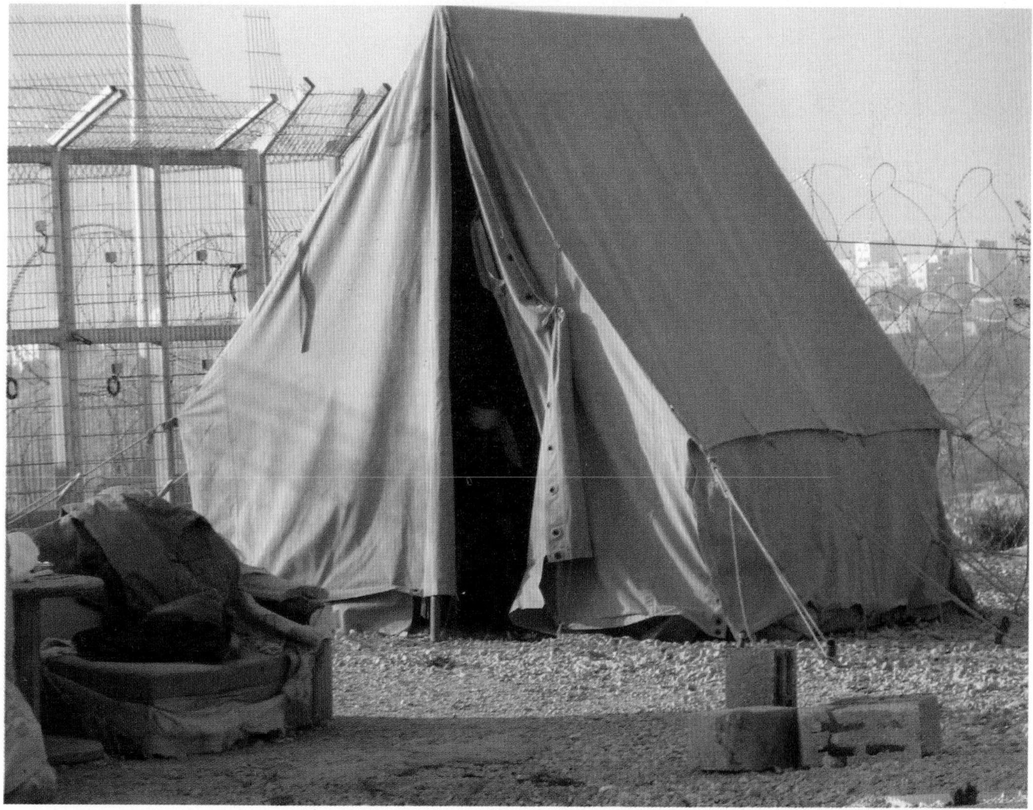

Soldiers hold Ashraf blindfolded in a tent as punishment for not responding to their questions.

and a lawyer, and I took some photos. When pressed, the soldiers explained that they had asked Ashraf if he wanted to return to his village and he said nothing. Then they asked if he wanted to return to the outpost and he said nothing. Now they were detaining him temporarily as punishment for not responding to their questions. When asked when he would be released they said they hadn't decided yet but maybe in half an hour. Abdallah felt that rather than cause a big scene we should wait and hope they were telling the truth.

We sat down next to the gate. I prayed the soldiers would not hurt Ashraf, not sure if I could bear watching, while unable to try and stop it. But they left him alone, and after about 40 minutes they removed his blindfold and handcuffs and escorted him to the gate. He walked through with a sheepish smile, clearly moved that we had waited to ensure his release. We drove back to Abdallah's house—half of which he's donated as a home for Israelis and internationals to have their own space in the village. We told Abdallah we'd see him next Friday, and started the long journey back to Haris.

Ashraf is released.

Paralysis, Prophets, & Forgiveness

Monday, February 19, 2007

Five years ago, 9-month-old Mohammed and his grandmother were in their West Bank home when it began to fill with nerve gas from a nearby military base. The army had moved in on a hill near their home in the Skan Abu Absa suburb of Ramallah, and would frequently shoot all over the surrounding area, sometimes in retaliation for Palestinian gunfire from a hill away from the suburb. As the gas seeped into his living room, Mohammed began to shake violently before suffering a stroke, which caused extensive paralysis. When his grandmother ran to pick him up, she, too, inhaled the gas, and felt an acute burning sensation all over her body. When she realized her grandson had stopped moving, she pleaded with the soldiers outside to open the road out of her town and raced Mohammed to the hospital. There, he was diagnosed with severe neurological deterioration resulting in a vegetative state. The Palestinian Ministry of Health and the United Nations Relief and Works Agency conducted extensive tests on Mohammed and his parents to determine with certainty the cause of his condition. After a full genetic investigation, doctors concluded that Mohammed's state was neither hereditary nor due to a chromosomal abnormality, but a result of the poisonous gas.

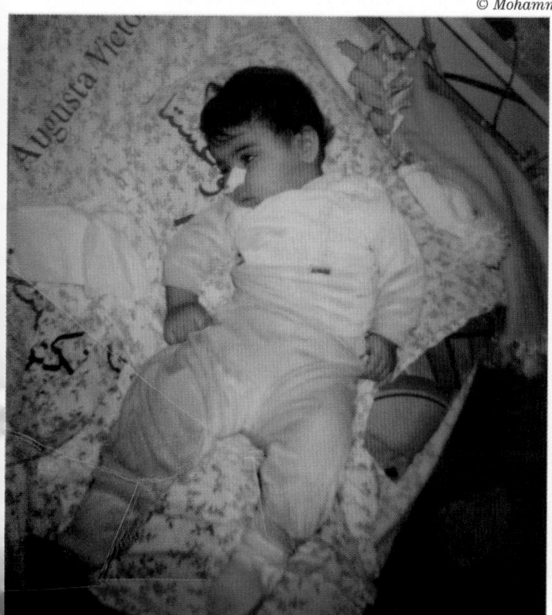

9-month-old Mohammed was paralyzed from poisonous gas shot by soldiers into his home.

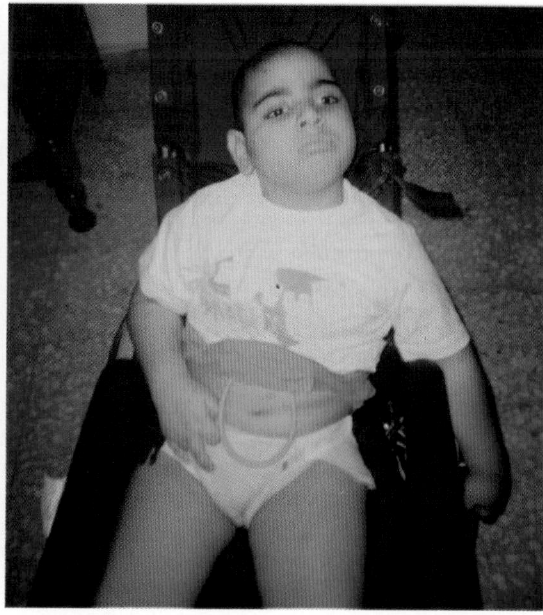

Mohammed today, age 6, eats through a tube connected to his stomach.

I met Mohammed's father, Zaim, waiting at a checkpoint near Haris. He'd hesitated to publicize his son's story for fear of harassment from the army. He said his family was suffering enough—their personal tragedy only began with the gassing. After Mohammed's injury, Zaim's father went from being a strong healthy 47-year-old to an emotional and physical wreck, and died one year later from stress and heart problems. Mohammed, now 6 years old, continues to suffer from severe neurodevelopmental delay, poorly controlled seizure disorder, loss of sight, and inability to eat normally. He eats via a tube poking directly into his stomach and survives on a special formula, "Pediasure," which is not available in Israel/Palestine, so Zaim travels to Jordan every 3 months to bring the formula and anticonvulsants that Mohammad requires. Each time Zaim crosses back to the West Bank, he must pay Israeli customs taxes on the formula, totaling hundreds of dollars a year. This is in addition to countless other expenses: land travel, adult diapers, maintaining Mohammed's customized bed (to prevent bed sores), medicine, and round-the-clock care. Zaim and his wife spend so much money taking care of Mohammed that they have no money left to take legal action against the Israeli army for poisoning their son.

Even if Mohammed's family had enough money for a lawsuit, however, there is little reason to think they would win. Tragic stories like Mohammed's are all too common in the West Bank. I recently interviewed Moussa, a young paraplegic who lost the use of his legs 5 years ago at the age of 19 when a soldier shot him in the colon. Last Monday, Moussa began experiencing severe pain from an infection in his wound, which his doctor warned could become systemic if not treated immediately. There was a risk that the infection would reach Moussa's back, developing into gangrene, and poisoning his blood. Unfortunately, no West Bank hospital was equipped to treat Moussa, and on Tuesday his doctor referred him to a hospital in Jordan. In 2 days the family renewed Moussa's passport and obtained a transfer from the Palestinian Ministry of Health to receive treatment in Amman. But as the family was preparing to leave, on Thursday, Israel refused the sick wheelchair-bound young man permission to leave the West Bank for unspecified "security reasons." When Moussa's doctor explained that waiting could mean the difference between life and death, the Israeli District Coordination Office invited the family to appeal the decision, but only 3 days later, after the Jewish Sabbath.

We put Moussa's family in touch with Physicians for Human Rights, who got him to Jordan before his infection became fatal. But Moussa will still never walk again, nor will my neighbor and friend Issa, who was shot by soldiers outside his home in May 2001 as he ushered children in from the streets during an army invasion. In spite of his handicap, Issa remains committed to working nonviolently against the Occupation.[22]

Almost 3 years ago, Issa wrote an open letter to the two nameless soldiers who shot and paralyzed him. It was published in *Haaretz* and elsewhere, and I've copied it below:

> I remember you. I remember your confused face when you stood above my head and wouldn't let people come to my aid. I remember how my voice grew weaker, when I said to you: `Be humane and let my parents help me.' I keep all those pictures in my head. How I lay on the ground, trying to get up but unable. How I fought my shortness of breath, which was caused by the blood that was collecting in my lungs, and the voice that was weakened because my diaphragm was hurt. I won't hide from you that despite this, I had pity for [you]. I felt that I was strong, because I had powers I didn't know about before.

[22] For more on Issa, see p. 220.

That was exactly 3 years ago. I rushed out of the house in order to distance the village children from the danger of the tear gas. They were used to playing their simple games on the dusty streets of the village while the pregnant women watched over them and chatted. I didn't believe that your weapons contained live bullets or dumdum bullets, which are prohibited under international law. I was able to protect the children and get them away from your fire, and I don't regret that.

I pity you for having become murderers. Since I was a boy, I have hated killing, hated weapons and hated the color red, just as I hate injustice and fight against it. That is how I have understood life since I was a boy, and that, in the same spirit, is what I have taught others. I gave all my strength for the sake of peace and justice and for reducing the suffering that is caused by injustice, whatever its origin. Yes, I pitied you, because you are sick. Sick with hate and loathing, sick with causing injustice, sick with egoism, with the death of the conscience and the allure of power. Recovery and rehabilitation from those illnesses, just as from paralysis, is very long, but possible. I pitied you, I pitied your children and your wives and I ask myself how they can live with you when you are murderers. I pitied you for having shed your humanity and your values and the precepts of your religion and even your military laws, which forbid breaking into homes and beating civilians, because that undermines the soldier's morale, his strength and his manhood.

I pitied you for saying that you are the victims of the Nazis of yesterday, and I don't understand how yesterday's victim can become today's criminal. That worries me in connection with today's victim—my people are those victims—and I am afraid that they too will become tomorrow's criminals. I pity you for having fallen victim to a culture that understands life as though it is based on killing, destruction, sowing fear and terror, and lording it over others. Despite all that, I believe that there is a chance for atonement and forgiveness and a possibility that you will restore to yourselves something of your lost humanity and morality. You can recover from the illnesses of hatred and the lust for revenge, and if we should meet one day, even in my house, you can be certain that you won't find me holding an explosive belt or concealing a knife in my pocket or in the wheels of my chair. But you will find someone who will help you get back what you lost.

You will find a soft and delicate infant here, whose age is the same as the second in which you pulled the trigger and who will never see his father standing on his feet but who is full of pride and power, even if he has to push his father's chair, having no other choice. Even though I have reasons to hate you, I don't feel that way and I have no regrets.

–Issa Suf

May 15, 2004, the third anniversary of my being wounded[23]

Issa is Arabic for Jesus, who is also revered as a prophet in the Muslim faith. Some would say it's a suitable name for a man who believes in responding to injustice with passionate nonviolence and forgiveness. Mohammed and Moussa (Arabic for Moses, who is also considered a prophet in Islam) never wrote a letter like Issa's, but they and their families welcomed me, a Jewish American, into their homes with gentle kindness and openness. Struggling for peace and survival in spite of great personal tragedies, the three prophets' namesakes and their families, like so many Palestinians paralyzed physically (as well as emotionally, spiritually, and economically) by the Occupation, are among the true—albeit often forgotten—heroes of Palestine.

[23] Gideon Levy, "'I pity you for becoming murderers,'" *Haaretz* (July 7, 2004).

Witness in Palestine

Nablus Invasion: Occupied Homes & Minds

Sunday, March 4, 2007

At around 1 a.m. on Sunday, February 25th, hundreds of Israeli soldiers in military vehicles surrounded Nablus and invaded the city, imposing a total curfew and seizing control over local television and radio headquarters, from which they broadcasted their mission: to capture or assassinate eight fighters from Al-Aqsa Martyrs' Brigades, the armed wing of the Fatah movement. Meanwhile, no news was allowed out of the stations about the invasion, so several colleagues and I decided to enter the city as witnesses. After one week in Nablus, I composed a series of three reports on what I had experienced. This is the first:

I don't know where to begin. It would make sense to start at the beginning, but the beginning was ages ago, long before I arrived. Nor is there any end in sight. I was dropped

Jeeps surround Nablus Old City and impose curfew.

into life in Nablus for one short week and I'm not sure if I'll ever recover. As I write from a place of safety, the people of Nablus continue to struggle, not just with the nightly incursions, bombings, and assassinations, but also simply to remember their own humanity in spite of the most inhumane treatment. I'm trying to rediscover my own, to revive the parts of me now polluted with anger, or worse—shut off, as if a part of me is dead. And I was there for just one week.

We arrived last Sunday to help volunteers from the Union of Palestinian Medical Relief Committees (UPMRC) deliver food and medical services. The 40,000 residents of the Nablus Old City were trapped in their homes, inside a war zone, unable to go to work or school, or even to buy food for their families. According to many families, this invasion posed a greater threat than those of the past because it was coming on top of an already desperate economic situation caused by the US-led embargo after the Hamas elections. Whereas in the past, residents would stock up on food and supplies in case of an invasion, these days people hardly have enough to meet their current needs. Many are working to buy bread for that very day, so the invasion was not only leaving them out of food, but preventing them from going out to make the money they need to buy more.

The normally busy streets of the Old City market are abandoned.

The Medical Relief volunteers led us into the Old City. Families called to us from windows above the twisted cobbled streets: "We have no more food!"; "My baby needs milk!"; "My mother has diabetes and is out of insulin!" As we rounded each corner, we would call, "Internationals! Medical Relief!" knowing soldiers were less likely to shoot foreigners breaking curfew than others.

Nablus Old City residents call out their windows that they need food and medicine.

Sometimes we would round a corner and find ourselves face to face with soldiers, jumpy and angry, their US-made guns pointed at us: "Go back!" "Put away your camera!" Often they were holding back large muzzled dogs. My heart was beating and knees shaking so fast I was sure I would collapse, but we followed

the Medical Relief volunteers' lead. They were not interested in challenging the soldiers' actions and authority, just in getting treatment and food to people who needed it. I recognized that this is one major difference between resistance work and humanitarian aid.

Sometimes the soldiers allowed the medical volunteers through. Often they didn't. As night fell and soldiers refused our passage to the hospital, we decided to call it a day and hoped we'd have more luck in the morning. As we were making our last bread delivery, eight soldiers walked by our group with one Palestinian. The man spoke quietly as he passed us: "I am being used as a human shield."

Using civilians as human shields is a serious violation of international law, and we immediately called *B'tselem* and Machsom Watch to file reports and hopefully help free the man. One Israeli contact explained that the practice is so common that we probably couldn't stop it before the man would be replaced with another, and another after that.[24] We

Soldiers take over neighborhoods in the Old City.

wanted to check with the man's family to see if there was anything else we could do, but the army had blocked off their whole neighborhood.

It was with an unshakeable feeling of helplessness that we checked into the Crystal Hotel that night, bombs exploding in the Old City nearby under a heavy rainstorm. We were woken at 6 a.m. by the jeeps driving through the streets announcing curfew. We met the medical relief workers and began making rounds again. Many families needed bread. One

A mother and her child are finally permitted to enter the Old City and to carry bread to hungry families along their way home.

[24] Israel's widespread practice of using Palestinians as human shields is outlined in "Human Shield: Use of Palestinian Civilians as Human Shields in Violation of High Court of Justice Order," *B'tselem* (Jerusalem, 2002), pp. 2, 19.

child had a broken arm and needed treatment. Occasionally while we were visiting families, soldiers would barge in with dogs, herd everyone into one room, and search the rest of the house. I would try to amuse the children to distract them, or maybe to distract myself. I tried to imagine what it would be like to have my home raided and my possessions destroyed, to be made a prisoner in my own house. Most raids ended quickly but some houses were occupied for days on end. We couldn't reach the families in them but heard stories from neighbors and medical workers.

Soldiers blindfold and lead away a man to interrogation.

The Dilal family's home had been occupied, and 20 people were stuffed into one room for almost 48 hours. Among them were two elderly people with heart problems, one pregnant woman, and eight small children. The rest of their home had been transformed into a military base where soldiers could rest and meet between operations.

The Awad family was also confined to one room of their home while soldiers took over the rest of the house. One floor was reportedly transformed into an intelligence center, another into a prison, and the basement into a makeshift interrogation center. We had already begun to hear stories from young men returning from interrogation—affectionately referred to as "Hell" in Arabic—while others went missing. In alleys we would find men handcuffed and blindfolded, being led into jeeps while soldiers aimed their guns in our direction as an unspoken warning against speaking or photographing. I kept my camera hidden, knowing that one Reuters cameraman had already had his film taken at gunpoint.

UPMRC volunteers were also starting to disappear, including one man named Alaa, with whom we had delivered bread a few hours before. I had last seen him while I was carrying one of two sick children from the clinic back to their home, since their parents could not

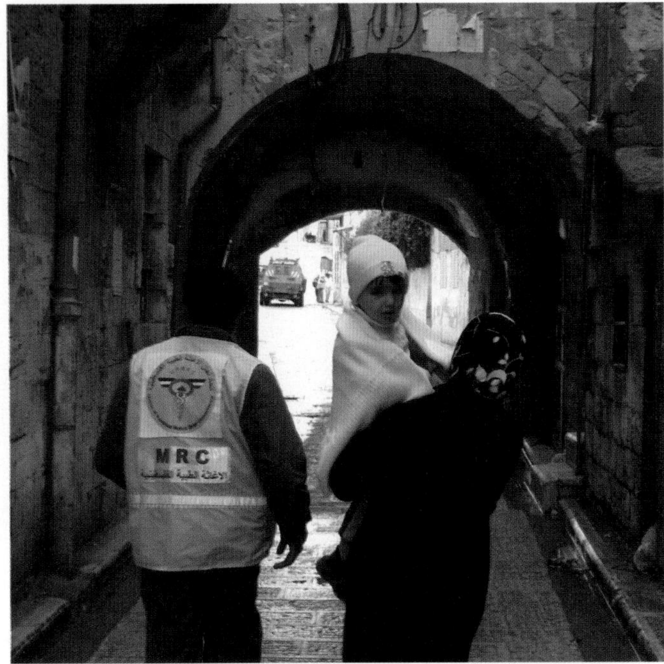

UPMRC volunteers accompany a mother and her child to an ambulance in violation of the curfew.

come to get them. After we'd delivered the kids and were walking away, we heard shooting from close behind us, just beyond the children's house. Within minutes, we learned that an unarmed man named Anan Tibi had been shot dead on his roof, and his unarmed 20-year-old son Ashraf's elbow had been blown off by a dumdum bullet. After the shooting, soldiers entered the house and detained young Ashraf, who was in shock. When Alaa and a doctor attempted to enter the home to bring the father's body down to an ambulance, soldiers detained them both. They held the doctor for several hours and then let him go. They kept Alaa in custody, saying he "looked suspicious."

Alaa and Ashraf were eventually released, and we took their reports the next day. Ashraf was in the hospital, surrounded by friends and family. He agreed to tell us his story:

> On Monday around noon, my dad went up to the roof to check on the water, which was not working. I sensed some movement outside and through the window I saw soldiers. I ran upstairs to warn my dad that the army was near, and as I spoke the words a dumdum bullet hit my right elbow, shattering it. My dad ran towards me to save me. When he looked back towards where the bullet had come from, he was shot in the neck by a sniper, and then in the head.

Ashraf Tibi

Anan Tibi

> I called for help and tried to give my dad CPR. When the ambulance arrived, it was surrounded by jeeps on all sides and prevented from reaching our home. The soldiers took me into one of their jeeps while my father was still bleeding seriously. They held me for an hour and a half before taking me to an ambulance. One soldier bragged that he was the one who shot me and my dad, and followed me to the ambulance in a jeep by himself. My family told me afterwards that after the soldiers made sure of my dad's death, they allowed the medical workers to carry him down.

The water tank next to which Anan Tibi was standing when he was shot dead on his roof

Ashraf pointed to a smiling picture of his father that hung on the wall opposite his hospital bed. I asked our translator how Ashraf knew CPR. He explained that Ashraf is an Emergency Medical Volunteer, and the type of person who risks his own life to save others. We asked Ashraf if he had a message for the American people. His response: "We are not terrorists—the soldiers will not find what they're looking for here. We are civilians, and we want to be left alone so that we may live."

There was a great deal of misinformation surrounding Ashraf's story in the Israeli and international media. Some news sources claimed he and his father were armed; others said they were walking around, breaking curfew. I visited the roof, I saw the bloodstains, I spoke to the medical volunteers who evacuated the men.[25] It is so crucial to get these stories out, especially as the media seems to have already moved on from the story.

The view from Anan Tibi's roof of the building (behind the bare trees) from which he and his son were shot

---

[25] Ashraf's interview and other excellent footage of the events described above are available from the Research Journalism Initiative. *www.ResearchJournalismInitiative.net*

Witness in Palestine

Nablus Invasion: Human Shields & Medical Obstruction

Monday, March 5, 2007

Most of the jeeps pulled out late last Monday night, but we all knew they would be back. Israeli officials announced that the operation was not over, as they had not yet achieved their objectives. Typically the army will withdraw for several hours or a whole day, hoping to draw out the wanted men. Soldiers will remain in occupied houses, where they typically set up sniper nests.

During the invasion, soldiers trashed countless local shops.

Despite the lingering soldiers, the withdrawal gave the city a chance to move and relax a bit before the next strike. We took the chance to document the destruction and take reports from victims and their families. Our first stop was Al-Watani Hospital, one of many that had been surrounded during the invasion. According to the director, soldiers set up a checkpoint for everyone coming into or out of the hospital, and questioned several patients after checking them. He worried about the psychological and physical effects of even mild interrogation on patients already frail with sickness.

In the hospital we met family members of Ghareb Selhab, a man who had been in critical condition since the day before. According to his son, Ghareb was in the bathroom when his home began to fill with tear gas. He gasped to his wife that he could not breathe, and went into cardiac arrest. The family immediately called for help, but soldiers prevented the ambulance from reaching Ghareb's home for over an hour. By that time, Ghareb had stopped breathing and fallen into a deep coma. When they reached the hospital, he had no pulse and it was too late. Doctors hooked him up to a breathing machine but, knowing it was hopeless, yesterday the family decided to pull the plug. He was 47 years old, the father of seven.

Normally UPMRC volunteers serve as a backup if ambulances can't get through, but as luck would have it, while Ghareb was breathing his last independent breath, the army was raiding the UPMRC. Soldiers came into the clinic with dogs and herded all the doctors and internationals into one room while they searched the building. My colleagues Nova and Yara overheard someone being beaten next door.

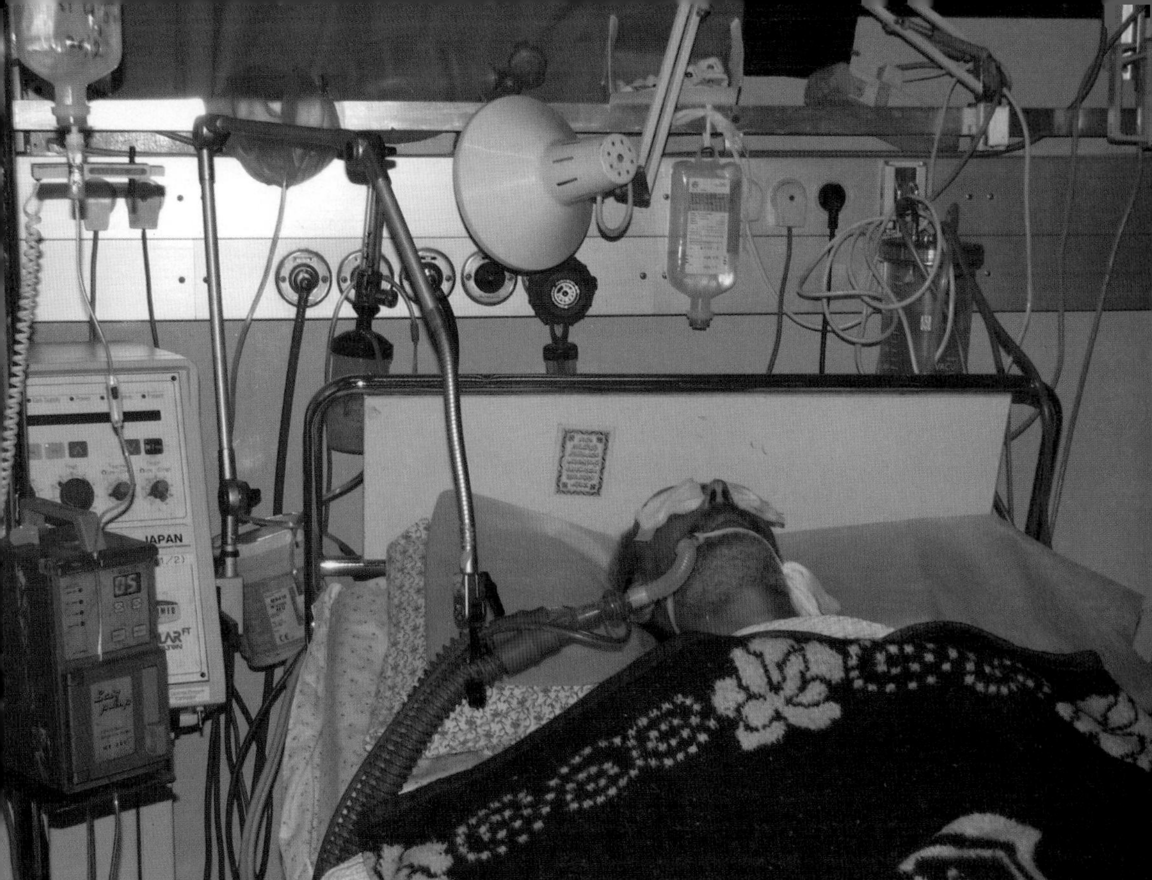

Ghareb, a 47-year-old father of seven, was tear-gassed in his home, causing him to go into cardiac arrest. Soldiers prevented ambulances from reaching him in time to save him.

The raid was just another instance of the army detaining medical relief workers. We interviewed Alaa from the UPMRC about his detention on Monday when he tried to evacuate Ashraf's father. Alaa said the soldiers handcuffed him and held him in a jeep for 7 hours. They scolded him when his hands shook (he has a weak pulse condition), and hit him whenever he raised his head. Alaa was released 5 miles south of the city at midnight, but was back delivering medicine with UPMRC on Wednesday, when the soldiers reinvaded Nablus and curfew was imposed again

The second invasion seemed heavier than the first, with even more soldiers and jeeps around every corner. More and more families were going incommunicado, which, we understood, meant that their homes were being occupied. Sometimes people would call for help and when we arrived at their houses nobody would answer the door. Had they left their homes? Neighbors would assure us that they were still inside. We would yell to the soldiers that we knew the families were there and we just wanted to deliver medicine. After some insisting sometimes the soldiers would answer; sometimes not.

At one point we were made to wait 40 minutes outside an occupied home. As we waited, soldiers escorted detained men in and out, including one group of 10 medical volunteers from the Red Crescent Society and the UPMRC. After half an hour they let the medical relief workers go on the condition that they would leave the area and stop distributing medicine.

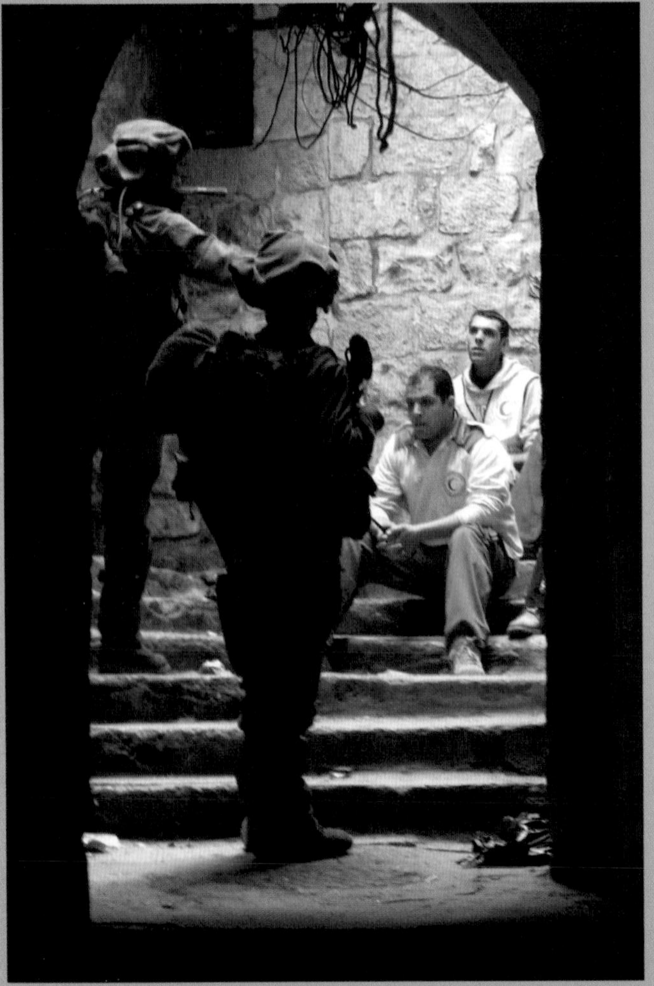

Medical Obstruction

Top left: Alaa, a UPMRC volunteer who was detained and beaten while delivering medical services because soldiers said he "looked suspicious"

Top right: Soldiers confiscate the IDs of medics and refuse to return them for one hour, preventing the volunteers from delivering medical services.

Left: Soldiers detain 10 medical workers outside an occupied house. After half an hour, the medics were released on condition that they leave the area and stop delivering medicine.

Sometimes the detention was unofficial. Soldiers once demanded at gunpoint the IDs of the four volunteers whom we were accompanying and then refused to give them back for a full hour. Because it's extremely dangerous to be caught breaking curfew without an ID, we were forced to wait. Meanwhile, a diabetic was waiting for his insulin, which we were on our way to deliver. The soldiers said they were checking the IDs, but spent the hour chatting, eating lunch, and taking pictures of us waiting.

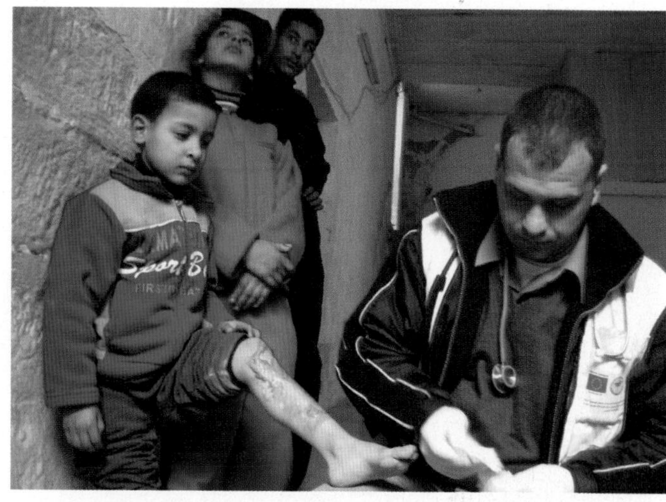

A UPMRC doctor delivers medical treatment to a boy with serious burns. Soldiers detained the doctor several times during the invasion.

There were so many stories that I stopped writing them down. But one that stuck with me came from Nova and Yara, who were delivering bread and medicine with three friends from the UPMRC when a group of soldiers called them over. One by one, our UPMRC friends were ordered to open their jackets, pull their pants down, turn around, and put their hands up against the wall. Nova and Yara averted their eyes as the men were forced to strip in front of them. The soldiers let them go afterwards, but we have scarcely seen our friends since—I can only imagine their embarrassment, in a culture where modesty and gender boundaries are so important.

Something about humiliation is worse than physical punishment. I've heard stories of young women detained, photographed naked, and threatened that if they don't collaborate with the army (as spies), their pictures will be distributed, shaming them and their families beyond repair. This can be more effective than bribery and even torture. Many of the detainees are young people, sometimes not more than 13 years old, who say they aren't questioned about the wanted men at all. Instead, soldiers use various techniques to encourage them to collaborate.

It's strategic to target the young and weak. We discovered an 11-year-old girl named Jihan who was taken from her home to serve as a human shield after her father and older sister proved too strong-willed to cooperate. The army came for her at night and made her walk in front of 10 armed soldiers as they went from house to house in the Old City. When she protested, they threatened to arrest her.

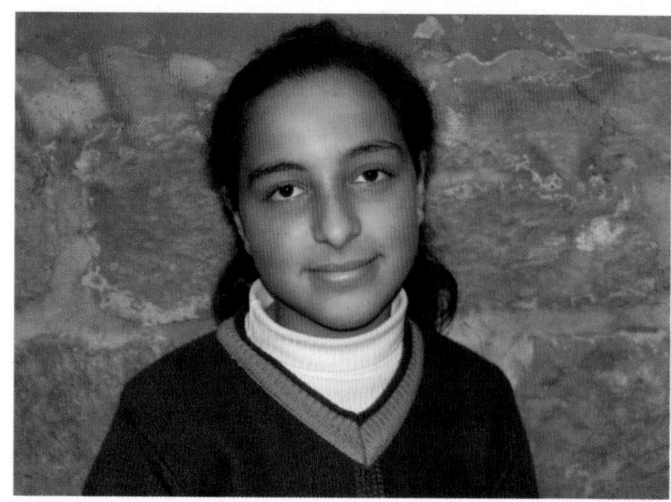

Jihan, 11 years old, was used by Israeli soldiers as a human shield.

A family sits in front of the hole that soldiers broke in the wall to enter the family's home. The child with the black hat was also used as a human shield.

Jihan was not the only young human shield used this week. One family told us how the soldiers invaded by breaking a hole through their wall, herding 27 family members into one room, and forcing two young men to open doors in front of them as they raided the rest of the neighborhood. After 6 hours, the women and older men were released while the young men being used as human shields and all the other men were handcuffed and taken away. One of those men, Abdallah, told us what happened:

> We were five in total, ages 17 to 30. They led us away from our home through the hole that they'd made in our wall. It was hard to climb through the hole without the use of our hands. Then we had to walk up the steep and rocky hill behind our house, which was also very difficult with our hands behind our backs.
>
> The soldiers brought us to a home in the Raas Al-Ain quarter. We were not allowed to use the toilet at all for the next 10 hours, but my need was very urgent during most of that time. After the first couple of hours, we asked when our hands would be untied—we were having pain in our shoulders, especially my brother who is overweight so he cannot remain so long with his hands stretched behind. A soldier came behind us and instead of opening our hands he tied the handcuffs tighter as punishment for asking. It was very painful for us. Soon I could not feel my hands and I asked another soldier if he would loosen the cuffs. He said we would be released soon.

> Instead, we were taken into jeeps, blindfolded, and driven to Huwwara military base south of Nablus. The *Muhabarat* (Israeli Intelligence) were waiting there and when we arrived they took off our blindfolds, looked at our IDs, checked them, and asked a few questions: What's your name? Where are you from? What do you do? We answered their questions in 2 minutes, and then they put the blindfolds back on for 6 more hours. You cannot know the feeling of being detained, handcuffed, and blindfolded for 17 hours. Try closing your eyes and tying your hands for just one hour—it will feel like an eternity, and you will begin to feel you are losing your mind.
>
> Between 9 p.m. and 3 a.m. they led us around to different jeeps. We kept tripping because we could not see anything or use our hands. At 3 a.m. they took off our blindfolds and handcuffs, gave us a paper saying in Hebrew that we'd been at Huwwara, and told us we could go. We could not understand the logic of detaining and handcuffing us all that time without food, water, or access to a toilet just to ask us a couple silly questions that they probably already know the answers to.
>
> Because of the curfew there was no transportation so we had to walk the 8 km [5 miles] back to Nablus. Actually, we ran part of the way because we were scared—there are many dogs on the road, plus we were afraid of being caught in clashes between Palestinians and the army. We arrived at home almost 2 hours later, around five in the morning.

The soldiers returned twice more to Abdallah's house during the invasions, and they will probably be back. The third time they destroyed many things in the house, turning over furniture and breaking glasses and windows. As illustrated by Abdallah's story, it's not clear whether the raids and detention are so much about getting information as general harassment, or at best callous disregard for residents' rights.

Hussein, a vegetable seller, 2 days after he was used by soldiers as a human shield

We documented another raid that took place at a student dormitory of Al-Najaa University. The soldiers arrived at 4:15 a.m., threw sound bombs, and threatened that unless everyone evacuated the building, it would be destroyed on top of them. Students and family residents fled outside in their pajamas and were brought to the basement of a nearby building. Women and children were kept in one room, while all of the men—some as young as 14—were handcuffed and made to sit in another room. For the next 6 hours, the 30 men were forbidden to speak, open a window for fresh air, or even lean against a wall to sleep.

When the soldiers left after 10 a.m. (without undoing the men's plastic hand-cuffs—neighbors came to help free them), the

A graduate student and her family describe their experience being woken up and detained from 4 a.m. to 10 a.m. with other students from an Al-Najaa University dormitory.

The Al-Najaa student dormitory's doors, windows, light fixtures, and elevator were left in shambles after an army raid.

Student dorm rooms were turned upside-down by soldiers looking for wanted men.

students and families returned to find their homes in shambles. Each flat had been raided: soldiers had used bombs to blast open doors, windows were shattered, light fixtures were dangling from their sockets, and the elevator had been blown apart. Bedrooms were turned upside-down, textbooks and assignments strewn across the floor, pictures and pop-star posters ripped from the walls. Like every other raid throughout the invasion, no wanted people were found in the building. But how many more fighters were created?

These reports of detention, raids, human shields, and the obstruction of medical treatment may seem repetitive. I record them here not only because I believe they each deserve to be heard, but more crucially because, with enough reports, these seemingly arbitrary instances of harassment can no longer be dismissed as isolated incidents or unfortunate side effects of conflict, but must be recognized as unspoken policies of the Israeli army. If the intention is security for Israeli citizens, these policies are not only ineffective but, in my opinion, severely counterproductive. If the intention is to frighten the people of Nablus, then this is terrorism and should be recognized and condemned as such.

Nablus Invasion: Resistance, Hypocrisy, & Dead Men Walking

Tuesday, March 6, 2007

What most struck me about the Nablus invasion wasn't the killing of unarmed civilians. It wasn't the deliberate obstruction of medical workers and ambulances, or the indiscriminate detention of men, or the occupied houses and curfews. What I will remember for the rest of my life is the steadfast resistance of the people of Nablus.

I came to Palestine to document and intervene in human rights abuses and to support nonviolent resistance to the Occupation. As I delivered bread and medicine with medical relief workers throughout the invasion, I wondered if I was really fulfilling my mission. Wasn't handing out aid simply accommodating and enabling the curfew?

An experienced Israeli solidarity organizer named Neta Golan eventually clarified things for me. She explained, "It's very good to distribute bread and medicine to needy people, but the real power and purpose of what you are doing is something else. First and foremost, you are supporting Palestinians who are breaking curfew. That is nonviolent resistance. And as you move around in spite of the army's indiscriminate imposition of house arrest, you empower others to do so as well. If the army knows there are dozens or even hundreds of civilians in the streets, and that several of them are internationals, they cannot shoot anything that moves, which they have done during curfews in the past."

Drivers and pedestrians break curfew, refusing to become prisoners in their own city.

Women in the Old City go out to get food for their families in spite of a curfew.

Neta was right. Simply being outside was a powerful form of nonviolent resistance. But the Palestinians didn't need much empowering: from the first day of the invasion, I saw many civilians on the streets and in cars driving through the city, defying the army simply by carrying on some semblance of daily life.

Some Palestinians went a step further in defiance. Once, when I was attempting to enter part of the Old City to deliver bread with a UPMRC volunteer named Firas, we were stopped by the army. Firas waited 10 minutes and then said, "Anna, come with me." He grabbed as many bags as he could carry, and began walking past the jeeps. I grabbed 12 pounds of bread and scrambled after him past the soldiers, who had come out of their jeeps and were yelling, "Hey! Stop! What are you doing? We said you can't enter!" Firas kept walking steadily and I turned around to the soldiers. "We're delivering bread to hungry people. What are you going to do, shoot us?" They were speechless and held their fire.

As we walked away, Firas smiled at me and said, "Next time it will be easier." Indeed, when we returned with more bread, the soldiers told us we could go this time but only for 5 minutes. "Sure," we said and kept walking, knowing the teenage soldiers were trying to salvage some power in the situation.

Resistance was creative and ubiquitous. When we got tired of speaking English loudly as a way of reminding soldiers that internationals were around, one Palestinian girl suggested that we sing her favorite song, "I Will Always Love You," by Whitney Houston. So we sang together as we came around corners to soldiers breaking into houses, annoyed at us for disturbing their raids. I hoped that singing would be both nonthreatening and humanizing in the eyes of the soldiers, while still achieving our objective. When the army prevented medical workers and internationals from entering the Old City, the volunteers gathered posters and paint and put together an impromptu demonstration, documented by all the reporters who were also barred from the Old City. The protesters sat yelling cheers in front of an occupied hospital until they were gassed from jeeps.

The most powerful demonstration came a week later in honor of Women's Day. The Women's Union in Nablus organized a rally and march in conjunction with the Public Committee Against Closure, the UPMRC, the Union of Health Committees, and other local groups. Hundreds of Palestinians, mostly women, gathered and marched to Huwwara checkpoint carrying flags and pictures of sons, husbands, brothers, and fathers who are wanted or imprisoned, or have been killed by the army. Hundreds of women held their ground as soldiers equipped with riot gear attempted to push the crowd back.

My colleague Nova recognized one of the soldiers from the invasion, because our last interaction with him had been so memorable. A few days before, we had been accompanying a doctor on duty when the soldier forbade our group to pass. He explained,

"That man is not a doctor. He's a killer." We were incredulous, and I prompted him to explain further. "An Arab killed my friend, and this man is an Arab."

I replied, "I'm sorry to hear about your friend, but that doesn't mean that all Arabs are killers." He was unmoved. He was also not alone. The soldier who had tried to prevent Firas and me from delivering bread had also shamelessly pronounced his wrath against Arabs. Certainly there are racists everywhere in the world, but it's particularly disturbing to listen to such hatred coming from a teenager who has been handed an M16 and near impunity in the land of the people he despises.

Of course, most of the soldiers didn't offer such remarks and probably considered themselves charitable to the Palestinians, given the circumstances. One soldier who detained us for half an hour bragged about all the food and medicine he'd allowed through. He couldn't understand what the Palestinians were still complaining about. I asked him where he was from.

"Tel Aviv."

"So if armed Palestinians invaded Tel Aviv, shut the entire population in their homes, and allowed aid workers to bring around food and medicine, you wouldn't complain?"

He said that was different. I asked how. He changed the subject. I asked him how long he was going to punish my colleague and me by detaining us on the street. He said he wasn't punishing us, that we just had to wait a little while, which was normal. I asked:

Israeli soldiers handcuff and detain Palestinians.

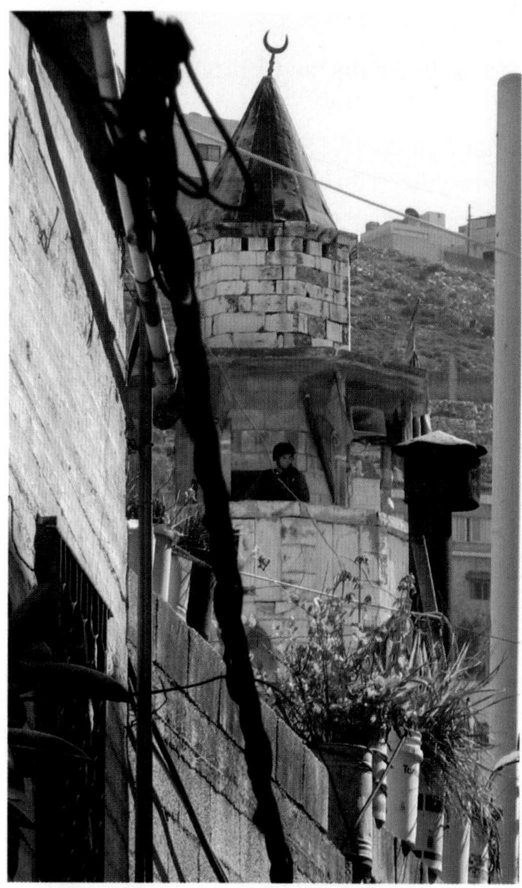

A soldier stands watch over the city from a minaret.

"So if armed Palestinians stopped you outside your house, demanded your ID, and prevented you from going to work, you would consider that normal?" He changed the subject again.

The Occupation and invasions have been happening for so long that soldiers forget that they are illegal occupiers with no legitimate authority in the area. Even according to agreements signed by Israel, Nablus is in Area A, the 12-17% of the West Bank where Israelis are forbidden to enter according to the Oslo Accords. Ironically, Oslo is among the agreements that Israel and the rest of the world are demanding that Hamas recognize in order for the Palestinian population to regain the lifeline of international aid that was pulled a year ago.

It's always illuminating to switch the names around. Israel arms teenagers and sends them into Palestinian cities, where they frequently kill unarmed civilians. What happens when armed Palestinian teenagers enter an Israeli city? Israel violates Oslo every day, but the Palestinian government will not be recognized or returned its own tax dollars until it fully accepts the same agreement (an agreement that, by the way, falls vastly short of international law and full human rights for Palestinians). Israel justifies major offensives against Palestinian fighters. What about Palestinians who target Israeli fighters, the occupying soldiers themselves? Armed struggle against illegal occupation forces is actually protected under international law, whereas Israel's occupation practices are not.[26]

I met some of the hunted the day before I left Nablus, including a leader of the Al-Aqsa Martyrs' Brigades, whom I'll call Majid. An acquaintance pointed a colleague and me to where a group of them were sitting and drinking juice in the Old City. They welcomed us and brought us sweet coffee. Majid was a soft-spoken man not much older than 40, while

---

[26] In his book *Sharing the Land of Canaan*, Mazin B. Qumsiyeh clarifies what violence is and isn't protected under the Declaration of Principles of International Law of 1970:

"All states are under a duty to refrain from any forcible action that deprives people of their right to self-determination ... [and] where forcible action has been taken to suppress that right, force may be used in order to counter this and achieve self-determination." Qumsiyeh, p. 108.

Qumsiyeh cites numerous UN resolutions that "have affirmed the legitimacy of the struggle of people for liberation from colonial domination and alien subjection, 'by all available means including armed struggle' (e.g. UN General Assembly Resolutions 3070, 3103, 3246, 3328, 3481, 31/91, 32/4 and 32/154).... The right of resistance is internationally recognized, but not the right of indiscriminate use of violence" or the targeting of civilians.

most of the other wanted men were mere teenagers, curious and excited to meet foreigners. Majid raised his voice just once during our conversation, to yell at one of the boys for trying to take my picture on his cell phone. He said it could be extremely dangerous for soldiers to find evidence of our meeting if the men were caught or killed, and he refused my business card for the same reason.

After a while, I asked Majid if he had a message to the people of America. He thanked me for the opportunity and began to speak slowly in Arabic, so that I could understand. I reconstructed his words below from detailed notes:

> I am from the Palestinian armed resistance to the Occupation. I am opposed to violence against civilians, whether they are Palestinian or Israeli, Muslim or Jewish. I hate fighting, but when soldiers invade our homes, our land, and our lives, it is our duty to resist them, to resist the theft of our water, our self determination, and our dignity. We are human just like you. We want to live, to have families, a normal life. But if we must fight to our death to protect what is ours, our land, the future of our children, we are ready to do so.
>
> I invite you to look at maps and statistics of this conflict over time. I lament the killing of innocent people on both sides, but the tremendous disproportion of land and water rights, civil liberties, and civilian casualties on the two sides is undeniable. The international community calls us terrorists, but we would welcome any objective international presence to bear witness to what is happening here and come to their own conclusions. Is beating unarmed children, medical workers, and even internationals not terror? Is taking advantage of lulls in violence—when the press isn't watching—to accelerate expansion of settlements in land and water rich areas not a crime?
>
> Palestinians have coexisted harmoniously with Jews in the past, and we are ready to do so again. After all, Jews are our brothers and sisters, people of faith just like us. As our party Fatah has said many times before, we are ready to live in peace with Israel if there can be a just and viable resolution to the issues of borders, distribution of water, settlements, Jerusalem, and the refugees. These are our conditions, and they are our rights.

Majid is a dead man walking, but he will continue to resist as long as he can, as will all the people of Nablus in their own ways. I relay Majid's message not to defend violence, but because I believe his perspective has a right to be heard.

Different sides of any conflict deserve to have a voice, but the mainstream media is unlikely to pick up Majid's speech, just as they haven't picked up anything but the most sensational aspects of the invasion. They haven't mentioned the way beautiful old houses were destroyed by soldiers digging for nonexistent tunnels. They haven't mentioned the walls of the Old City that were broken

Soldiers destroyed every room of the house that a groom was preparing for his bride.

Military vehicles damaged the water pipes of the Old Ciy, losing days worth of precious water.

Soldiers trashed the 400-year-old Turkish Baths after using the building as a military base. The baths are a cultural and economic center of the city, and supported several local families.

down by Israeli hummers too wide to fit down the narrow streets, and the water pipes along the walls that were busted and sprayed throughout the curfew, depleting the city of several days worth of its precious water supply. They haven't mentioned the 400-year-old Turkish baths that soldiers used as a military base between operations, and then destroyed from top to bottom. Several families depended on income from that cultural treasure, which we found in ruins with playing cards left by the occupying soldiers all over the floor.

The media haven't mentioned the house that was burned from the inside, or the wanted men's families who were beaten and detained, or the 15-year-old boy who was shot in the wrist with a rubber bullet while he was out buying bread for his family. They haven't mentioned that the jeeps returned every night, even after Israel announced that the operation was over. I would like to tell you about each of these things in detail, but with every passing hour there are new tragedies to report and attend to, and as it is I can hardly keep up... but what is the alternative? Silence would be tantamount to admitting that nothing can be done.

Steadfast in Bil'in

Friday, March 9, 2007

Two weeks ago, shortly before the army invaded Nablus, the villagers of Bil'in held a demonstration commemorating the second anniversary of their weekly nonviolent protests against the Wall. Organizers worked day and night to prepare. Abdallah, coordinator of the Popular Committee Against the Wall in Bil'in, unfurled and hung what was undoubtedly the world's largest Palestinian flag along one side of the main street. On the other side, villagers mounted an impressive photo exhibition with images of 2 years of village resistance, and constructed a large, symbolic scales-of-justice, fake coffins, and clothes hanging from nooses to illustrate the death of Palestinian freedom and nationhood.

Palestinians, Israelis, and internationals met outside Abdallah's house, easy to pick out from the Israeli flag that soldiers had painted on the street outside it. Soon we began to march. Soldiers met our large and diverse crowd at the gate in front of the Wall. Protesters climbed on top of the gate waving flags and giving speeches, while soldiers contemplated what to do. Eventually, one soldier pushed one of the protesters, who fell off the gate.

© IWPS

Abdallah and the author prepare signs for the 2-year anniversary demonstration in Bil'in.

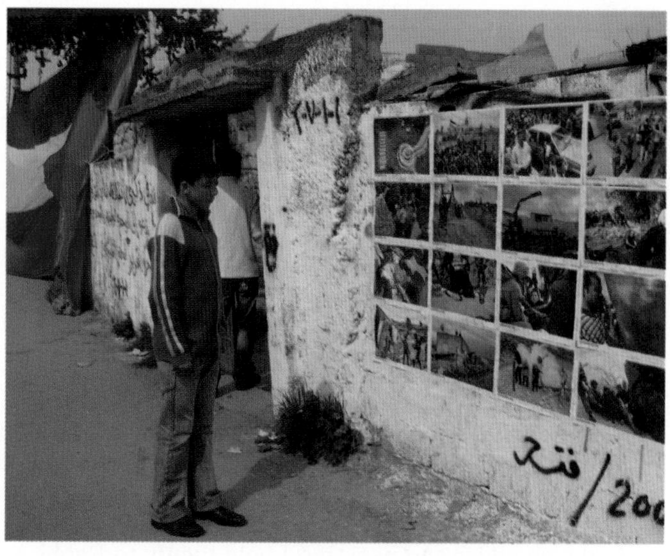

A photo exhibition commemorates 2 years of weekly nonviolent demonstrations against the Wall in Bil'in.

The crowd held its breath. Thankfully, the protester was not hurt—but he was angry, and with frustration banged his flag stick on the helmet of the soldier who had pushed him.

This seemed to be the reaction the soldiers were waiting for and within seconds they were hurling sound bombs and tear gas as the hundreds of protesters dispersed. Several village boys began to throw stones at the soldiers, but Abdallah and his colleagues refused to let this be the end of the demonstration and called on demonstrators to return peacefully to the gate. Those of us who could come back into position did, although over half of the demonstrators had been trapped down the hill towards the village, after soldiers moved in following the tear gas. Our group was smaller, but so was the soldiers'. I spotted Abdallah advancing to-wards the Wall with his wife Majida and her friend, and next to them something I'd never seen before: a water cannon.

I'd heard about police hosing civil rights demonstrators in the United States in the 1960s, but I was shocked to see a massive tank-like machine raise its cannon and fire out a strong blast of water towards Abdallah and the two women. They fell to the ground and Abdallah screamed, clutching his leg, which was spattered with blood from gravel that had ricocheted up with the water. I rushed to his side to ask if he was ok. He nodded, but his face betrayed the pain he was in. Suddenly a soldier grabbed Abdallah's arm as if he intended to arrest him, and I threw myself on top of my friend, as did Majida and Yonatan, an Israeli activist. The soldier wasn't prepared to carry off all four of us so he backed off, and then Majida recognized an opportunity: the gate was unguarded.

Majida sprang up and began pushing open the gate between her village and the Wall. Yonatan, Abdallah, and I ran to help her. It was halfway open before the soldiers could catch up to us, and they immediately began pushing back. We were gaining on them until they began hitting our hands with batons. Frightened, I quickly withdrew my throbbing hands, but when I saw Majida still pushing I was inspired and went around to pull from the other side. The tug-of-war was symbolic—the Wall still stood behind us—but it felt good to exercise our determination, and the soldiers eventually relented.

I quickly realized, however, that the soldiers were moving out of the way of the water cannon that was aiming at us. I ran to protect my camera, knowing inside that really I was protecting myself. Shaking like crazy, I watched my friends and colleagues tumble over one another as the massive stream struck them down. But they would not be moved. Three of them sat down in front of the gate linking arms.

I shoved my camera into a plastic bag and went to sit with them, arms linked. Others joined us. Soon we were so many that an outer circle had formed around our inner one. To my left was Rabbi Arik Ascherman from Rabbis for Human Rights, to my right were internationals, and in front of me were Abdallah and his colleagues. Sitting there, we—people of Palestine and the world—were asserting Bil'in villagers' right to remain on their land. It felt good, but I knew what was coming.

First they tried sound bombs. My ears rang, but only one of our group—a cameraman who was hit in the back with one of the exploding bombs—was moved from our circle. Then, as if in slow motion, I watched the water tank point its cannon towards our sit-in and I braced myself to experience what I had just seen from the outside. "Water!" someone yelled, and we threw our heads down and shut our eyes. The blast hit me like a ton of bricks in the shoulder and neck but I held tightly to Rabbi Ascherman's arm and waited for it to be over. When the water stopped, we lifted our heads to find the whole group still intact, steadfast.

The Israeli army hoses Palestinians, Israelis, and internationals holding a sit-in on Bil'in village land.

Rabbi Ascherman began appealing to the soldiers to think about what they were doing. I watched a Bil'in villager hoist Uri Avnery onto his shoulders so that the renowned Israeli journalist and peace activist, now 83, could project to the soldiers as well. I was moved to speak as well. "We do not want to hurt you," I said to the soldiers. "These people are defending their land and their livelihoods, which is their right. But we will not use violence against you, and you do not need to respond with violence."

Soon the water cannons were aimed and firing again. This time the rush hit me straight in the head, and I screamed out in pain. When it stopped, my head throbbed and everything was spinning. Our guard was down as we recovered and suddenly soldiers snatched two internationals from our group, saying they would only be released if we ended our sit-in. The organizers were ready to head back anyway so we called it a day.

The soldiers did not keep their word—they didn't release our friends and within minutes things were back to stones versus bullets, gas, and bombs. We were caught in the middle, and I suddenly found myself amidst a fog of tear gas and unable to breathe. All the gas-countering vinegar in my bandana had washed out during the hosing, so each gulp of air brought in more stinging gas. I began gasping and gagging. I groped around and found a person nearby who would stay with me until I recovered. Soon I could walk again and found my way back to the village, wondering how on earth Bil'in villagers do this every week.

Tear gas canisters collected by children from Bil'in after a nonviolent demonstration against the Wall

Witness in Palestine
War & Irony on Hebron Hilltops

Saturday, March 10, 2007

No matter how bad things become in the north West Bank, it's never as bad as in Hebron. I'm back in the ancient city exactly 2 years after my last visit, to participate in several solidarity activities, among them school patrol in Tel Rumeida. This small Palestinian neighborhood is home to some of the most violent ideological settlers in Hebron. Tel Rumeida settlers, who have moved into local homes by force, frequently parade around the streets with guns, terrorizing the remaining Palestinian residents. Every day, local children on their way to school dodge sticks and stones thrown by settler children (and their parents) as soldiers watch on indifferently. I was among several internationals who accompanied the students to document and even shield them from the attacks.

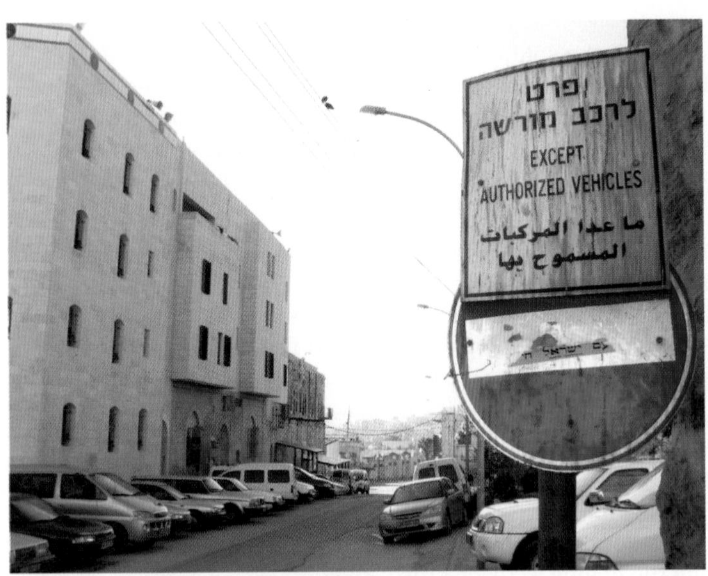

A sign warns against "unauthorized" vehicles in front of Beit Hadassa illegal settlement on Shuhada Street, a major thoroughfare from which Palestinians are now banned. In Tel Rumeida neighborhood, only Jews (i.e. soldiers and settlers) are allowed to drive; Palestinian cars are not even allowed in.

Today my station was on Shuhada Street, which used to be a major Palestinian thoroughfare before settlers moved in down the road and blocked it to non-Jews. Settler cars and military vehicles frequently drive through Tel Rumeida, but Palestinians are not allowed to use cars in the neighborhood. They are banned from even walking on the main street, so they wind their way through a cemetery to get from their neighborhood to the city. More than 2,000 small businesses around the Old City and Tel Rumeida have closed down, and the once-thriving cultural and economic center is now a ghost town.

We watched the schoolchildren advance cautiously down the road where Israeli flags hung from street lamps and nearly every Palestinian home had a star of David spray-painted outside. Out of one house came Jamilya, whose mother was recently attacked by a settler girl who then incited a mob to come rip the family's door off. Their windows are

Above: *Palestinians have caged in their windows to block stones thrown by settlers, but some still get through.*

Right: Settler graffiti reads, "Gas the Arabs!" outside a Palestinian home.

caged like all others on the street, to block stones; occasional cracks show where small rocks still get through. At the military station, Jamilya climbed a set of stairs to her right and then entered school via a narrow stone path that was just reconstructed after settlers destroyed it for a third time. More kids came from the opposite direction on a dirt path, passing a Palestinian house with graffiti across the main gate that read: "Gas the Arabs!"

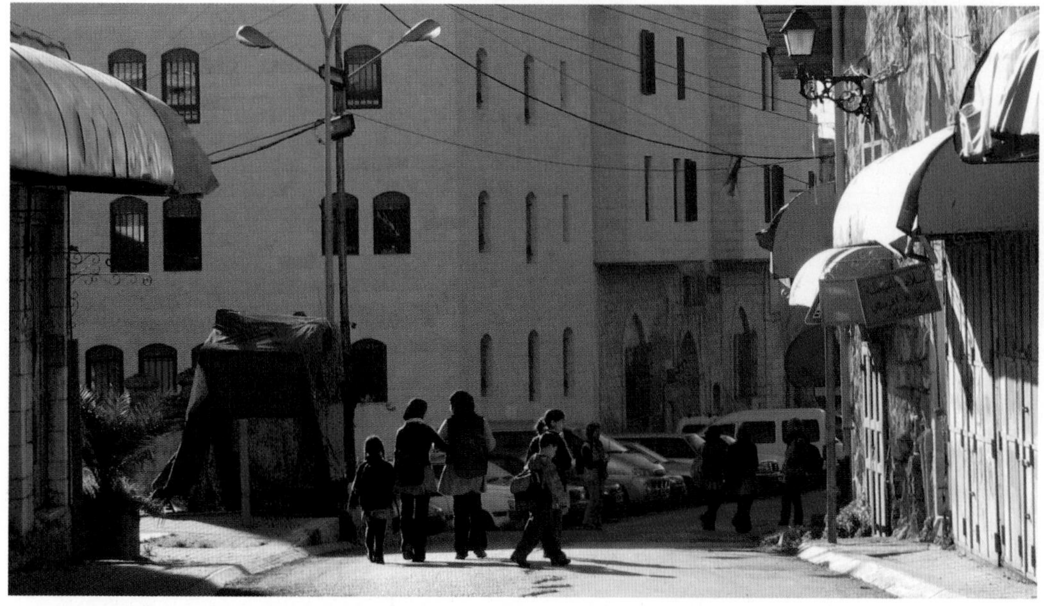

Schoolchildren walk past illegal settlements, anti-Arab graffiti, and army bases on their way to school.

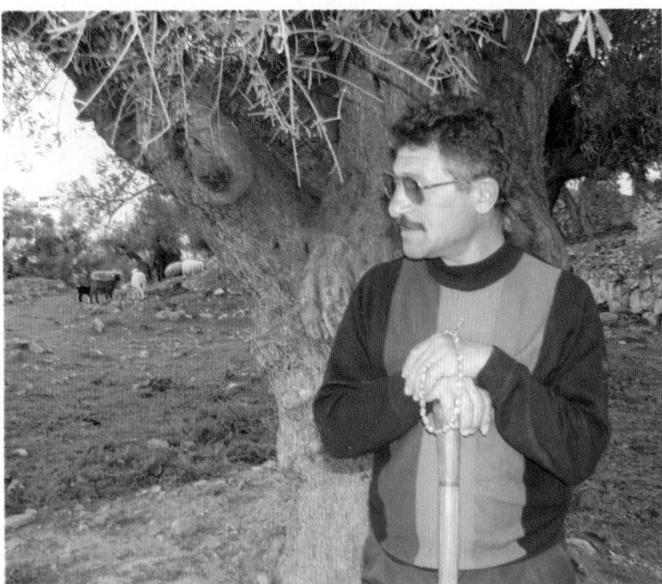

Abu Thelal watches over his sheep in the olive groves outside his house, which settlers trespass almost daily.

An Israeli activist and local children play marbles on the Palestinian olive groves that violent ideological settlers trespass almost daily.

An Israeli friend of mine named Cheska showed me around the olive groves between Tel Rumeida settlement and the school, where a few Palestinian families are still struggling to survive. Cheska introduced us to a shepherd named Abu Thalal, who welcomed us into his home. He said he's grateful for Israeli allies like Cheska, and has even tried reaching out to the settlers who trespass on his land every day. Abu Thelal said that when a settler once asked him for a cigarette, he didn't hesitate to hand one over, and even prepared tea for the two to drink together, as is customary when strangers visit an Arab home. Shortly after, Abu Thelal was shocked to see the same man and his children throwing stones at his house. He shrugged after he finished the story. "There are good Israelis and bad Israelis, just like there are good Palestinians and bad Palestinians."

From Abu Thelal's home you can see the mosque and temple where Abraham was buried. The groves and ruins surrounding Abu Thelal's home are not just old; they look and feel biblical. Cheska said she once watched in horror as settlers celebrated the Jewish holiday *Lag B'Omer* by making a bonfire (one of the symbols of the holiday) on the ancient land, and burning Palestinian flags in it.

Jewish holidays continue to translate into Palestinian suffering in the West Bank. This past week was Purim, so closure (increased travel restrictions that—among other things—invalidate many previously-issued permits) was imposed on the entire West Bank Palestinian population so that soldiers could go home to celebrate with their families. Hebron-based human rights groups needed extra help with their patrolling today because it's Shabbat, when attacks are more frequent because settler children don't have school.

Last week, one settler child ran down the street flailing his arms and throwing stones at Palestinians in every direction. Soldiers prevented internationals from photographing, saying, "It's okay, it's Purim. He's just drunk."

Soldiers also didn't intervene when settlers rioted in Hebron during the Jewish holiday of Sukkot a few years ago. Rioters attacked the homes of local Palestinians, who were under curfew because of the Jewish holiday. One of the damaged homes belonged to Hana'a and Feryal Abu Haykal and their 11 children, one of whom was injured by the rioters.[27] I met the Abu Haykals, who live right between a military outpost and Tel Rumeida settlement. Their windows are caged, much of their land has been declared a "closed military zone" (although settlers frequently trespass on it without consequence), and they've removed the staircase to the roof so that soldiers will stop coming to use it for surveillance. Settlers, who want the large well-situated house for themselves, have done everything they can to scare away the family, but the Abu Haykals just won't give up.

The youngest of the Abu Haykal children, a bubbly 17-year-old girl, met us at the door and welcomed us in for tea. When we asked about school, she explained that all 10 of her older brothers and sisters are engineers, but she wants to study psychology. We met 5 of her siblings, but most of the others are studying or working abroad. One of the sisters at home offered to teach us a relaxation technique she's been working on. One brother discovered that—adjusting for time-difference—he was born precisely 10 hours after I was. I told him that when I was his age I was eating breakfast, and he thought that was funny.

Two of the Abu Haykal's 11 children chat with international observers in front of the metal detector and checkpoint through which they must pass on their way to school.

A mural in the Abu Haykal home. The Abu Haykals have been violently attacked by settlers who covet the family's house, but the family remains on their land, steadfast.

[27] *AIC*, pp. 37-38.

The Abu Haykals have lived in their home since the neighborhood was Jewish, before Zionism and the Hebron Massacre of 1929. Settlers claim they are reclaiming Jewish territory, yet the Jewish families who left have issued joint statements demanding that the settlers leave and stop all violence against their former neighbors.

Many Jewish Israelis like Cheska have spoken out against settler violence in Hebron. Many of them came with us today on a joint action to rebuild destroyed houses in the South Hebron hills. Across the south West Bank there are dozens of tiny villages where Palestinians live in caves, tents, and small stone houses surrounded by rolling hills where they graze their sheep every day. Many years ago, fundamentalist Jews began settling hilltops all over the south Hebron hills, and they frequently harass or even physically attack the shepherds on their land and in their villages. Settlers from the illegal outposts have poisoned village water sources with dead chickens and dirty diapers, and cemented over cave entrances. They run down the hills into villages wearing masks and carrying baseball bats or large guns.

To add insult to injury, the Israeli army has been demolishing Palestinian structures across the south Hebron region, most of them homes and bathroom facilities. The pretext is that the shepherds didn't secure Israeli building permits before constructing the rooms and outhouses on their land. The caravans of violent settlers who have snuck onto surrounding hilltops (also without permits) are meanwhile encouraged with subsidies, infrastructure, and protection from the Israeli state to flourish on land that does not belong to them, even though the outposts are illegal according to international and Israeli law.

Hundreds of rural Palestinians' homes and caves have been bulldozed, and many families have fled to escape what can accurately be described as ethnic cleansing. Still, despite tremendous obstacles, several villages remain, refusing to leave their ancestral land. One such village is Qawawis, where I spent the day rebuilding homes that the army had recently demolished. Organized by *Ta'ayush*, a joint Jewish-Palestinian human rights group from Israel, dozens of Israelis, internationals, and Palestinians came together to build foundations, stone walls, and rooftops for the four families of Qawawis and other

Palestinians and Israelis work together to rebuild a demolished house.

Right: Qawawis villagers rebuild the village houses, sheep pens, and bathrooms that were demolished by the Israeli army. Illegal Israeli outposts stand untouched on the hilltops in the background. The four families of Qawawis have been repeatedly attacked by violent ideological settlers, but the villagers refuse to be ethnically cleansed from their ancestral land.

nearby villages. We mixed cement, formed assembly lines, and chatted together throughout the beautiful, exhausting day. When we were finished, I headed back to Hebron.

Re-entering Tel Rumeida, soldiers searched my bag and person for weapons. Beyond the checkpoint I could see settler children and their parents carrying M16s as they walked home from synagogue. I reflected on the irony of being checked to enter a street where armed fundamentalists known for violence are granted virtual impunity.

One soldier clarified the dynamic for me. He explained, "I'm Jewish, so I have to protect the Jewish people." I told him I was Jewish too, but that security could only come from protecting everyone's rights. His eyes lit up when I said I was Jewish:

"So this is your land too! Don't you know we are the children of Abraham?"

His question reminded me that many of the soldiers patrolling Hebron are settlers themselves. Many of the guns used to terrorize Tel Rumeida Palestinians are from the Israeli army, purchased from American weapons manufacturers with my own tax dollars.

Army jeeps patrol Tel Rumeida, where settlers have hung Israeli flags outside Palestinian homes. The Israeli army and settlers work together, employing a variety of methods to gradually transfer land and resources from Palestinians to Jews.

It is always tempting to blame Israel's sins on the religious settlers, whom most Israelis don't identify with anyway. But the reality is that Jewish-only settlements and outposts could not be established or maintained in the West Bank without Israel's political, financial, and military support. The Israeli government, whose job it is to enforce the law, instead enjoys a symbiotic relationship with the fundamentalist settlers. Both have a strong interest in controlling as much West Bank land as possible, with as few Palestinians on it as possible. The *Alternative Information Center* cites four main methods employed by Israel for land confiscation in the Occupied Territories: "the seizure of land for military needs, the designation of land as 'state land,' the definition of land as 'absentee property,' and expropriation of land for 'public needs.' All these methods serve a single purpose: the transfer of land from Palestinian to Israeli ownership."[28]

Of course, Israel's expansionist policies are made possible by support from my own government. Democratic and Republican administrations alike have consistently provided the aid and political clout necessary for Israel to continue appropriating Palestinian lands and resources. Similarly, the trend of cooperation between Israeli settlers and their government has been consistent regardless of which major Israeli party was in power. As the foreign minister under Yitzhak Rabin's first government, Yigal Allon of the "left-wing"

---

[28] Ibid, at 29.

Labor party offered substantial political support to settlements in the east Hebron area, trying to prevent Palestinian development in sections of the West Bank that were to be incorporated into Israel according to the Allon Plan. Having too many Palestinians on certain coveted sections of the West Bank could threaten the "Jewish character" of Israel once those portions of land were annexed.

Settlers in Hebron are subject to a different legal system altogether from their Palestinian neighbors. Jewish settlers are subject to Israeli law, while Palestinians are subject to military law. Therefore, they have different rights and face different legal consequences for the same crime. In every scenario, the Israeli law is more lenient. The rare times they are tried and convicted, settlers generally enjoy relatively light sentences. For example, a settlement leader Rabbi Levinger spent just 10 weeks in jail for killing an unarmed Palestinian merchant. If a Palestinian were convicted of manslaughter, he could easily face life in prison.

Tonight around the dinner table, internationals who had stayed in Tel Rumeida today discussed which of the day's incidents to include in the daily media report. Volunteers didn't think it was worth mentioning that settlers had spat at Palestinians and trespassed on Abu Haykal's land, because such incidents are so common. They did report on the group of settler kids who used sticks and stones to attack four young Palestinian schoolchildren, none over the age of eight, while border police physically prevented internationals from intervening.

As we spoke, I kept thinking about Nablus. Jewish fundamentalists once tried to set up camp in Nablus city but they were driven out by the city's armed resistance. It was one of the few clear Palestinian victories of the Second Intifada. What would have happened if the people of Hebron had used more violent resistance back in 1967 when the settlers arrived? Nablus fighters are called terrorists, and Hebron's fighters would surely be demonized as well. Still, knowing now what wasn't known then, could we really blame them for taking up arms to prevent the takeover of their city? Those were the thoughts swirling through my head tonight as I prepared to return to my relatively peaceful existence in Haris.

Settler children strut down Shuhada Street, banging on families' doors and spitting at Palestinian and international passersby.

Witness in Palestine

Existence is Resistance: Challenging the Assault on Ordinary Life

Monday, March 12, 2007

One week after I left Nablus, I found myself again looking out across the city's majestic sunlit hills, this time from one of the highest mountains in the West Bank. In all my reporting on Israel's invasion and human rights violations, I never mentioned how beautiful the ancient city is, from the surrounding mountains to the enchanting Old City, so easy to get lost in. Both remind me of Damascus.[29] My last day in Nablus I had the chance to discover another one of the city's gems: Al-Najaa University. I was immediately charmed by the old architecture mixed with modern sculptures on the main campus, but what inspired me most was watching thousands of students return to the frantic bustle of daily university life so soon after soldiers had released the city from siege. Resilience is a defining feature of Palestinian identity in my experience, and I was impressed but not surprised to see Palestinians so determined to get an education even under the most difficult of circumstances.

Nablus

[29] One pessimistic Palestinian pointed out the similarity early during my stay, claiming that the Nablus invasion was practice for an attack against Syria.

The night before visiting Al-Najaa, I had passed by the empty campus—which had been abandoned since the siege—in a taxi, driving home with the family that was hosting me. I had grown quite close to the couple and their five children, and I felt happy and comfortable in their home, which their three daughters had covered with posters of Che Guevara, David Beckham, Shakira, and other teenage idols. As we were driving and chatting, jeeps suddenly appeared around us, coming from all directions. We panicked. Was there a curfew? Would we be shot for being outside? Screeching to a halt, we tried to back up to the neighborhood we'd come from, but jeeps were swarming in that direction as well. Where were we supposed to go?

Palestinian students return to school after a week under siege.

The jeeps left as quickly as they had come. We realized later that the army had been conducting a practice invasion to train new soldiers, as they've done recently in other parts of the West Bank.[30] I will never forget that feeling of being suddenly surrounded, the confusion and panic, the helplessness. There was something about sitting together to a cheerful family breakfast the next morning that felt like a kind of nonviolent resistance, too: the insistence on ordinary life and pleasures no matter what havoc Occupation Forces are wreaking just outside.

I returned to the Nablus region a week later to accompany a teacher named Addawiya and her family to plow land they haven't been able to work for 6 years due to soldier harassment. The next plot over hasn't been plowed in 26 years for the same reason, and many of its olive trees have desintegrated from neglect. There are Israeli military posts on all the highest West Bank peaks, among them the mountain where Addawiya's land lies. As we cleared away stones that had covered the land over the last half dozen years, Addawiya told me about the day she was picking olives with her

Addawiya's family plows their land for the first time in 6 years.

---

[30] Polly Bangoriad, "Israeli army units fake usurpation of Palestinian villages for 'practice,'" *International Middle East Media Center* (March 16, 2007).

brother when the soldiers came and threatened to shoot her brother if he didn't leave the land immediately. He persisted in picking olives until the soldiers began shooting into the air to show that they were serious, at which point he ran off terrified. Addawiya was left alone, and on her hands and knees pleaded for her life, sure she was going to die. Her fear was not unjustified. Three years ago, Addawiya's sister was taking a walk on the family's land near the village with her husband when a group of soldiers jumped out from the foliage and opened fire on him. The 33-year-old teacher died instantly.

After years of neglect, the olive trees that used to surround Addawiya's land are now gone. The plot was abandoned for 26 years after soldiers from the nearby army base began threatening and violently attacking local farmers.

The Israeli army came and apologized to Addawiya's family. Apparently they were intending to assassinate a wanted man and shot the wrong guy. Addawiya's sister, who was 23 and pregnant at the time, is now a 26-year-old going on 60. With nobody to support her and two young children to raise, she had to move back in with her mother. Incidentally, the mother invited me to move in too when we returned from plowing (as an unmarried and childless 27-year-old woman, I'm practically an old maid around here). I declined politely, and we began the journey back to Haris.

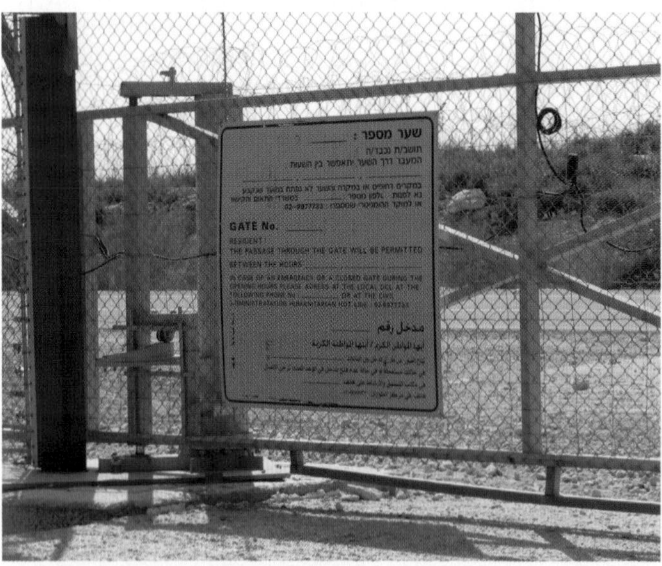

Signs along the Wall imply that farmers will be permitted to access their land on the other side of the barrier, yet in practice many of these signs are never even filled out, let alone followed.

Our first stop along the way was Huwwara, the southern checkpoint out of Nablus city, where as usual hundreds of students from Al-Najaa and other universities were waiting unhappily. They were squeezed together uncomfortably under a small roof, trying to get shelter from the rain as they waited for clearance to leave the city. I remembered passing through Huwwara a few days earlier on a trip accompanying other farmers in the area. Since the solidarity effort was organized by the Israeli group Rabbis for

Human Rights, we were driving in an Israeli car with yellow license plates, so we didn't even slow down as we breezed through on the Israeli-only road parallel to the one where Palestinians had been waiting for hours.

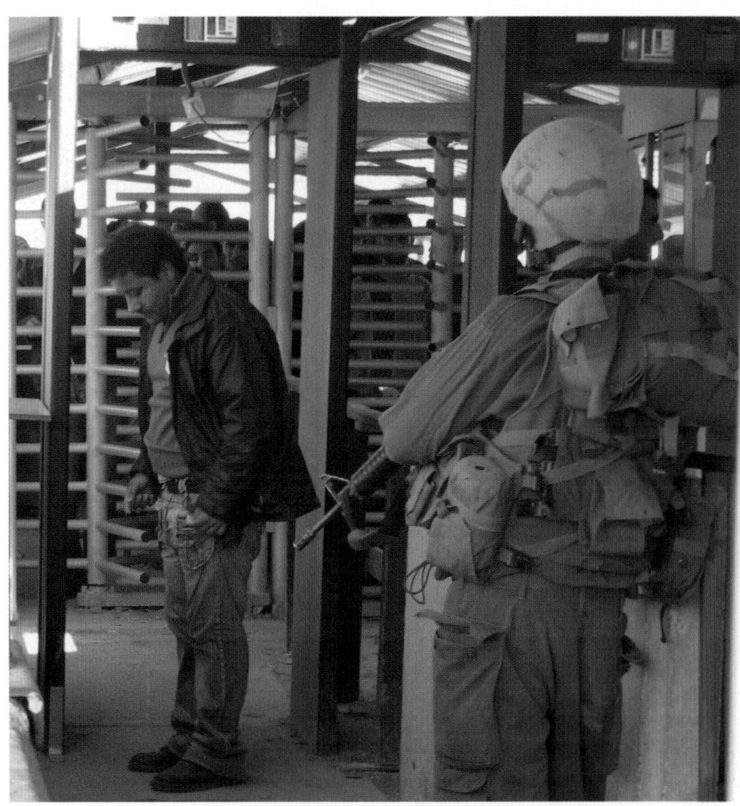

Screening at Huwwara checkpoint

On the way back from Addawiya's land, a colleague and I decided to stay at Huwarra to observe the checkpoint and document any human rights violations. There was already one sick man whom the army had refused to let pass and we took his story. At first, the soldiers didn't seem to mind our presence, but after some time one soldier told us we weren't allowed to stand where we were. He pointed to a line drawn on the floor nearby and said we could stand behind it. We began to protest, but quickly realized a fight would translate into longer waiting time for the Palestinians being processed by the same soldier, so we walked a few paces to the other side of the line. Ten minutes later, a different soldier informed us it was illegal to be observing the checkpoint at all, so we would have to leave immediately. We didn't even dignify his absurd claim with a response. He stood next to us awkwardly repeating himself a few times and then eventually went away.

We were approached by a third soldier, speaking only Hebrew. When we said we couldn't understand, he told us in broken English that it was illegal to be there if you didn't speak Hebrew. This was a new one. A fourth soldier showed up to translate the third soldier's original message, which was that we could stay but were not allowed to take pictures. He regretted to inform us that he would have to delete my photographs. At that point we decided we preferred to leave rather than lose the photos, so we began to walk away. As expected, the soldier didn't chase after the supposedly "illegal" pictures. Just before we left, we saw the sick man previously denied passage try his luck with a different soldier at a different machine and get through.

Israel claims that its checkpoints are for the security and safety of its citizens. One of the things making this claim so difficult to believe for those observing the institutions is how inconsistent and seemingly arbitrary the army's actions and "laws" so frequently are at checkpoints. The sick man got through on his second try. Had that failed, he could have sprung for an expensive taxi ride to an alternative checkpoint 10 miles north that is scarcely monitored at all (when we passed through on the way to Addawiya's land there were no soldiers in sight). The whole trip north and then around again would cost him several hours and paychecks, but he could exit his city with relative certainty. Anyone who's spent time in the West Bank knows that if you're desperate and you have enough money, you can get anywhere. There is always an alternative road, even into Israel, even with the Wall, which is full of holes so as not to hinder settlers commuting to Israel.

As our shared taxi from Huwwara to Haris left the checkpoint, the driver pulled up next to several drivers to ask how Zatara was. Zatara is a permanent checkpoint between Huwwara and Haris, but there's an alternative road through Jama'iin, which drivers take when the checkpoint line is too long or slow. The drive takes much longer, and is painfully bumpy and curvy. When our driver chose the detour, the woman next to me grimaced and took out some plastic bags, which she spent the ride vomiting into. I rubbed her back, not knowing what else to do, thinking about the short, straight, paved road that could have eased her suffering.

Soldiers have surrounded the Haris bus stop with old roadblocks, making it difficult to wait in the sheltered bus stop.

The taxi eventually dropped us off near the Haris bus stop, which soldiers have surrounded with large concrete cubes left over from the roadblock that used to block our village. The blocks mean that waiting Palestinians cannot easily get from the sheltered bus stop to the road, so at least one traveler must always wait on the road to spot and flag down cars, even when it's raining. Each time I'm forced to drench my backpack and jeans waiting to start a day's journey, I think about what Israel has to gain by making it hard even to sit at a bus stop, or by turning what could be a smooth drive home into a nauseating miserable one. I think about why the roadblocks were set up to begin with outside Haris.

The motivation behind Israel's actions is made clear to me every day when strangers call or approach us desperate for help getting a visa to Europe or North America. They say they can't take it anymore. First Israel took their land, then their sons, and now their dignity. What Israel wants more than anything isn't to harm Palestinians; it wants the Palestinians to leave. Israel is the first to admit that the "demographic problem" of too many Palestinians in an exclusively Jewish state threatens Israel more than any suicide bomber ever could.

Addawiya told me she wanted to leave as we were walking back from her groves. I asked her where to, and she told me it didn't matter—she wasn't going anywhere. "Because no country will give you a visa?" I asked, and she shook her head. "Because that's what they want us to do. They want us to flee as we did in 1948, so that the Jewish National Fund can again expropriate our land and reserve it for Jews only. But I won't leave. I will stay here because it's my right and it's my duty, to myself and to my children." For Addawiya, like so many others, simply staying in her village and working her land is resistance. It won't make it onto headlines or the six o'clock news, but it is there, it is strong, and it is not going away.

Thursday, March 15, 2007

Olfat Nimer of Qira village, near Haris, was diagnosed with kidney failure as a young child and, after an unsuccessful transplant in 1993, had been flushing her body, using dialysis, every 4 hours for the past 14 years of her life. One month ago, after a year of international sanctions against Palestine, the hospital that was supplying Olfat with dialysis solution ran out and her parents were forced to start diluting their remaining liquid. In less than 2 weeks, Olfat's situation deteriorated significantly. Because Nablus was under siege at the time, Olfat's family could not reach the medical facilities there for treatment. By the time the curfew was lifted and Olfat could reach the hospital, her chest was so full of liquid that she was past the point of recovery. She died 2 days later, at the age of 19.

Olfat's family agreed to let me publish their story with the hope that it might prevent other such incidents. They said nobody should have to experience what they have. Yet even in their village of 1,000, there are almost half a dozen cases of kidney failure, a disproportionately high percentage likely due to the stagnant water that Qira villagers are forced to purchase from Israel because they no longer control the fresh water native to their own land. According to an article by one Qira villager in *The Nation*:

> Every summer the Israeli company that supplies water to our village and that provides about 53% of the total Palestinian domestic water supply deliberately cuts off our water, thus generating a crisis. [In the summer of 2005, we] had no water for more than three continuous weeks, despite the summer heat. Water reductions and total cuts force villagers to find alternative water sources. We collect rainwater in cisterns during the winter, but by the start of the summer, the cisterns, unfortunately, run dry. Palestinian communities are thus obliged to purchase additional water from expensive and unsanitary tankers.[31]

Israel controls all of the water in the West Bank and Gaza. It collects the Palestinians' water and then sells it back to them at a price higher than many can afford. Prime Minister Olmert's recent "Convergence Plan" aims to maintain Israeli control over the two main West Bank aquifers: the lower Jordan River basin and the eastern mountain aquifer.[32] The latter is expected to be trapped in the Seam on the western side of the Wall, along with 62 springs and 134 wells. The Oslo Accords stipulated that just under 20% of the land's water sources should go to Palestinian inhabitants of the Occupied Territories; meanwhile, 24% is reserved for the illegal Jewish settler population, which is less than a tenth of the size of the Palestinian one. Since Israel (which gets what's left) controls all the water, Palestinians often end up with even less than their allotted fifth. In Hebron, for example, 85% of the

---

[31] Fareed Taamallah, "A Thirst for West Bank Water," *The Nation* (June 9, 2006).

[32] John Dugard, "Implementation of General Assembly Resolution 60/251 of 15 March 2006 Entitled 'Human Rights Council,' Report of the Special Rapporteur on the situation of human rights in the Palestinian territories occupied since 1967," *United Nations Human Rights Council*, A/HRC/4/17 (January 29, 2007).

A sign from the Women's Zionist Organization of America and the Jewish National Fund (JNF) boasts about Israeli water projects in the Jordan Valley. One-third of the water in Israel/Palestine is controlled by the JNF and thus explicitly reserved for Jews.

water is allotted to 500 illegal settlers, while the remaining 15% is divided among the city's 120,000 Palestinians. One-third of the water in Israel/Palestine is controlled by the Jewish National Fund and thus explicitly reserved for Jews.[33] Overall, Israeli citizens actually use 89% of the total water resources, including 65% of the water taken from the Jordan River (the other 35% is shared by Syria, Lebanon, and Jordan; Palestinians have had no share since 1967).[34]

Israel's disproportionate distribution of water sources was just one of several factors that led to Olfat's death. The international sanctions were another; were it not for the US-led economic embargo, Olfat's hospital likely would not have run out of dialysis solution. As it is, the World Health Organization reported the absence (or less than one month's supply) in the West Bank of not only Olfat's dialysis solution type, but more than one third of the items listed on the Ministry of Health's Essential drug list.[35]

Even without the correct dialysis solution, Olfat still might have survived if her family had been able to reach the medical facilities in Nablus quickly. According to the Union of Health Work Committees, restriction of movement is the single greatest factor threatening Palestinians' health.[36] Unable to reach hospitals, many Palestinians are forced to settle for substandard health care, and at times they are unable to obtain any treatment at all. Pregnant women, for instance, often cannot reach prenatal facilities, resulting in high infant and maternal mortality rates.[37] Mobility restrictions prevent many Palestinian children from receiving basic vaccinations. Of all West Bank households, 37.9% have problems accessing health services because of Israeli closure, 41.9% have such problems due to military checkpoints, and 14.5% are separated from their medical facilities by the Wall.[38]

I learned about Olfat's story from my friend Fareed, a peace activist from Qira who began researching kidney failure when his daughter Lina developed the condition a few

---

[33] Qumsiyeh, p. 88.

[34] "Water Resources," PWA; As cited in *PASSIA* 2007, pp. 315-316.

[35] "Coping with Crises: Palestinian Authority Institutional Performance," *World Bank* (November 2006); As cited in *PASSIA* 2007, p. 331.

[36] Personal correspondence with the Union of Health Work Committees, Ramallah. www.hwc-pal.org

[37] When this book went to press, the Palestinian infant mortality rate was 2.4% (of live births), and the Palestinian maternal mortality rate was 12.7 per 100,000 births. "Health Status in Palestine," *Ministry of Health* (2005); As cited in *PASSIA* 2007, p. 330.

[38] "Impact of the Israeli Measures on the Economic Conditions of Palestinian Households," Palestinian Central Bureau of Statistics (April-June 2005); As cited in *PASSIA* 2007, p. 331.

years ago at the age of two. Qira was under curfew at the time, so Lina and her family were trapped in their home for 6 days before they could finally set off to the hospital in Nablus. The city's southern checkpoint Huwwara was closed, so Lina's mother carried the toddler over the western hills. Lina was desperate for a kidney transplant, and in 2005 another IWPS volunteer named Anna, this one from South Africa, offered to give the child one of hers. The transplant was successful, and Lina is now a happy, healthy 5-year-old girl.

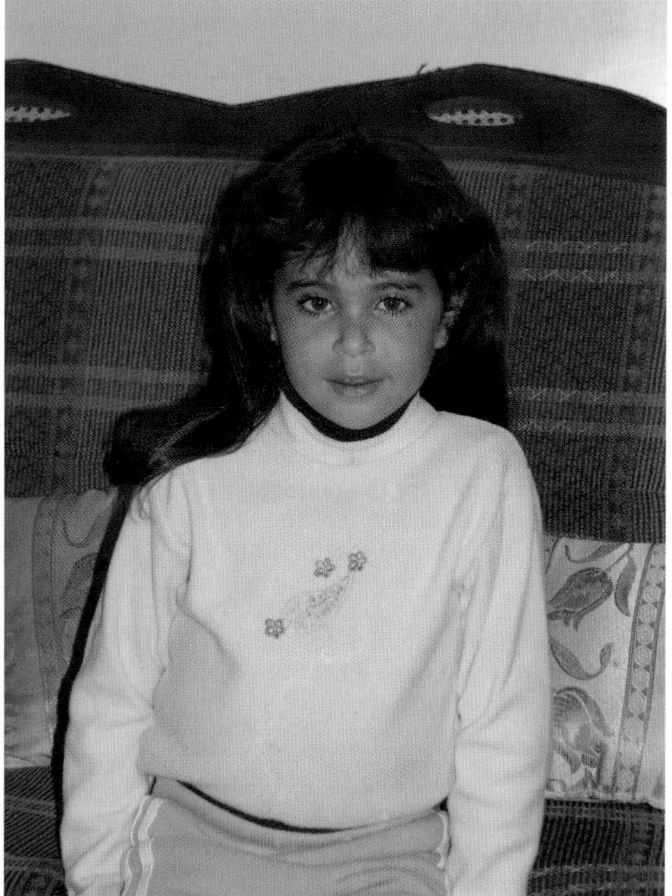

Lina

Fareed showed off the marks on his living room wall recording the young girl's growth, which had been stunted before the operation. He said with the number of Palestinians killed on a daily basis, children like Lina should have no problem finding donors, but the PA hasn't developed an efficient distribution program. An organizer at heart, Fareed hopes to form a union to address the problem. Meanwhile, an organ donation system does exist in Israel, and Fareed reminded me of Ahmed Ismail Khatib, a 12-year-old boy from Jenin who was killed in 2005 by Israeli soldiers who mistook his toy gun for a real one. Ahmed's parents donated their son's organs to six needy Israelis. Among the recipients—mostly children—were Jews, Palestinians, and a Druze girl. Ahmed's mother told journalists, "We have no problem whether it is an Israeli or a Palestinian [who receives Ahmed's organs, if] it will give them life." Said Ahmed's father: "I have taken this decision because I have a message for the world: that the Palestinian people want peace—for everyone."[39]

Ahmed's parents' extraordinary gesture of kindness and forgiveness offers hope for a future that is based on sharing rather than pure self-interest. Although Israel/Palestine's water resources are finite, the health and security of the Israelis and the Palestinians is not a zero-sum situation. Cooperation and a fair distribution of land and resources will be key to ending the bloodshed on both sides of the Green Line.

[39] "Palestinian's organs go to Israel," *BBC News* (November 8, 2005).

Witness in Palestine

The Crime of Being Born Palestinian

Dawud

Wednesday, March 21, 2007

Almost 2 weeks ago, my friend Dawud, a high school English teacher from Kafr 'Ain, called me nearly in tears to report that a checkpoint hold-up had cost him his 6-month-old son. Shortly after midnight on March 8th, Dawud's baby began having trouble breathing. Dawud and his wife Samaa quickly got a taxi to take their son to the nearest hospital in Ramallah in order to put him into an oxygen tent, which had helped him recover from difficult respiratory episodes in the past. As the family was rushing from their village to Ramallah, they were stopped at Atara checkpoint, where an Israeli soldier asked for the father's, mother's, and driver's IDs. Dawud explained to the soldier that his son needed urgent medical care, but the soldier insisted on checking the three IDs first, a process that usually takes a few minutes. Dawud's was the only car at the checkpoint in the middle of the night, yet the soldier held the three IDs for more than 20 minutes, even as Dawud and his wife began to cry, begging to be allowed through.

Samaa holds a picture of her son Khalid, who died at Atara checkpoint.

After 15 minutes, the baby's mouth began to overflow with liquid and my friend wailed at the soldier to let them go, that his baby was dying. Samaa's screams were getting higher and higher, and she begged the soldier to at least look at her baby. Instead, he demanded to search the car, even after the IDs had been cleared. At 1:05 a.m., 6-month-old Khalid Dawud Fakaah died at Atara Checkpoint. As the soldier checked the car, he shined his flashlight on the dead child's face and, realizing what had happened, finally returned the three ID cards and allowed the grieving family to pass.

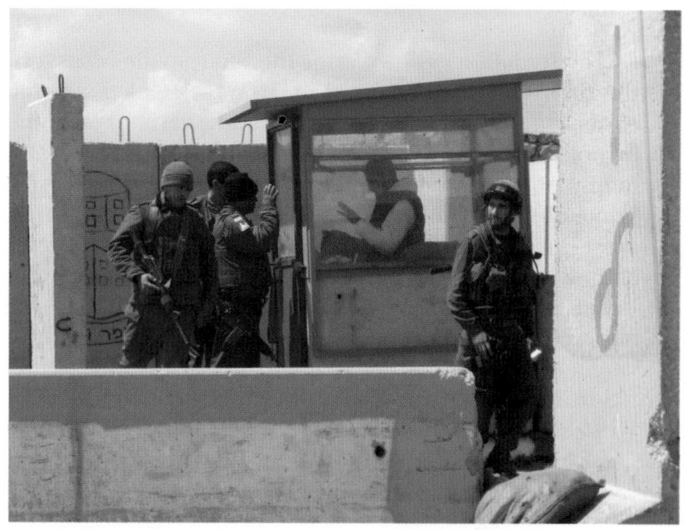

Soldiers hold up a Palestinian traveler at Atara checkpoint.

Checkpoints and ID cards. Mention these words and anyone who has lived under apartheid can produce dozens of horror stories like Dawud's. South Africa employed a similar system with its former apartheid "Pass Laws," which the South African government used to monitor the movement of black South Africans. Blacks had to carry personal ID documents, which required permission stamps from the government before holders could move around within their country. Similarly, Palestinians in the West Bank are required to carry Israeli-issued ID cards that indicate which areas, roads, and holy sites they are or are not allowed to access. And, just as in South Africa, the system of ID cards is used not only to restrict movement, but also so that the army can arrest or detain Palestinians at will. Jewish inhabitants of the West Bank (like all Jewish Israelis) have ID cards specifying their "Jewish" nationality, thereby exempting them from the restrictions imposed on Palestinians in the West Bank, and granting them automatic permission to access the modern roads and holy sites from which most Palestinians are banned.

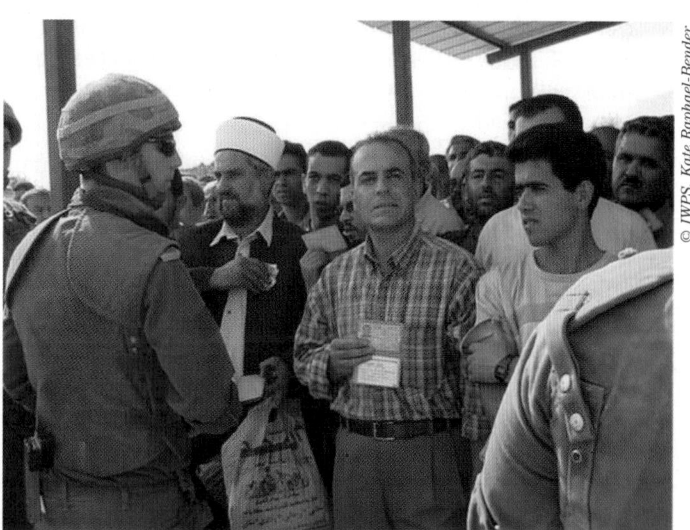

The Israeli government monitors the movement of Palestinians in the Occupied Territories through a system of Israeli-issued ID cards, indicating which areas, roads, and holy sites the carriers are allowed to access. Palestinians without Israeli-issued ID cards are unable to work, study, or travel for fear of imprisonment or deportation.

Forty-seven years ago today, on March 21, 1960, hundreds of black South Africans gathered in Sharpeville, South Africa and marched together in protest of the racist and dehumanizing pass law system. Police fired on the unarmed crowd, killing at least 67 and injuring almost three times as many, including men, women, and children. Witnesses say that most of the people shot were hit in the back as they fled.

Nearly half a century after the Sharpeville Massacre, pass laws still plague the lives of the oppressed. Every day I meet West Bank Palestinians living without permits and ID cards, either because Israel never granted them residency on their land, or because soldiers or police confiscated their IDs as punishment or harassment. I recently interviewed the family of Ibrahim, a 20-year-old veterinary student who was arrested 3 years ago for the crime of not having an Israeli-issued ID card. Ibrahim's parents were born and raised in the West Bank and own land in their small village of Far'ata, where I interviewed them. In 1966, as newlyweds, the couple moved to Kuwait where they began working. The year after, Israel occupied the West Bank and shortly after took a census. Any Palestinians who were not recorded due to absence—whether studying abroad, visiting family, or anything else—became refugees. Israel stripped Ibrahim's parents and hundred of thousands of other Palestinians of their right to return to their homes and land, and effectively opened up the West Bank to colonization by any Jews who were willing to come.

Israel's census strategy of 1967 bears a striking resemblance to the Absentee Property Law that Israel employed after the 1948 expulsions. The law says that non-Jews who left present-day Israel at any point during the War of 1948 forfeit their rights to their property, with no possibility of appeal or compensation. Therefore, the property that was left behind by Palestinians who fled the expulsions of 1948 was transferred to the State of Israel.[40] To this day, the Jewish National Fund and the Israeli state collectively own about 93% of the land of Israel. This land is exclusively reserved for the Jewish people and is virtually impossible for the owners of the land themselves—the 1947-1948 refugees—to go to, let alone get back.

When I say 93% of "the land of Israel," I am referring to land within the internationally recognized 1967 borders of Israel. Interestingly, the text of the Absentee Property Law itself refers to the West Bank and Gaza strip as the "Land of Israel that is outside the territory of Israel." In fact, in common Israeli parlance, the "Land of Israel" is something quite different from the "territory of Israel." This classification of the West Bank and Gaza as an inherent part of Israel began long before 1967, and makes the territories' occupation less than 2 decades later either a tremendous coincidence or entirely unsurprising.

To this day, Palestinians like Ibrahim's parents who were in the wrong place during the 1967 occupation and census must apply for what is called "family reunification" from the Israeli Ministry of the Interior in order to reside legally in their own homes and villages. In May 2002, Israel suspended the processing of family reunification applications for residency in Israel. The Interior Minister explained that the growth in the non-Jewish population of Israel due to family reunification was becoming a threat to the "Jewish character" of the state.[41]

Family reunification applications for residency in the Occupied Territories were also frozen last year after the Hamas election, including the applications of Ibrahim and his family. The family had returned legally to the West Bank in 1998, when the Oslo Accords had projected that Palestinians would have their own state. But when Israel's Occupation and settlement expanded, Ibrahim and his parents and five siblings were left with even fewer rights than the Palestinians with West Bank residency. Although the Palestinian Authority agreed that Ibrahim and his family could live in Far'ata (and the PA even

---

[40] The exact period stated in the law is between November 29, 1947 and September 1, 1948. The *Nakba* continued after this point, but mostly in the north and the Negev, outside of the West Bank and Gaza. *PASSIA* 2007, p. 291.

[41] *PASSIA* 2007, p. 294.

provided them with free education and health care), they still needed permission from Israel.

The Israeli government monitors the movement of Palestinians in the Occupied Territories through a system of Israeli-issued ID cards, indicating which areas, roads, and holy sites the carriers are allowed to access. Palestinians without Israeli-issued ID cards are unable to work, study, or travel for fear of imprisonment or deportation.

Ibrahim began veterinary school at Al-Najaa University in 2000, but had to commute over the Nablus hills, since soldiers manning the checkpoints would never allow him to enter the Palestinian city without an Israeli-issued ID card. On March 23, 2004, during Ibrahim's last semester before graduation, the Israeli army caught him walking to school inside Nablus and put him in prison. This Friday marks 3 years exactly that Ibrahim—now 23—has been in jail, his only crime being that he has no Israeli-issued ID card. The first year, Israel imprisoned Ibrahim within the West Bank, but for the past 2 years he has been held inside Israel, a violation of international law: Occupiers cannot hold prisoners and detainees from the occupied population in the land of the occupying power, because of how severely it limits prisoners' rights.[42] Israel's policy of imprisoning Palestinians in Israel means that their families often cannot visit them without permits to enter Israel, and they cannot have a Palestinian lawyer from the Occupied Territories because most of them don't have permits to practice law in Israel. Ibrahim's father, for example, is a lawyer but can do nothing to help his son. Since he returned from Kuwait, he has worked as a shepherd, unable to go anywhere outside his village safely without an Israeli-issued ID.

Ibrahim's situation is worse than most. Since most of his family members don't have ID cards, they cannot even apply to enter Israel to visit him. Ibrahim's sister gained residency a long time ago through marriage, but even she cannot visit her brother since it is impossible to prove to Israel that she is related to a person with no official name or identity.

"Nobody from the family has seen Ibrahim in 2 years," his mother Hanan told me. "I send him gifts and receive news via the mother of another West Bank inmate in the same jail, a friend who is occasionally permitted by Israel to visit her son. Ibrahim is not even allowed to use the phone." Hanan began to cry. "He's the first thing I think about when I wake up and the last thing before I go to sleep. I cannot bear to imagine him there in prison, perhaps for the rest of his life, knowing how much he must be suffering, knowing that I can do nothing to help him. He did nothing wrong. His only crime is that he was born a Palestinian."

[42] Fourth Geneva Convention, Article 76 of Part III Section III.

Hanan has six children altogether, three of whom decided to settle in Jordan, where they could enjoy citizenship (Palestinians in the West Bank before 1967 had Jordanian ID cards), and Hanan hasn't seen them in 9 years. She wept again as she told me she has grandchildren and sons and daughters-in-law whom she has never met. Even if she wanted Jordanian citizenship now, she's lost her chance, having stayed outside Jordan for so long. And the family members who returned to claim their land and rights in the West Bank are now stateless, like so many millions of other Palestinian refugees in the diaspora.

In recognition of the tragic events of the 1960 Sharpeville Massacre, the UN declared May 21st the International Day for the Elimination of Racial Discrimination, pushing states around the world to redouble their efforts to combat all types of racism and ethnic hatred. Yet within Israel, ethnicity still determines nationality, resource allocation, and rights to land ownership. There are discriminatory laws separating Palestinian families in Israel and threatening to revoke Palestinians' Israeli citizenship.[43] Tel Aviv University Medical School just announced a rule that de facto targets Palestinian prospective students.[44]

In the rest of the so-called "Land of Israel," the ethnic discrimination is much worse, from segregated roads to separate legal systems. Defenders of Israel's policies argue that such discrimination is only self-defense. On some level this is correct: if the Jewish state desires to control the territory that it has for more than two-thirds of its history, and to remain the state exclusively of the Jewish people, and to be democratic as well, it must find a way to create a Jewish majority on a strip of land in which the majority of inhabitants are not Jewish. There are only so many possible solutions: there's mass transfer (as was tried successfully in 1948, and is currently advocated by Israeli Minister of Strategic Threats Avigdor Lieberman), there's mass imprisonment (10,000+ Palestinians are being held in Israeli jails as I write), there's genocide, or there is apartheid. The more humane alternatives of Israel withdrawing to the 1967 borders or becoming a state of its citizens are not even on the bargaining table.

Apartheid failed in South Africa and the United States and it will fail in Israel and Palestine. Ethnocentric nationalism failed in Nazi Germany and it will fail in Zionist Israel. But until they do, the Ibrahims and baby Khalids of Palestine are counting on you and me to do something, to say something, since they themselves cannot. We cannot wait for things to get worse. The apartheid and ethnic cleansing have gone on long enough.

---

[43] Justin Podur, "A State of all its Citizens: An interview with Jamal Zahalka," *Znet* (February 28, 2007).

[44] Tamara Traubmann, "Tel Aviv medicine faculty ups minimum age to 20," *Haaretz* (March 15, 2007); Visit *www.Adalah.org* or *www.MossawaCenter.org* for information about minority rights in Israel.

Held at Einab Junction: Inside Israel's New Terminals

Friday, March 23, 2007

One new development of the Occupation since my last stint with IWPS in 2005 is the presence of Israeli terminal-style buildings, which have replaced several military checkpoints. I first encountered one of these terminals in January of 2006, after visiting a women's cooperative in Tulkarem to purchase several bags of embroidery for friends in the US. Because there are no reliable postal services in the West Bank, and because I did not want to risk the products being damaged or confiscated by Israeli airport security if I transported them in my luggage, I knew I would have to send them to the US from a post office in Israel. I had traveled from Tulkarem to Tel Aviv once in the past by taking a shared taxi to the nearby Einab junction, where I had walked from the Palestinian road to the Israeli one and caught transport into Israel.

This second time, I was traveling with my backpack and six plastic bags full of embroidery, and I assumed the trip would be as straightforward as it had been in the past. When I arrived at Einab junction, I found a large new building, fortified by several layers of metal fences, walls, and gates. The first layer reminded me of rural parts of the Wall—wire fence reinforced with electric sensory wire and razor wire with a heavy iron gate. The gate was open but there was nobody to be seen on the other side. I walked through and came

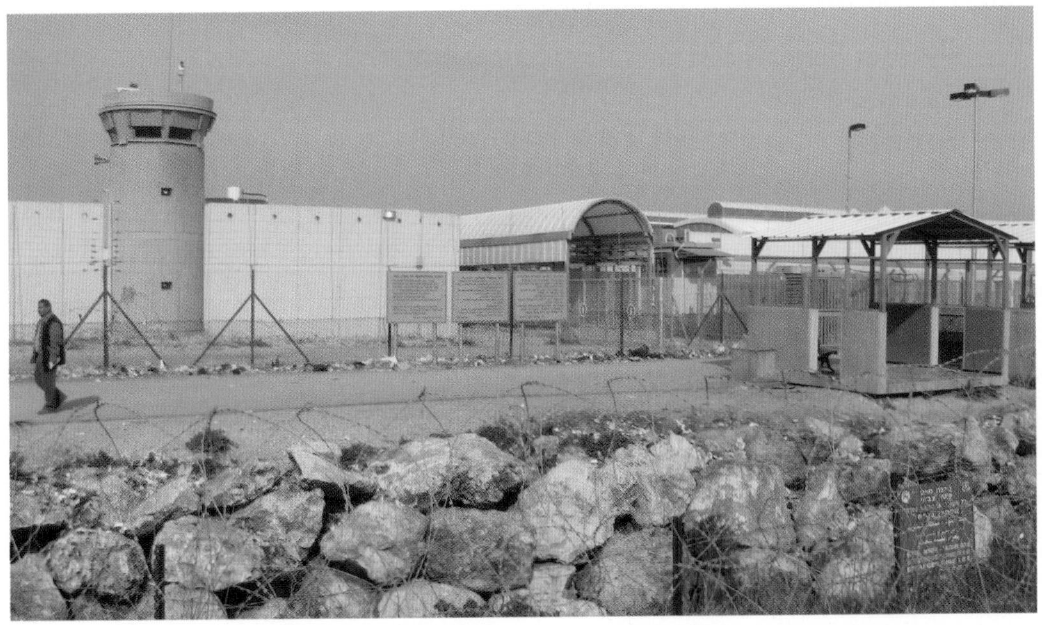

Israel has replaced many checkpoints inside the West Bank with terminal buildings.

The second gate of pre-screening before entering the terminal building at Einab

to two large iron turnstiles surrounded by a wall of iron bars. The turnstiles were locked. Frustrated, I put down my six bags to rest for a moment. Maybe someone would come back? I waited, but still there was nobody.

I called out. "Hello? Anybody out there?"

"Please wait a moment," a staticky voice above me blared, and I looked up to find a speaker attached to the turnstile. I didn't have much choice but to wait. Whoever was operating the turnstiles didn't seem to be in much of a hurry, so I took out my camera.

"Excuse me!" the voice snapped.

"Yes," I answered as I took my first photo.

"Please put your camera away immediately!"

"Please let me in immediately," I answered, as I framed a second shot.

"I said to wait," said the voice, and I answered, "And I am waiting."

The light above the turnstile turned from red to green and I put away my camera and picked up my bags to walk through. It was difficult squeezing into the tight rotating cage with all my bags, and by the time I'd made it to the other side, I was hot and cranky. I had yet to see a human face.

In front of me was a metal detector, surrounded by iron bars. I began to walk through but the voice called out from another speaker above, "Stop!"

The third phase of pre-screening before entering the terminal building at Einab

I continued through the metal detector and yelled, "What?!" into the air, wondering where he was watching me from.

"Go back and put down your bags."

I sighed and went back through the metal detector and set down my six bags, which were feeling heavier by the minute. I took the opportunity to take another picture. The soldier didn't bother protesting this time, but ordered me to walk through the metal detector again.

I tried to pick up my bags again but he ordered, "No, without your bags." I walked through. Nothing happened.

"Now, go back."

I closed my eyes with a sigh, walked back, picked up my six bags, and walked through again before he could give me the order to do so. Somehow this seemed so much worse than the turnstiles and metal detectors I had seen at Huwwara checkpoint. At least there you could see the people humiliating you. Or maybe it was more upsetting because I wasn't used to being the one humiliated.

Beyond the metal detector was another set of turnstiles, locked again. I took a deep breath and stared at the red light, hoping to see it turn green rather than let the guard hear my voice crack if I spoke. Thankfully, the turnstile buzzed and I squeezed through to reach the building itself. That was the end of the pre-screening. Now it was time for the *real* screening.

The inside of the building reminded me of an airport terminal—high ceilings and multiple floors, and multilingual signs for travelers. The ones here read, "Prepare documents for inspection" in Hebrew, Arabic, and English. The signs didn't clarify where one was supposed to go, however. There were a series of five doors with red lights on top, and I called out, "OK, my documents are ready... Now what?"

This time nobody answered, so I asked again. Again, nothing. I set my bags down, pissed off. My back was hurting, I was sweating, and I didn't know where I was or what was going to happen to me. Instead of taking a deep breath, I screamed at the top of my lungs, "Is anybody there?! Hellooooooo!"

Eventually a second staticky voice came through from a speaker on the wall. "Please proceed to the door."

"Which door?"

"The one on the left."

"Left of what? Where are you?"

"I can see you," the voice said. "Walk backwards and go left."

I saw a door behind me on the left and carried my bags over to it. Above the door was a red light, which I stared at. Nothing happened. I was ready to cry. "Now what?" I yelled. Silence. I yelled again, even louder.

"What am I supposed to do?!"

"Calm down!" yelled a cheerful soldier walking by on an upper level above me. He was finishing a conversation on his walkie-talkie, and put up his hand for me to wait. I glared at him. "Go there," he pointed to another door near the one I was standing at, and began to walk away.

"No, please!" I blurted out, forgetting our policy of not pleading with soldiers. "You're the first human face I've seen and I'm starting to lose it."

He motioned towards the door and promised that if I stood there, the light would eventually turn green. I picked up my bags, approached the door, set them down, and waited. Eventually, the light turned green, this time accompanied by a little buzz that unlatched the full iron door. I expected to find a soldier on the other side, but as the heavy door slammed behind me I found myself in a tiny room with white walls, no windows, and a second iron door. That door eventually buzzed as well, and I struggled to open it as I held my bags, settling to kick one in front of me instead.

The next room had three walls and a double-paned window with a soldier on the other side. The soldier asked for my ID and I slipped it under the glass. He tried to make small talk and asked me what part of the United States I was from. I told him flatly, "For the first time in my life, I want to blow someone up."

He must not have heard me because he let me through to the next tiny windowless room. The next buzzing heavy door led out into the other open-spaced side of the terminal, where I picked up the pace, hoping to get out finally, an hour after I'd arrived. No such luck.

One more soldier behind a window beckoned for my passport again. "Where's your visa?" he asked, not finding the stamped slip of paper issued by Israel when the passport itself is not stamped. I answered truthfully, "They told me at the airport that there were none left and that it would be OK." As the words came out, I realized how absurd this sounded, and I kicked myself for falling for it when I'd flown in the week before. How could the airport run out of visa sheets? Wasn't it more likely that they were deliberately trying to inhibit my travel in Palestinian areas?

It was hard to blame the soldier, since, for all he knew, I'd snuck in over the hills of Jordan. "Whatever," I sighed. "Call airport security—I promise I'm in the system."

I knew it would be a while, so I sat down again. I thought I was past the point of anger until I noticed a line of 25 or so Palestinians waiting outside to come in from the other direction, heading back to Tulkarem. Had they been waiting there all this time? Why weren't they being processed? I asked the guard holding my passport and he said he'd tend to them after I left.

It was one thing to feel frustrated and humiliated, but another to know that my ordeal had held up dozens of Palestinians from getting back to their homes and families. "No," I said. "Are you telling me that in your fancy new facility you can't process people coming in two directions? Don't let the problem with me delay these people any longer."

Dozens of Palestinians wait to be screened in the terminal at Einab junction inside the West Bank on their way home from work.

Dozens of Palestinians wait to be screened in the terminal at Einab junction inside the West Bank on their way home from work.

He told me not to worry, that the Palestinians were used to waiting. This made me even more upset. I insisted that I would rather wait longer myself, and eventually he beckoned the group forward. I marveled as they waited patiently and yet somehow not submissively, beacons of dignity next to my defeated and angry presence. I took out my camera and took a few photos. Within seconds, a guard appeared next to me—in person, nothing but air between us!—and said sternly, "Come with me."

I told the guard I wasn't carrying my bags another step unless it was out the door; he agreed to carry them. I followed the guard back towards the section of the terminal from which I had just come. We passed through the windowless rooms and into a new room with crates on the floor. From there, the guard opened another, even heavier iron door, and motioned for me to pass ahead of him. Expecting the guard to follow me in, I turned and instead found him placing my bags into the crates. Realizing that soldiers were going to go through my bags, I demanded to be present during the search to ensure that nothing would be damaged or stolen. "That's not possible," the guard said flatly, and the door slammed shut between me and my belongings.

I kicked the door with frustration, realizing that all my contact information for Palestinian organizers and friends was still on my computer. I realized that I still had my phone in my pocket and quickly called my friend Kobi, an Israeli activist. I told him where

I was and asked if he might call Machsom Watch on my behalf. He said he'd do what he could and we hung up.

I looked around the room. It was empty except for a chair and an empty crate on the floor. There were no other doors, but there was a two-paned window with a soldier watching me from the other side of it. "What are you looking at?" I snapped at the soldier, and he walked out of view. Another soldier appeared, a young woman. She spoke into an intercom so that I could hear her through the window. "Please take off your clothes and put them in the container on the floor."

It took a moment for the words to sink in. Once they had, I looked the soldier straight in the eyes, and I began to undress. I removed each piece of clothing slowly, not once taking my eyes off hers. I watched her with a look of hurt, not anger. I wanted her to see that she was not just searching me—she was humiliating me. Several times she looked away. When I was down to my underwear, the soldier stopped me; she said that was enough. A part of me wished that she hadn't. Perhaps if I were completely naked, she would more likely recognize the extent of my humiliation and her role in it.

The booth in which Palestinian women may be strip-searched, at a checkpoint in the West Bank

The iron door behind me buzzed and the soldier told me to place the crate containing my clothes and phone into the room where I had last seen the guard. My other belongings were long since gone, and I could hear soldiers in the next room going through them. When I got back to the room, the soldier in the window was gone. I sat down on the chair and waited. The soldiers next door were chatting and laughing. I imagined them examining my personal photographs and letters. I was too upset to sit still. I stood up and started pacing back and forth in the small room. I had to do something—anything—to express my emotions. If I could hear them, then they could hear me. I began to sing.

I sang an old song that I'd learned at summer camp as a child. Its words were meaningless, but I sang it at the top of my lungs. Within seconds, the female soldier was at the window, looking very alarmed. I waved. I sang that stupid song until my voice hurt. It felt good to sing—I felt empowered. It was easier to act like a crazy person than a prisoner. If I was unpredictable, then they had lost the power to control me.

Half an hour passed. Or was it an hour? My energy had worn off and I sat down miserably on the chair. I was so tired. The soldiers were gone from the next room now. What was taking them so long? It was cold in the room, and I had nothing to cover myself with. I began to shiver and rock back and forth on the chair. I had no more energy to yell. I began to cry. I cried for a long time. Eventually, the female soldier appeared in the window. I could tell she felt bad for me. I looked away. The door buzzed and she instructed me to open it. On the other side was a jacket and a cup of water. I put on the jacket and drank the water to soothe my throat, but I was unimpressed. I didn't want a jacket or water. I wanted my freedom to leave. I wanted my dignity back.

Time passed. I stopped looking at the soldiers and talking to them. I stopped thinking of ways to pass the time or express myself. I didn't even feel like myself anymore. I felt empty, defeated. I just sat and waited, with a feeling of profound loneliness.

After what felt like an eternity, the iron door buzzed and I opened it to find all my clothes and bags in a large pile brimming over the tops of the containers. The soldiers had emptied every single item separately into the crates. The papers from my notebook were strewn about loosely. Each piece of embroidery had been removed from its protective wrapper and crumpled into a pile. A can of tuna had been opened and left amidst the hand-sewn garments. Even the boxes of Turkish delight—a soft sticky candy covered with powdered sugar, which I'd brought from Turkey for my Israeli friends in Tel Aviv—had been opened and rummaged through.

The only thing stronger than my anger was my desire to leave. I sat down miserably and folded everything back into my bags. I was crying uncontrollably, but I bit my tongue each time I was tempted to speak. When I was dressed and ready, I stood up, collected myself, and tried to open the door. It was locked.

"The door's still locked," I informed the soldier watching through the window.

"Yes, please wait a little longer."

"Why?" I asked. "You saw everything I have. You know I'm not a security threat, and surely you know by now that I have a visa."

"I'm sorry but you're going to have to wait," she said.

I couldn't hold myself back any longer. I lost it. I opened up my bags and took out what was left of my canned tuna. With my fingers, I began to spread the oily fish all over the window.

"What are you doing?" asked the soldier, alarmed.

"You don't respect my stuff, I don't respect yours," I answered.

Next, I opened a box of Turkish delight. "I'm not going to stop until you let me out," I announced as I began mashing the gummy cubes into the hinges of the iron door. I took out a black marker and began to write "Free Palestine" in large letters on the wall.

"OK, OK," said the soldier's voice over the intercom. "You can go now." The door buzzed.

I gathered my bags and walked out. A soldier was waiting for me on the other side. He gave me my passport and said I was free to leave. I called Kobi as soon as I was outside. He said it was the US Consulate that had helped get me released. The army claimed they were holding me because of the photographs I had taken inside the terminal. Interestingly, they hadn't bothered to delete the images from my camera when they had searched my bags.

I told Kobi what had happened to me and what I had done. I felt as if I had lost a part of myself inside that terminal as I had slowly lost control. Kobi reminded me that even the option of losing control was a sign of privilege—Palestinians who behaved as I had would not likely have been freed. I tried to imagine what it would be like to endure such an invasive screening every day of my life.

Kobi told me a story about his Palestinian friend, Sara, whom he'd met in Maryland. Sara would frequently travel back and forth between her home in Palestine and the United States, where she was studying. Each time she returned to Palestine, she was able to walk right through the checkpoints. She had enough confidence to just assert her will and go through, simply by the fact that she was used to being treated like a person. And each time, after a few months in Palestine, she would lose that ability.

In just a few hours I had gone from empowerment to craziness to submission to destructiveness. What would I become after months of such treatment? What about a lifetime of the even worse treatment that Palestinians experience?

It was dark outside the terminal as I hung up the phone. I had been held for 3 hours, and there were no more buses running. I could see the lights of a settlement on a nearby hill. I began walking in what seemed like the direction of Tel Aviv. I stuck my thumb out to the occasional passing car, and eventually a settler stopped. He moved his gun out of the front seat so that I could get in. Feeling lousy about it, I accepted a ride to the nearest bus stop from where buses were still running to Tel Aviv. I boarded the first bus out and cried the whole way back to the city.

Witness in Palestine

The Untold Stories: Tragic, but Not Tragic Enough to Notice

Sunday, March 25, 2007

Today I visited my friends Dawud and Samaa in Kafr 'Ain for the first time since they lost their 6-month-old baby at Atara Checkpoint. Dawud told me how the soldier insisted on searching under the car, behind the wheels, and in the trunk before taking 3 minutes to bring back the IDs that had already been cleared. They told me what happened after they got through the checkpoint: After confirming at the hospital in Ramallah that nothing could be done to revive their child, they returned to their village. On the way back they passed Atara checkpoint and the same soldier, who again stopped their car. "Where's your baby?" he inquired.

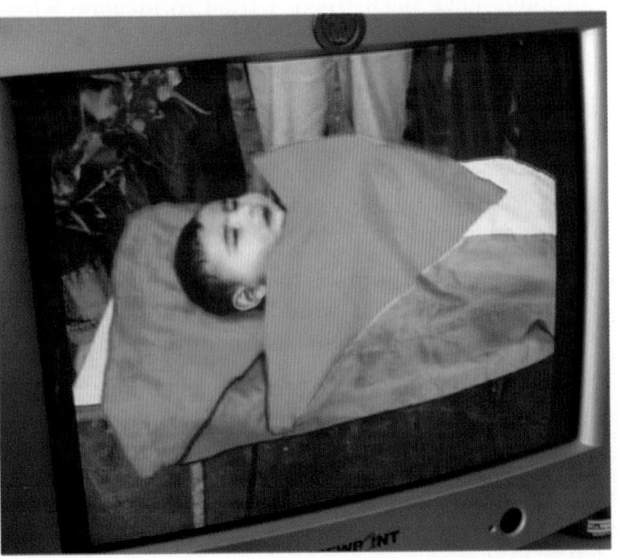

Khalid Dawud Fakaah, 6 months old, died at Atara checkpoint when he was prevented from reaching the hospital.

Samaa knits yarmulkas for Jewish Israelis to bring in an extra 5 shekels (just over US$1) a day for her family.

"He died."

"Why?" the soldier asked.

Dawud tried to remain calm. "Because you prevented us from passing. He died because he couldn't reach the hospital in time, because of you."

The soldier shook his head. "This is not from me, this is from Allah," and let them pass.

Samaa tried to hold back tears as her husband retold their story to me and Gideon Levy, a well-known Israeli journalist, who had come to take the report for *Haaretz*. Samaa kept her hands busy knitting yarmulkes (round skullcaps worn by many observant Jewish men), which she said she sells to Israeli merchants for 5 shekels apiece (about

US$1.15). She can make about one per day. It was heartbreaking to hear the details of the story from Dawud, who just one month ago was asking me when I would come visit Kafr 'Ain for pleasure, not just to take a report. He said there was more to Palestine than the sob stories. But today was all about grief. We watched a video of the funeral in silence, and saw Samaa break down and say she couldn't take it anymore. She'd already lost two sons to natural causes, but apart from moderate and treatable asthma, Khalid had been a happy and healthy little boy.

Last time I visited Kafr 'Ain I took reports from one family after another about nightly raids by the army. A 14-year-old girl told me how the soldiers woke up her family in the middle of the night with sound bombs, forced everyone out in their pajamas with no shoes and isolated the young girl to question her before enclosing the mother and children in their living room and ransacking the house. She showed me where the soldiers had detonated small explosives in her room and in the family's well.

A 14-year-old girl (left) and her three younger sisters sit in the room where they were held with their mother for several hours while soldiers ransacked their home.

Another family told me how they were woken with sound bombs, rushed outside, and the young men were stripped, handcuffed, and forced to lie on their front lawn in the cold before being taken to a neighbor's living room for interrogation. The neighbor's family was meanwhile locked in their bedrooms with the lights off, warned against any sound or movement.

Left: Soldiers rummaged through one family's photographs.

Left middle: A family in Kafr 'Ain that was locked in their bedrooms with the lights off and warned against any movement as soldiers transformed their living room into an interrogation center for neighbors

Above right: Another family was woken with sound bombs and rushed out into the cold. The men were stripped, handcuffed, and taken to a neighbor's home for interrogation.

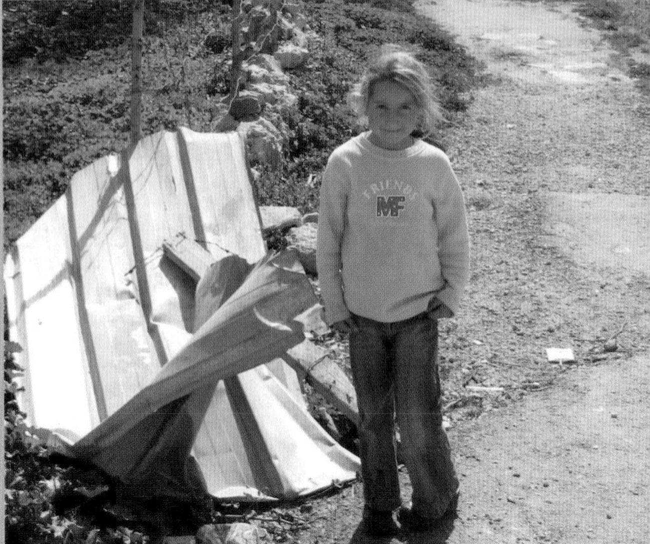

Left: A girl in Kafr 'Ain stands in front of the gate to her house, destroyed by jeeps during a night raid.

There were more stories. Too many, in fact. Eventually I had to stop taking reports, partially because I had to be somewhere, but more because as I recorded the stories I had a sinking feeling that the raids were simply too common, too unremarkable to catch anyone's attention. This would not be a human rights report that any legal or humanitarian organization would follow up on.

Major operations in Nablus or Ramallah make headlines, but incursions into many small West Bank villages are just a part of daily life. For example, for the past 2 months, the army has come nightly to Marda village, throwing sound bombs, arresting men, abducting boys. Soldiers steal IDs and refuse to return them until their holders give the names of kids in the village who put stones in the settler road that cuts through Marda. They spontaneously shut the village down without prior warning, preventing residents from entering and visitors from leaving. Two weeks ago soldiers broke into the house of a family with three sons. The middle son Ahmad, 19, was studying for an English exam the next day when he heard soldiers outside. He told me the story:

> I left my books to go see what all the commotion was about. There were about 14 soldiers total surrounding my house, and three jeeps. Soldiers were kicking our front door and throwing sound bombs. When the soldiers saw me, they grabbed me and began to hit me. My parents and my brother Qutaiba—he' s only 13—tried to intervene but the army pushed my mom and dad to the ground and hit Qutaiba in the stomach. Each time my little brother tried to stand up they would punch him in the gut again, and my mother began screaming for them to stop. It seemed like each time she screamed they beat him again. Suddenly my mother began to wail and I saw that two soldiers were covering Qutaiba's face with their hands so that he could not breathe, suffocating him until his face began to turn red. Eventually they allowed him to breathe.

I asked Qutaiba what happened after that.

> The soldiers blindfolded and handcuffed me and Ahmad and brought us in their jeeps to the entrance of our village. They dragged me out of the jeep by lifting my cuffed hands behind my back, which hurt my shoulders. Several soldiers beat me with their fists, bats, and guns, and then they started asking me questions about which village boys were throwing stones. I told them I was cold and sick, and one soldier said that this was nothing; he would punish me to the point of death. They took my cap and began throwing it above my head, laughing, making fun of me. After half an hour they got bored and left me to walk home. They drove away with my brother still blindfolded and handcuffed in the jeep.

Ahmad picked up the story where Qutaiba had left off:

> It was terrible listening to my little brother being beaten, and I was almost grateful when they drove away with me. The soldiers took me to the Ariel police station, where they beat me for several hours all over my body, especially in my head and temples. All the time I was blindfolded so I could not anticipate where the next blow was coming from. It was very scary. One soldier put his boot in my mouth. I asked the commander for some water and he told me to go to hell. Suddenly one of them kicked me very hard in the groin and everything went black. The next thing I knew they were splashing my face with cold water, and when they saw I was awake they began to beat me again, accusing me of throwing stones, destroying settlers' cars, and being a member of Hamas. After 4 hours they finally let me go.

Ahmad's father Rasmi cut in:

> When my son came home after 1 a.m., it looked as if he had taken a blood shower. He had to go into school the next day but his English teacher let him postpone the exam. I teach my children good values, to respect others and never to use violence. But how can they continue to be peaceful when they are constantly surrounded and threatened by so much brutality? I'd like to live peacefully with the Jewish people. They build their state, and we build ours. They take care of their children, and I take care of mine. I lived in Chicago for 15 years. I know that in America it's a sin to hit your children. Here, soldiers can hit other people's children and nobody says a thing! But even if they kill my children, I will not kill theirs. These are my values, what my parents taught me and what I teach my children.

Qutaiba, 13, was blindfolded, handcuffed, taken from his home, and beaten by soldiers invading Marda.

As Rasmi spoke, a car drove by and the whole family jumped. They laughed nervously when they realized it was just a neighbor. Rasmi said the soldiers returned 3 days later and took Ahmad again, this time with his older brother Samiah. They blindfolded and handcuffed them, and brought them to an abandoned warehouse off the main road. Ahmad was still fragile from his fresh head wounds, but the soldiers beat him and his brother nonetheless, first in silence, then cursing them and accusing them of harboring weapons. When it began to rain, the soldiers brought the young men outside, removed their jackets, and began hitting them again. Eventually they let the boys go, after stealing all the money in Samiah's wallet, 70 Jordanian dinars and 60 Israeli shekels. This in addition to 400 shekels that they stole from the house the first time, all together the equivalent of more than US$200 (not to mention the CDs and toys that they broke when they ransacked the home). They also took the university documents that were in Samiah's wallet.

Although the villagers of Marda call us more than most, it's not because Marda is worse off than other villages. It's because many people in the other villages have given up on us. We recently met a 56-year-old grandmother named Hilwe who was shot in the face 3 weeks ago by soldiers hiding behind a corner in her village, Qarawat Bani Hassan. One rubber-coated bullet (don't let the name fool you; rubber bullets can—and do—kill) grazed her face, tearing and detaching a segment of her right nostril, disfiguring her and requiring 20 stitches. I asked Hilwe what the soldiers were doing in her village and she shrugged, "They come every day. It's nothing special." I asked why nobody had called IWPS and Hilwe's brother answered straightly, "What are you gonna do, write a report?"

We encouraged the family in Qarawat to call us more, but I won't blame them if they don't. How much are we really helping by writing these reports that policymakers and even most activists will never read? How much are we just creating false hope and forcing families to relive painful episodes that they'd rather try to forget? The best we can do is to offer our services and be honest about what we can and cannot do. We cannot bring criminals to justice; we cannot get innocent men out of jail; we cannot keep the soldiers from invading, or settlers from stealing land. All we can really do is document incidents and offer sympathy, and occasionally remind soldiers that we are watching.

Even our home village seems to have given up on us. The jeeps still come, but nobody calls. Yesterday I heard by chance from a friend that a boy from Haris says he was kidnapped by soldiers because he was wearing too much olive green. The soldiers reportedly said that that color is reserved for the army. They drove him onto a quiet road between our village and Kifl Haris, made him take off all his green clothes (everything but his underwear), and left him half-naked to hitch his way back. He hid behind the olive trees until a Palestinian driving by took pity on him and brought him some clothes.

Hilwe, a 56-year-old grandmother, wa... the face by soldiers invading Qar... Hassan.

Like Ahmad's and Hilwe's, the Haris boy's story will never make headlines. But there will always be the stories that do get out. Gideon Levy followed up on our report of the 11-year-old human shield in Nablus, a story that eventually made it to the *New York Times* and other mainstream media. The Israeli army finally said it will look into the charges.[45]

It is the brave voices of Israelis like Levy that give me the most hope f... Israeli mainstream society. I remained stoic through dozens of human ri... the past weeks and months, but I finally broke down when I learned tha... voices had been lost. Eight days ago, Israeli linguist and political a... died of a stroke in New York City. Tanya was a staunch defende... dedicated to exposing to her fellow Israelis and to the world th... against the Palestinian people. Tanya wrote extraordinary b... spent time on the front lines of the movement here in Pal...

In our last correspondence, Tanya confessed wit... Israel because she couldn't bear to remain after h... Gaza and Lebanon. She had eventually quit h... employers "made life impossible" as punishme... hear such an extraordinary activist apologi... most of us can ever hope to.

Brave Israeli dissidents like Tany... has done extensive research on t... plans to leave Israel for the UK b... it "increasingly difficult to liv... growing faster than it ever h... come out, even if it takes an... power is covering up the tru... Israel's historic and present... hidden forever.

[45] While some s... fact the inva... cautious." H...

[46] Jonny Paul...

Witness in Palestine

Prelude to the Third Intifada?

Wednesday, April 4, 2007

It's been almost 2 weeks since I last wrote. Things have been awful on the ground here in Palestine, leaving little time for reflection. As usual, Passover—the Jewish holiday elebrating freedom from ession—has been accompanied htened restrictions on rs. While Jewish Israelis nearby, travel within the s become difficult, if or everyone except breeze by the Calling the ost offices for the gently tals

Passover—the Jewish holiday celebrating freedom from oppression—was accompanied by extra checkpoints and restrictions on Palestinians, like all Jewish holidays.

According to the Palestinian Center for Human Rights' weekly report, the army has—among other activities—killed 4 Palestinians (including a sheep herder), injured 10, conducted 21 incursions into West Bank Palestinian communities, arrested 37 Palestinian civilians (including 5 children), and demolished two houses... all in the past week.[47] A woman watching the demolition of her sister's house was attacked by a police dog. Settlers moved back into an evacuated settlement in Nablus, while several hundred took over a massive building in the heart of Hebron. Israel immediately deployed soldiers to protect the new settlement. The nearby Abu Haykal family, friends whom I visited last month in Tel Rumeida, had their car torched by Hebron settlers. All in all, it was an average week in Palestine.

The ongoing brutality and harassment are fueling a growing tension that I predict will one day explode into a third intifada. The signs are there—intense frustration, and an even stronger determination to throw off the Occupation's yoke. There are demonstrations all over the West Bank, sometimes several per day. Israel's excessive force and continued colonization are unsustainable, because the Palestinians will never stop resisting. To stop resisting is to have no future—it is national suicide. The worse the Occupation becomes, the stronger the resistance will become.

Although it is not reported as such, most of the current Palestinian resistance has been nonviolent. At the Arab American University of Jenin, the "Green Resistance" student group succeeded in banning the Israeli-produced *Tapuzina* fruit juice from the AAUJ campus, part of a growing Palestinian campaign to support local products rather than paying for their own Occupation. My neighbor Abu Saed in Haris, whose trees have been uprooted by settlers three times over the past month, continues to replant them week after week, with support from Rabbis for Human Rights and IWPS. Two weeks ago, more than 350 people—Palestinians, Israelis, and internationals—gathered for the first-ever Palestine International Bike Race from Ramallah to Jericho, an event organized by the East Jerusalem YMCA for people from all over the world to protest human rights violations in Palestine and demand freedom of movement for Palestinian civilians.[48] The event was projected to be the longest ever international sporting event protesting the Occupation, but Israeli jeeps cut the race short by closing traffic to two-wheelers and the "Bikes not Bombs" enthusiasts were forced to turn back.[49]

Near the Quaker Friends School where the bike race commenced is a cultural center where dozens of Palestinian youth come together every week to make short films and dance together. The Occupation not only threatens Palestinians' homes, land, livelihoods, time, and future, but also their creativity and expression, sometimes intentionally.[50] Palestine's unique cultural heritage is evidence of Palestinians' history on the land that Israel now claims, and confirmation of their identity as a people distinct from those in

---

[47] "Weekly Report: On Israeli Human Rights Violations in the Occupied Palestinian Territory," No. 12/2007, *Palestinian Centre for Human Rights* (March 28, 2007).

[48] "EJ YMCA organizes the Palestine International Bike Race," *YMCA News* (March 23, 2007).

[49] For photographs and a participant's account, read "Bikes vs. Bombs," by Martinez (March 23, 2007). *www.palsolidarity.org/main/2007/03/23/bikes-vs-bombs*

[50] Israel has directly targeted sources of Palestinian cultural pride, like when an exhibition of Palestinian art, plays, and dress fashion at Bir Zeit College was closed by an Israeli military governor on grounds that "expressions of Palestinian culture are dangerous political acts." Chomsky, *Fateful*, p. 145; For other examples of attacks on Palestinian culture, see Finkelstein, *Image*, p. xxv.

Palestinians dance to celebrate their culture, which the Occupation threatens to destroy.

other parts of the Arab world. When I visited the Ramallah cultural center, students explained to me that, for them, "art is not a luxury—it's a must." Art is a tool to prevent Palestinian culture from being lost or distorted, and students described how they would meet in secrecy to practice quietly during invasions and curfews as their own form of creative nonviolent resistance.

In the Salfit region where we live, a new center has been established to conduct workshops in strategic communication, peace-building, conflict resolution, and nonviolent resistance. I spoke with the director, Fuad, who explained that nonviolent resistance in Israeli jails (such as hunger strikes) has recently increased, and that many Palestinians—particularly those returning from prison—have been building what he called "a nonviolent movement for freedom, equality, democratic values, and human rights." His organization aims to develop human rights and democracy awareness workshops and resistance trainings, but they lack the proper funding to do so. Fuad told me his own story of transformation from a soldier in Arafat's "*Sabahtash*" army to a committed nonviolence advocate after his brother was killed. Fuad was particularly inspired by the First Intifada, during which many parts of Palestinian society joined in nonviolent civil disobedience to demand freedom with one loud voice. When I told Fuad that IWPS could offer no financial support,[51] he replied, "We have no money, but our strength is in our beliefs: our commitment to nonviolence. Violence kills the spirit, pushing it towards more violence or submission, but nonviolence will always prevail in the end."

Fuad said he chose to work in the Salfit area because of its history of nonviolent resistance. Indeed, over the past week there were a number of major actions in our often forgotten rural region. On Land Day, hundreds gathered in the village of Rafat to protest the Wall that is slowly enclosing their village. When they found the fenced gate of the Wall unguarded, they grabbed hold of it and began to rock it, back and forth, all together, until finally the gates exploded open. When the soldiers arrived, protesters retreated to their homes, not a single stone thrown. They had made their point: Rafat will not accept collective imprisonment.

The next day in the town of Salfit, a group of demonstrators found the Wall unguarded and began removing the electric sensory wire that lines the fenced sections. Soldiers arrived quickly and began shooting into the air, but protesters held their ground and raised

[51] Although *you* could help—please contact *fuad_alramal@yahoo.com* if you think you might be able to contribute funds or other resources to the new center for nonviolence.

Demonstrators from Salfit remove the electric sensory wire lining of the Wall that has cut their town off from their main road and land, and then raise the Palestinian flag above the Wall.

Palestinian flags above the Wall that encages them. Salfit, too, will not accept collective imprisonment. Nor will the rest of the West Bank, where many other actions took place over Land Day weekend. In Qaffin town in the north, thousands of demonstrators gathered and marched and danced their way to the Wall to show their spirit and resolve to resist the illegal barrier and Occupation. In Nablus, hundreds marched to Beit Furik, one of the six city exits—all army checkpoints—through which men 16 to 45 years old are not allowed to pass without a special Israeli-issued permit that can only be obtained outside the city. The march, organized in part by the Nablus Women's Union and a society for local disabled

Nablus residents march through and occupy Beit Furik checkpoint.

Organized in part by a society for disabled people, the march was open to everyone and very diverse.

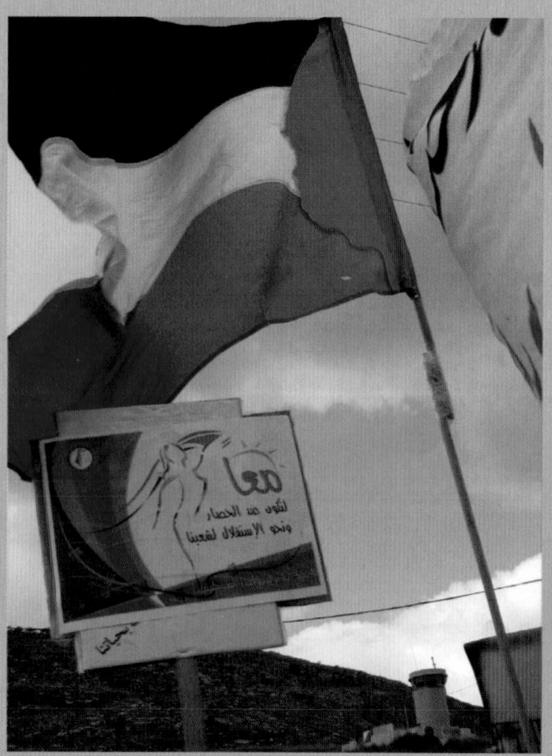

The march was organized in part by the Nablus Women's Union

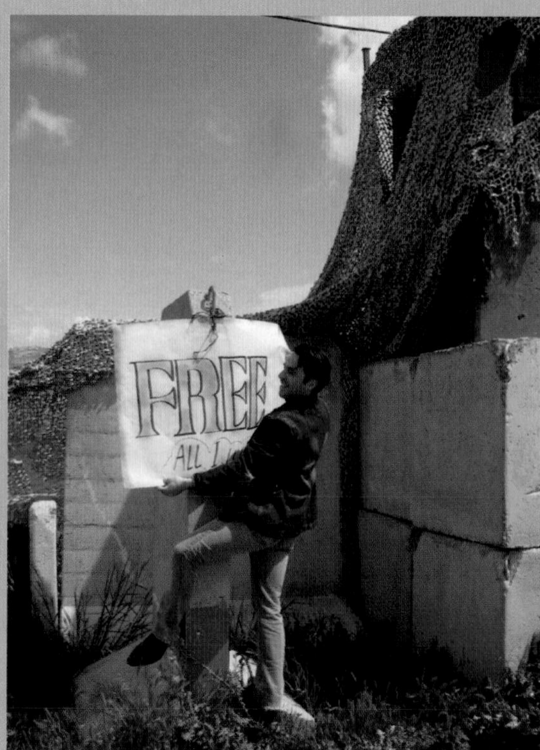

Nablus residents occupy Beit Furik checkpoint.

Nablus resisdents occupy Beit Furik checkpoint.

people, continued *through* the checkpoint past stunned soldiers unable to hold the cheering protesters back. The demonstrators then occupied the checkpoint, first by sitting down and later by climbing atop the waiting pens and hanging Palestinian flags and freedom signs around the base.

Gross injustice is unsustainable. It cannot be normalized, because there will always be resistance. The Third Intifada will come. It may be nonviolent like the first, or it may be more like the second. The Israeli government and army are doing their best to divert Palestinian energies. It is no coincidence that Israel began construction at the Temple Mount holy site in Jerusalem just as warring religious and secular Palestinian factions were coming to a truce, setting off yet another round of conflict between them. Israel prefers that Palestinians fight one another rather than their oppressors, but Palestinians in the West Bank and at the negotiating table are struggling to work together against their common enemies: Zionist racism and the Occupation. United, they will prevail. If the Third Intifada does not succeed, there will be a fourth. And then a fifth… as many as it takes.

Witness in Palestine

The Bedouins & their Unrecognized Villages

Thursday, April 5, 2007

A few weeks ago I participated in a solidarity visit to the Bedouins in the Negev desert. There are more than 150,000 Bedouins in Israel, the majority of whom live in villages that Israel has never recognized. These Bedouins are citizens of Israel, pay taxes, and many of them serve in the army, but since their communities are unrecognized, they receive no services from the State; many of their villages have no roads, no electricity, no running water or sewage system, no schools, and no medical facilities.

The Bedouins were part of the Palestinian Arab population living in Palestine long before Zionist immigration began. More than 80% of the Bedouin population fled during the *Nakba*. The Bedouins in Israel today are the descendents of the 10,000 or so who stayed, some of whom fought alongside Zionist forces with the promise that they could be a part of the new Jewish state.

Now, almost 60 years later, most of their communities have never been recognized and they live as second-class citizens, the poorest minority in Israel.[52] The forced expulsions continue, primarily through house demolitions, denial of services, and land confiscation.

A Bedouin village

[52] "Third or fourth-class citizens" might be more accurate if you account for other Palestinian citizens of Israel and foreign immigrants, whose communities are at least recognized even if the services they receive are minimal compared to those granted to Jewish citizens. There is also discrimination within the Jewish population targeting Sephardic, Mizrahi, and Ethiopian Jews, even though they collectively outnumber the more elite European Ashkenazi Jews.

Amos

More than 42,000 Bedouin homes are "illegal" according to the Israeli Ministry of the Interior. The Bedouins are widely known to be a small and peaceful population, so there is no pretext that Israel is pushing Bedouins out for "security." The dispossession of the Bedouins is patently about one thing: land. The Bedouins have one thing that Israel desires: land.

I learned about the Bedouins from an Israeli activist named Amos, who had organized our trip from Tel Aviv to the desert. Along the ride, Amos told me the history of Israel's policies towards the nomadic population. In the 1950s, Israel adopted a policy of concentrating the many Bedouin tribes into a small 20 mile by 20 mile section of the Negev, known as the Siyag Zone. This freed up the majority of the desert for Jewish settlement and development. In the 1960s, Israel pushed the traditionally rural Bedouins in the Siyag Zone out of their decentralized villages and into towns, where they would occupy less land. The Bedouins currently live on about 85,000 acres and are fighting for rights to 100,000 more, a small fraction of their original land. If Israel succeeds in moving them all into towns, the Bedouins will be left with just 25,000 acres.

We began our tour in the village of Al-Nasasra, home to 25 Bedouin families. The ride into Al-Nasasra was a bumpy one, and Amos explained that villagers are forbidden to pave their village roads, even at their own expense. He also pointed out to me how cheaply the houses had been made, usually with stacks of stones or even sheets of metal. He said the villagers are not legally permitted to build on their land, so in anticipation of their homes being destroyed, they use only cheap materials. Many roofs in Al-Nasasra are made of asbestos, in spite of the health risks. The villagers simply cannot afford to invest in more expensive materials for a house that will eventually be destroyed.

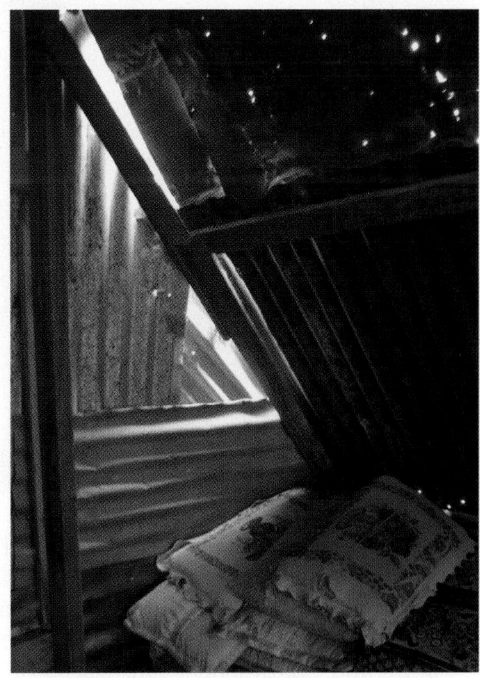

Many Bedouin homes are constructed with cheap materials. Anticipating their homes being demolished by Israel, the Bedouins cannot afford to invest in stronger materials.

On our arrival at the village center we were welcomed into a large tent with mattresses and pillows spread out over the ground. Our hosts passed around tea and coffee while we got acquainted with the other Israelis and internationals who had come for the day. The head of the village council gave a short history of Bedouins in Israel, similar to the one I'd heard from Amos. He added that for the first 20 years after their tribe's relocation to the Siyag Zone, local children had to walk 3 miles each way to

Bedouin children outside their homes in Al-Nasasra

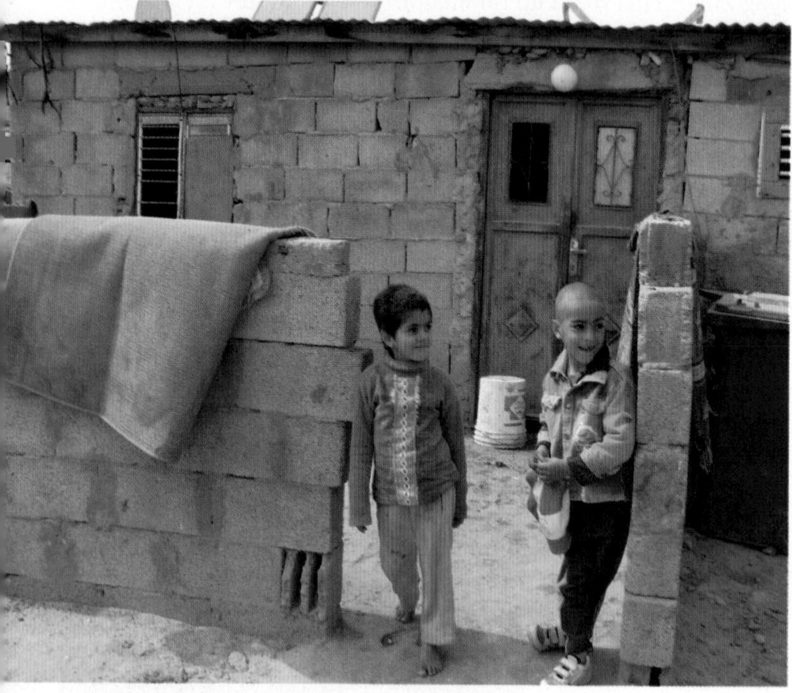

attend school since the government would not provide school buses.[53] He remarked on the irony of being denied services and recognition in the very village that Israel had forced the tribe to move to in the 1950s. Now, in exchange for recognition, Israel is demanding that the villagers give up all their agricultural land—their livelihood. The councilman explained that the families were willing to compromise, to move again, but Israel has refused to provide an alternative place where the tribe can live peacefully and continue its traditional, rural way of life.

A representative from the nearby village of Asira spoke about her village, which has existed since the Ottoman era. Bedouin families lived in the area hundreds of years before Israel was created, but the Jewish state views them as foreigners. The government talks about the "Bedouin problem" the same way it talks about perceived threats from Lebanon and Iran. Israel's settlement of Jews aims at expansion, whereas its resettlement of Bedouins aims at concentration and displacement. As in the Jordan Valley, the government will redistribute hundreds or even thousands of Bedouins' acres to a single Jewish family, saying it's for the preservation of the "Jewish character" of the state. The speaker commented that these tactics foster anger between Jews and Palestinians. She clarified, "We are not opposed to Jewish settlement in the Negev, but why must it be at our expense?"

---

[53] Transport was provided starting in 1980.

Government policies also fuel tensions between different tribes. Israel will resettle one tribe on the land of another, provoking feuds that undermine Bedouin unity and the ability to stand up for themselves collectively. The Asira representative explained, "Israel tries to separate us from other Bedouins, and from our brothers and sisters in Northern Israel, the Occupied Territories, and the Diaspora. They call some of us Arabs, some of us Palestinians, and some of us Bedouins. But we are all three, and this is one struggle against racial discrimination and ethnic cleansing."

Jewish communities in the Negev (like the kibbutz above) are encouraged to flourish and grow, while Bedouin communities are systematically deprived of services and displaced.

Amos was the next to speak and he addressed the internationals in the group, stressing how important it is that we petition our own governments to put pressure on his government to change its policies. He spoke about the conflict between law and morality, pointing out that the laws governing Bedouins are not about punishing or preventing a crime; they are about land acquisition. He explained to his fellow Jewish Israelis, "These people's actions may be illegal, but they are justified. With no alternative place to go, Bedouins cannot exist on their land without breaking the law. A Bedouin baby is born, and before it can speak or cry it is already breaking the law."

I gave a brief speech in Arabic on behalf of the internationals in the room, and then we walked around Al-Nasasra to meet families and document their living conditions. Many families had found demolition warnings stuck to their doors last fall, demanding that they leave. The villagers insisted on feeding us like royalty before we left, which was hard to accept when I learned that they hadn't hired a lawyer to appeal the demolition orders because they couldn't afford one.

The villagers of Al-Nasasra send us off with an extraordinary meal, in spite of their personal struggles to make ends meet.

Twail Abu Jarwal village, partially demolished by Israel

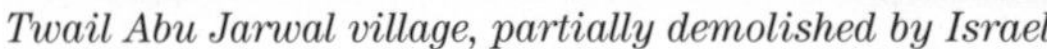

One villager of Twail Abu Jarwal tells us the story of his tribe.

Our next stop was Twail Abu Jarwal village, home to a Bedouin tribe that was relocated to a village in the Siyag Zone in 1951, and then relocated again less than 10 years later. The second time, they were placed in a Bedouin town called Lakia on land belonging to another tribe. The people of Twail Abu Jarwal asked Israeli authorities to allow them to live somewhere where they would not displace anyone else, but Israel refused. The tribe members decided to return to their original land, where they have lived for the past 7 years, despite repeated demolitions. One villager told us his tribe's story:

> Twail Abu Jarwal survived 1948 but we were moved 3 years later, with the promise that we could return soon thereafter. That was 50 years ago and they never kept their promise. We finally took the initiative to return home ourselves, and the army comes periodically to destroy all the houses. They came six times last year. They wake us up at 5 a.m. with enough soldiers to conquer half the country, and there's nothing we can do to stop them. After the first several times, they started taking away the broken pieces of our homes so that we could not rebuild with them. During the winter we have to sleep in tents. We live as if in the Middle Ages, in a modern state that claims to be democratic.
>
> We offered to move and even suggested three alternative village sites, but they were all rejected. Israel should be ashamed to talk about equality after 60 years of systematic discrimination. Instead of investing money in new roads and houses for illegal settlements in the Occupied Territories, the government should be giving full rights to its own citizens. The settlers get fancy houses, satellite TV, and swimming pools, but Israel doesn't even give us drinking water.
>
> We are not asking for favors or special treatment; we are asking for our basic rights. We know that even if Twail Abu Jarwal were recognized, we would not receive equal rights anyway because we are not Jewish. But after seeing my home demolished five times, I say forget equality—just give me a place to live!

I asked Amos why Twail Abu Jarwal had been targeted even more than other villages, and he answered without hesitation: "What Israel wants least of all is for Palestinians to reconnect to their historic land, because this makes their expulsion even harder. Israel

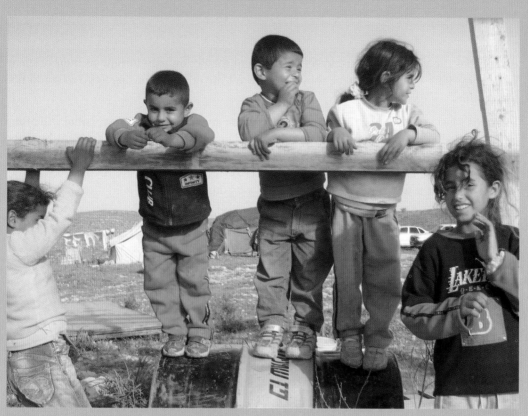

Children in Twail Abu Jarwal play among the ruined and half-built houses.

demolishes the village so as not to set a precedent for Bedouins returning to their original land. They don't do it to be mean; they simply want the ethnic cleansing to go as smoothly as possible."

Amos's last statement clarified for me why, when given the opportunity, Israel will often purchase Bedouins' land from them, something I'd heard before. One villager in Al-Nasasra pointed out the irony: "Whenever a Bedouin agrees to sell his land, Israel is ready to buy it. Would you buy a car from someone who didn't own it? Israel doesn't recognize that the land is ours, but it will recognize that the land *was* ours after we've sold it to them."

Anticipating inevitable dispossession, some Bedouins have given up, sold their land, and moved away "voluntarily"—an ethnic cleansing success story. But tens of thousands more remain, steadfast in the struggle to preserve their land and way of life.

A Bedouin shepherd grazes his sheep in the Negev.

Sewage Tsunami & Strangulation in Gaza

Friday, April 6, 2007

Last week, the walls of an overburdened cesspool in northern Gaza collapsed, flooding a nearby Bedouin village with up to two meters of raw sewage. At least five people drowned to death, with dozens more left sick, injured, or missing.

Predictably, the international community's fingers are pointed at the Palestinian Authority, which was warned of the danger of Beit Lahia treatment plant's flooding but did not take the necessary steps to ensure the villagers' safety. To many, it's just another example of how the Palestinians are incapable of ruling over themselves. But the PA is only part of the problem. In fact, funds were secured long ago for transferring the dangerous sewage pools, but according to the Palestinian Centre for Human Rights (PCHR), the project "was delayed for more than two years due to delays in importing pipes and pumps from abroad as a result of the closure imposed by[the army] on the Gaza Strip. In addition, [Israeli] military operations in the project area prevented workers from free and safe access to the area to conduct their work."[54]

After the supposed "withdrawal," Gaza remains encaged by a fence and under Israeli military control. Gazans who approach the "free-fire zone" near the fence risk being shot by snipers.

Almost two years ago, Israel claimed to be withdrawing from Gaza, and yet, according to the Human Rights Council report commissioned by the UN, Gaza has "remained under the effective control of Israel." Israel continues to control Gaza's air space, sea space, and borders, closing down Gaza's border crossings for long periods of time. Rafah, the only border crossing where Palestinians can enter Egypt, has been open only 14% of scheduled times, so Gazans (including students and sick people needing treatment in Egyptian hospitals) have had to wait sometimes for weeks on end to get through either way. Last December, Israel promised to allow 400 trucks a day to pass through Karni crossing, which links the Gaza Strip to Israel, to deliver desperately needed food and medical supplies and to allow Palestinian produce to reach foreign markets. The promise has yet to be kept, though, and

[54] *Palestinian Centre for Human Rights. www.pchrgaza.ps/files/PressR/English/2007/20-2007.htm*

An Israeli army base and tank next to Gaza

After the supposed "withdrawal," Israel still controls Gaza waters and maintains regular bans on the Gaza fishing industry, which tens of thousands of civilians depend on.

the effects on the local economy have been "disastrous," according to the Human Rights Council Report. The report continues: "In effect, following Israel's withdrawal, Gaza became a sealed off, imprisoned and occupied territory."[55]

Last week, over 50 fishermen were arrested in Gaza when they tried to go fishing and Israel opened fire on their small fishing boats.[56] Israel maintains regular bans on fishing off the Gaza coast, paralyzing the Palestinian fishing industry, which tens of thousands of civilians depend on.[57] Palestinians inside Gaza are subjected to a brutal regimen of ground invasions (two last week), frequent pot-shots from snipers, and aerial bombardments. All in all, Israel has killed more than 700 Gazans (including hundreds of women and children) since the celebrated "withdrawal." And yet, Israel's apologists still cite the "withdrawel" as evidence that Palestinians can't take advantage of a good opportunity if it falls into their laps.

---

[55] John Dugard, "Implementation of General Assembly Resolution 60/251 of 15 March 2006 Entitled 'Human Rights Council,' Report of the Special Rapporteur on the situation of human rights in the Palestinian territories occupied since 1967," *United Nations Human Rights Council*, A/HRC/4/17 (January 29, 2007).

[56] Michael Hess, "Fifty Gaza Fisherman [*sic*] Arrested by the Israeli Army," *BBSNews* (March 26, 2007).

[57] According to *B'tselem*,

"In addition to shooting, in recent months Israel Navy crews have used a new method of humiliating and abusing the fishermen.... [In] many cases ... the sailors stopped fisherman off the coast, particularly opposite Rafah, forced them to go further out to sea and then ordered them, under threat of firearms, to undress and swim dozens of meters in the sea to the navy ship, despite the bitter cold. The sailors threatened to shoot anyone who did not want to jump in because he didn't know how to swim. The fishermen were ordered to swim to a rescue float that the soldiers threw into the water, but the soldiers yanked at the float just before the fishermen reached it. After being taken on board, the ship sailed to Ashdod Port. On the way, the fishermen were kept on deck in their soaked underwear, exposed to the wind and the spray of water. At the port, the fishermen were held for from fourteen to twenty-four hours, their hands cuffed and their eyes covered, and interrogated. In some cases, they were given military clothes and were offered food and a hot beverage. At the end of the interrogation, they were taken back to the ship and returned to where their boat had been anchored. The sailors then forced them to undress again and swim to their boat. In some instances, their clothes had been blown into the sea, so they had to make their way to shore in their soaked underwear. In rare cases, the fishermen were returned to the Gaza Strip via Erez Crossing."

"IDF prohibits fishing off Gaza coast and abuse [*sic*] fishermen," *B'tselem* (February 23, 2007).

Recently, perhaps the most paralyzing feature of life in Gaza is the poverty resulting from more than one year of international economic sanctions against Palestinian civil servants. Doctors, teachers, elected officials, and other government workers (on whom about a quarter of the population is financially dependent[58]) have not been fully paid in more than one year, pushing the population into a humanitarian crisis. Over 80% of Gazans are living below the official poverty line, and basic infrastructure is deteriorating.

Some may wonder why the international community should be held responsible for financially supporting the Palestinian population to begin with. The late Tanya Reinhart articulated the reason during her last lecture in France. She explained that Europe, like the US, had no right to cut off money, food, and medicine from the Palestinians because the aid "was not an act of generosity which Europe could either carry on or not.... It was a choice which had been made to take on the obligations imposed by international law on the Israeli occupier to see to the well-being of the occupied populations. Europe chose not to oblige Israel to respect its obligations, and preferred to pay money to the Palestinians. When it put an end to this, it breached international law."[59]

The United States, Europe, and Israel (which has withheld US$55 million per month in taxes collected from Palestinians on behalf of the PA for the past year, more than half a billion dollars in total) say they will only return the Palestinians' lifelines if Hamas agrees to three conditions: (1) renouncing violence, (2) accepting previous agreements, and (3) recognizing Israel. These conditions sound reasonable enough, but are painfully ironic for anyone living on the ground here. True, Hamas has not sworn off violence once and for all, but has Israel? In the past year, Palestinians have killed 27 Israelis, most of them soldiers. During that same period of time, Israelis have killed 583 Palestinian *civilians*.[60] Hamas has held fairly consistently to a *unilateral* ceasefire since January 2005, when it announced its transition from armed struggle to political struggle. Actions speak louder than words. Hamas says it reserves the right to use violence, but has more or less stopped attacking Israelis. Israel claims that all it wants is peace, yet the daily invasions and assassinations continue.

The second condition involving previous agreements is hard to take seriously given Israel's consistent disregard for the same agreements that it expects Hamas to accept. According to the Oslo Accords signed by both Israel and the PLO in 1993, there should have been a Palestinian state by 1998. During those 5 interim years, however, Israel instead appropriated more land, nearly doubled the number of settlements, and managed to violate every single clause of the agreement.[61] When will the US demand that *Israel* adhere to previous agreements in order to receive the billions of US tax-dollars handed over every year?

---

[58] "Humanitarian Update, Occupied Palestinian Territory. Special Focus: Emerging Humanitarian Risks," *OCHA* (January 2006); As cited in *PASSIA* 2007, p. 322.

[60] *Middle East Policy Council* (April, 2007). *www.mepc.org/resources/mrates.asp*
"Numbers do not include Palestinian suicide bombers (or other attackers) nor do they include Palestinians targeted for assassination, though bystanders killed during these assassinations are counted. However, [Israeli] soldiers killed during incursions into Palestinian lands *are counted*. Data collected from *B'tselem* (the Israeli Information Center for Human Rights in the Occupied Territories), the Palestinian Red Crescent Society, and the Israeli Ministry of Foreign Affairs."

[61] "Israeli Author, Peace Activist Tanya Reinhart Dies at 63," *Democracy Now!* (March 19, 2007).

The last and crucial condition is that Hamas must recognize Israel. The question is, what exactly is meant by "Israel"? Does "Israel" mean a place where Jewish people are respected and secure, or is it something else? Israel defines itself as "the state of the Jewish people," not the state of its citizens. Palestinian citizens of Israel don't have the same rights as Jews, because so many laws are aimed at further "Judaizing" the country.[62] Israel has an artificial Jewish majority that was created and is maintained through various forms of ethnic cleansing. Israel's very existence as a Jewish state is conditional upon the dispossession and either expulsion or bantustanization of the indigenous Palestinian population. If you ask one of these Palestinians if he recognizes the right of such an Israel to exist, a country built on his land that explicitly excludes him and discriminates against him, and that Palestinian says "no," is he being racist or anti-Semitic? Or is he himself defending against racism and anti-Semitism? (After all, Arabs are Semites, too.[63])

Furthermore, Israel cannot specify what exactly it wants Palestinians to recognize because Israel doesn't actually recognize itself. Israel has refused to clarify its own borders, because they keep expanding as the Jewish state establishes more settlement "facts on the ground." In spite of all these things, the PLO actually agreed to recognize Israel, renounce terror, and sign agreements with Israel almost twenty years ago. Israel responded with continued colonization and resource confiscation in the Occupied Territories and bombardment of Lebanon to root out the PLO, which was becoming dangerously moderate.[64] Hamas, too, has indicated that it would consider peace if Israel withdrew to its internationally recognized 1967 borders, leaving Palestinians with less than a quarter of their historic homeland, but Israel says full withdrawal is out of the question. It is Israel who has yet to recognize Palestine's right to exist, not the other way around.

One more point of irony is that Israel justifies the ongoing siege of Gaza as a response to the capture of Corporal Gilad Shalit even though such collective punishment is cruel, hypocritical, and in breach of international law. Just last week, the Israeli army abducted and imprisoned 29 Palestinians, including one child. The week before that they took 37 Palestinians, including five children. The week before that they took 61, and the week before that 63, and the week before that 107. Israel has "captured" ("kidnapped" would be a more appropriate word, since most of the abductees were civilians) at least 860 Palestinians this year, and it's only April.[65] Palestinians are illegally holding one Israeli, and Israel is illegally holding more than 11,000 Palestinians, including about 40 elected officials and almost 500 women and children.[66] If the Israeli army is justified in starving and bombarding 1.3 million Gazans to avenge the capture of one of their fighters, what could the families of 11,000 Palestinian political prisoners claim is justified?

In reality, Israel is holding more than 1.3 million Palestinians prisoner with its ongoing siege of Gaza. Most of them are refugees, corralled into one of the most densely populated places in the world where many can practically see their land through the cage around

---

[62] For information about discrimination against Palestinians with Israeli citizenship, see p. 169 or visit *www.Adalah.org* or *www.MossawaCenter.org*

[63] Strictly speaking, a "Semite" is a person who speaks a Semitic language (Qumsiyeh, p. 6); The Semitic language family includes Hebrew, Arabic, Aramaic, Maltese, and many others.

[64] For a discussion on the events leading up to the first invasion of Lebanon and the invasion itself, see Noam Chomsky's classic, *The Fateful Triangle.*

[65] For week by week statistics, visit *www.pchrgaza.ps*

[66] *Mandela Institute for Human Rights & Political Prisoners. www.mandela-palestine.org*

Corralled into one of the most densely populated places in the world, some refugees in Gaza can see the land that their families fled—much of it now empty and uncultivated—through the fence around them.

them, but are forbidden from ever returning because they are not Jewish (I, on the other hand, could go live there next month if I wanted to). The Beit Lahia sewage treatment plant was designed in the 1970s to serve up to 50,000 people, but the local population has since risen to 200,000. The "sewage tsunami" is as much a result of population density as anything else. In comparison, the land-rich West Bank feels like paradise, but perhaps not for long. As the Wall continues to snake around West Bank towns and villages, cutting inhabitants off from their land, jobs, schools, hospitals, and each other, Israel's intention seems clear: those Palestinians who won't leave the West Bank altogether will be squeezed into bantustans, each of them a new Gaza. Meanwhile, any Palestinian who makes the slightest motion to resist will be branded a racist and anti-Semite, even though the worst racism and anti-Semitism are directed towards them by Israel, not the other way around.

Deir Yassin Continues

Monday, April 9, 2007

Fifty-nine years ago today, the militant Zionist Irgun and Stern Gang systematically murdered more than 100 men, women, and children in Deir Yassin. The Palestinian village lay outside the area that the UN had recommended be included in a future Jewish state, and the massacre occurred several weeks before the end of the British Mandate, but it was part of a carefully planned and orchestrated process that would provoke the flight of 70% of the Palestinian population to make way for an ethnically Jewish state.

Adnan holds a map of his village Lajjun, from which he and his family were violently expelled in 1948. Although they are Israeli citizens, Adnan and his family have never been allowed to return.

Deir Yassin was just one of more than 400 Palestinian villages depopulated and destroyed by Jewish forces in 1948 (or shortly before and after). I recently visited the ruins of a Palestinian village called Kafrayn in present-day Israel on a tour with *Zochrot*, a group of Jewish and Palestinian citizens of Israel that works to educate people about the *Nakba*.[67]

Our group met in the home of Adnan, a refugee from another village called Lajjun, who now lives in the town of Um Al-Fahim in Israel. A well-dressed man in his late sixties, Adnan welcomed us into his living room when we asked to hear his story. His grown son brought around fresh strawberries and fancy chocolates before sitting down to translate as his father began to speak:

[67] *Zochrot. www.nakbainhebrew.org/index.php?lang=english*

I remember Lajjun as if in a dream. I was only seven years old when the men with guns came, but I still remember certain things so clearly. I remember my school, and the name of my teacher. I remember we had a community center for visitors, and the village was very excited because an English ambassador was planning a visit. We worked for weeks renovating the big gardens in anticipation. I remember our village had a strong spring and a sophisticated water system. Israel has succeeded in convincing the world that Palestinians were primitive and uneducated until the Zionists arrived, but that is propaganda. We even had developed agricultural tools like trucks to turn corn. We were well-educated and we had good relations with our Jewish neighbors living in a kibbutz a few miles away.

Then the soldiers came. I remember them shooting from atop a mountain, bullets flying over my head as we ran. We fled to a town called Taybi, taking nothing with us—we had no time, and we assumed we would be back when the war was over. In Taybi we had to borrow woolen tents to live in. Eventually we found our way to Um Al-Fahim with thousands of other refugees, and we've been here ever since. Our village had 44,000 dunums [more than 10,000 acres] of agricultural land and they took every last one of them. We are citizens of Israel, but never allowed to return to our land and our homes nearby. We are refugees in our own state.

Between 1948 and 1966, Palestinians in Israel lived the way Palestinians now live in the West Bank and Gaza. We were prisoners in our homes in Um Al-Fahim, under frequent curfew and controlled by checkpoints. Although certain restrictions have been lifted, as non-Jews we are still generally restricted from more than 93% of the land in Israel, owned by the state or the Jewish National Fund. That includes my land, my village. They've surrounded it with a fence and won't even let us go pray in the mosque, one of the only structures still standing. The mosque belongs to the nearest kibbutz now, so Jewish kibbutzniks can visit it when they please.

How can Israel call itself a democracy when I cannot go to my land simply because I am a different ethnicity from my Jewish neighbors? What kind of a democracy is this where political parties are not allowed to challenge the Zionist exclusivist framework,[68] but they *can* challenge the rights of the indigenous population to stay here? Israel's Deputy Prime Minister and Minister of Strategic Threats Avigdor Lieberman, who immigrated from Moldova in the seventies, is talking about kicking out the Palestinian citizens of Israel, we who've been here for hundreds if not thousands of years! The Jewish people know catastrophe and suffering. They work for justice in their own lives… why not in all of our lives?

About one-third of all Palestinians with Israeli citizenship are internal refugees from 1948 like Adnan and his family.[69] They live as second-class citizens, receiving fewer services than their Jewish counterparts. Israel spends an average of 4,935 shekels (US$1,372) for each Jewish student per year, compared to 862 (US$240) per Arab one.[70] In

---

[68] For details on official exclusion of non-Zionist political parties in Israel, see Appendix IV.

[69] *Al-Awda* FAQs on Refugees. *www.al-awda.org/faq-refugees.html*

[70] According to the *Guardian Unlimited*, "In the 2002 budget, Israel's housing ministry spent about £14 [$27] per person in Arab communities compared with up to £1,500 [$2,950] per person in Jewish ones." During the same year, the Israeli health ministry used less than 1% of its budget towards developing healthcare facilities in Arab communities; "Worlds Apart," *Guardian Unlimited* (February 6, 2006).

Driving around with Nakba survivors trying to find villages that no longer exist

Left: Um Al-Fahim town in present-day Israel is home to 48,000 Palestinian citizens of Israel, most of whom are internal refugees denied equal services to Jews or the right to return to their homes.

the words of the Israeli parliamentarian Jamal Zahalka, "Israel is a democratic state for its Jewish citizens, and a Jewish state for its Arab citizens."[71]

Several elderly Um Al-Fahim residents accompanied us on our tour to Kafrayn. It was a strange thing, driving around in a bus looking for a village that no longer exists. Before we'd reached Kafrayn, one elderly Palestinian named Muneeb jumped up and began motioning outside the window: "That's it! That's my village!" I turned to see a large hill covered with trees. Like so many others, Muneeb's village (near Kafrayn) had been emptied of Palestinians and then planted over with fast-growing Jerusalem pines by Zionists who would later brag about "making the desert bloom."

A Palestinian Nakba survivor visits the land from which he was violently expelled.

Muneeb pointed excitedly towards one part of the hill: "That's where I used to walk to school! And that's where we'd go to fetch water! And that—that's where my house was…"

Suddenly Muneeb's voice cracked and he looked down, embarrassed. "I shouldn't have come here today," he confessed after

[71] Dina Awad, "An Inside Job: Arab Israeli parliamentarian calls Israel's bluff," *NOW* (March 15, 2007).

Signs read "Welcome to Military Base 105" and "Danger: Firing Area – Entrance Forbidden!" near the ruins of Kafrayn village. There are no soldiers in sight, but villagers are forbidden from returning.

he had regained his composure. "It's too emotional. You were here thousands of years ago and you miss your land," he spoke to the Jews in our group, "I was here 50 years ago and I miss my land."

What most struck me about our drive was how bare everything was. Nobody was living in Muneeb or Adnan's villages, or anywhere near them. Their villages had been turned into forests, military bases, and pastures, controlled by kibbutzim sometimes many miles away. One Israeli on the tour explained to me that Israel typically develops large land-intensive projects to maintain control over empty areas where it doesn't want Palestinians to settle. When we arrived in Kafrayn, we found several empty fenced-off areas. One was labeled "Welcome to Military Base 105." Another posting said "Danger: Firing Area—Entrance Forbidden!" A third sign read "Cattle-Grazing Land."

The former site of Kafrayn village is fenced off and designated as military and grazing grounds. Most Palestinian refugees' land remains empty but is controlled by kibbutzim or the Jewish National Fund.

"So they let cows live here but not Arabs?" I asked my new friend.

"Cows don't have nationalist aspirations," he smiled. "Besides, do you even see any cows around here?" He was right—there were no cows in sight, nor soldiers for that matter.

More than 100 Israelis and internationals accompany Palestinian refugees to Kafrayn village, razed and destroyed in 1948.

One common misconception about the Palestinian refugees' right of return is that its implementation would create a new refugee crisis by displacing most Israelis. In fact, according to Dr. Salman Abu Sitta, a former member of the Palestine National Council and researcher on refugee affairs, "78% of [Jewish Israelis] live in 14% of Israel. The remaining 22% ... live in 86% of Israel's area, [on] Palestinian land. Most of them live in a dozen or so Palestinian towns. A tiny minority lives in Kibbutz [*sic*]... Thus, only 200,000 Jews exploit 17,325 sq km (6,700 sq miles), which is the home and heritage of 5,248,180 refugees, crammed in camps and denied the right to return home." In other words, the vast majority of Palestinian refugees could return to their land without displacing more than about 3.5% of Jewish Israelis.[72]

The issue is not about space; it's about demographics. Allowing Palestinian refugees to return would change the ethnic character of Israel. Rather than being the state of the Jews, it might have to become the state

A girl walks with her father through the ruins of the Palestinian village from which her grandparents were violently expelled. She, like all non-Jews in Israel, continues to live as a second-class citizen in the Jewish state.

[72] Data collected from Dr. Abu Sitta's highly recommended *Nakba* Map, available at *al-awdacal.org/shop.html*

of the people who live in it, some of whom are Jews, some of whom aren't. But until that happens, the most people like Muneeb and Adnan can look forward to is an occasional tour with Jewish fringe activists every few decades. Some of the Kafrayn expulsion survivors who accompanied our tour had not been back since 1948—almost 60 years. They wandered around, as if in a dream, pointing out where the old cemetery and school used to be. One survivor, Abu Ghasi, recalled his story for the group:

> We had all heard about the Deir Yassin massacre a few days before, so when the Zionist forces arrived and began shooting, we all ran. Those of us who survived took shelter in a nearby village, and soon we heard the blasts that we knew were our homes being exploded. After the Jewish forces had moved on, we returned to find our village completely obliterated. It was clear we had no alternative but to move elsewhere, and eventually we settled in Um Al-Fahim.

Abu Ghasi points out where the cemetery used to be.

The place where the schoolhouse used to stand

An old woman from the nearest kibbutz spoke with the survivors and all agreed that their communities had gotten along well before the expulsion. They reminisced about a school bus driver they had shared, and the woman confirmed their story about the Zionist forces razing and bombing Kafrayn. The tour ended with a communal lunch between survivors, kibbutzniks, and the rest of the group next to Kafrayn's old springhouse and main water source.

Somebody had painted "Death to Arabs" in Hebrew on the springhouse, but we didn't let that keep us from enjoying the spring's natural beauty as several people got up to speak. One Jewish woman who had immigrated from Canada to Israel 27 years ago said it took her 2 decades to really understand the truth about Israel's past and present. One man asked an old kibbutznik if he thought his Palestinian former neighbors should be allowed to return, but the kibbutznik was unwilling to give a straight answer, saying it was complicated. The questioner responded with frustration, saying, "We are here on 100,000 dunums [almost 25,000 acres] of empty land. We have in Israel many internal refugees from this land that lies empty. Why not give families just one of their thousands of dunums to let them come back to their homes?"

Hebrew graffiti on the Kafrayn springhouse reads "Death to Arabs."

A Kafrayn survivor addressed the kibbutznik as well: "Look, we all want peace. It's very easy to say, but peace requires making an effort. I've lost 60 years on my land. How can you expect me to live in peace with the Jews if they refuse to give me back my land and my rights?" Another refugee echoed his sentiments: "Peace does not look like one type of person enjoying land and others forbidden. If you want peace, let's share everything. Let's live together."

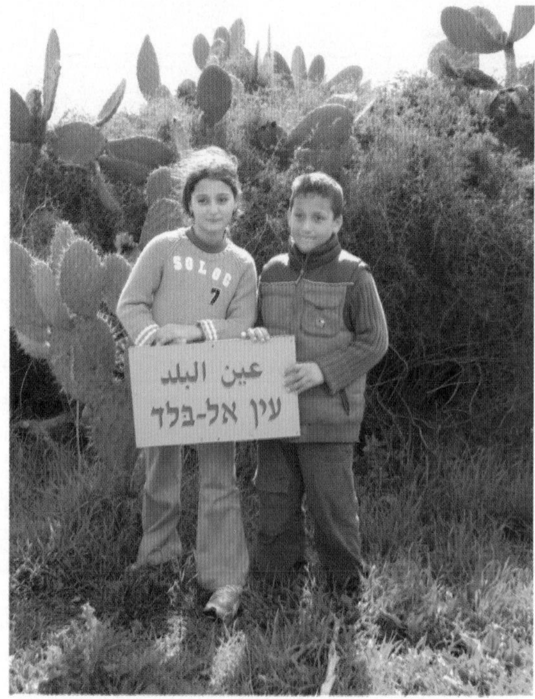

The grandchildren of refugees who fled Kafrayn in 1948 visit their village for the first time.

Tubas, the Jordan Valley, & the Economics of the Occupation

Palestinian actors illustrate the harassment they experience daily at military checkpoints.

Thursday, April 12, 2007

This week I attended an event commemorating Palestinian Prisoners' Week at Al-Far'a refugee camp in Tubas, the only West Bank area I had never visited. Palestinian actors had set up a makeshift checkpoint through which everyone attending the event had to pass. Mock soldiers pointed their guns in our faces and screamed in Hebrew for us to get back. Although I knew they were only acting, I could not help but be frightened. It was a helpful reminder. Although I had seen the same thing happening at countless checkpoints, I had always been looking on from the outside, and still have never really experienced firsthand the sort of harassment that Palestinians face daily. I suspect that the actors had been told to focus on the Western attendees for precisely that reason, to show us the abuse from which we are shielded. It was very effective.

Past the checkpoint, hundreds of locals and visitors were watching performers depict typical scenes of interrogation, abuse, and torture in Israeli prisons and detention centers. Some of the actors wore blindfolds, handcuffs, and chains and gave moving monologues about the injustice of abuse and imprisonment without trial in an occupier's land. Others played Israeli soldiers and guards. Afterwards, young Palestinian boys danced Debka, a traditional Palestinian dance, as a symbol of the proud persistence of Palestinian culture in the face of enormous hardships.

The event took place in a former prison and torture center. Afterwards, spectators toured the old holding rooms, which were haunted by past inmates and painted over with graffiti and prisoner shadows. There I met a mother holding a framed picture of her son, who is currently being held in Israeli jail along with more than 11,000 other Palestinians. Near the old torture chambers was a holding center converted into an art studio, where I

Above and bottom left: Palestinian performers depict scenes of interrogation, abuse, and torture that are common in Israeli prisons.

Right: Families visiting a former prison and torture center hold pictures of their loved ones being held in Israeli prisons today.

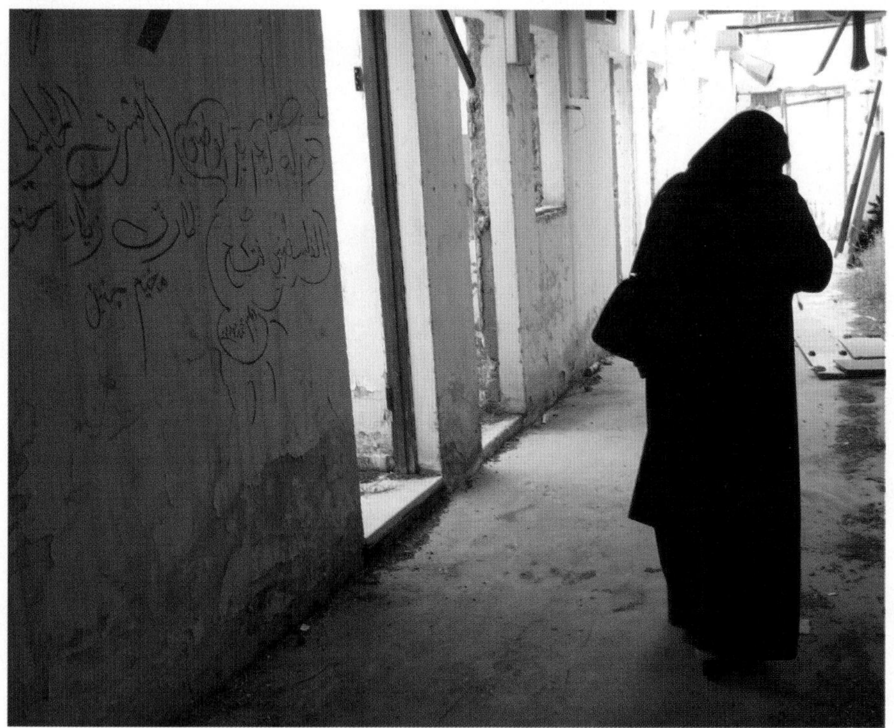

Families of prisoners tour an old prison and torture chamber (pictured below).

met Morshid Graib, an artist whose many stunning images depicting the suffering of his people were on display. His paintings and the performances reminded me once again of the extraordinary creativity of the Palestinians in their resistance to the Occupation.[73]

[73] To contact Morshid Graib or purchase his paintings, call him at (972) 599 716 987 or contact him by email via Jamil at *valley4@gmail.com*

Morshid Graib illustrates the roots of the Palestinian refugees in their villages, from which many were expelled in 1948 and 1967.

Graib illustrates the "arm-breaking policy" developed by Israel's former prime minister Yitzak Rabin.

The next day I was going on a tour of the Northern Jordan Valley, about 6 miles from Tubas as the crow flies. By road it's more like 13 miles, via Tayseer checkpoint, but that road is only for Israeli settlers and Palestinian residents of the Jordan Valley. I was forced to reach my destination the long way around, via Ramallah, in the center of the West Bank. It's hard to comprehend the absurdity of such a detour without looking at a map. Rather than driving 20 minutes, I was forced to travel 6 hours southeast through three checkpoints the first day, and then 4 hours back up through two checkpoints the next day to reach the other side of Tubas's eastern mountains—10 hours instead of 20 minutes.

The hills between Tubas and the Jordan Valley as seen from both directions (Left: Tubas; Right: Jordan Valley) Most Palestinians and internationals have to go hours or even days out of the way to travel from one to the other, since the 13-mile road between the two is closed to everyone but settlers and the few remaining Palestinian residents of the valley.

I was cranky from the long ride when I got to Ramallah, but a kind shop-owner noticed my malaise and took me into his store for tea and fresh pastries. His name was Ali, and he spoke near-perfect English. Ali, a native East Jerusalemite, lived in the United States for 19 years. He studied civil engineering at Illinois Institute of Technology and was one of the top engineers behind a major Chicago public transportation project. For 19 years, Ali flew back to Israel every 3 months to renew his Jerusalem ID, which wasn't automatically renewed—although he and his family were born and raised in the city—because he is not Jewish. After Ali acquired US citizenship, he continued returning every three months until one day Israel revoked all Jerusalem IDs of Palestinians with another citizenship. This was the first Ali had heard of such a law, but without warning his ID was confiscated and he was barred from ever returning to the city where his home and family remain (of course, the Jewish Americans who immigrate and become Israelis never suffer penalties for dual citizenship). An extremely successful and well-educated engineer, Ali now works at a souvenir shop selling trinkets in Ramallah. He cannot get normal work because he doesn't have a West Bank ID, either.

The Jordan Valley is like East Jerusalem in that most Palestinians are not even allowed to enter it. Those who live there do so in constant fear that their houses will be razed or their identification cards confiscated (which would render their presence in the Jordan Valley illegal). Such tactics have already pushed most of the Palestinians out of the area.

There were 350,000 Palestinians living in the Jordan Valley before 1967; now there are 50,000. More than 85% of the Jordan Valley population fled after violent expulsions during the first 5 years of the Occupation. According to US President Jimmy Carter, "Israeli customs officers keep lists of their [the evicted Jordan Valley Palestinians'] names and are careful to prohibit their crossing any international checkpoint into the occupied territory, where they might lay claim to their homes and farmland."[74]

According to our tour guide, Fathi, who is from the area, the ethnic cleansing continues today as more and more Israeli Jews move in and Palestinians move out. Israel no longer accepts applications from Palestinians to move into the Jordan Valley, only out of it. (A one-way transfer is occurring out of the rest of the West Bank as well: Since the outbreak of the Second Intifada, Israel has not approved the relocation of a single Gazan to the West Bank, although Palestinians *have* been forcibly transferred in the other direction.[75]) Jordan Valley Palestinians who spend too long outside of the region lose their residence permits for the valley, just as Ali did for East Jerusalem. And as in East Jerusalem, Israel's annexation is so advanced that many Israelis don't even realize the area is occupied. Israelis come to the valley on vacation to enjoy the bountiful fruit orchards, the desert mountains, and the Dead Sea. The modern highways are lined with palm trees and nicely-groomed settlements. And there is hardly a Palestinian in sight.

At one point our tour bus stopped at a juice stand and we could just barely hear Fathi's voice over the zoom of settler and vacationer cars speeding by: "I am 40 years old and from the Jordan Valley, but I have only seen the Jordan River twice in my life, on my way to and from Jordan. They say it's about resistance, but Israel controlled this area strictly with checkpoints decades before suicide bombs or the intifadas began. As a Palestinian, I'm not allowed to go to the river, or even to the Dead Sea—that precious natural wonder which scientists now say will be gone in 12 years due to overuse. The valley is reserved for Jews and tourists. But it belongs to Palestinians as far west as Bethlehem, Jerusalem, and beyond."

Traditionally, Palestinian families used to live in the Jordan Valley during the wintertime because of the mild climate and fertile land. But now, of the 30% of the West Bank that the valley covers, half is controlled by Israeli settlements, and almost all the rest is split between military closed areas, border closed areas, and environmental "green" closed areas. The closed area strategy is familiar to anyone who has studied urban development in East Jerusalem: Israel declares large "closed" or "green areas" and bulldozes all the Palestinian homes and buildings within them. After they've remained empty for a few years, the state begins to settle Jewish Israelis inside.

Some of these "closed areas" in the Jordan Valley are villages where Palestinians have been living for generations. We visited Fasayel, a Palestinian village that Israel has refused to recognize for 40 years since the Occupation began. Because Fasayel is unrecognized, villagers aren't allowed to build or even repair their own homes. They have no water infrastructure for the same reason. The village recently got electricity, but the electric poles are under demolition order since they were built without a permit. In nearby Al-Jiflik village, Israel has refused permits to build a school, insisting that families should either move or bus their children more than an hour each way to Tubas. In peaceful response, the

---

[74] Carter, p. 195.

[75] Kate Coakley and Marko Divac Öberg, "Israel's Deportations and Forcible Transfers of Palestinians Out of the West Bank During the Second Intifada, Occasional Paper 15" *Al-Haq* (April 2006).

Above left and right: An outhouse and a home in Fasayel village, which is unrecognized by the Israeli government. Many such structures in the village are under demolition order.

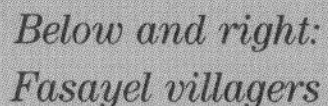

Below and right: Fasayel villagers

Fasayel villagers

teachers of Al-Jiflik started holding classes in a large village tent. Last year, Al-Jiflik finally constructed a real schoolhouse, which students will use until Israel tears it down.

Outside Fasayel we saw two gardens about 400 sq ft each, prominently labeled "USAID." On its website, the United States Agency for International Development (USAID), the largest international nongovernmental organization partnered with the US government, boasts about the US$1.7 billion in economic assistance that the US government has provided Palestinians primarily through USAID projects altogether over the past 15 years.[76] But looking at the small plots, the effort seemed somehow a token one as I considered the fact that the US government gives *twice* that sum to Israel *per year*, facilitating the Occupation that has prevented Palestinians from developing any type of real infrastructure themselves. Perhaps rather than seeing US-initiated projects providing education, healthcare, water, and economic development in Palestinian areas, Palestinians would prefer to see the US end its military aid to Israel, funding used to cut Palestinians *off* from the very schools, hospitals, and water supplies that USAID seeks to provide. The source of aid that

USAID garden outside of Fasayel

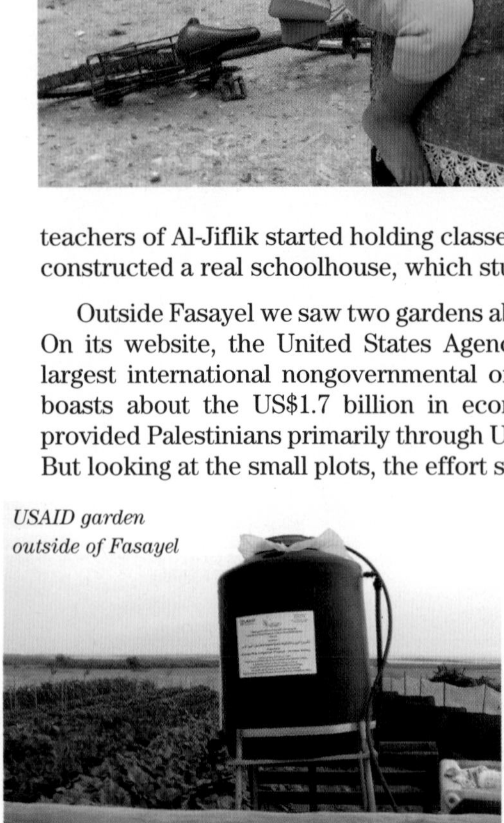

[76] *www.usaid.gov/wbg*

funds the little gardens outside Fasayel—US tax dollars—is the same source supplying the bulldozers that Israel will likely one day use to destroy the entire village. It is the same source helping to fund the settlements that have surrounded Fasayel and appropriated its land. Would USAID's goals of "promoting peace and security" not sooner be achieved by the US government conditioning Israel's billions of annual aid on its respecting international law and human rights for everyone in the region?

About 4,500 Palestinians live in Fasayel and Al-Jiflik combined. That's nearly the total population (6,300) of Israeli settlers in the *whole* of the Jordan Valley. And yet, that small number of settlers, living in 36 settlements, controls the land where tens of thousands of Palestinians reside. Some settlements are just a family or two, but have taken over huge expanses of Palestinian farmland. Naama settlement replaced a Palestinian refugee camp and is home to 172 Israelis controlling more than 2,500 acres. Just 4% of the valley remains for its 50,000 Palestinian inhabitants. That includes the city of Jericho and a few built-up Palestinian villages, but leaves next to nothing for agricultural use. This has been devastating for the agriculture-based society and explains the mass exodus of Palestinians even after Israel's overtly violent expulsion tactics ceased. Having lost their livelihoods, Jordan Valley farmers can either move west, or stay and work as settlement laborers on their own land.

Sparsely populated settlements occupy vast amounts of land belonging to Palestinian families who have been forced to leave.

In Fasayel we met a young man named Zafar, who works full-time packing grapes into boxes at Beit Sayel settlement, because his family has lost all their land. Zafar said that workers are paid between 30 and 50 shekels (between US$7.50 and US$12.50) for an 8-hour work-

A Palestinian who packs produce in a Jordan Valley settlement describes the difficult working conditions for Palestinian laborers, many of whom are children.

day, depending on their age: 50 for adults and 30 for child laborers, some of whom are younger than 10 years old. He said there's no contract, no insurance, no holiday or sick pay, but they work like slaves because it's the only alternative to leaving. We asked Zafar if he supported the boycott of Israeli products even though that could indirectly affect his job and he answered unhesitatingly: "Yes. I hope everyone will boycott. I only work for the settlement because I have nowhere else to work—they took all our land."

The Jordan Valley's "Forgotten Wall"

Along our tour we met a farmer named Abu Hashem who used to be one of the richest landowners in Palestine. Of his original 2,000 acres, only 17 are left after Israel built what Fathi calls "the Forgotten Wall." East of the major settler highway is a barrier similar in shape and effect to Israel's better-known Wall snaking throughout the western half of the West Bank, although this one was built back in 1971. From his modest house, Abu Hashem can see past the wall across the thousands of his acres that he can never return to, spanning all the way to the Jordan River.

Palestinian crops rot in the fields since Palestinian farmers cannot bring people from outside to work the land (if they still have land). Farmers are also unable to transport the crops due to checkpoints, and unable to sell them due to Israeli monopolies that dominate the market.

Abu Hashem's sons alternate each year between going to university and working on the farm to support the family. Abu Hashem would hire Palestinian laborers so his sons could study full-time, but Israel prohibits Palestinians from bringing in outside workers. Another farmer we met said he needs 50 farmers to cultivate his land, but he only has 10, since so many locals have left. Settlements, on the other hand, are free to bring in as much cheap labor from the rest of the West Bank as they like, so long as the Palestinians head back west when they're done so as not to disrupt the Judaizing demographic trend.

Much of the produce harvested by cheap Palestinian laborers in Israeli settlements is then exported by the company Carmel-Agrexco, half of which is owned by the Israeli state, and which took in US$750 million last year alone.[77] Anyone who claims that Israel is not profiting from the Occupation need only take a tour of the Jordan Valley to see truck after truck of local goods being sent off to the European market. Carmel-Agrexco boasts about transporting produce from the Jordan Valley (which they often refer to as "Israel" on origin-of-product labels) to the United Kingdom in 24 hours, when it takes Palestinians three times as long just to get it through checkpoints. Israel has consistently prevented Palestinians from exporting their own produce, so it rots on its way from one village to another, while Europeans enjoy fresh "Israeli" citrus and avocados and the Israeli state's money pool increases.

As always, Palestinians find ways to survive. We visited an agricultural cooperative Ein Al-Beida where local farmers have pooled their dwindling resources in order to feed their communities without relying on settlement products. Two representatives of the cooperative told me that Israel controls all the water in the Jordan Valley (as in the rest of the West Bank), and only allows the farmers to use running water once a week, not nearly enough to sustain their crops in the desert heat (meanwhile, the residents of certain settlements enjoy swimming pools to cool off from the same desert heat). In addition, when the farmers do manage to produce enough to sell outside their communities, Carmel-Agrexco and other Israeli companies simply lower their prices until the Palestinians are run out of the market. Then, secure in their monopoly, the companies raise their prices back up.

Israeli politicians and analysts have called the Jordan Valley "Israel's second priority," after Jerusalem. The most convincing reason for its importance is not border control. Carmel-Agrexco is just one of many companies profiting heavily from the Occupation, in the fertile and lucrative Jordan Valley and beyond. Electric, gas, and water providers have done particularly well for themselves by providing for Palestinians, who have to either buy directly from Israel or pay taxes to Israel for foreign goods. The latter isn't always an option anymore, so millions go straight from Palestinians' pockets into Israel's.[78] Outside financial support for Palestinians eventually feeds into the Israeli economy on top of the billions in aid that Israel already receives from the United States, more than enough to offset most of

[77] "Companies Supporting Apartheid and Occupation: Carmel-Agrexco and Checkers," *Worldwide Activism, Palestinian Grassroots Anti-Apartheid Wall Campaign* (January 20, 2007).

[78] In his book, *Epidemic of Globalization*, Palestinian political economist Adel Samara describes how military orders catered to Israel's economic interests within days of Israel's 1967 conquest of the West Bank and Gaza.

"Military orders cut the occupied territories off from the rest of the world, making Israel their main supplier (90 percent of the occupied territories' imports come from or through Israel). Thus the wages paid to the workers were returned to Israel as payments for Israeli consumer goods. By absorbing the labor force, while at the same time pursuing a policy of rejecting Palestinian applications for licenses to start productive projects, the Israelis were able to destroy the occupied territories' economic infrastructure, thus facilitating the integration of the latter's economy into that of Israel."

Adel Samara, *Epidemic of Globalization* (Glendale, CA: Palestine Research & Publishing Foundation, 2001), pp. 115-116; As cited in Jonathan Scott, "The Niggerization of Palestine" *Black Agenda Report* (November 1, 2006).

Markets in the Jordan Valley are filled with produce grown on Palestinian land but which local Palestinians are forced to buy from Israeli companies like Carmel-Agrexco that exploit the land themselves, reaping heavy profits from the Occupation.

the Occupation's costs. Coupled with tax collection, a captive cheap unprotected labor source, and often unchecked industrial expansion using stolen land and resources, the Israeli economy as a whole has been profiting from the Occupation for many, many years.[79]

Surprisingly—or perhaps not so surprisingly—it is difficult to find this information collected all in one place, but the Women's Coalition for Peace in Israel is working to create just such a resource.[80] Meanwhile, Israel's claims that the near-annexation of almost a third of the West Bank is required for "security" are generally accepted, with few people stopping to ask who the real winners and losers are. Does Israel seek to protect lives, or to protect profits? The same question might be asked about the United States. Is the war in Iraq for the benefit of the citizens of the United States, or is it for large industries and private contractors? As in America's war on Iraq, the real driving force behind Israel's policies in the Jordan Valley and all of the Occupied Territories is not security; it's power, control, and money. The winners include the Israeli state, the private sector, the economic settlers, and the ideological fundamentalists. The losers are too numerous to name: They are the millions of Palestinians living under brutal military occupation. They are the Israelis who live in fear, and who mourn the victims of Palestinian armed resistance. And they are the American people, who continue, mostly in ignorance, to foot the bill for so much of the carnage.

---

[79] Even in the early 1980s, considering the $600 million per year in export sales to the Palestinian controlled market and another $500 million in tourism, experts put the potential loss to Israel of abandoning the Occupied Territories as over US$1 billion per year; Thomas R. Stauffer, *Christian Science Monitor* (Jan. 13, 1982); As cited in Chomsky, *Fateful*, p. 46 (see also p. 114).

[80] The best compilation of information available when this book went to print was available at *www.alternativenews.org/aic-publications/the-economy-of-the-occupation.* The Coalition of Women for Peace will eventually have a full report on their website: *coalitionofwomen.org/home*

Monday, April 23, 2007

Shortly after I arrived back at the IWPS house in January, we started a project with the Israeli Committee Against House Demolitions (ICAHD) to document the ongoing displacement of Palestinians in and around the Salfit region. For 3 months, we have been interviewing residents of each village in the area to document their stories. As the Wall expands in Salfit, many residents are receiving notices of impending demolitions or land confiscation. Deir Ballut, for example, is expected to lose all of its land to the south, including the village's most fertile areas, which the mayor called "the heart of Deir Ballut." In preparation for the Wall, soldiers recently uprooted 200 olive trees belonging to Lamis and her husband (the couple who lost their twins after a hold-up at Deir Ballut checkpoint in 2003). Public buildings are also under threat: the new Deir Ballut boys' school remains under demolition order and the old one was shut down for lack of funds from the PA due to international sanctions. The village still has no medical clinic.

Not far from Deir Ballut is the village of Kafr Ad-Dik, similarly rich with land and also expected to lose most of it (80%) to the Wall. Long ago, Israel outlawed construction outside the central parts of Kafr Ad-Dik and nearby Bruqin, so residents of both villages live crammed together, as if they were in a

Forbidden from building on most of their land, residents of Kafr Ad-Dik and Bruqin live crammed together as in refugee camps. The villages' fresh water source has been polluted with sewage from Ariel settlement.

refugee camp, despite the abundance of land visible from their rooftops. The fresh water stream that runs through Kafr Ad-Dik has been polluted by sewage from the nearby settlement of Ariel, and Israel has limited the village water allotment to as little as 21 liters per day (the World Health Organization recommends 100 liters as a bare minimum, and Israeli per capita consumption reaches 350).[81]

Across the Wall's path from Kafr Ad Dik is the village of Sarta, where five houses have already been demolished in preparation for construction of the illegal barrier. Other houses have pending demolition orders. Sarta's mayor took us to visit the different families whose homes Israel has threatened. One family said that they were told by soldiers to apply for a permit to build onto their house, which they did, but Israel never responded. That was 10 years ago. The family showed us a Star of David that soldiers had painted on the side of their house.

Almost all of the tiny village of Izbat At-Tabib is threatened with demolition, including the village town hall, mosque, entrance gate, and bus stops. There are even orders to destroy the stone walls that separate villagers' plots of land. The families in Izbat At-Tabib came to the area in 1948 after being expelled from their village of Nubsor located in present-day Israel.[82] Israel is now demanding that the families relocate for a second time, this time to the nearby town of Azzun.

Azzun itself is now only half of its original size, having lost the other half of its land in 1948. The most recent demolition in Azzun was of a new swimming pool along with its changing rooms and water purification facilities. The Israeli army's explanation was that the town had not secured an Israeli building

Almost all of the tiny village of Izbat At-Tabib is threatened with demolition, including the village town hall, mosque, entrance gate, and bus stops, and even the stone walls that separate villagers' plots of land.

[81] Fareed Taamallah, "A Thirst for West Bank Water," *The Nation* (June 26, 2006).

[82] "Izbat At-Tabib: a Palestinian village under the threat of eviction," *Applied Research Institute – Jerusalem* and *Land Research Center* (March 19, 2007).

permit for the pool, the same reason given for the current orders to demolish the nearby children's playground and small amphitheater. As in many towns and villages, Azzun has tried going to court to stop the demolition of its buildings, but on the rare occasions when villages win their cases, it doesn't make any difference; the destruction continues unabated.

Each village that we visited had a different story, but all had one thing in common. When we would ask for population size, they would give us two numbers: the population living in the village at the time, and the total population of the village. The latter population was often more than twice the former. Israel's various actions have had at least one universal effect on the villages of Salfit and its environs: residents are moving away, fleeing the violence and economic hardships that render life under occupation insufferable.

It doesn't take more than comparing the maps over time to recognize that the gradual dispossession and displacement of Palestinians in Salfit are only the continuation of a larger, historic trend of transforming historic Palestine into an exclusively Jewish state. While Jews owned only 6% of the land in historic Palestine before the War of 1948, now, less than 60 years later, Israel controls more than 90% of that land. One ethnic population is being displaced to make way for another: this is ethnic cleansing, which the US State Department defines as "the systematic and forced removal of the members of an ethnic group from communities in order to change the ethnic composition of a given region." Israel's version of ethnic cleansing is reminiscent of the displacement of the American Indians in North America.

Of course, the terminology is not the important thing. It matters what is happening, not what we call it. That said, categories such as "ethnic cleansing" may offer a framework with which we can evaluate Israel's policies and determine an appropriate response.

The Israeli army demolished Azzun's swimming pool along with its changing rooms and water purification facilities. The nearby playground and children's theater are also under demolition order.

Children in Sarta stand next to graffiti (that reads "Israel" in Hebrew) painted by soldiers on their house.

A Sarta villager whose home was demolished for lack of a permit

Mohammed from Sarta stands with his wife and daughter outside the tiny house that they moved into after their house was destroyed by the Israeli army.

Mohammed visits the ruins of his house, which was destroyed by the Israeli army.

Explicit recognition with such words is also symbolic. In his book, *The Ethnic Cleansing of Palestine*, Israeli historian Ilan Pappe writes:

> To deny the reality of the ethnic cleansing is an insult to the Palestinian people and morally repugnant, like Holocaust denial. One does not have to equate the two events to see that this erasure of history is wrong. It is a denial of the very humanity of the victims, who did not deserve their suffering. And those who go down this road have no business accusing others of racism.[83]

Part of the resistance to recognizing the ethnic cleansing that Israel is committing in the Occupied Territories may stem from an aversion to recognizing the ethnic cleansing that occurred before the Occupation began. Former Israeli prime minister Menachem Begin pointed out this connection when he was questioned about the legitimacy of settlement in the Occupied Territories:

> Either Zionism was moral from its inception ... and then it is moral to settle in all parts of the land of Israel [meaning Israel plus the West Bank, Gaza Strip, and East Jerusalem]; or ... our settlement activity today is not moral, and then we must make amends for what we did the last 100 years in the land of Israel.[84]

Early Zionist leaders were explicit about the expulsions they would carry out to achieve their goals. Joseph Weitz, the director of the Jewish National Land Fund, wrote:

> It must be clear that there is no room in the country for both peoples.... If the Arabs leave it, the country will become wide and spacious for us.... The only solution is a Land of Israel... without Arabs. There is no room here for compromises.... There is no way but to transfer the Arabs from here to the neighboring countries, and to transfer all of them, save perhaps [a few].[85]

David Ben-Gurion, the first prime minister of Israel, himself proclaimed, "With compulsory transfer we [will] have a vast area [for settlement].... I support compulsory transfer. I don't see anything immoral in it."[86]

Contrary to the widely held belief that the 1948 expulsions were an unintended and tragic consequence of the war, instigated by Zionists in spite of themselves, historians have now concluded that the expulsions were not circumstantial. "Rather," writes Pappe, "It is the other way around: the objective was the ethnic cleansing of the country [that] the movement coveted for its new state, and the war was the consequence, the means to carry it out."[87]

Even the area that the UN proposed for a Jewish state had a non-Jewish majority.[88] Recognizing the imperative of expulsion, Zionist leaders developed several plans to remove

---

[84] Sasson Sofer, *Begin: Anatomy of Leadership* (NY: 1988), p. 128; As cited in *AIC*.

[85] Benny Morris, *The Birth of the Palestinian Refugee Problem, 1947-1949* (Cambridge, 1988), p. 27; As cited in Finkelstein, *Image*, p. 86.

[86] Benny Morris, *Righteous Victims: A History of the Zionist-Arab Conflict, 1881-1999* (1999); As cited in The Origin of the Palestine-Israel Conflict, published by Jews for Justice in the Middle East, third edition. *www.cactus48.com*

[87] Ilan Pappe, "The 1948 Ethnic Cleansing of Palestine," *Journal of Palestine Studies*, issue 141 (2006).

[88] Finkelstein, *Image*, p. 85.

the native Palestinian population. One such plan was code-named Plan D, Operation Dalet, and is described by Pappe in *The Ethnic Cleansing of Palestine*:

> Military orders were dispatched to units on the ground to prepare for the systematic expulsion of Palestinians from vast areas of the country. The orders came with a detailed description of the methods to be used to forcibly evict the people: large-scale intimidation; laying siege to and bombarding villages and population centers; setting fire to homes, properties, and goods; expelling residents; demolishing homes; and, finally, planting mines in the rubble to prevent the expelled inhabitants from returning.[89]

In addition to evicting and intimidating the Palestinians, and bombing, burning, and looting their villages, Zionist forces committed acts that are defined as war crimes—such as rape and massacres—"in almost every Arab village occupied by [them] during the War of Independence." The former director of the Israeli army archives counted at least 20 large-scale massacres (more than 50 people killed), and another 100 or so small-scale massacres (1-49 people killed) perpetrated by Zionist forces against the native Palestinian population, inducing them to flee.[90]

As historical scholarship renders the crimes perpetrated by Zionists during Israel's "War of Independence" harder and harder to refute, Israel's apologists are now arguing that the events of 1948 were tragic, but what's done is done. They criticize the Palestinians for holding on so stubbornly to the dream of returning to Palestine rather than accepting their displacement and integrating as much as they can into their new countries.[91] Besides, Israel's apologists argue, surely Israel's crimes pale in comparison to the larger atrocities committed by the Nazis or the colonizers in the Americas. It was a long time ago, they say, and it is time to move on.

Not so. The ethnic cleansing of Palestine is happening right now. Not only have the massacres and expulsions of the past never been officially acknowledged, but the *Nakba* continues today with every destroyed home and Palestinian emigrant. However, the unwavering resistance and resilience of the remaining Palestinian population have, so far, ensured that Israel's ethnic cleansing of Palestine remains incomplete. It is up to all of us to ensure that the Palestinians' steadfast struggle for survival and freedom has not been in vain.

[89] Meir Pail, *From Haganah to the IDF* [in Hebrew] (Tel Aviv: Zemora Bitan Modan, n.d.), p. 307; Gershon Rivlin and Elhanan Oren, *The War of Independence: Ben-Gurion's Diary*, volume 1 (Tel Aviv: Ministry of Defence, 1982), p. 147; As cited in Ilan Pappe, "The 1948 Ethnic Cleansing of Palestine," *Journal of Palestine Studies*, issue 141 (2006).

[90] *Hair* (May 6, 1992); As cited in Finkelstein, *Image*, p. 110.

[91] It is curious that such a criticism should come from supporters of Zionism, which is itself based on a dream that was held onto for thousands of years to return that same land.

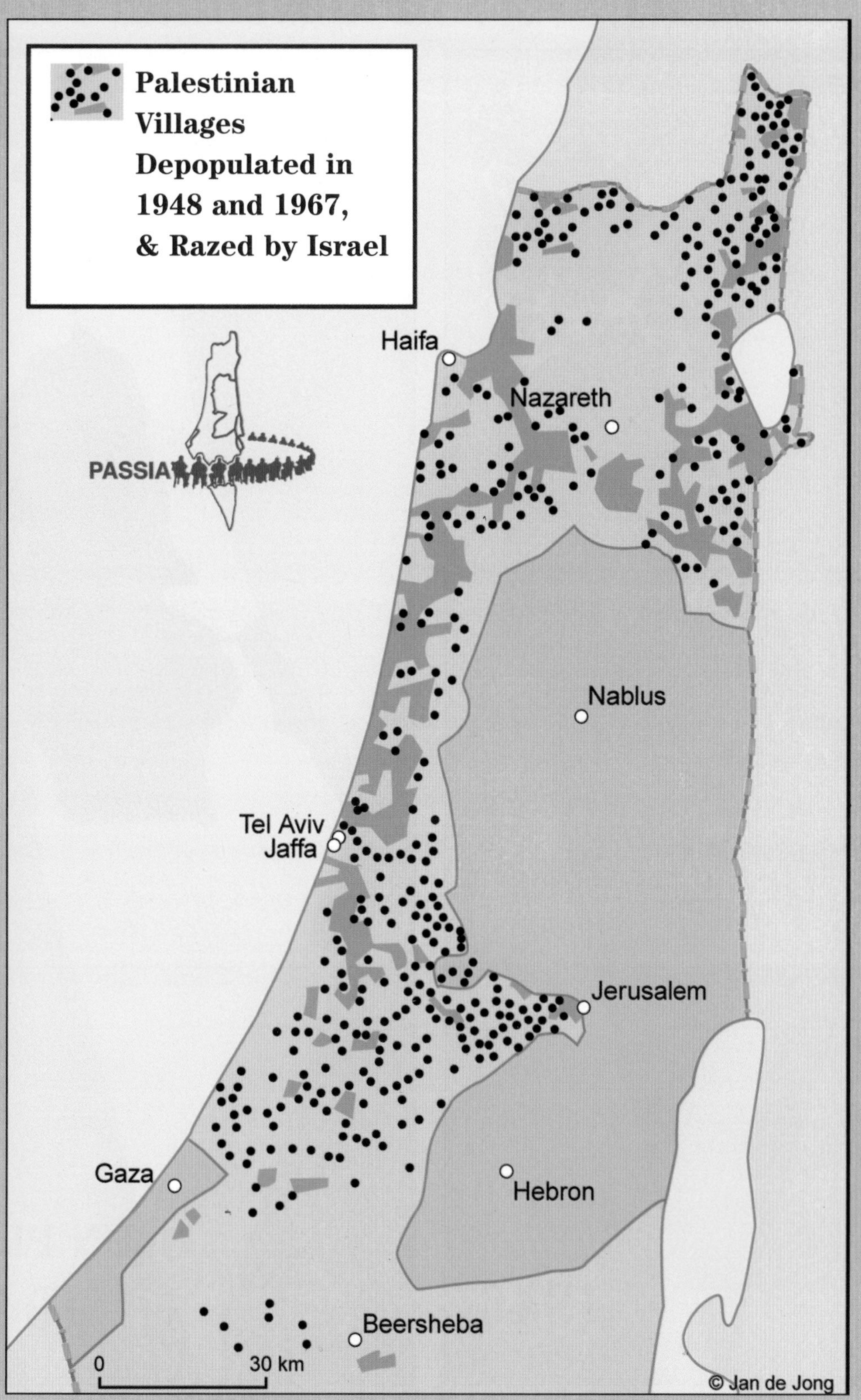

Modified by Hüseyin Ruhi Uğural

Palestinian loss o

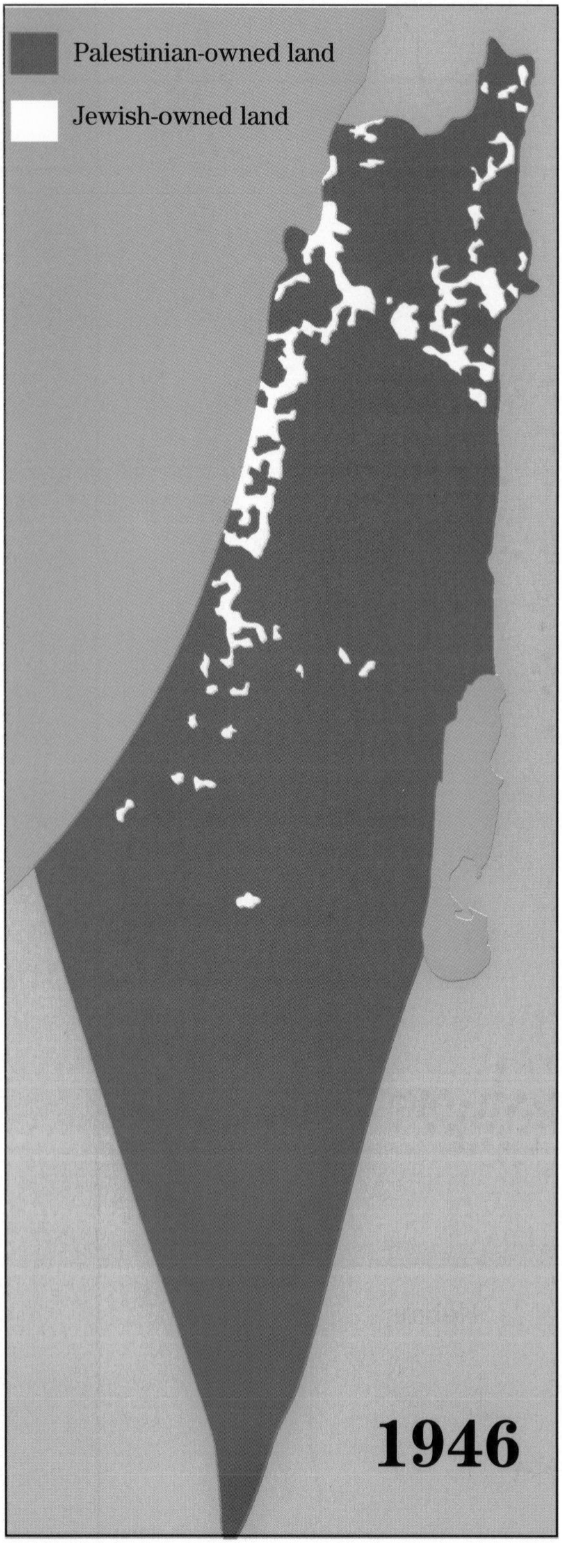

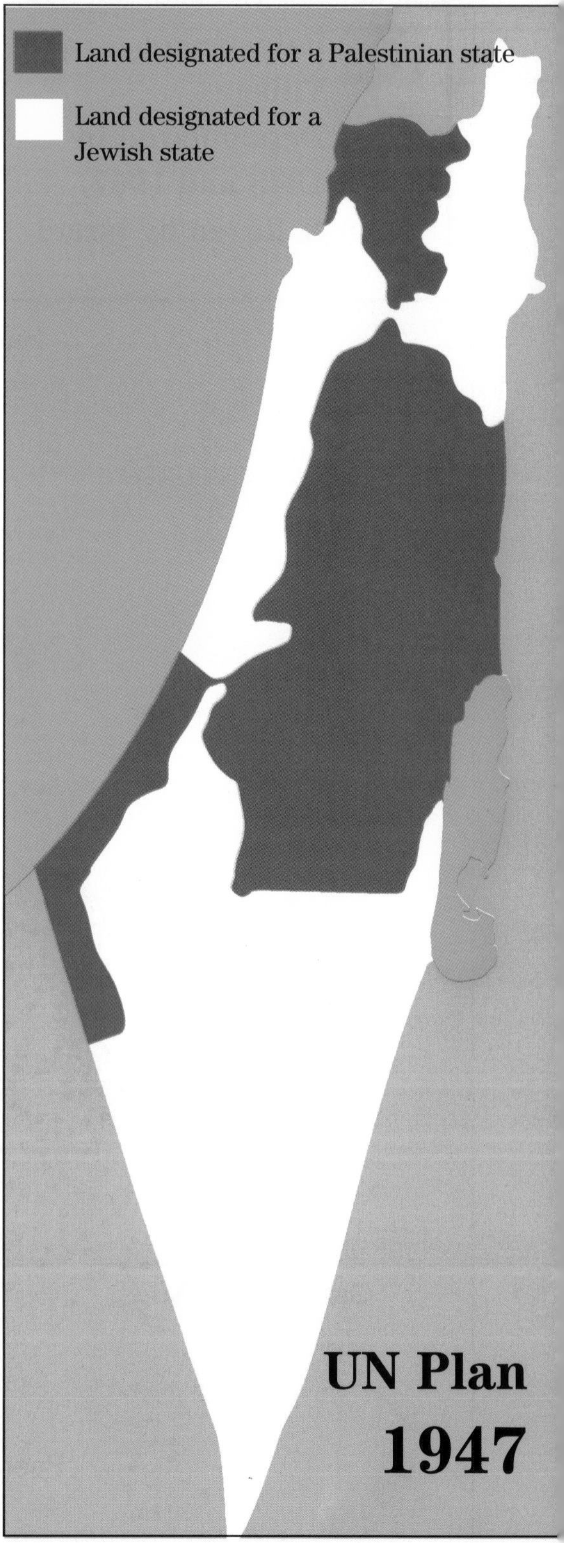

and, 1946 - 2007

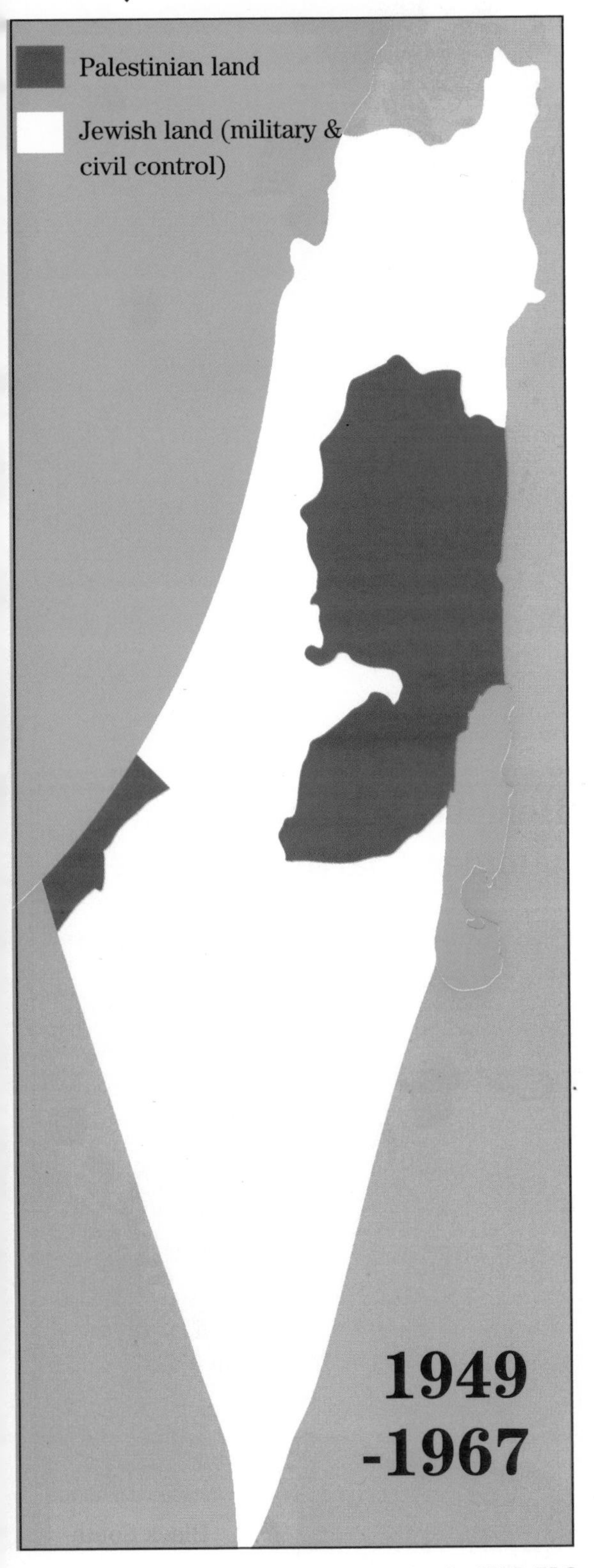

Original version by NAD-PLO
Adapted from Oren Medicks 1999

Palestinian land

Jewish land (military & civil control)

2007

As published in *Occupation Magazine*
Modified by Engin Çoban

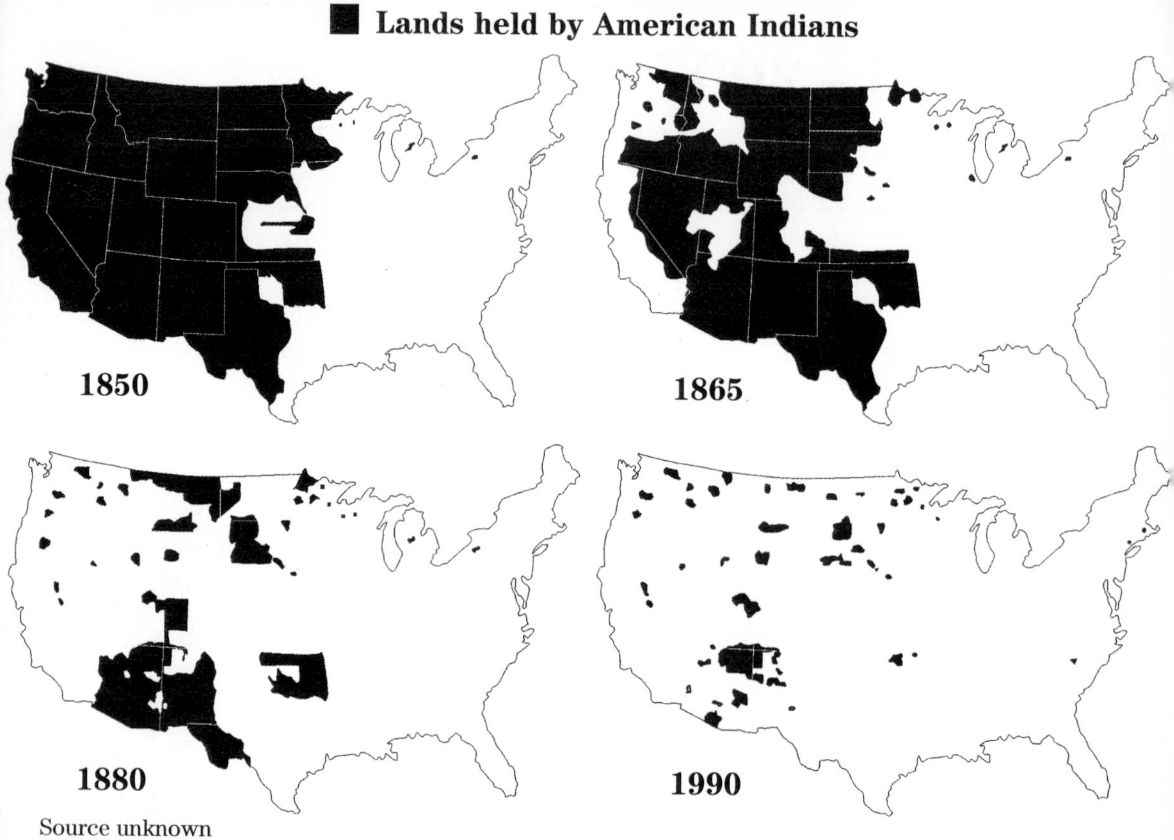

Lands held by American Indians

1850

1865

1880

1990

Source unknown
Modified by Engin Çoban

Israel's policies of displacement and segregation are not unique to Israel. They are classic strategies of colonization, reminiscent of the displacement of American Indians in the Americas, and apartheid (Afrikaans for "separation") in South Africa (see the Conclusion for a discussion on the applicability of the term "apartheid" in Palestine).

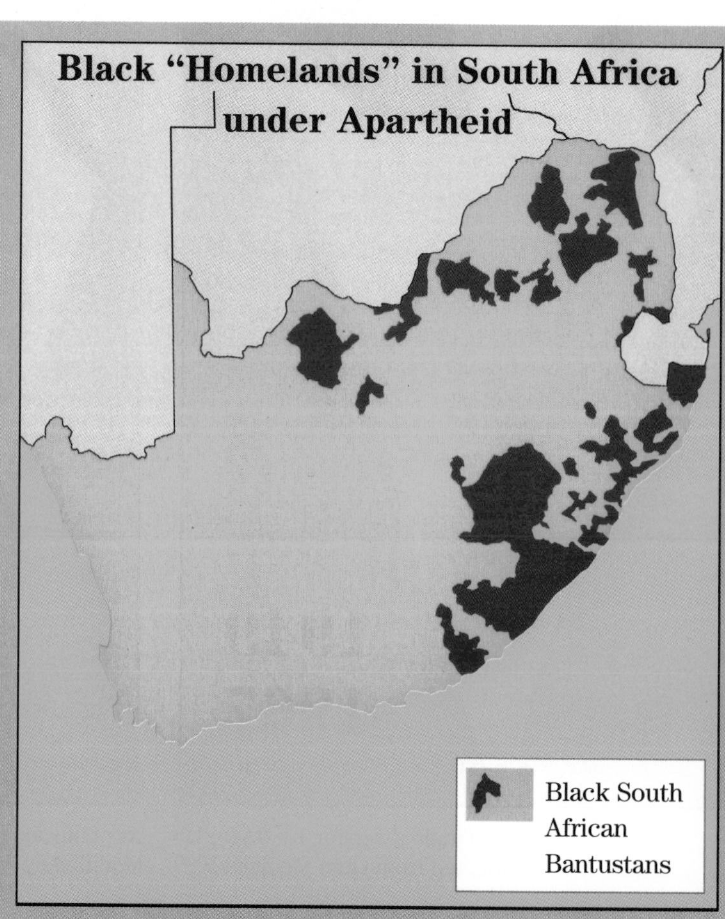

Conclusion

Six weeks after I left Palestine, people around the world commemorated the 40-year anniversary of Israel's Occupation of the West Bank, Gaza Strip, and East Jerusalem. In Washington DC, thousands from all backgrounds and faiths gathered to protest the US government's role in perpetuating the conflict through unconditional military and economic aid to Israel. Dozens of Zionists came as well to counter our demonstration. They accused Arab protesters of being anti-Semitic terrorists. The Jewish protesters they called "self-hating Jews."

I recognized the term from my experiences lecturing on Palestine. Although my presentations were mostly well-received, there were still many people who came to undermine my talks, some of whom accused me of "self-hatred." Some felt so threatened by my exposure of Israel's discriminatory policies that they charged me with "generating another Holocaust." But in my presentations, as in this book, the most basic point I have tried to get across is precisely that the Israel/Palestine conflict is *not* a war about Judaism or religion, but a war about land and water. Such is the reality of most wars in the world, but the mistaken belief that this war in particular is about ethnicity or religion prevents people from recognizing that the Israeli government's current policies of occupation and annexation in the Palestinian territories are consistent with the desire for control of resources, not religious or cultural freedom.

The mistaken perception of this conflict as an ancient religious war also makes it seem too complicated to resolve and keeps many people from getting involved and taking a side. The conflict is certainly complicated—both Jews and Palestinians have been victimized throughout history, both peoples are deeply traumatized and mistrustful, and once some kind of resolution is reached the healing process is likely to be a long one—but certain things are clear. The Occupation, for example, is harming both Palestinians and Jewish Israelis, and bringing about its end is a necessary step in the path towards a just peace. I used to put balance above everything in my approach to this issue, but now I realize that balance has its limits. Neutrality is especially important at the outset of research; it is critical to examine things from different perspectives. But when something is deeply harmful and immoral, I believe it is more important to take a stand against injustice than to claim the moral high ground of the dispassionate observer.

In addition, much of the impassioned debate surrounding the issue is based not on its complexity, but on misinformation. There is often, for example, great controversy between people who attend my talks regarding the history of the Israel/Palestine conflict, yet there is virtually no controversy among historians. When Zionist and Israeli state and army archives were declassified in the 1980s, Israeli historians dispelled countless falsehoods about the 1948 War. Historians have debunked the claims that Palestinians refugees left on

Arab orders[1] and that Zionist forces were at a military and numerical disadvantage,[2] to take just two examples. Ongoing research has corrected countless other false claims about the conflict, many of which I discuss in Appendix IV: Myths and FAQs. Yet misinformation about this conflict is so widespread that many of the myths live on, sometimes through the dishonest rhetoric of top American officials.[3]

There is also little controversy in the international political arena regarding the illegality of the Occupation and certain necessary steps required to resolve the ongoing conflict. In spite of what the (largely contrived) controversy presented in US mainstream media and public forums would have you believe, there is actually international consensus as to what a realistic solution would entail:

- Israeli withdrawal from the Occupied Territories
- Two independent states with secure and viable borders
- A shared capital in Jerusalem
- The right of Palestinian refugees to return to their homes in Israel or to the new Palestine if they so choose, or to receive compensation for their losses

The Palestinians joined that international consensus 20 years ago, forfeiting 78% of their historic homeland to Israel—a tremendous compromise. For two decades, only Israel and the United States have consistently rejected this consensus.[4] Not only that, but the latter consistently uses its powerful veto to block UN attempts to enforce the very laws that Israel, the US, and all other member states have signed.

So what happens when negotiations consistently fail and near consensus in the United Nations is not enough to enforce the law? There is a common tendency to think that the solution is educating mainstream Zionist Americans and Jewish Israelis to help their community and political leaders recognize the error of their ways. I am very much in favor of dialogue with Zionists, as I am with all communities, but I do not believe that the very people and countries perpetuating the conflict (through economic and political support) are going to be the ones to stop it. This should come as no surprise: In the words of Martin Luther King, Jr., "Freedom is never voluntarily given by the oppressor; it must be demanded by the oppressed." We cannot wait for the Zionists in Israel, the US government, and around the world to wake up and realize the injustice of the Occupation. That is not where change will come from. So where *will* change come from?

---

1 See Appendix IV, Myth #3 for documentation.

2 According to Israeli historian Ilan Pappe in *The Ethnic Cleansing of Palestine*, "When Operation Dalet was put into effect, the Hagana had more than 50,000 troops at its disposal, half of which had been trained by the British army during the Second World War." According to Israeli historian Ilan Armitzur: "There was never a moment in the 1948 Palestine war that the Jewish forces suffered a numerical inferiority against the Arab forces which they fought." Ilan Armitzur, *The Origin of the Arab-Israeli Arms Race: Arms, Embargo, Military Power and Decision in the 1948 Palestine War* (New York University Press, 1996), p. 62; As cited in Qumsiyeh, p. 41.

3 Senator Hillary Clinton, for example, has denounced anti-Semitism and incitement for hatred in Palestinian textbooks many times, in public forums and in correspondence with the president, even though the findings of academic and government studies in Israel, the US, and Europe directly contradict her claims. See Appendix IV, Myth #7 for details on the myth compared to research findings.

4 See Appendix IV, Myth #6 & FAQs #1-2 for documentation and details.

The answer to that question was clarified for me at the 2007 International Conference on Nonviolence, which I attended in Bil'in before I left Palestine. Guest speakers at the conference included Palestinian politicians and resistance leaders, European parliamentary members, and a Nobel peace prize laureate. But it was the common words of the three Jewish Israeli speakers—historian Ilan Pappe, journalist Amira Hass, and political analyst and activist Jeff Halper—that stressed the futility of waiting for change from Israeli society and affirmed the importance of grassroots struggle in realizing an end to the Occupation. Hass, who has spent decades educating fellow Israelis about the Occupation as a writer for the mainstream newspaper *Haaretz*, explained that she no longer believes it is enough for Israelis to know what is happening. In fact, many Israelis do know, but that does not mean they are ready to make bold sacrifices to effect change.[5] Hass concluded that the Occupation will continue as long as it remains profitable for Israel, which, historically, US aid and Israel's exploitation of Palestinian labor and resources have always ensured.[6]

Pappe and Halper concurred that the world cannot wait for the Israeli leaders to come to their senses; Israel will not change unless it is has to. Norman Finkelstein wrote in 2003:

> Israel will withdraw from the Occupied Territories only if Palestinians (and their supporters) can summon sufficient force to change the calculus of costs for Israel: that is, making the price of occupation too high. The historical record sustains this hypothesis. Israel has withdrawn from occupied territory on three occasions: the Egyptian Sinai in 1957 after Eisenhower's ultimatum, Sinai in 1979 after Egypt's unexpectedly impressive showing in the October 1973 war, and Lebanon in 1985 and 2000 after the losses inflicted by the Lebanese resistance.[7]

To the list could be added Israel's "withdrawal" from the Gaza Strip in 2005 and from Lebanon again in 2006. Both followed heavy armed resistance, not constructive diplomacy. Sadly, it is Israel's military and political setbacks that seem to have produced the most willingness to change course. This is not to say that all military force against Israel is justified, only that it is unrealistic to think that the absence of such violence would lead to a change in Israel's behavior.

It is clear that the international community must join Palestinians in exerting appropriate pressure on Israel until it adheres to the laws that the United Nations and the international community have been unable to enforce for the last half-century. There are many different ways of exerting pressure. Perhaps the most effective would be diplomatic pressure, for example placing conditions on aid to Israel. Israel receives more aid from the United States than do sub-Saharan Africa, Latin America, and the Caribbean combined.[8] Figures range from an annual $3 to $10 billion, depending on how and what you count. If tax-free donations, government guaranteed loans, free weapons, and gifts are counted, US aid to Israel reaches about $22 million *per day*.[9] Israel could not continue its expansionist policies without that aid. Yet interestingly, although Israel is the highest recipient of US

---

5 The same could certainly be said for Americans, most of whom oppose the Iraq War but are unprepared to dedicate themselves fully to bringing about its end.

6 See p. 349-350 for details about the economics of the Occupation.

7 Finkelstein, *Image*, p. xxxiv.

8 Mission Statement, *If Americans Knew*. *www.ifamericansknew.org*

9 "US foreign aid to Israel," *MIFTAH* (May 20, 2002). *www.miftah.org*

foreign aid, it is the only country that is not held accountable for the way it uses the aid. Were the US to monitor the uses of its aid to Israel and to insist on compliance with international law and human rights, Israel would have to comply.[10]

But again, are Palestinians to continue waiting another 60 years or more for the US to challenge Israel? What can *we* do, the people of the world, without an army or billions of dollars but with growing numbers and international consensus on our side?

When a collection of Palestinian civil society groups was asked that very question, they called for boycott, divestment, and sanctions (BDS) against Israel until it complies with international law. BDS is a nonviolent way for the international community to educate others and to mobilize and put pressure on Israel in a style similar to that used against South Africa when apartheid reigned there. According to Jeff Halper, Israel's Occupation and Wall classify as apartheid because they meet precisely the definition of the word: separation of populations in a regime under which one population permanently dominates another.[11] *B'tselem*, the Israeli Information Center for Human Rights in the Occupied Territories, writes:

> Israel has created in the Occupied Territories a regime of separation based on discrimination, applying two different systems of law in the same area and basing the rights of individuals on [whether they are Jewish or Arab].... The regime is the only one of its kind in the world, and is reminiscent of distasteful regimes from the past, such as the Apartheid regime in South Africa.[12]

In the words of South African Archbishop Desmond Tutu:

> Israeli governments [have] reserved 93% of the land—often expropriated from Arabs without compensation—for Jews through state ownership, the Jewish National Fund and the Israeli Lands Authority. In colonial and then apartheid South Africa, 87% of the land was reserved for whites. The Population Registration Act categorized South Africans according to an array of racial definitions, which, among other things, determined who would be permitted to live on the reserved land.[13]

In the case of South African apartheid too, grassroots organizations led the international opposition; only later did governments follow suit. In fact, divestment took 30 years to become a strong force against South Africa, but the anti-apartheid movement targeting Israel has recently been advancing much more quickly. With the denouncement of Israeli apartheid by US President Jimmy Carter and the Special Rapporteur to the UN Commission on Human Rights John Dugard[14]—in addition to Halper, *B'tselem*, Tutu, and countless others—churches, universities, unions, and other communities around the world have started taking action and passing divestment resolutions of their own. And, of course,

---

10 For an example of US threats to suspend aid actually affecting Israeli policy, see President Jimmy Carter's book, *Palestine: Peace not Apartheid*, p. 132.

11 Jeff Halper, speech at the 2007 International Conference on Nonviolence (Bil'in, April 19, 2007).

12 "Land Grab," *B'tselem* (May 2002); As cited in Finkelstein, *Image*, p. xx.

13 Desmond Tutu, "Apartheid in the Holy Land," *Guardian* (December 21, 2006).

14 Carter entitled his 2006 book on the Israel/Palestine conflict, *Palestine*: Peace *Not Apartheid*, while Dugard condemned Israel's apartheid practices in the "Implementation of General Assembly Resolution 60/251 of 15 March 2006 Entitled 'Human Rights Council'" as well as his article "Israelis adopt what South Africa dropped," *The Atlanta Journal-Constitution* (November 29, 2006).

thousands of other groups and individuals are contributing to the worldwide anti-Occupation movement in other useful ways. Various ideas for internationals to get involved are listed in the next section.

I am optimistic that there will someday be peace in Israel/Palestine. My optimism comes not only from international advocacy, but largely from my experience on the ground there. Resistance in Deir Ballut, Budrus, and other parts of Palestine has succeeded in raising awareness about the Occupation and even changing the planned route of the Wall, something neither the United Nations nor the International Court of Justice was able to do. More and more Israeli soldiers are coming forward with stories about their service in the Occupied Territories, refusing to take part in Israel's discriminatory policies any longer. And polls consistently show that the majority of people on both sides of the Wall favor an end to the violence and a path towards reconciliation. The indications that peace is just waiting to break through the mutually destructive Occupation are unmistakable.

Appendix I: What You Can Do

As a math student and later an English teacher, I never imagined I would end up doing political activism. I didn't see myself as the type of person who could write or speak articulately about important world issues, and I found those who could to be intimidating. After I witnessed the realities of daily life under the Occupation, I felt a responsibility to speak out publicly against my government's role in the atrocities, but I was still very hesitant and it took me almost 2 years to take the next step. I finally dared to put myself out there when I realized one day that, no matter what, I am the expert on at least one thing: my own experience. Simply reaching out and telling my story was enough to inform thousands. I also realized that whereas reading and hearing about the Israel/Palestine conflict leaves me feeling hopeless and discouraged, being a part of the movement (in Palestine and in my own country) and watching it progress and grow reminds me every day that change is possible. Those who consider themselves too inexperienced or pessimistic to take action on this issue may be pleasantly surprised should they one day take the chance...

1. ***Do Your Own Research.*** Go beyond mainstream media sources. Appendix II provides a list of resources that have helped me gather alternative information on the conflict.

But remember that knowledge about Palestine is meaningless if you don't use it. Palestinians don't need more people feeling sorry for them; they need people to take *action*. Don't put off acting until you know everything—you never will. Here are some ideas for next steps in getting involved:

2. ***Go to Palestine.*** It will change your life. Just being there in solidarity and sharing your experiences with people back home is one of the most effective actions you can take. You can go as a solidarity volunteer or just to tour and see for yourself:

Solidarity organizations for internationals in Palestine include:

- International Women's Peace Service (IWPS): *www.iwps.info*
- International Solidarity Movement (ISM): *www.palsolidarity.org*
- Christian Peacemaker Teams (CPT): *www.cpt.org/hebron/hebron.php*
- Ecumenical Accompaniment Program in Palestine/Israel (EAPPI): *www.eappi.org*

Organizations (one international, one Palestinian, and one Israeli) giving tours of the West Bank:

- Birthright Unplugged: *www.BirthrightUnplugged.org*
- Global Exchange: *www.GlobalExchange.org*
- Holy Land Trust (Bethlehem): *Travel.HolyLandTrust.org*
- Israeli Committee Against House Demolitions (ICAHD): *www.icahd.org*

3. ***Join the Boycott, Divestment, and Sanctions (BDS) Campaign against Israel.*** When Palestinians were asked what they most wanted from the international movement against the Occupation, they called for boycott, divestment, and sanctions against Israel until it complies with international law. BDS is a nonviolent way for the international community to mobilize and put pressure on Israel in a style similar to that

used against South Africa to help end apartheid there. For a list of companies profiting in different ways from the Occupation, visit *www.InterfaithPeaceInitiative.com/ProfitingFromOccupation.htm*

You can boycott or divest from US companies, international arms producers, Israeli Bonds, Israeli products, and more. Individuals with pension funds, universities, labor unions, municipalities, insurance companies, and churches are just some of the types of groups that can take part. To learn what organizations have already divested and how your community can do it too, visit *www.bds-palestine.net.* Or download a Global Exchange Toolkit (details below) for details on creating a divestment petition, passing a divestment resolution, and everything in between.

4. ***Get Involved Locally.*** Palestine solidarity groups are organizing around the world. Many organizations in the US are listed at *www.endtheoccupation.org* and *www.unitedforpeace.org*. If your campus, church, high school, or workplace doesn't have a group, start one. Organize a teach-in in your school, church, or even home. Speakers from *Wheels of Justice (www.justicewheels.org)* travel around the US giving eyewitness accounts from Palestine and Iraq—invite them to your community. Open a dialogue with people around you about Palestine. Show them the maps, which tell much of the story. In a grassroots struggle such as this one, public opinion changes one person at a time. You have the ability to affect others in your community—so use it! For talking points and organizing details, download a Global Exchange Toolkit (details below) and see "Confronting Misinformation" and "How to Organize a Teach-In."

5. ***Contact Local Media.*** Write a letter to the editor or an op-ed for your local newspaper, or call you local TV or talk radio stations to protest any biased coverage you observe. As long as media consumers accept everything they are fed, there is no incentive for producers to go beyond superficial coverage that often only reinforces myths and stereotypes. For media contact information, visit *www.congress.org/congressorg/dbq/media* or *www.pmwatch.org/pmw/contact/media.asp.* For talking points and tips on writing, download a Global Exchange Toolkit (details below) and see "Letter to the Editor How-to."

6. ***US Citizens: Call, Write, and Meet with Your Representatives.*** Demand that the US government hold Israel accountable for its violations of human rights, international law, and US law: the US Arms Export Control Act prohibits the use of US-supplied weapons to target civilians. Urge that military aid to Israel be cut off as is required by US law. To find your representatives and contact them, visit *www.congress.org* and enter your zip code. Read the dos and don'ts for communicating with elected officials (including how to prepare, framing the issue, and following up), listed in the Global Exchange Toolkits (details below).

Highly recommended: The Global Exchange Activists Toolkits give excellent instructions and tips for all of the above actions as well as many others, including holding town hall meetings, organizing demonstrations, fundraising, and publicizing events. Download a free copy at *www.GlobalExchange.org/Countries/Mideast/Palestine/Toolkits.html* or call (800) 497-1994 ext. 251.

More ideas for getting involved can also be found at *www.qumsiyeh.org/WhatYouCanDo*

Appendix II: Resource Guide

Note: See also organizations listed in Appendix I.

Israeli/Palestinian:

Adalah, Legal Center for Arab Minority Rights in Israel: *www.Adalah.org*

Addameer, Prisoners Support & Human Rights Association: *www.Addameer.org*

Al-Haq, Palestinian Legal & Human Rights Organization: *www.AlHaq.org*

Alternative Information Center (AIC), A partnership of Israelis & Palestinians: *www.AlternativeNews.org*

Breaking the Silence, Israeli ex-soldiers tell stories about the Occupation: *www.BreakingTheSilence.org.il*

B'tselem, Israeli Information Center for Human Rights in the Occupied Territories: *www.Btselem.org*

Coalition of Women for Peace, including Machsom Watch, Women in Black, New Profile, & others: *www.CoalitionOfWomen.org*

Gush Shalom, Israeli Peace Bloc: *www.Gush-Shalom.org*

Haaretz, Mainstream Israeli Daily Newspaper: *www.Haaretz.com*

IndyMedia, Alternative news source by Israeli activists: *www.IndyMedia.org.il*

Mandela Institute for Human Rights, Human rights organization focusing on the plight of political prisoners: *www.Mandela-Palestine.org*

MIFTAH, NGO in East Jerusalem promoting human rights, democracy, & peace: *www.miftah.org*

Mossawa Center, Advocacy Center for Arab Citizens in Israel: *www.MossawaCenter.org*

Occupation Magazine, News & commentary from people against the Occupation: *www.kibush.co.il*

Palestine Monitor, Information from Palestinian civil society to the foreign press: *www.PalestineMonitor.org*

Palestinian Academic Society for the Study of International Affairs (PASSIA): *www.passia.org*

Physicians for Human Rights, Israel/Palestine Chapter: *www.phr.org.il/phr*

Public Committee Against Torture in Israel: *www.StopTorture.org.il/eng*

Rabbis for Human Rights (RHR), Israeli rabbinic campaign against discrimination & inhumane conduct, giving voice to the Jewish tradition of human rights: *www.rhr.israel.net*

Zochrot, Israeli citizens raising awareness of the *Nakba*: *www.NakbaInHebrew.org*

International:

Amnesty International, Worldwide campaign for human rights: *www.Amnesty.org*

Electronic Intifada, Leading Palestinian portal for information on the Israel/Palestine conflict: *www.ElectronicIntifada.net*

European Jews for a Just Peace, Federation of Jews: *www.ejjp.org*

Palestine Remembered, Extensive information on the *Nakba*: *www.PalestineRemembered.com*

Research Journalism Initiative, Providing students a direct link to regions of conflict abroad: *www.ResearchJournalismInitiative.net*

United Nations Office for the Coordination of Humanitarian Affairs (OCHA): *www.ochaopt.org*

North American:

Cactus48, Offering the complete text of the Origin of the Palestine-Israel Conflict by Jews for Justice in the Middle East: *www.Cactus48.com*

If Americans Knew, What Every American needs to know about Israel/Palestine: *www.IfAmericansKnew.org*

Jewish Voice for Peace (JVP), Activists inspired by Jewish tradition to work for peace, social justice, & human rights: *www.JewishVoiceForPeace.org*

Not In My Name (NIMN), Jewish organization committed to a peaceful & just resolution of the conflict: *www.nimn.org*

Recommended Books (& primary works cited in this book):

Jimmy Carter, *Palestine: Peace Not Apartheid* (New York: Simon & Schuster, 2006).

Noam Chomsky, *Fateful Triangle: The United States, Israel, and the Palestinians*, updated ed. (Cambridge: South End Press, 1999).

Norman Finkelstein, *Beyond Chutzpah: On the Misuse of Anti-Semitism and the Abuse of History* (Univ. of California Press, 2005).

Norman Finkelstein, *Image and Reality of the Israel-Palestine Conflict*, 2nd ed. (New York: Verso, 2003).

Jews for Justice in the Middle East, *The Origin of the Palestine-Israel Conflict*: *www.cactus48.com*

Ilan Pappe, *The Ethnic Cleansing of Palestine* (Oxford: Oneworld Publications, 2006).

Mazin Qumsiyeh, *Sharing the Land of Canaan* (London: Pluto Press, 2004).

Tanya Reinhart, *Israel/Palestine: How to End the War of 1948* (New York: Seven Stories Press, 2002).

Appendix III: Brief History

Important note: *This brief time line is intended as an overview for people unfamiliar with the Israel/Palestine conflict and is* not *meant to be a thorough account of the region's history.*

1897: The World Zionist Organization, the first formal organization devoted to Zionist principles, is founded with the goal of establishing a Jewish homeland in historic Palestine (present-day Israel and the Palestinian Territories). At the time, Palestine is under Ottoman rule and Jews make up less than 2% of its population.

1914: Britain promises the Palestinians independence if they will lend support against Turkey in World War I.

1917: With help from the Palestinians, Britain captures Palestine from the Turks. Britain issues the Balfour Declaration endorsing the creation of a Jewish national home in Palestine, so long as it does not violate the civil and religious rights of the existing non-Jewish communities.

1920s: Following World War I, Britain receives Palestine and present-day Jordan as a mandate from the League of Nations. Palestinians oppose the idea of an exclusively Jewish state on their land and protest Zionist immigration with a general labor strike and violent attacks.

1939–1947: Jewish immigration escalates in response to Nazi persecution and atrocities in Europe. Britain tries to restrict the immigration. In protest, Zionists organize underground gangs and launch hundreds of violent attacks against British and Palestinian officials and civilians. Palestinian opposition to Zionism continues.

1947: Britain hands the problem over to a United Nations Special Committee on Palestine, which, following pressure from the US, proposes allocating 54% of the land to Jews (who owned about 6% of the land at the time) and 46% to Palestinians (who owned about twice that—over 90%). Zionist leaders accept the Partition Plan publicly, although they are clear in personal correspondence that partition is only the beginning of realizing the Zionist dream encompassing all of historic Palestine (see Appendix V for quotations). The Palestinians reject the proposal. War breaks out.

1947–1948: Recognizing the impossibility of establishing a Jewish state in a land with a non-Jewish majority, Zionist forces launch a series of operations including Plan Dalet, inducing the flight of some 750,000 Palestinians (75% of the indigenous Palestinian population). After the British pull out at the end of the mandate period, Zionists declare the State of Israel on May 15th, 1948, which is to be remembered as "Independence Day" for Jewish Israelis and the "*Nakba*" (Catastrophe) for Palestinians.

That same day, multiple Arab countries invade the self-declared state in the second phase of the war. Israel emerges victorious and soon enacts laws to officially expropriate the Palestinian refugees' property and bar their return. The UN General Assembly passes Resolution 194, stating that "refugees wishing to return to their homes and live in peace with their neighbors should be permitted to do so at the earliest practicable date."

1949: The initial borders of Israel are established along what will become known as the "Green Line," encompassing 50% more territory into Israel than was originally allotted for a Jewish state by the UN Partition Plan, a total of 78% of historic Palestine. The West Bank and Gaza Strip, the remaining 22%, come under Jordanian and Egyptian control, respectively.

1950–1967: Border incidents and hostilities between Israel and surrounding countries continue.

1967: Egypt blockades the Straits of Tiran. In response, Israel attacks Egypt, Syria, Iraq, and Jordan and, within 6 days, occupies the West Bank, Gaza Strip, Sinai Peninsula, Golan Heights, and Arab sector of East Jerusalem. About 320,000 Palestinian civilians are displaced, more than half of them for the second time. Israel immediately begins establishing Jewish-only settlements in the West Bank, Gaza, and East Jerusalem.

Six months later, the UN Security Council passes Resolution 242, stressing the "inadmissibility of the acquisition of territory by war" and calling for the "withdrawal of Israeli armed forces from territories occupied," affirming the necessity for "freedom of navigation through international waterways" and "a just settlement to the refugee problem." Israel maintains positions in the occupied territories and prevents the old and new refugees from returning to their homes and land.

1973: On the Jewish holy day of Yom Kippur, Egypt and Syria attack Israeli positions in the occupied Sinai and Golan Heights. With significant US economic and military assistance, Israel succeeds in forcing the Egyptians and Syrians back.

1979: Having suffered heavy losses there during the 1973 War, Israel returns the Sinai to Egypt in exchange for normal diplomatic relations and Israeli access to the Suez Canal.

1980: The Israeli Knesset (Parliament) adopts the Jerusalem Law, officially annexing East Jerusalem into Israel.

1981: Israel accelerates the establishment of Jewish-only settlements in the Occupied Territories.

1987–1993: The first major Palestinian uprising against the Occupation begins, continuing for 6 years. Known as the First Intifada, it is largely nonviolent. The Israeli military response is harsh. For example, Defense Minister Yitzhak Rabin (who would later become Israeli Prime Minister) orders soldiers to break the bones of Palestinian youth. Many of the tens of thousands injured are under ten.

1988: Yasser Arafat, the top representative of the Palestinian people, officially recognizes Israel's right to exist and renounces violence.

1993–1996: Israeli and Palestinian representatives sign the Oslo Accords, leading to the withdrawal of Israeli troops from Gaza and most West Bank cities and towns. Israel embarks on an accelerated settlement program, building thousands of new housing units in the West Bank and doubling the settler population there.

1994: A Jewish American settler in Hebron massacres 29 Palestinians praying in a mosque. Israeli troops place Hebron Palestinians, but not the settlers, under curfew. Shortly thereafter, the first Palestinian suicide bomber blows himself up inside Israel. Brutal attacks against Israelis continue until the present, often correlating with Israeli brutality in the Occupied Territories.

2000: Negotiations for a final settlement at Camp David II (see Appendix IV for a map and details) are unsuccessful. Sharon's September visit to the Temple Mount with 1,000 soldiers sparks riots that escalate into the Second Intifada. By the end of the year, 42 Israelis and 327 Palestinians have been killed.

2001: Negotiations at Taba are unsuccessful. Violence from both sides surges in the Occupied Territories. Over the course of the year, 190 Israelis and 577 Palestinians are killed.

2002: The Arab League, composed of 22 Arab countries, proposes peace, normal relations, and regional integration with Israel in exchange for an end to the Occupation and a "just solution" to the refugee problem. Israel rejects the offer and begins unilateral construction of the Wall. Over the course of the year, 422 Israelis and 1072 Palestinians are killed.

2003–2004: The "Quartet" (US, UN, EU, and Russia) develop a "Roadmap to Peace." The Palestinians pledge full support; Israel rejects key sections. Over the course of both years, 295 Israelis and 1,547 Palestinians are killed.

2005: Israel evacuates 8,000 settlers from Gaza, meanwhile constructing new housing units for 13,000 more settlers in the West Bank. Israeli troops withdraw from Gaza but retain control of free-fire zones with snipers, as well as crossings, airspace, and coastline.

2006: Hamas defeats Fatah in the democratic legislative elections after holding to a unilateral ceasefire for more than one year. The US and EU cut off aid and declare an embargo on the Palestinian government, on which Palestinian civil society is dependant. Poverty soars to unprecedented levels. Interfactional violence breaks out between Hamas and Fatah.

In June, 2 days after Israeli soldiers capture two Palestinian soldiers in Gaza, Gaza militants kill two soldiers and capture one. Israel launches a 5-month attack on Gaza leaving 8 Israelis (6 soldiers and 2 civilians) and 400 Palestinians (mostly civilians) dead. Hamas temporarily breaks its ceasefire in June but quickly resumes it, even as the bombardment of Gaza continues.

2007: Fatah and Hamas officially agree to share power, but interfactional violence continues.

Sources: Jimmy Carter, *Palestine: Peace Not Apartheid* (New York: Simon & Schuster, 2006), plus online sources: *Columbia Encyclopedia, BBC, MidEastWeb for Coexistence R.A., CBC News, MIFTAH, Christian Century, Jerusalem Fund, PalestineHistory.com, Double Standards Palestine and Israel Timeline*, and *Middle East Policy Council.*

Appendix IV: Myths & Frequently Asked Questions

Myth #1: This is an ancient war between Jews and Muslims.

The Israel-Palestine conflict actually began quite recently. Jews and Palestinians had traditionally coexisted with little if any conflict between them before Zionist immigration began. European settlers started purchasing land from absentee Arab owners for exclusive Jewish labor and settlement, leading to the dispossession of the non-Jewish peasants living on that land.[15]

This is not a conflict of the Jewish people versus the Muslim people. First of all, 20% of Palestinians worldwide are Christians, and they are subject to the same restrictions as their Muslim counterparts. Israel has a strong peace movement calling for an end to the mutually-destructive Occupation, and many Jews find Zionism itself antithetical to Jewish principles.

Hasidic Jews protest Zionism in Washington DC.

Myth #2: Jewish Israelis are the descendants of the original inhabitants of Israel/Palestine.

Before the Hebrews first migrated there around 1800 B.C., present-day Israel/Palestine was inhabited by Canaanites. The Jewish kingdoms ruled for 414 years, just one of many periods in the land of Canaan. Palestinians are the descendents of intermarried Canaanites and Arabs who arrived in the 600s.[16]

---

15 Don Peretz, *The Arab-Israel Dispute* (New York: Facts on File, 1996); As cited in *The Origin of the Palestine-Israel Conflict*, published by Jews for Justice in the Middle East, third edition. *www.cactus48.com*

16 *The Origin of the Palestine-Israel Conflict*, published by Jews for Justice in the Middle East, third edition. *www.cactus48.com*

Genetic studies have shown that Sephardic Jews (descendents of Canaanites who migrated to the Iberian peninsula and then to North Africa and the Middle East) are actually closer to Palestinians than they are to Ashkenazi Jews (concentrated in Eastern Europe). This is because Ashkenazi Israelis are largely the descendents of Turkic khazars (of Slavic ancestry) who converted to Judaism in the 700s or 800s, not the descendents of Canaanites. According to geneticist Dr. Mazin Qumsiyeh, "the Zionist concept of 'return' is flawed, at least with respect to Ashkenazi Jews ... Return implies that one's ancestors originated from the area in question."[17]

The idea that anyone has claim to land based on blood or religion rather than geography is inherently problematic and dangerous, but for those inclined to argue on the basis of ancient inheritance, it is instructive to know that Palestinians have as much—if not more—ancestral claim to the land as Jews do.

Myth #3: The Palestinian refugee problem was created when Palestinians fled on radio orders from Arab leaders to move out of the way of an attack.

When Zionist and Israeli state and army archives were declassified in the 1980s, the myth that Palestinians left their homes voluntarily in 1948 was refuted by Israeli historians, who monitored countless broadcasts and found "not a single order or appeal, or suggestion about evacuation from Palestine, from any Arab radio station, inside or outside Palestine, in 1948." In fact, the only Arab orders recorded were for Palestinians to stay put.[18] Israeli historian Ilan Pappe writes:

> It is ironic that the "orders from above" theory should enjoy a kind of afterlife in the U.S. The Zionist community [there] is actually rather insulated from the complex public debate about Zionism in Israel. Our U.S. pro-Israel crowd looks a little backward when they keep repeating these myths. They are still digging out the same debating points they used thirty and forty years ago. They are perhaps more an embarrassment than a help to Israel's cause.[19]

Myth #4: Israel is a democracy.

Israel is the state of the Jewish people, not the state of its citizens. Non-Jewish citizens are excluded from many things granted automatically to Jews. Palestinian citizens of Israel are largely prevented from buying or leasing 93% of the land in Israel, much of it owned by the Jewish National Fund and thus exclusively reserved for Jews. Although they pay taxes, Palestinian citizens of Israel living in non-Jewish neighborhoods receive only a fraction of the resources and services granted to Jewish neighborhoods. Palestinian citizens of Israel *are* allowed to vote, and they can even run for office, unless they run on a platform advocating that Israel become the state of all of its citizens rather than the state only of the Jews, in which case they can be disqualified.[20] A 1989 High Court case challenging the law

---

[17] Qumsiyeh, pp. 20-29.

[18] Erskine Childers, British researcher; As quoted in Sami Hadawi, *Bitter Harvest* (Scorpion Publishing Ltd, 1983); As cited in *The Origin of the Palestine-Israel Conflict*, published by Jews for Justice in the Middle East, third edition. *www.cactus48.com*

[19] Ilan Pappe, *The Ethnic Cleansing of Palestine* (Oxford: Oneworld Publications, 2006).

[20] For information about discrimination against Palestinians with Israeli citizenship, see p. 169 or visit *www.Adalah.org* or *www.MossawaCenter.org*

found that "it is necessary to prevent a Jew or Arab who calls for equality of rights for Arabs from sitting in the Knesset [Israeli Parliament] or being elected to it." One Justice stated that a political party should be disqualified if it advocates "a state, as all democratic states, of the totality of its citizens, without any advantage to the Jewish people as such."[21]

Moreover, more than one third of the people living under Israeli rule are denied Israeli citizenship and the rights and protections that come along with it, including the right to participate in the government that controls their lives. These are the Palestinians in the Occupied Territories. The government in which non-Jews in the Occupied Territories *can* participate is not allowed to do basic things like control its people's own borders, security, or finances.

It is worth noting that Israel *is* a democracy for Jews. In other words, Israel is an ethnocracy.

Myth #5: The return of the Palestinian refugees would mean the displacement of Jewish Israelis, and is therefore impossible.

Dr. Salman Abu Sitta, a former member of the Palestinian National Council and the founder of the Palestine Land Society, has conducted extensive research on the possibility of refugees returning to their villages, many of which no longer exist. At an international convention on the right of return in July of 2006, he clarified his findings in five illustrative points:

- The land of the refugees, roughly 93% of present-day Israel, is currently inhabited by 1.5% of Israeli Jews.
- Of the more than 500 Palestinian villages from which the refugees were expelled, 90% are still vacant (many planted over with trees), 7% are partially built-over, and just 3% are completely built over—those in Tel Aviv and West Jerusalem.
- A full 97% of the refugees live within 62 miles of their homes, and 50% of them live within 25 miles. Many can see their land from their camps but cannot go there.
- The population density of Gaza is roughly 15,500 people/square mile, while Gaza's refugees' land nearby is practically empty—fewer than 16 Israelis/square mile. There are fewer Jews in the half of Israel closest to Gaza (from Ramleh to Eilat) than the population of a single Gaza refugee camp. Israel has welcomed as many Russian immigrants as there are Palestinian refugees in Lebanon and Gaza combined, and has been clear that it would make room for millions more Jewish immigrants if such a possibility arose.[22]

The issue is not about space; it's about demographics. The issue is that allowing Palestinian refugees to return would alter the ethnic character of Israel.

Myth #6: Israel has no genuine partner for negotiations or peace.

The most common example cited as "proof" that Palestinians don't want peace is Yasser Arafat's rejection of the offer presented by Israeli Prime Minister Barak at Camp David in

[21] Shapiro, *Jerusalem Post* (December 15, 1989); *Yediot Ahronot* (December 15, 1989); As cited in Chomsky, *Fateful*, p. 507

[22] *Al-Awda's* 4th International Convention (San Francisco: July 2006). *www.al-awda.org/abusitta.html*

2000. Widely perceived as generous, in fact the proposal fell far short of Israel's responsibilities to the Palestinians under international law in numerous ways:

- The proposal suggested that Israel annex 10% of the West Bank, including some of its most fertile and water rich areas, also home to more than 80,000 Palestinians.
- The proposal kept Israel in control of the West Bank's border with Jordan, thereby creating a defacto Palestinian island within Israel.
- The proposal offered the Palestinians control over the Arab sections of Jerusalem, but kept all of the city—as well as 85.3% of settlers—under Israeli sovereignty.
- The proposal specified that the Palestinian state would not control airspace or water, and could not have an army.
- The proposal cut the Palestinian state into three separate cantons: the Gaza Strip, the north West Bank, and the south West Bank. Gaza had no clear territorial link to the West Bank.

Projection of the West Bank Final Status Map presented by Israel, Camp David, July 2000

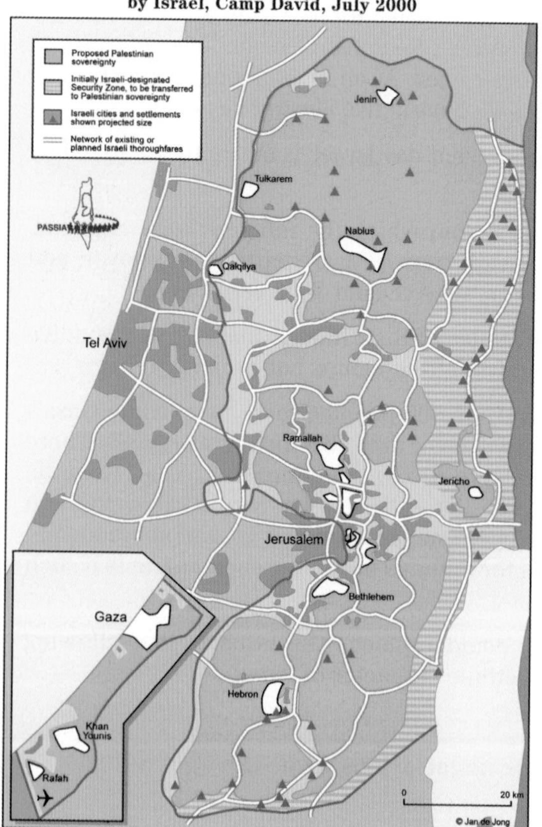

- The proposal denied Palestinian refugees their right to return to their homes and land to live in peace with their neighbors.[23]

Arafat's rejection of Barak's offer does not seem so shocking when you see a map of what the final effect would have looked like. President Jimmy Carter writes about Camp David: "There was no possibility that any Palestinian leader could accept such terms and survive, but official statements from Washington and Jerusalem were successful in placing the entire onus for the failure on Yasir Arafat."[24] Even Barak's foreign minister Shlomo Ben-Ami—a key player at Camp David—later admitted publicly: "If I were a Palestinian I would have rejected Camp David as well."[25]

One could argue that Arafat *should have* agreed to the proposal because now the Palestinians are even worse off, but that's not a logic I hear employed by many Palestinians I've talked to. Most of them say they would prefer being forced into oppression than signing away their rights to freedom. Maybe this way they can still hope for change.

---

[23] Boston Coalition for Palestinian Rights, 2002. *www.bcpr.org/break.html*

[24] Carter, 152.

[25] John Mearsheimer and Stephen Walt, "The Israel Lobby: Mearsheimer and Walt Respond to Criticisms," *London Review of Books* (May 11, 2006); As cited by Scholars for Peace in the Middle East. *www.spme.net*

In fact, Israel has been offered peace in exchange for compliance with international law several times, and rejected each offer. Here are some examples:

- In the mid-1970s, the Palestinian Liberation Organization (PLO) endorsed a comprehensive peace with Israel in exchange for its full withdrawal from the West Bank and Gaza. Israel rejected the offer.[26]
- In March 2002, Saudi Crown Prince Abdullah, along with all 21 other members of the Arab League, proposed not only peace but normal relations and regional integration with Israel in exchange for an end to the Occupation and a "just solution" to the refugee problem. Israel rejected the offer.[27]
- Israel effectively rejected the Saudi Initiative a second time when the proposal was included as part of the "Roadmap" announced by the UN. Wrote Carter, "The Palestinians accepted the road map in its entirety, but the Israeli government announced fourteen caveats and prerequisites, some of which would preclude any final peace talks."[28]

The Palestinians long ago joined the international consensus advocating two states based on the 1967 borders, shared Jerusalem, and a just solution for the refugees. Fatah recognized Israel's right to exist and renounced terrorism in 1988.[29] Hamas has also announced its willingness to establish peace with Israel along its internationally recognized borders. Hamas leader Ismail Haniyeh told *Newsweek* and the *Washington Post*:

> If Israel withdraws to the 1967 borders, then we will establish a peace in stages. We will establish a situation of stability and calm which will bring safety for our people ... a long-term hudna [ceasefire].[30]

Israel has refused to negotiate with the democratically elected Palestinian government of Hamas for three official reasons: (1) failure to renounce violence, (2) failure to recognize and abide by previous agreements, and (3) failure to recognize the right of a state besides one of its own to exist in historic Palestine. Interestingly, Israel is guilty of all three of the very things for which it faults Hamas.[31]

Myth #7: Palestinian textbooks incite hatred against the Jewish people.

There is a widely held belief that Palestinian textbooks demonize Israelis and teach Palestinian children to hate Jews. This particular myth originated with Itamar Marcus, an Israeli settler who founded an organization called the Center for Monitoring the Impact of Peace. Marcus' claims have been refuted by Israeli, American and European studies that examined the actual content of Palestinian texts.[32]

---

[26] Finkelstein, *Image*, p. 176.

[27] Ibid, at xxi.

[28] Carter, p. 159.

[29] *PASSIA* 2007.

[30] Yitzhak Ben-Horin, "We don't want to throw them into the sea," *Israel News* (February 25, 2006). *www.ynetnews.com*

[31] See pp. 329-330 for an elaboration on this point.

[32] Len Traubman, "Reports on Palestinian kids' hatred grossly exaggerated," *Jewish News Weekly of Northern California* (February 6, 2004).

In response to pressure from Congress to investigate the issue, the US government commissioned the Israel-Palestine Center for Research and Information to convene a team of professional educators—Israeli, Palestinian and American—to explore the allegations. Their 2003 report concluded: "[The Palestinian] textbooks do not incite against Israel or against peace" and "the overall orientation of the curriculum is peaceful despite the harsh and violent realities on the ground.... Religious and political tolerance is emphasized."[33]

In Europe, the prestigious Georg Eckert Institute for International Textbook Research facilitated research into the allegations. The Hebrew University's Harry S. Truman Research Institute for the Advancement of Peace and the Palestine-Israel Journal of Politics, Economics and Culture have published studies on the texts. Committees of the US Senate and the European Parliament have both held hearings on the matter. It seems no people's textbooks have been subjected to as much scrutiny as those of the Palestinians.

Yet time and again, independently of one another, researchers have found no incitement to hatred in Palestinian textbooks. It seems the original allegations were based on Egyptian or Jordanian textbooks and false translations.[34] A Middle East Working Group of the European Union found the textbooks "free of inciteful content ..., constituting a valuable contribution to the education of young Palestinians."[35]

If anyone's textbooks deserve scrutiny, perhaps it's those of the Israelis. Professor Dan Bar-Tal of Tel Aviv University concluded from a study of 124 textbooks that "over the years, generations of Israeli Jews [have been] taught a negative and often delegitimizing view of Arabs." Bar-Tal reported two major themes of Arab characteristics. One implied a "primitiveness" and an "inferiority in comparison to Jews." The other presented Arabs as violent, brutish, untrustworthy, cruel, fanatical, treacherous, and aggressive.[36]

In an article entitled, "Learning all the wrong facts," *Haaretz* reporter Akiva Eldar cites numerous studies concluding that many Israeli textbooks not only dehumanize Arabs, but are entirely devoid of the word "Palestinian." Also alien to many educational materials was the Green Line to distinguish Israel from the Palestinian territories. Those maps that do outline the West Bank often refer to it as "Judea and Samaria" or "Palestine-*Eretz Yisrael*," i.e. part of the "Land of Israel." Some official Israeli maps include Israeli settlements but *exclude* Palestinian towns, even those within Israel.[37]

Myth #8: Israel only uses violence as a last resort, to defend itself and to prevent terror attacks.

Human rights organizations have documented extensive disproportionate and indiscriminate use of force by the Israeli army over 40 years. For example, according to *Amnesty International*, most of the children killed by soldiers in 2002 were attacked "when there was no exchange of fire and in circumstances in which the lives of the soldiers

33 "Reviewing Palestinian Textbooks and Tolerance Education Program," *Israel/Palestine Center for Research and Information*, submitted to the Public Affairs Office US Consulate General (Jerusalem, 2003).

34 Roger Avenstrup, "Palestinian textbooks: Where is all that 'incitement?'" *International Herald Tribune* (December 18, 2004).

35 Akiva Eldar, "Reading, writing, and propoganda," *Haaretz* (September 10, 2004).

36 Traubman, *Jewish Weekly News of Northern California*.

37 Akiva Eldar, "Learning all the wrong facts," *Haaretz* (December 9, 2004).

were not at risk."[38] *B'tselem*, the Israeli Information Center for Human Rights in the Occupied Territories, described the situation as follows:

> In every city and refugee camp that they have entered, IDF soldiers have repeated the same pattern: indiscriminate firing and then killing of innocent civilians, intentional harm to water, electricity and telephone infrastructure, taking over civilian houses, extensive damage to civilian property, shooting at ambulances and prevention of medical care to the injured.[39]

Israel also uses humiliation tactics, as in the town of Halhul where town notables and other men were taken from their homes to the town square by soldiers in the middle of the night, where they were "ordered to urinate and [defecate] on one another, and also to sing *Hatikva* ['The Hope,' the national anthem of Israel] and to call out 'Long Live the State of Israel.' ... Some were even ordered to lick the earth." Other Palestinian detainees and civilians have reported being forced to crawl on all fours and bark like dogs. Children were made to slap their parents. Soldiers wrote numbers on the arms of Palestinian prisoners on Holocaust Remembrance Day.[40] Israeli settlers reportedly "caught an old man who had protested when his lands were taken and shaved off his beard—just what Polish anti-Semites did to Jews."[41]

FAQ #1: There are many terrible things happening around the world. Why should Americans care so much about this particular conflict?

Whether they know it or not, Americans are deeply involved in the Israel/Palestine conflict because they are Israel's financial sponsors. US tax-payers are funding Israel's aggression and therefore have a right and a responsibility to demand that those tax dollars not be used to violate international law and human rights.

The US government also perpetuates the conflict by preventing the United Nations from taking decisive action against Israel's crimes. A University of Cambridge study found that the US veto has ensured that Israel enjoys "virtual immunity" from the enforcement measures typically adopted by the UN against countries committing identical violations of international law.[42] According to President Carter:

> The United States has used its U.N. Security Council veto more than forty times to block resolutions critical of Israel. Some of these vetoes have brought international discredit on the United States, and there is little doubt that the lack of a persistent effort to resolve the Palestinian issue is a major source of anti-American sentiment and terrorist activity throughout the Middle East and the Islamic world.[43]

---

[38] "Killing the Future," *Amnesty International*, pp. 1-2, 16; As cited in Finkelstein, *Chutzpah*, p. 113.

[39] "A Deadly Pattern," *B'tselem*, press release (March 12, 2002); As cited in Qumsiyeh, p. 117.

[40] Zvi Barel, *Haaretz* (January 20 & 30, 1983); Edward Walsh, *Washington Post—Boston Globe* (February 18); David Richardson, *Jerusalem Post* (February 18); Aharon Bachar, "Do not say: We did not know, we did not hear," *Yediot Ahronot* (December 3, 1982); As cited in Chomsky, *Fateful*, pp. 130-131.

[41] "The Gangrene of the Occupation," *Al Hamishmar* (February 19, 1982); As cited in Chomsky, *Fateful*, p. 142.

[42] Mark Weller and Dr. Barbara Metzger, "Double Standards," *Negotiations Affairs Department, Palestinian Liberation Organization* (September 24, 2002); As cited in Finkelstein, *Image*, p. xviii.

[43] Carter, pp. 209-210.

FAQ #2: Why does the US continue to give Israel so much aid and political support?

The main reasons for US support of Israel can be summed up as follows:

1. The second most-powerful lobby in the US is the "Zionist Lobby" (often mislabeled the "Jewish Lobby" even though it is composed of many non-Jews, and many Jews oppose it), led by the American Israel Public Affairs Committee (AIPAC).[44] Described in the *New York Times* as "the most important organization affecting America's relationship with Israel,"[45] AIPAC has more than 100,000 US members and an annual budget of as much as $40 million,[46] which it uses to promote US policy aligned with Israeli interests. AIPAC has successfully defeated numerous senators who were perceived to be insufficiently pro-Israel.[47] Senator William Fulbright once wrote:

> AIPAC ... and its allied organizations have effective working control of the electoral process. They can elect or defeat nearly any congressman or senator that they wish, with their money and coordinated organization.[48]

University of Chicago professor John Mearsheimer and Harvard professor Stephen Walt published a controversial article entitled "The Israel Lobby," outlining various ways in which the lobby's control over US politics actually functions to the detriment of US strategic interests.[49]

2. Some argue that the US would never pursue another country's interests above its own and that US support for Israel is due to the countries' twin interests in military and spin-off development projects and the storage and base facilities that Israel provides for US forces targeting oil-rich countries in the region.[50]

Still others believe that it is a combination of the Zionist Lobby and US strategic interests that perpetuates US support for Israeli violations of international law.

3. No small number of American industries are profiting from US support for Israel. Most notable among these are US arms manufacturers. In addition to American weapons that are donated to Israel, two-thirds of US financial aid to Israel is earmarked for purchase of more US arms.

Other groups profiting from the conflict include the oil industry, Arab leaders, and US elected representatives who receive generous election donations for maintaining the status quo or increasing US unconditional support for Israel.[51]

4. Finally, American public opinion about Israel tends to be sympathetic for two reasons: First, people are rightfully sensitive to the tragic plight of Jews throughout history.

---

44 Daniel Kurtzman, "AIPAC listed 2nd most powerful group on Fortune list," *Jewish News of Greater Phoenix* (November 28, 1997).

45 As cited on AIPAC's homepage: *www.aipac.org*

46 "AIPAC Holds National Meeting Amid Spy Scandal Investigation," *Democracy Now!* (May 25, 2005).

47 Mitchell Kaidy, "Tiny Israel's Giant U.S. Lobby Goes Unmentioned in Campaign Finance Hearings," *Washington Report on Middle East Affairs* (December 1997), p. 42.

48 J. William Fulbright, *The Price of Empire* (London: Pantheon Books, 1989), p. 183; As cited in Qumsiyeh, p. 168.

49 John Mearsheimer and Stephen Walt, "The Israel Lobby," *London Review of Books* (March 23, 2006).

50 Ibid, at xiii.

51 See Qumsiyeh, *Sharing the Land of Canaan*, pp. 203-204 for details about each of these groups.

Against this historic backdrop, people are resistant to criticizing Israel and seeing Jews as anything other than the victims.

Second, although American tax-payers give more foreign aid to Israel than to any other country in the world, many remain largely ignorant of the uses of this aid and therefore do nothing to change it. This is due in large part to what many—myself included—perceive as a US mainstream media pro-Israel bias, which is documented extensively by the organization *If Americans Knew*. One of the group's studies found that the Associated Press reported deaths of Israeli children even more often than they occurred but failed to cover 85% of the deaths of Palestinian children. Another study on the *San Francisco Chronicle* made 30 mentions of Israeli children dying for every 20 who died (i.e., some deaths were reported more than once), but reported on only 1 in 20 deaths of Palestinian children. Studies on the *New York Times*, ABC, CBS, NBC, and other media sources revealed similar trends. Stories about torture, hunger strikes, Israeli refuseniks, and the Palestinian nonviolence movement were also grossly underreported. As long as Americans remain ignorant of Israeli's atrocities, they are unlikely to pressure their government to stop funding them.[52]

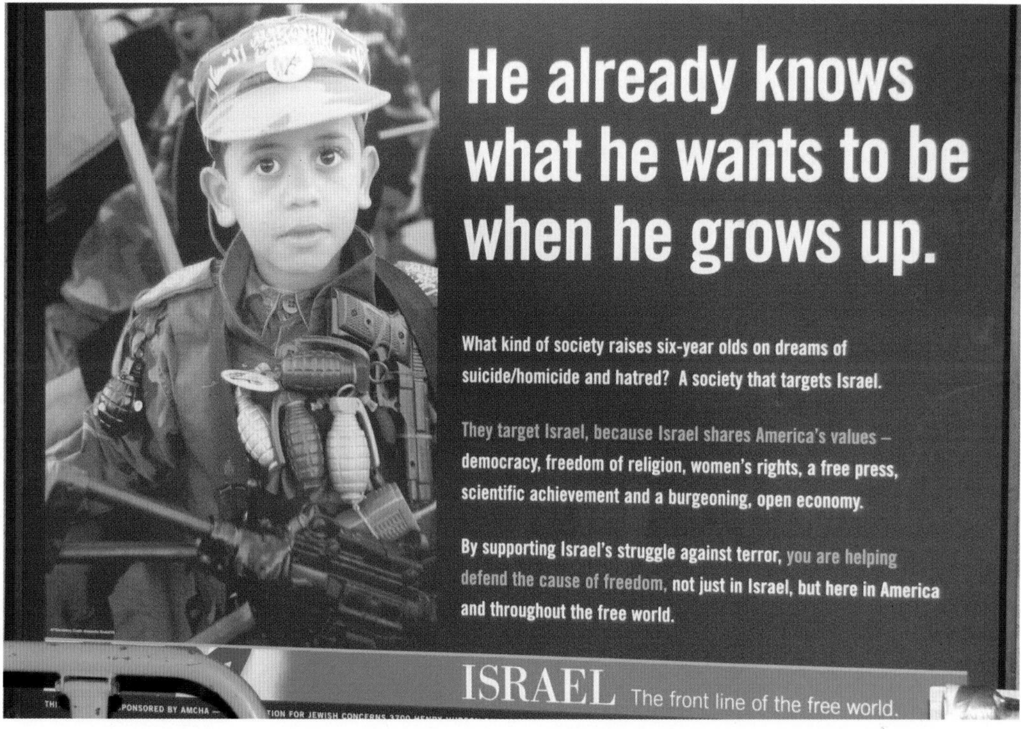

It is not surprising that most Americans remain ignorant of Israel's crimes given the prevalence of media asserting claims like the one below (which I encountered at a Washington DC metro station in June 2007). The subtitle reads: "What kind of a society raises six-year-olds on dreams of suicide/homicide and hatred? A society that targets Israel. ***They target Israel because Israel shares America's values****—democracy, freedom of religion, women's rights, a free press, scientific achievement and a burgeoning, open economy. By supporting Israel's struggle against terror,* ***you are helping defend the cause for freedom****, not just in Israel, but here in America and throughout the free world. —ISRAEL. The front line of the free world."*

---

[52] *www.IfAmericansKnew.org*

Appendix V: Quotations from Prominent Figures

Early Zionist leaders on the fulfillment of Zionism

We shall try to spirit the penniless population across the border by procuring employment for them in the transit countries while denying any employment in our country. Both the process of expropriation and the removal of the poor must be carried out discretely and circumspectly.[53]

—Theodor Herzl, the founder of Zionism, 1897

We must expel the Arabs and take their places and if we have to use force to guarantee our own right to settle in those places—then we have force at our disposal.[54]

—David Ben-Gurion, Israel's founding father and first prime minister, 1937

In Palestine we do not propose to go through the form of consulting the wishes of the present inhabitants ... The four great powers are committed to Zionism and Zionism, be it right or wrong, good or bad, is rooted in age-long tradition, in present needs, in future hopes, of far profounder import than the desires and prejudices of the 700,000 Arabs who now inhabit that ancient land.[55]

—Lord Balfour, British Foreign Secretary, author of the Balfour Declaration, promising a "homeland for the Jews" in Palestine, 1919

Zionist colonization, even the most restricted, must either be terminated or carried out in defiance of the will of the native population.[56]

—Vladimir Jabotinsky, founder of revisionist Zionism, 1923

I support compulsory transfer. I do not see in it anything immoral ... The Arabs will have to go, but one needs an opportune moment for making it happen, such as a war.[57]

—David Ben-Gurion, Israel's founding father and first prime minister, 1937

---

[53] Raphael Patai, *The Complete Diaries of Theodor Herzl* (New York, 1961), p. 88; As cited in Finkelstein, *Image*, p. 176, footnote 19.

[54] Nur Masalha, *Expulsion of Palestinians*, p. 66; As cited in "What leading Israelis have said about the Nakba," *Institute for Middle East Understanding* (May 9, 2007).

[55] Edward Said, *The Question of Palestine*; As cited in *The Origin of the Palestine-Israel Conflict*, published by Jews for Justice in the Middle East, third edition. *www.cactus48.com*

[56] Vladimir Jabotinsky, *The Iron Wall: We and the Arabs*; As cited in Qumsiyeh, p. 75.

[57] Ilan Pappe, *The Ethnic Cleansing of Palestine* (Oxford: Oneworld Publications, 2006).

During the War of 1948

In the Negev we will not buy land. We will conquer it.[58]

—David Ben-Gurion, Israel's founding father and first prime minister

These operations can be carried out in the following manner: either by destroying villages (by setting fire to them, by blowing them up, and by planting mines in their rubble), and especially those population centers that are difficult to control permanently; or by mounting combing and control operations according to the following guidelines: encirclement of the villages, conducting a search inside them. In case of resistance, the armed forces must be wiped out and the population expelled outside the borders of the state.[59]

—From Operation Dalet, adopted by the Zionist leadership in 1948

[Capturing the village] without a fight, [Zionist forces first] killed about 80-100 [male] Arabs, women and children. The children they killed by breaking their heads with sticks. There was not a house without dead.... One soldier boasted that he had raped a woman and then shot her. One woman, with a newborn baby in her arms, was employed to clear the courtyard where the soldiers ate. She worked a day or two. In the end they shot her and her baby.[60]

—Eyewitness soldier of the massacre at Ad-Dawayima village in October of 1948

Early Zionist leaders on Partition

The debate has not been for or against the indivisibility of Eretz Israel [the "Land of Israel," including the West Bank and Gaza]. No Zionist can forgo the smallest portion of Eretz Israel. The debate was over which of two routes would lead quicker to the common goal.[61]

I have no doubt that our army will be among the world's outstanding—and so I am certain that we won't be constrained from settling in the rest of the country, whether out of accord and mutual understanding with the Arab neighbors or otherwise.[62]

After the formation of a large army in the wake of the establishment of the state, we will abolish partition and expand to the whole of Palestine.[63]

—David Ben-Gurion, Israel's founding father and first prime minister, 1937

---

[58] Benny Morris, *The Birth of the Palestinian Refugee Problem, 1947-1949* (Cambridge, 1988), p. 170.

[59] The English translation is in Walid Khalidi, "Plan Dalet: Master Plan for the Conquest of Palestine," *Journal of Palestine Studies*, issue 1 (1988), pp. 4-20; As cited in Pappe, "The 1948 Ethnic Cleansing of Palestine," *Journal of Palestine Studies*, issue 141 (2006).

[60] Morris, p. 230; As cited in Finkelstein, *Image*, p. 76.

[61] Quote from 1937. Arlosoroff memorandum; As cited in Chomsky, *Fateful*, p. 162.

[62] Yosef Gorny, *Zionism and the Arabs, 1882-1948: A Study of Ideology* (Oxford: Clarendon, 1987), p. 260; As cited and expanded in Finkelstein, *Image*, p. 15.

[63] Quote from 1937. Remi Kanazi, "Transferring the Truth," *AIC* (September 20, 2005).

The partition of the Homeland is illegal. It will never be recognized.... It will not bind the Jewish people. Jerusalem was and will forever be our capital. Eretz Israel [the "Land of Israel," including the West Bank and Gaza] will be restored to the people of Israel. All of it. And forever.[64]

—Menachem Begin, 6th Israeli Prime Minister, 1954

After the establishment of Israel

In our country there is room only for the Jews. We shall say to the Arabs: Get out! If they don't agree, if they resist, we shall drive them out by force.[65]

—Ben-Zion Dinur, Israeli Minister of Education and Culture, 1954

Why should the Arabs make peace? If I was an Arab leader, I would never make terms with Israel. That is natural: we have taken their country. Sure, God promised it to us, but what does that matter to them?... They only see one thing: we have come here and stolen their country. Why should they accept that? They may perhaps forget in one or two generations' time, but for the moment there is no chance.[66]

—David Ben-Gurion, Israel's founding father and first prime minister, 1956

Leading up to the 1967 War and the Occupation

[Israel must] invent dangers, and to do this it must adopt the method of provocation-and-revenge ... And above all—let us hope for a new war with the Arab countries, so that we may finally get rid of our troubles and acquire our space.[67]

—Moshe Sharatt, Israeli Prime Minister in 1953-1955

In the case of the new war, we must avoid the historic mistake of the War of Independence [1948 War] and, later, the Sinai Campaign. We must not cease fighting until we achieve ... the territorial fulfillment of the Land of Israel.[68]

—Yigal Allon, Interim Prime Minister in 1969, Architect of the Allon Plan

---

[64] Menachem Begin, "The Revolt" (New York: Schuman, 1951), p. 335; As cited in Chomsky, *Fateful*, p. 161

[65] *History of the Haganah*; As cited in Sam Bahour, "Israel at 58: A Failed Experiment," *Electronic Intifada* (May 15, 2006).

[66] Nahum Goldmann, *The Jewish Paradox* (New York: Grosset & Dunlap, 1978); As cited in *The Origin of the Palestine-Israel Conflict*, published by Jews for Justice in the Middle East, third edition. *www.cactus48.com*

[67] Livia Rokach, *Israel's Sacred Terrorism* (AAUG Press, 1986); As cited in *The Origin of the Palestine-Israel Conflict*, published by Jews for Justice in the Middle East, third edition. *www.cactus48.com*

[68] Michael Brecher, *Decisions in Crisis* (Berkeley: 1980), p. 100; As cited in Finkelstein, *Image*, pp. 195-196.

Reflections on the 1967 War

I do not think that Nasser wanted war. The two divisions he sent to the Sinai would not have been sufficient to launch an offensive war. He knew it and we knew it.[69]

—Yitzhak Rabin, Israel's 5th Prime Minister, 1968

In June 1967, we again had a choice. The Egyptian Army concentrations in the Sinai approaches do not prove that Nasser was really about to attack us. We must be honest with ourselves. We decided to attack him.[70]

—Menachem Begin, 6th Israeli Prime Minister, 1982

I know how at least 80 percent of all the incidents with Syria started. In my opinion, more than 80 percent ... It would go like this: we would send a tractor to plow ... in the demilitarized area, and we would know ahead of time that the Syrians would start shooting. If they did not start shooting, we would inform the tractor to progress further, until the Syrians, in the end, would get nervous and would shoot. And then we would use guns, and later, even the air force, and that is how it went.... We thought ... that we could change the lines of the cease-fire accords by military actions that were less than a war. That is, to seize some territory and hold it until the enemy despairs and gives it to us.[71]

—Moshe Dayan, Israeli Defense Minister, 1976

Quotes from modern Israeli leaders

It is the duty of Israeli leaders to explain to public opinion, clearly and courageously, a certain number of facts that are forgotten with time. The first of these is no Zionism, colonialization [sic], or Jewish State without the eviction of the Arabs and the expropriation of their lands.[72]

Everybody has to move, run and grab as many hilltops as they can to enlarge the settlements because everything we take now will stay ours.... Everything we don't grab will go to them.[73]

—Ariel Sharon, Israeli Prime Minister from 2001 to 2006

---

[69] *Le Monde* (February 28, 1968); As cited in *The Origin of the Palestine-Israel Conflict*, published by Jews for Justice in the Middle East, third edition. *www.cactus48.com*

[70] "Address by Prime Minister Begin at the National Defense College," *Israeli Ministry of Foreign Affairs* (August 8, 1982).

[71] "Interviews on the Golan Heights and on Jewish Settlements in Hebron," *Yediot Ahronot* (November 22, 1976); As cited in Finkelstein, *Image*, p. 187.

[72] Agence French Presse (November 15, 1998); As cited in "What leading Israelis have said about the Nakba," *Institute for Middle East Understanding* (May 9, 2007).

[73] Quote from 1998. Ibid, at 147.

The vision I would like to see here is the entrenching of the Jewish and the Zionist state.... I very much favor democracy, but when there is a contradiction between democratic and Jewish values, the Jewish and Zionist values are more important.[74]

—Avigdor Lieberman, Israeli Minister of Strategic Threats, 2006

Former Israeli leader on Jewish resistance to British occupation

Neither Jewish ethics nor Jewish tradition can disqualify terrorism as a means of combat ... First and foremost, terrorism is for us a part of the political battle being conducted under the present circumstances, and it has a great part to play ... in our war against the occupier.[75]

—Yitzhak Shamir, 7th Israeli Prime Minister

Modern Israeli historian on the discrepancy between the collective understanding and the reality illustrated by these candid quotations

When it comes to the dispossession by Israel of the Palestinians in 1948, there is a deep chasm between the reality and the representation. This is most bewildering, and it is difficult to understand how events perpetrated in modern times and witnessed by foreign reporters and UN observers could be systematically denied, not even recognized as historical fact, let alone acknowledged as a crime that needs to be confronted, politically as well as morally. Nonetheless, there is no doubt that the ethnic cleansing of 1948,. the most formative event in the modern history of the land of Palestine, has been almost entirely eradicated from the collective global memory and erased from the world's conscience.[76]

—Ilan Pappe, prominent Israeli "New Historian," 2006

Gandhi on Palestinian resistance

I am not defending the Arab excesses. I wish they had chosen the way of non-violence in resisting what they rightfully regard as an unacceptable encroachment upon their country. But according to the accepted canons of right and wrong, nothing can be said against the Arab resistance in the face of overwhelming odds.[77]

—Mahatma Gandhi

---

[74] *Scotsman* (October 23, 2006); As cited in Ali Abunimah, "World silent as fascists join Israeli government," *Electronic Intifada* (October 25, 2006).

[75] Yitzhak Shamir, *Hehazit*, LEHI, the "Stern Gang" (1943); translated in *Middle East Report* (1988); As cited in Chomsky, *Fateful*, pp. 485-486.

[76] Ilan Pappe, "The 1948 Ethnic Cleansing of Palestine," *Journal of Palestine Studies*, issue 141 (2006).

[77] Martin Buber and Paul R. Mendes-Flohr, *A Land of Two Peoples* (University of Chicago Press, 2005); As cited in *The Origin of the Palestine-Israel Conflict*, published by Jews for Justice in the Middle East, third edition. *www.cactus48.com*

Glossary

Absentee Property Law: An Israeli law by which people who fled their land in present-day Israel at any point during the War of 1948 forfeit their rights to their property, with no possibility of appeal or compensation. Through this law, the property belonging to more than 750,000 Palestinian refugees of 1948 was transferred to the Jewish National Fund and to the State of Israel, which now, collectively, own 93% of Israel. Much of the 93% is reserved exclusively for Jewish people, excluding not only the owners of the land who are now in other countries (and are prevented from returning) but also Palestinians with Israeli citizenship.

administrative detention: The common practice of arrest or detention without charge or trial, indefinitely renewable under Israeli law but forbidden by international law.

Al-Aqsa Martyrs' Brigades: The military wing of Fatah Party.

Ariel (settlement): The largest settlement in the Salfit region and the third most populous Israeli settlement in the West Bank (after Ma'ale Adumim and Modiin Ilit), home to 17,000 settlers.

bantustans: The "homelands" designated for black South Africans under apartheid. The term is now often used to describe segregated territories denied real authority or power, such as the isolated Palestinian areas of the West Bank.

Bil'in: West Bank village of about 1,800, the site of ongoing weekly nonviolent protests against the Wall since February 2005. A center of popular nonviolent resistance, Bil'in hosted the International Conference on Nonviolence in 2006 and 2007.

building permit: A license that Palestinians must obtain from Israeli authorities (except in areas under PA control) in order to be able to build on their own land. Palestinian applications for building permits are extremely expensive (about $20,000) and rarely successful.

checkpoint: Barrier manned by Israeli soldiers or border police to monitor Palestinian movement. Most West Bank checkpoints are between Palestinian towns and villages.

Checkpoint Watch: An international and Israeli campaign to document and to prevent abuses of power by Israeli soldiers at checkpoints inside Palestinian areas.

Citizenship Law: An Israeli law denying citizenship or residency to West Bank or Gaza Palestinians married to Israeli citizens (typically Palestinian). The law also denies Israeli citizenship to children born of an Israeli citizen and a non-Jewish resident of the Occupied Territories. If families can obtain special permission from the Israeli Minister of the Interior, children can live with their Israeli parent in Israel until age 12, at which point they will be uprooted and forced to leave the state.

closure: A period of time during which all Israeli-issued permits for Palestinian movement are cancelled, including permits into Israel, to East Jerusalem, between the north and south West Bank, and to Palestinians' land, schools, workplaces, and hospitals. The Israeli army usually imposes closure after violent attacks and during Jewish holidays.

curfew: A period of hours, days, weeks, or even months when entire communities of Palestinians are forbidden to leave their homes for any reason at any time, except a few hours a week to get food. Curfews are imposed by the Israeli army, and Palestinians caught outdoors risk being shot. As an example, the 11,000 men, women, and children in Dheisheh refugee camp near Bethlehem are under curfew an average of 4 months a year.

Deir Ballut Peace Camp Against the Wall: A December 2003/January 2004 solidarity encampment of Palestinians, Israelis, and internationals on threatened land in Deir Ballut village to protest, document, and publicize construction of the Wall.

Deir Yassin: A pastoral Palestinian village where Zionist forces murdered more than 100 Palestinian men, women, and children in 1948 as part of Operation Dalet.

direct action: Physical action to resist or undermine a function of an oppressive force. Examples include dismantling a roadblock that immobilizes a population or blocking a bulldozer that is being used to uproot trees or demolish homes. Direct action differs from educational campaigns and political lobbying, which are other tactics favored by progressive organizations.

economic settlers: Israeli settlers who choose to live in the Occupied Palestinian Territories primarily because of the financial benefits offered by the Israeli government, such as tax breaks and housing subsidies. Settlers who live in Palestine for non-economic reasons, by contrast, are called "ideological settlers."

ethnic cleansing: "The systematic and forced removal of the members of an ethnic group from communities in order to change the ethnic composition of a given region," as defined by the US State Department.

family reunification: The ability of Palestinian families to live together on their land, granted or denied at the discretion of the Israeli Minister of the Interior. Shortly after Israel occupied the West Bank, Israeli authorities took a census. All those not counted in the census due to absence—whether studying abroad, visiting family, or anything else—became refugees, losing their right to return to their homes, land, and families. Palestinian refugees wishing to return must apply for family reunification, but by 2006, Israel had suspended the processing of family reunification claims as punishment for the election of Hamas and on the grounds that permitting relatives of Palestinian citizens of Israel to obtain citizenship was a threat to the "Jewish character" of the state.

Fatah: An Arabic acronym for "Movement for the National Liberation of Palestine" and the most prominent faction of the Palestine Liberation Organization (PLO), headed by Yasser Arafat until his death, and by Mahmoud Abbas since then.

flying checkpoints: Mobile checkpoints erected without warning anywhere within the Occupied Territories to monitor and restrict Palestinian movement.

Fourth Geneva Convention: An international treaty protecting civilians in occupied areas from mistreatment and occupied land from colonization in times of war. The treaty was adopted by the international community—including Israel—in 1949, in reaction to the Nazi atrocities of World War II. Among other things, the Fourth Geneva Convention forbids degrading or dehumanizing treatment, coercion, corporal punishment, torture, confiscation of property, collective punishment, and the obstruction of movement.

Gaza (Strip): A narrow strip of Palestinian territory bordering northeast Egypt, home to about 1.4 million Palestinians under continuous Israeli occupation since 1967. Although Israel claims to have withdrawn from Gaza in 2005, it remains under Israeli control.

Goldstein, Baruch: An Israeli settler and army reservist from Brooklyn, New York, who massacred 29 Palestinians praying in a mosque in Hebron in 1994.

Green Line, the: The internationally recognized border between Israel and the territories it has illegally occupied since 1967.

Hamas: An Arabic acronym for "Islamic Resistance Movement" and the dominant Islamic political organization in the Palestinian Territories. Initially tolerated—if not encouraged—by Israel as an alternative to the PLO, Hamas has been responsible for a number of attacks on Israeli soldiers and civilians. Hamas won an upset victory during the 2006 elections on a platform calling for economic reform and an end to corruption in the Palestinian Authority. The party consists of a civilian wing that runs numerous health clinics and welfare and educational institutions, and a military wing that had held fairly consistently to a unilateral ceasefire for almost 2.5 years when this book went to press. Hamas is ideologically opposed to the existence of an exclusively Jewish state in historic Palestine.

Haris: A West Bank village of about 2,800 in which the International Women's Peace Service (IWPS) office and volunteers are based.

human shields: Civilians used to shield combatants during an attack, in violation of the Fourth Geneva Convention. The Israeli army frequently uses Palestinians as human shields during invasions, a practice known as the "neighbor procedure" in Israeli military parlance. "Human shields" can also refer to people deliberately using their own bodies to shield others from harm.

ideological settlers: Israeli settlers who choose to live in the Occupied Palestinian Territories for political or religious reasons. Settlers who live in Palestine for economic reasons, by contrast, are called "economic settlers."

internally displaced refugees: Palestinians who fled their villages in 1948 but remained in the area that became Israel. These Palestinians were granted Israeli citizenship but never allowed to return to their homes and villages. Now totaling more than a quarter of a million, they have yet to be officially acknowledged by Israel to be part of the refugee problem.

International Solidarity Movement (ISM): A Palestinian-led organization that welcomes international volunteers to join Palestinians in resisting the Occupation using nonviolent direct action methods and principles.

International Women's Peace Service (IWPS): An organization of internationals dedicated to documenting and nonviolently intervening in human rights abuses in the West Bank, and supporting the Palestinian nonviolent movement to end the Occupation.

intifada: The term, meaning "shaking off" in Arabic, used for the two large-scale Palestinian uprisings directed at ending the Israeli Occupation, the first from 1987 to 1993 and the second starting in September 2000.

Jewish National Fund (JNF): "The caretaker of the land of Israel, on behalf of its owners—Jewish people everywhere," according to its website. The JNF expropriated land of Palestinian refugees from the 1948 War and reserved it for Jews only.

Jewish settler highways: Large roads built by Israel on Palestinian land to connect Jewish-only settlements with one another and with Israel proper. Palestinian use of settler highways is generally limited or forbidden.

***Kach* and *Kahane Chai*:** Two closely-related far-right Zionist organizations advocating the forcible expulsion of Palestinians from Israel and the Occupied Territories. Both the US and Israeli State Departments list *Kach* and *Kahane Chai* as illegal terrorist organizations.

Land of Israel (Eretz Yisrael): The term, as distinct from the internationally recognized "territory of Israel," meaning all of historic Palestine—including the West Bank and Gaza—in Israeli parlance.

Law of Entry to Israel: Israeli law issued in 1952 that has been used extensively to control the number of Palestinians living in Jerusalem and Israel. The following restrictions apply to Palestinian Jerusalemites but not to Jewish Jerusalemites: (a) those wanting to travel abroad must obtain an Israeli re-entry visa or else they lose their right to return to their homes and families; (b) those who apply for or carry residency or citizenship anywhere else can no longer reside in Jerusalem; (c) those living "abroad" (including in the West Bank and Gaza) for 7 years or more can no longer reside in Jerusalem; and (d) children can inherit Jerusalem residency rights paternally but not maternally.

Mas'ha Peace Camp Against the Wall: An action that began in May 2003, in which thousands of Palestinians, Israelis, and internationals camped out together in Mas'ha village in protest of the Wall. The encampment continued for 4 months until August 2003, when over 70 activists were arrested when they tried to prevent bulldozers from razing land in preparation for the Wall in front of Munira's house.

Munira's house: A Palestinian house on the outskirts of Mas'ha village built by Hani Amer. Hani, his wife Munira, and their six children live surrounded on all sides by the Wall and fences installed by the Israeli army.

***Nakba*:** The term, meaning "the Catastrophe" in Arabic, referring to the flight of three quarters of the indigenous Palestinian population during the War of 1948 (Israel's "War of Independence") as a result of violent expulsion campaigns (such as Operation Dalet) carried out by Zionist forces.

Operation Dalet (Plan D): The formalized plan for the systematic expulsion of Palestinians from present-day Israel, adopted by the Zionist leadership in early 1948.

Oslo Accords (Oslo II): The agreement signed by Israel and the PLO in 1995, establishing a Palestinian Legislative Council and dividing the West Bank into three jurisdictional sections, still applicable in theory but largely ignored: Area A (17.2% of the West Bank) came under full Palestinian control, Area B (23.8%) came under Palestinian civil control and Israeli military control, and Area C (59%) came under full Israeli civil and military control.

outposts: Structures—often uninhabited trailers or a few mobile homes—established on Palestinian land without official Israeli state recognition, as precursors to new or expanded government-subsidized Jewish-only settlements.

refuseniks: Conscientious objectors who either refuse to serve in the Occupied Territories or refuse to serve in the Israeli army altogether.

right of return: The right of Palestinian refugees who fled during past wars to return to their land in or occupied by Israel. The right was established with United Nations General Assembly Resolution 194, which has been reaffirmed more than 130 times since it was originally passed in 1948. The resolution states, "Refugees wishing to return to their homes and live at peace with their neighbors should be permitted to do so." Israel has its own right of return—the "Law of Return," which welcomes any Jew in the world to settle in Israel and obtain Israeli citizenship—but rejects the idea of non-Jews coming back to their homes, land, and families.

roadblocks: Concrete blocks or very large dirt piles installed by the Israeli military to inhibit vehicular movement on Palestinian roads. When this book went to press, there were approximately 450 roadblocks throughout the Occupied Territories.

Salfit (district): A rural West Bank region with over 60,000 inhabitants, almost half of them Israeli settlers. IWPS is based in Haris village in Salfit.

Seam: The term for the area of the West Bank between the Wall and the Green Line. Approximately 375,000 Palestinians will be stranded in the Seam if the Wall is completed as projected. To the east, Palestinians in the Seam are cut off from the rest of the West Bank by the Wall. To the west, they are denied rights in Israel because, as non-Jews, they cannot acquire Israeli citizenship. Palestinians in the Seam need permits to continue living in their own homes, while Jewish Israelis are free—and often encouraged—to settle the land.

settlements: Colonies exclusively for Jewish Israelis, built and sustained by the Israeli government on Palestinian land outside of Israel.

Wall: Israel's unilaterally constructed, rapidly expanding "Security Fence," made of different combinations of fence, electric sensory wire, sniper towers, razor wire, and concrete. The International Court of Justice declared the Wall illegal in July of 2004, but Israel has continued its construction. More than three times the length of the actual border between the West Bank and Israel, the Wall weaves through the former, annexing large amounts of fertile land and water sources into Israel, isolating Palestinian towns and villages, and separating hundreds of thousands of Palestinians from their schools, their social services, their land, and each other.

West Bank: The bulk of the Palestinian Territories, bordered by Jordan to the east and Israel to the north, west, and south. The West Bank is home to more than 2.5 million Palestinians and approximately 500,000 Israeli settlers, including those living in annexed East Jerusalem.

Women for Life (WFL): A Palestinian women's organization established in Salfit with the objective of empowering rural women in their struggle for freedom and equality. WFL projects have included legal and leadership workshops, job training, domestic violence awareness, and creative nonviolent resistance to the Occupation

Yanoun: A West Bank Palestinian village, formerly home to about 300 Palestinians until violent settler attacks drove villagers to evacuate in October 2000. About 90 villagers have returned to their homes in Yanoun on the condition that Israeli and international activists maintain a constant presence in the village.

Zionism: Controversial term used in this book to refer to the political ideology that supports an exclusively Jewish state in historic Palestine.

Sources: International Women's Peace Service, Haaretz, Jewish Virtual Library, Hanitzotz Publishing House, CIA World Fact Book, Washington Report on Middle East Affairs, Applied Research Institute of Jerusalem, and the Palestinian Academic Society for the Study of International Affairs.

Index

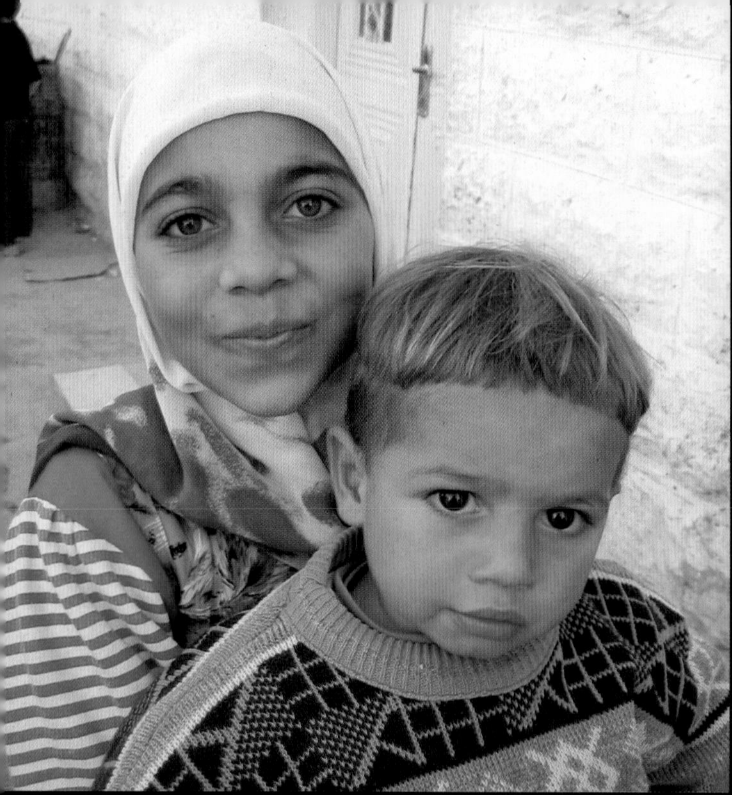

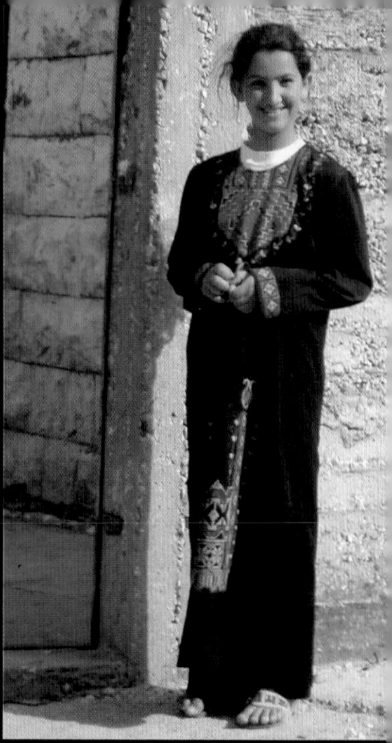

Born Under Occupation

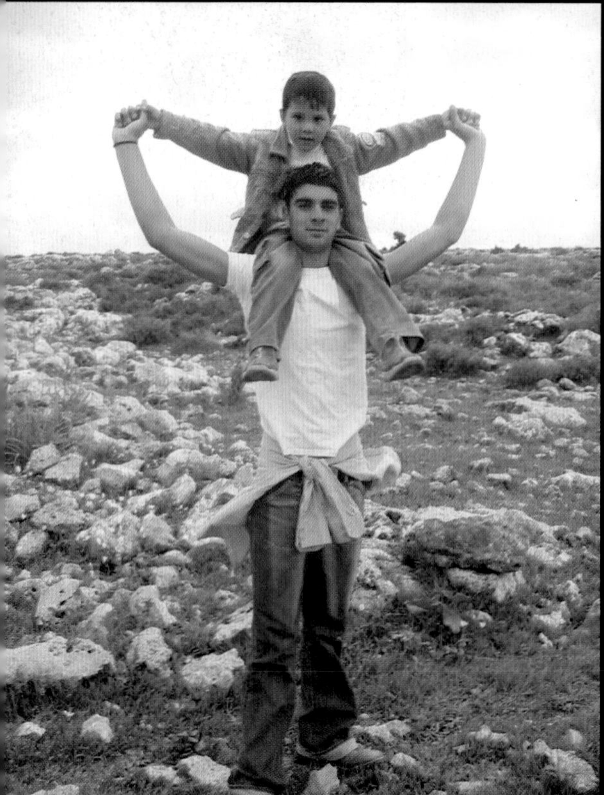

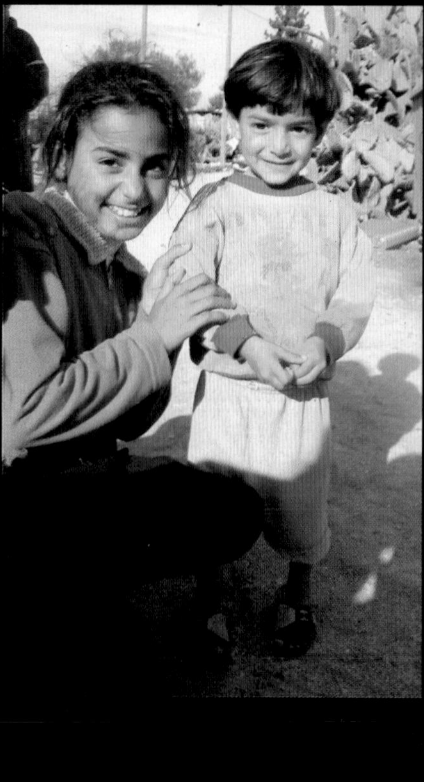

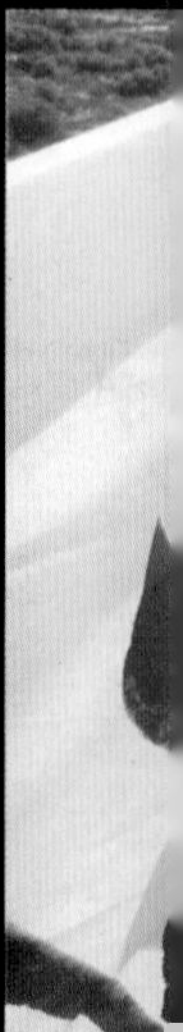

Anna Baltzer was born in 1979 and raised in Berkeley, California and Austin, Texas. She graduated from Columbia University with a degree in Mathematics and Economics, but today she divides her time between teaching, traveling, and activism. Anna first traveled to the Middle East in 2003 while on a Fulbright grant in Turkey. Since then, she has traveled to the West Bank every year as a volunteer for the International Women's Peace Service, documenting human rights abuses and supporting nonviolent resistance to the Occupation. For information on Anna's work, DVD, and educational tours, or to join her email list to receive eyewitness reports from Palestine, visit *www.AnnaInTheMiddleEast.com*